A Man After God's Own Heart

A Man After God's Own Heart

The Life of David

R. T. Kendall

Christian Focus

© R. T. Kendall

ISBN 187792 382 0

Published in 2001, reprinted 2002
by Christian Focus Publications,
Geanies House, Fearn, Ross-shire,
IV20 1TW, Great Britain.

www.christianfocus.com

Cover design by Owen Daily

Contents

Dedication

To R.V. and Joy

Preface

One of the happiest things to happen to me during our twenty-five year ministry at Westminster Chapel is Christian Focus. I never will forget the day I was first approached by Malcolm Maclean, and it led to a happy relationship and a number of books.

This book is sermons that have been edited to make them read slightly better. They were originally preached at Westminster Chapel on Sunday evenings from October 4th 1987 to June 11th 1989. They are presented in this book and I hope they will be a blessing to you.

I have a number of people to thank. First, Margaret Downing, who has edited nearly all of the sermons. I thank also Malcolm Maclean for his encouragement in this production, which has been no small task. And my warmest thanks also to William Mackenzie, the publisher of Christian Focus Publications.

This book is lovingly dedicated to Dr and Mrs R.V. Reese of Fitzgerald, Georgia. R.V. and Joy are like family to us, and R.V. in particular has looked after my ailing father over the years that Dad has lived in Fitzgerald.

R T Kendall
Westminster Chapel,
London
January 2001

1

Introduction

I have a wonderful father. As I write these lines, he is in a nursing home in Fitzgerald, Georgia. He has Alzheimer's disease. The last time I saw him, he hardly knew me. But nearly every time I see him I think of the influence he had on me, which began when I was a small boy and my Dad reading Bible stories to me – or telling them to me from his own memory.

One of those stories was the life of David, with particular reference to David killing Goliath. My Dad had a way of telling the story – which I heard again and again – that made me attracted to the character David more than I would have otherwise experienced. I wish I could in some way dedicate this book to my Dad, but I have already dedicated a book to him once before. If my Dad were able to read, he would certainly love this book.

But there are other reasons I am thrilled to have had the privilege of presenting this book. The main reason: David wasn't perfect. Some people want their heroes to be perfect, but it is good once in a while to have a hero who is not perfect. When I know that God could use a man like David, he can use any of us. No man was so godly in all of Scripture, but no man sank so low. It is absolutely incredible. A man who was one of the great military, political, and spiritual leaders of the Bible was very human indeed. But a point at which I identify with David most of all is that he was not the perfect parent. My greatest sense of guilt is my own neglect of our two children as they grew up – because I was so busy in the Lord's work. David was one of the worst fathers in the Bible, and it will come out in the second part of this book. And when I think of how much God loved David, this gives me great consolation.

I was once asked to be interviewed for the Billy Graham organisation and they made a video – asking me all kinds of questions. The questions ranged from how I prepare sermons, how I view the church in Britain, what did I believe about the Holy Spirit and other things. And then the director said, 'We have sixty more seconds to use on this tape – how shall we use it?' Then the director said, 'Tell us a little bit about your family and your being a father.' I replied that they would not want me to speak on this – that I am not a success as a father, indeed I am failure as a father. The last thing they would want is my comments on a subject like that. I went on to say that I spent the early years at Westminster Chapel neglecting my children because I thought that putting my church first was putting God first, and I now believe that I would have preached just as well – perhaps better – had I put the family first and not sermon preparation, etc. About that time the director said 'Cut!' It turned out that he was filming the whole time I said that. What is more, when the video was edited, that was only part they used! They said that my words would be an encouragement to other ministers who have been so busy and have not given the attention to family matters and that is why they felt they should use that part. I didn't mind, because I get comfort from knowing that David wasn't perfect.

There is one other thing I should mention. I never will forget it as long as I live: I had come to the end of the life of David in 2 Samuel 12, and it happened to be at Christmas time. I announced to the Deacons during the Christmas break that I would not be finishing the life of David when we come back in January after Christmas. Why? Because I had no heart to go into the sadness of David's life, knowing that Nathan's prophecy about the sword not leaving David's house made his whole life look so sad. I simply did not want to preach on it.

But something changed my mind. We were having a day of prayer and fasting in early January and it was during that time that the Lord seemed to speak to me and say: 'So you are not going to be preaching on the second part of the life of David? Don't you know that that is where most of your people are?' I was shaken rigid. The Lord somehow made me see that my own members are not perfect – that they would be encouraged for me to go on preaching. I did. I enjoyed preaching on the life of David after his fall and in all that he went through as a result of his sin than any other part of his whole life! That is absolutely true, and it made me see how God loved David just as much after he sinned as he did when he was in his days of glory.

I therefore trust that this book will be a blessing to every reader, every church leader, every backslider and even those who have never been saved. Because there is an evangelistic thread that runs right through the book that will tell anybody, if they don't know, how to become a Christian.

2

A Man After God's Own Heart

1 Samuel 13:14

When I was a boy, my father would tell me Bible stories at bedtime. The story I would ask him to tell me most often was the story of Joseph because it took such a long time, but the one I probably enjoyed the most was the story of David and Goliath. We will come to this exciting encounter later, but in this chapter I want to put David's life into perspective and to portray something of the *man*. David, who lived around 1000 BC, is the only person in the Bible whom God called a man after his own heart. Both the Old and the New Testaments record this fact. In 1 Samuel 13:14 Samuel said, 'The Lord has sought out a man after his own heart', and in Acts 13:22 Paul said, 'After removing Saul, he made David their king. He testified concerning him: "I have found David son of Jesse a man after my own heart."' God seemed to be saying, 'I really like this person', and God was clearly involved on a personal, if not even an emotional level.

David was a sensitive man, a man with deep feelings; he was a poet and a musician, and in the psalms he unashamedly bared his soul, expressing his inmost thoughts for the world to see. He was also Israel's greatest king and the greatest military leader described in the Bible. Yet, in a sense, I think these things are less important than the fact that he was a man God held in high esteem, a man he used, and a man in whom he confided. David revealed his intimate fellowship with God when he said, 'The Lord confides in those who fear him' (Ps. 25:14). It is a great honour to have someone confide in you – but to think that *God* would confide in a human being is amazing! David was one such person with whom he chose to share what was on his heart. Now we may feel a little jealous of David. I think I do, for I want to become a man after God's own heart above all else. Yet the beauty of it all is that God is no respecter of persons and he wants to esteem us all as highly as he did David.

How, then, does one become a person after God's own heart? If we return to Acts 13 and look at the rest of verse 22, we discover the secret. God said, 'I have found David son of Jesse a man after my own heart; *he will do everything I want him to do' [my* italics].

Will you do everything God wants you to do? Do you feel a desire to pray more, a desire to know more of his will and to have a greater measure of his Spirit, a desire for him to trust you so much that he confides in you? God says, 'I want you; I love you and if you will let me, I will confide in you. Come close and hear my heart beat, and let your heart beat with mine.' 'But how can I be *certain* if I am a person after God's own heart?' you may ask. Well, I will show you four things about David, and then you can see if your experiences of God match his.

First, we see that David was a *found* man. God himself used this term to describe him and said, 'I have found David son of Jesse a man after my own heart' (Acts 13:22).

Now you may wonder *why* God should go looking for someone? To find the answer, we need to look at the background to the story.

Israel had spoilt their relationship with God and their requests grieved him, particularly when they asked for a king. God had established a theocracy and had sent Israel a series of leaders who led his people as he directed. The prophet Samuel had given a lifetime of faithful service, but the Israelites wanted to cast him aside; this displeased God, for by rejecting the leader he had chosen, they had rejected his authority over them. Nevertheless, he eventually yielded to their request, and Samuel anointed Saul as Israel's first king.

But Saul proved to be an unsuitable leader: he was filled with pride (he took himself too seriously) that led him to disobey God, who finally rejected him (1 Sam. 16:1). God later described his feelings to the prophet Hosea, saying, 'In my anger I gave you a king, and in my wrath I took him away' (Hos. 13:11). Dr Lloyd-Jones used to say to me that the worst thing that can happen to a man is to succeed before he is ready. I think that this was exactly what happened to Saul: he became king before he was ready.

Samuel then went to Saul and told him of God's decision to replace him with a man after his own heart. He said:

'You acted foolishly. . . . You have not kept the command the Lord your God gave you; if you had, he would have established your kingdom over Israel for all time. But now your kingdom will not endure; the Lord has sought out a man after his own heart and appointed him leader of his people, because you have not kept the Lord's command' (1 Sam. 13:13–14).

The Bible says that God cannot stand a proud look (Prov. 6:17) and he will have nothing to do with arrogant people: 'God opposes the proud but gives grace to the humble' (Jas. 4:6). Like Saul, we readily fall into the sin of pride – a fault we often fail to detect in ourselves, although we are quick to spot it in others; but when we recognize this sin in ourselves, we take a great step forward in spiritual maturity.

Today God looks over the world he created and he sees it in turmoil, inhabited by people who are filled with pride, and he seeks men and women after his own heart who will do his bidding. He goes into hospitals, into offices and factories and asks, 'Is there anybody here who will do everything I want him to do?' He goes into homes, into schools and colleges and asks, 'Is there anybody here who will do everything I ask?'

Notice *God* does the seeking: he takes the initiative. Jesus said, 'No-one can come to me unless the Father who sent me

17

draws him' (John 6:44). 'The Son of Man came to seek and to save what was lost' (Luke 19:10). So when we are talking about a *found* man or woman, we mean that God himself came looking for that person.

Sadly many people are too proud to admit they are lost and need help. But Jesus came into this world looking for those who recognized they had problems: he looked for those who did not know their way; he looked for those who were confused and disillusioned; he looked for those who needed help. And these are the kinds of people he seeks today.

In Luke 15 there is the Parable of the Lost Sheep. Jesus told this story to illustrate the seeking heart of God and his joy in finding and recovering the lost. He said a shepherd had a hundred sheep: ninety-nine were safe in the fold, but one was missing. So he went out to look for it, and having found the wanderer, he returned rejoicing and called together his friends and his neighbours saying, 'Rejoice with me; I have found my lost sheep' (v. 6). Then Jesus added, 'I tell you that in the same way there is more rejoicing in heaven over one sinner who repents than over ninety-nine righteous persons who do not need to repent' (v. 7).

In the same chapter is the Parable of the Prodigal Son, who left home taking with him his share of his father's money, which he soon spent in reckless and extravagant living. We do not know how long he was away, but his family did not know where to find him and perhaps had given up hope of ever seeing him again. However, eventually, hunger forced the prodigal to return home. His father was overjoyed to see him and laid on a banquet, explaining to his eldest son, 'We had to celebrate and be glad, because this brother of yours was dead and is alive again; he was lost and is found' (v. 32). This parable makes the same point: God's heart is set on finding the one who is lost, and he rejoices in his recovery.

Maybe you know what it is to be in the Christian fold, but somehow you became loose and wandered away into the wilderness. Maybe you can recall the joy of your salvation, but you were tempted by worldly pleasures and fell into sin. Perhaps, after a while, your conscience almost ceased to trouble you, until one day you woke up and realized you were lost. God comes to you and says, 'I'm looking for you!' Jesus said, '[I] came to seek and to save what was lost' (Luke 19:10).

The second thing we learn is that David was a *feared* man. Saul came to fear David, and we can understand why. Think for a moment: how would you feel if you were king and a prophet came to you saying, 'You are finished; God is looking for a man after his own heart, and he will replace you as king!'? That is exactly what happened to Saul. Samuel told him, 'Your kingdom will not endure; the Lord has sought out a man after his own heart' (1 Sam. 13:14). Saul knew then that God had finished with him, but instead of repenting, pride quickly filled his heart and he thought, 'Samuel is not infallible; perhaps his prophecy about me is wrong.'

It was not long before David appeared on the scene, and after David killed Goliath, Saul heard singing that angered him:

When the men were returning home after David had killed the Philistine, the women came out from all the towns of Israel to meet King Saul with singing and dancing, with joyful songs and with tambourines and lutes. As they danced, they sang:

'Saul has slain his thousands, and David his tens of thousands.'

Saul was very angry; this refrain galled him. 'They have credited David with tens of thousands,' he thought, 'but me with only thousands. What more can he get but the kingdom?'
    And from that time on Saul kept a jealous eye on David' (1 Sam. 18:6–9).

The king's alarm continued to grow, and we read in 1 Samuel 18:12 that 'Saul was afraid of David, because the Lord was with David but had left Saul.'

When God is with a person, as he was with David, that individual becomes a threat, someone to be feared, as you will discover if you become a Christian. Unconverted people will secretly respect you but will not show it because they are afraid. So they will try to undermine your faith by mocking you and catching you off-guard. Why? Because you have someone in your life who is not in theirs, someone whom they hate: all unregenerate people, by nature, hate God. So remember, when you become aligned with the God of the Bible, others will see you as a threat.

A friend of mine from the United States told me how he became a Christian. His testimony clearly illustrates that others, even those closest to you, will not be happy to hear of your conversion:

> I did not go to church with the idea of becoming a Christian at all. In fact, I went for all the *wrong* reasons. But during the service, my heart was stirred; then the sermon really gripped me. As they sang 'Just as I am, without one plea', I fought the feeling that I needed to be converted, and I held onto the pew in front of me so tightly the blood vessels in my hand felt as if they were about to burst. But when they got to the fourth verse of the hymn, I did what I thought I could never do: I stepped into the aisle and walked down to the front and accepted Jesus as my Saviour. I can't describe the peace that filled me then.
>
> I couldn't wait to get home because I wanted to tell my mother what happened. When I got into the house, I said, 'Mom, guess what! I got saved.'
>
> She said, 'Your supper's ready.'
>
> 'Mom, you didn't hear me. *I* got *saved!*'
>
> 'I heard you. Your supper will get cold. Go in and eat it.'
>
> 'But Mom, I went to church tonight. I found Jesus; *I'm saved*!'

There was no answer, and to his dismay he realized that his own mother was not a Christian. He had thought she was and assumed she would be so glad he had become a Christian too.

When something is precious to you, you look forward to sharing it with others and think they will be as happy as you are. But instead of this, they will be afraid of you. However, God will be with you, as he was with David, and he can be your hero, for he too was a feared man.

Third, we see that David was a *fallen* man.

Perhaps, until now, you have been thinking, 'There is no point in believing I can be a person after God's own heart. He won't want *me*. Look what I have done!' Listen. I know of *nothing* more encouraging than this: the only person in the Bible described as 'a man after God's own heart' was far from perfect. In fact, David committed what was possibly the most serious, scandalous, single sin described in the Old Testament.

After he became king, David probably experienced what James Dobson calls 'a midlife re-evaluation' – in his case, the kind of crisis where a middle-aged man feels the need to be admired by a young, beautiful woman. We read how David succumbed to temptation in 2 Samuel 11:2–3:

> One evening David got up from his bed and walked around on the roof of the palace. From the roof he saw a woman bathing. The woman was very beautiful, and David sent someone to find out about her. The man said, 'Isn't this Bathsheba, the daughter of Eliam and the wife of Uriah the Hittite?'

The fact that Bathsheba was a married woman should have stopped David in his tracks. However, if we read on, we see that what happened was this: 'Then David sent messengers to get her. She came to him, and he slept with her' (v. 4).

Perhaps David and Bathsheba thought it would just be an 'afternoon affair' and their adultery would remain hidden. But a few weeks later Bathsheba sent a message to the king, telling him she was pregnant (v. 5).

No doubt David panicked a little at first, but then he decided that there was a solution to his problem after all. So he sent for Uriah and offered him weekend home leave, thinking that after Uriah slept with his wife, he would never discover that he was not the father of her child.

However, things did not go according to plan, for Uriah's conscience troubled him: 'I can't go home while my fellow soldiers are on the battlefield,' he thought.

When David discovered that Uriah had turned down his offer of leave, he did the unthinkable:

> In the morning David wrote a letter to Joab [the commander of his army] and sent it with Uriah. In it he wrote, 'Put Uriah in the front line where the fighting is fiercest. Then withdraw from him so that he will be struck down and die.'
>
> So while Joab had the city under siege, he put Uriah at a place where he knew the strongest defenders were. When the men of the city came out and fought against Joab, some of the men in David's army fell; moreover, Uriah the Hittite was dead (vv. 14–17).

David's sin was tantamount to murder, but God did not bend the rules for him: he was found out.

In fact, all those who are found by God, are also *found out*. So if you have done wrong and think you can escape the consequences of your sin, think twice! If you abuse a woman, step on people and hurt them, or lie about others to gain promotion, remember, you may seem to get away with it for a while, but it is not a good sign. Those who are *found* get *found out*, as David was to discover, for God revealed the truth to the prophet Nathan, and he went to David and exposed his crime (2 Sam. 12).

It is marvellous when God finds us out. It was certainly the best thing that could have happened to David.

Fourth, David was a *forgiven* man.
When Nathan confronted David, he repented of his sin and confessed, 'I have sinned against the Lord' (2 Sam. 12:13).

Then, having admitted his crime, he prayed for mercy. We can read David's prayer of heartfelt penitence in Psalm 51:

> Have mercy on me, O God,
>   according to your unfailing love;
> according to your great compassion
>   blot out my transgressions.
> Wash away all my iniquity
>   and cleanse me from my sin.
> For I know my transgressions,
>   and my sin is always before me.
> Against you, you only, have I sinned
>   and done what is evil in your sight. . . .'
> Cleanse me with hyssop [a plant used to sprinkle the blood of
>   the sacrifice], and I shall be clean;
>   wash me, and I shall be whiter than snow (vv. 1–4, 7).

The only thing that David could plead then was the blood of Jesus, because he foresaw Jesus' sacrifice on the cross. That is a fact, for he knew that the Mosaic law made no provision for pardoning an adulterer: the penalty for adultery was death by stoning; nor did it make provision for pardoning a murderer: the penalty for murder was also death by stoning. So David realized he was in deep trouble and his only hope was to throw himself on the Lord's mercy and cry, 'The sacrifices of God are a broken spirit; a broken and contrite heart, O God, you will not despise' (Ps. 51:17). David felt so grateful when Nathan told him, 'The Lord has taken away your sin' (2 Sam. 12:13) and he received God's forgiveness. And we too have so much for which we should be thankful, for we can plead the blood of Jesus, who bore our sins in his own body so that we might be forgiven. The Bible says, 'If we confess our sins, he is faithful and just and will forgive us our sins and purify us from all unrighteousness' (1 John 1:9).

3

Beyond Outward Appearance

1 Samuel 16:1–13

We instinctively judge by outward appearance, but we should all learn *not* to judge a book by its cover. Yet when I was looking for a girlfriend, that was exactly what I did: I picked the prettiest girl I could find. However, when I fell in love with Louise, I was blessed that she was just as lovely *inside*. If she had turned out to be empty-headed or spiritually barren, I would have been in trouble, because I just *had* to have her as my wife. Happily, God overruled in my case, but it is possible to make a very serious mistake when you judge by outward appearance alone. Yet we all tend to do it when determining who is worth knowing or when judging whether somebody is really a Christian.

Now this chapter should speak mainly to those who have experienced rejection. Have people passed you by? Perhaps, as a child, you remember how it felt not to be chosen for the football team or for a role in the school play. Perhaps your hopes of promotion at work have been dashed or you have been rejected because of your family background. Or maybe you may feel that you were overlooked when it came to receiving great privileges or fine gifts, and you stand back and watch others receiving all the acclaim.

I remember when I was at school in Ashland, Kentucky, the boys would pick sides for a game of football, but they always left me till last. Somebody then had to say, 'Well, who will take R.T.?'

'You take him.'

'No, you take him.'

And there I was, the player nobody wanted. It didn't do a lot for my ego!

However, I realize why they overlooked me: they were judging by appearances. It was the same when I went to high school. The school published an annual book containing photographs of the students. Pictures of some people, like the queen of the senior prom, or the star football player covered the whole page. One page contained pictures of students most likely to succeed, but I was never in the top fifty!

Samuel had the task of choosing the person whom God wanted to succeed Saul as king. We too must find out the person God wants, but we must remember that when God looks for someone, he does not judge by outward appearance: he looks on the heart. Although he was a mature man of God, Samuel still had to grasp this, but this is a lesson we must all learn.

Some years ago, when I was a pastor of a church in the state of Ohio, I noticed an unconverted man who came regularly to the Sunday evening service. As I preached the sermon each week, I looked at him and thought I could tell by his expression that he was about to give his life to the Lord. That was many years ago, and I am *still* praying for his conversion. Others, whom I felt were far less likely to receive the gospel, surprised me by responding to the altar call and accepting salvation. As the Bible says, 'Man looks at the outward appearance' (1 Sam. 16:7).

One of the most interesting stories I have heard is how Jim Kennedy led a man to Christ in Fort Lauderdale. I know the story well because the man concerned was Dr Freeman Springer, our dentist. One evening Jim and his wife Anne went to witness to him and to his wife in their home. Dr Springer was very courteous and invited them in. Jim presented the gospel to the couple and then asked, 'Would you like to receive the gift of salvation?'

'Yes, please,' they replied.

It was so easy. Nevertheless, Jim thought, 'I shall have to

pray with them; I can tell by their expressions that God is not at work here.'

'Are you *sure* you understand it all?' Jim asked.

'Yes, thank you.'

Jim and his wife then prayed with them, shook hands and left.

When they were in the car, Jim turned to Anne and said, 'That's one couple we will never see again.'

However, the next morning Dr Springer got out of bed and opened the blinds and daylight streamed into the room. 'It was then', he said, 'I realized I had eternal life.' His wife was converted too, and they were not only in church that following Sunday, they became soul-winners. When I last talked with Dr Springer, he had led more than seventy-five people to Christ. Yet Jim, going by outward appearance alone, had thought, 'Nothing is happening here.'

'Do not consider his appearance or his height . . . . The Lord does not look at the things man looks at. Man looks at the outward appearance but the Lord looks at the heart' (1 Sam. 16:7). This was what God told Samuel when he instructed him to look among the sons of Jesse for Saul's successor.

Why do you think God said this? Because Samuel was wrong. When Eliab, Jesse's eldest son, passed in front of him, and he saw how tall and how handsome he was, Samuel had said, 'Surely the Lord's anointed stands here before the Lord' (v. 6). He had thought he had found the right man, but God said, 'Wait!' Samuel had to learn to do things God's way.

Eliab too had a lesson to learn. He would have to realize that Samuel, a man of God, could make a mistake; the man God had chosen was not even present at the time. I wonder how Eliab felt when Samuel passed him by. For a moment he thought *he* was to be selected.

Perhaps you feel that your minister or members of your church have overlooked you. But remember they are only human; churches are filled with people who share your human failings, and like everyone else, Christians sometimes make mistakes.

I want us to consider four things about the task of the church from the story of how Samuel set about finding a new king.

First, we see the task of the church is to preach the gospel.

Samuel's task was to find the person God had chosen, and the task of the church is the same: to find those whom God is seeking. The church must hold out the bread of life to the hungry and the water of life to the thirsty; its task is to give everyone the invitation expressed in Revelation 22:17: 'The Spirit and the bride say, "Come!" And let him who hears say, "Come!" Whoever is thirsty, let him come; and whoever wishes, let him take the free gift of the water of life.'

At the beginning of 1 Samuel 16 the prophet was in mourning, because King Saul had disobeyed God, who rejected him (1 Sam. 15:26). Now Saul is a picture of the apostate church – a church that has rejected the faith. And though a church may have a fine building with splendid stained-glass windows, though it may have a cross above its doors and a great historic past, if that church is not preaching the gospel, God will reject it.

Many of us mourn over the conditions today, and it does not make our job any easier that many people do not believe that heaven and hell exist. Yet this has happened because the church, generally speaking, no longer preaches about heaven and hell and the doctrine of atonement by the blood of Jesus Christ; nor does it believe the Bible is infallible.

But there is always a danger of grieving too long and allowing our misery to paralyze us to the extent that we sit back and fail to do the work God has asked us to do. Remember, God said to Samuel, 'Stop mourning for Saul.' God doesn't stop working and he tells us, 'Get on with the task I gave you.'

Second, we need to see that the church should begin searching for the person God has chosen with a *general* call.

Here is the way God put it to Samuel: 'I am sending you to

Jesse of Bethlehem' (1 Sam. 16:1). The man whom God had chosen to succeed Saul was a member of Jesse's family, but Samuel did not know *which* of his sons it would be. God led Samuel a step at a time. He did not say, 'Go to Jesse and you will find that the seventh son, David, is the one I have chosen.' He said, 'Go to Jesse's family.'

God often sends us in a general direction and provides detailed instructions later. Maybe God is telling you to move in a general direction, but you respond by saying, 'I won't go until I know all the details.' That is disobedience. God does not lead us directly from A to Z, but from A to B, and from B to C. If you insist on wanting the details first, then God will pass you by. Remember, when God speaks to you, he will not tell you everything until you begin doing what he asks.

If you are not yet a Christian, your first step is to respond to what God says and move from A to B. He says, 'Receive Jesus Christ as your Saviour and Lord and confess him.' When you do that, God will take you from B to C. It is a great way to live: God will be with you; he will open the right doors and shut the wrong ones; moreover, he will *never* desert you.

Third, we must remember that the church seeking the person God has chosen, must move forward under the banner of the shed blood of Jesus Christ.

In 1 Samuel 16:3 God said, 'Invite Jesse to the sacrifice.' But Samuel was fearful, asking, 'How can I go? Saul will hear about it and kill me' (v. 2). Samuel had cause to be apprehensive, for Saul was vindictive and might well have tried to harm him had he heard that Samuel had anointed his successor.

Samuel was afraid then, and we have some reason to be alarmed today. You see, the devil was opposed to what Samuel was to do then, and he opposes anyone responding to the gospel now. We see him at work in the apostate church, which is often more anxious to keep people from being converted than it is in defending the faith God called it to uphold.

However, Satan hates and fears the blood of Jesus. There are two reasons for this.

First, the blood of Jesus spelt the devil's defeat. When Jesus was hanging on the cross, Satan thought he had successfully carried out the greatest plan since the dawn of history, and he and his hordes, if I may put it this way, were popping champagne corks and celebrating, shouting, 'We did it! We did it! Jesus is on the cross. He is going to die!' Only later did they discover that the blood that Jesus shed was God's way of saving the world and snatching it from Satan's grip. So he hates and fears the blood of Jesus.

He also knows that the blood of Jesus protects the Christian. Knowing Samuel was afraid of Saul learning that he was to anoint a new king, the Lord said, 'Take a heifer with you and say, "I have come to sacrifice to the Lord." Invite Jesse to the sacrifice, and I will show you what to do' (1 Sam. 16:2–3). If you are afraid, remember the great sacrifice that Jesus, the Lamb of God, made two thousand years ago. The blood that he shed on the cross will cover and protect you. So whenever you feel the fear of death or fear of Satan, just say, 'Lord Jesus, cover me with your precious blood.'

The second reason the devil fears the blood of Jesus is that when you become a Christian, Jesus' blood covers all your sins, and in God's eyes you are blameless. I do not know how great your sins are; perhaps they are comparatively small, nevertheless, they haunt you. They should, for God hates all sin, and when the Holy Spirit convicts you, you will feel awful. But if you repent and plead the merit of Jesus' blood, God will wash your sins away and never remember them again (Isa. 43:25).

Samuel continued his journey and when he arrived in Bethlehem, the elders came to meet him and asked fearfully, '"Do you come in peace?"

Samuel replied, "Yes, in peace"' (vv. 4–5).

You may wonder why the elders were afraid. However, people are often afraid when they first hear the gospel message: it is a natural reaction. Martin Luther once said, 'God uses sex to drive a man to marriage, ambition to drive a man to service and fear to drive a man to faith.' So fear gives way to faith, and faith in Jesus Christ always brings peace. In fact, whenever you obey the Holy Spirit, you will find peace.

The fourth thing we must learn is that the church does not determine who will become a part of it.

You will recall that when Samuel saw Jesse's eldest son Eliab, he looked at him and said, 'Surely the Lord's anointed stands here before the Lord' (1 Sam. 16:6), and for a moment Samuel thought that *he* was going to decide who was going to be the next king of Israel. However, as we have seen, he was wrong.

Sadly, sometimes a church will encourage only people whom it deems socially acceptable to join it. Yet, as we have already seen, judging by outward appearances is the way of the world. The world judges people by the colour of their skin, their looks, their clothes, their background, culture, education and occupation. However, the church has no right to do that.

The early Christians were wrong when they tried to fill the church with middle-class people and they grieved the Holy Spirit. But if you were to see a video replay showing the masses of people who followed Jesus, you would see the *common* people heard him gladly (Mark 12:37 AV), and Jesus owned them as his. I believe God is grieved that the church in Britain today is largely middle class. The late Dr Martin Lloyd-Jones once said to me, 'Christianity has not touched the working class of Britain.' It is a sad fact.

Samuel had to learn to follow the leading of the Spirit. God had not chosen Eliab, whose height and appearance were so impressive; he said, 'Don't look on the outward appearance.' Jesse then called Abinadab, the son next in age, but Samuel rejected him too. In fact, eventually seven of Jesse's sons passed before Samuel, and he began to think he had made an awful mistake: 'God told me to go to Jesse's house. I have seen all his sons, but God has not chosen any of them. How could I be wrong?'

There was only one other possibility; so he asked Jesse, 'Are these all the sons you have?' (v.11).

> 'There is still the youngest,' Jesse answered, 'but he is tending the sheep.'
>
> Samuel said, 'Send for him; we will not sit down until he arrives.'
>
> So he sent and had him brought in. He was ruddy, with a fine appearance and handsome features.
>
> Then the Lord said, 'Rise and anoint him; he is the one' (1 Sam. 16:11–12).

This passage shows us that although God had chosen David, his own father passed him over and rejected him.

Have your parents rejected you? Could it be that you have never enjoyed a good relationship with them? Has someone you held in high regard let you down and belittled you? If so, remember, God wants you and says, 'Maybe others have rejected you, but I want you; do *I* matter? I will not abandon you. Will *I* do?'

Samuel discovered that the most unlikely person was the one the Holy Spirit had chosen, and he anointed David. Today, as then, the church must follow the Holy Spirit's guidance. Man always looks at what seems religious and outwardly moral, but these things do not count in God's sight. He does not judge by outward appearance but looks at a person's heart.

4

The Anointing

1 Samuel 16:1–13

God had commissioned Samuel to do one of the most dangerous and daring things that ever a man did: to anoint David as king while the reigning monarch was still alive. It took great courage to seek out the person God had chosen and to anoint him, but Samuel obeyed the Lord, and having found David, he anointed him.

The Bible uses the word 'anointing' in several ways, but I will mention two of them. First, it uses the term in the sense of 'inauguration' – a ceremony when someone is instituted into office. This is an outward ritual, and when people think of the anointing in the Old Testament, they often think of this.

Such a ceremony took place when Samuel anointed David. Samuel took a horn – probably a ram's horn – that he had filled with freshly pressed olive oil, then he poured the oil on David's head. You can imagine how it felt when the oil ran down over his hair and onto his face, trickling down onto his shoulders and his clothes! David undoubtedly drew from this experience when he described Aaron's anointing as high priest in Psalm 133:

> How good and pleasant it is
> when brothers live together in unity!
> It is like precious oil poured on the head,
> running down on the beard,
> running down on Aaron's beard,
> down upon the collar of his robes (vv. 1–2).

As high priest, Aaron wore a robe that was ornate. Imagine olive oil dripping down on it! Why would anybody want to ruin such a beautiful garment? The answer is, the oil was far more important than Aaron's beautiful robe for it symbolizes the Holy Spirit, the secret of the power of God. And when I preach, I am aware that far more important than the notes I have prepared is the anointing of the Holy Spirit, and when he comes I must be willing to put my preparation aside and speak the word *he* gives me.

A second way in which the Bible uses the term 'anointing', then, is in the sense of what happens in a person's heart. In 1 Samuel 16:13 we read: 'Samuel took the horn of oil and anointed him in the presence of his brothers, and from that day on the Spirit of the Lord came upon David in power.' And far more important than the crown that would one day be placed on David's head was that inward anointing of the Holy Spirit.

The same remains true today: what happens inwardly is far more significant than any visible ritual. Baptism is one example of an outward ceremony in the church. Yet sadly, some people make a public profession of faith in Jesus whose hearts are barren, for they have never been converted. Another example of an outward ceremony in the church is the celebration of the Lord's Supper. However, when people partake of the bread and the wine, they need an inward discerning of the Lord's body and the anointing of the Holy Spirit.

'Anointing' is a word translated from the Greek word *chrisma* and refers to the application of oil or ointment. The term is derived from the root *chrio*, the word underlying 'Christ'. Jesus, the Son of God, was called Christ meaning 'Messiah' or 'the Anointed One'. Another word, *charismata*, sounds similar to *chrisma*, but its meaning is different and it is used in the Bible to refer mainly to the spiritual gifts that result from the anointing.

Sadly, this is a generation where people are often more

interested in the *charismata* than they are in the *chrisma*: they are often more interested in receiving the gifts than the Holy Spirit himself. (Paul discusses spiritual gifts in 1 Corinthians 12.) Moreover, they assume that if they have a gift they also have the anointing, but it is possible in a sense to have the gift *without* the anointing, as Jesus pointed out when, speaking of the Final Judgment, he said:

> 'Many will say to me on that day, "Lord, Lord, did we not prophesy in your name, and in your name drive out demons and perform many miracles?"
>
> Then I will tell them plainly, "I never knew you. Away from me, you evildoers!"' (Matt. 7:22–23).

The proof of this inward anointing is that it brings you in touch with Jesus Christ. He becomes central in your life, and you are not interested in some ecstatic experience for the sake of constantly feeling good, but you want to honour him.

When Samuel anointed David, God planted the root we read about in Isaiah 11:1: 'A shoot will come up from the stump of Jesse; from his roots a Branch will bear fruit.' Jesus said, 'I am the Root and the Offspring of David, and the bright Morning Star' (Rev. 22:16). So when God raised up David, he raised up a man from the tribe of Judah who was the forerunner of Jesus, his own Son. This event was so momentous that not only would it affect the whole of Israel, but it was deeply significant to the greater kingdom of God, and to this day it directly affects us all.

David's anointing was kept secret from Israel as a whole, for both he and Samuel would have been killed if the word leaked out. But Samuel did what he had to do, and performed the ceremony 'in the presence of [David's] brothers' (1 Sam. 16:13). But, as we have seen, the inward anointing that took place with David was the more important aspect of his anointing, and it was the real secret of his success.

It is the same with preaching. Do you know that the great Charles Spurgeon was not formally ordained as a minister?

He said, 'Their empty hands on my empty head will not add to my empty ministry.' Yet what Spurgeon *did* have was an anointing of the Spirit. Sadly, today we hear of many who are in the ministry who are neither called nor anointed.

David not only had a secret anointing but a secret *application* because the Spirit of God came upon David with the oil. The oil that dripped down over David's head was more than mere olive oil; in Psalm 89:20 God said, 'I have found David my servant; with *my* [my italics] sacred oil I have anointed him.' And this is what we must remember: it was *God's* holy oil, so David's anointing depended upon God and not on any external factors.

Let us consider this for a moment.

First, we see his anointing did not depend on circumstances in his country. As in the period of the judges, 'Everyone did as he saw fit' (Jdgs. 21:25). Israel was spiritually and morally bankrupt, and rebelling against God's rule, they demanded a king (1 Sam. 8).

Looking at the moral and spiritual state of the world around you today, you may say, 'It would be useless for the Holy Spirit's anointing to fall on me. Look how godless and immoral society has become! What can *I* do to change anything?' However, you must remember Israel was in a similar condition in David's day, but this did not prevent David from accepting his anointing.

Second, the anointing did not depend upon David's parents. Had it been left to Jesse, David would not have been anointed; he did not think for a moment that God would choose his youngest son and had, in fact, left David out in the fields looking after the sheep, as we see in 1 Samuel 16:

> Jesse made seven of his sons pass before Samuel, but Samuel said to him, 'The Lord has not chosen these.' So he asked Jesse, 'Are these all the sons you have?'
>
> 'There is still the youngest,' Jesse answered, 'but he is tending the sheep.'

Samuel said, 'Send for him; we will not sit down until he arrives.'

So he sent and had him brought in. . . .

Then the Lord said, 'Rise and anoint him; he is the one' (vv. 10–12).

Thus David could never say, 'My *father* chose me to be king of Israel', and his anointing did not depend on his parents.

The same is true for you, and if the Holy Spirit comes to indwell you, it will not depend on your parents. Perhaps you feel that you have not had a good upbringing and you have not been raised in a Christian home. But it is marvellous how God can step in and overrule your parents' influence on you. Yet conversely, you should realize that if you do have Christian parents, they cannot pass salvation to you. They can have you baptized and bring you up to attend church, but these things will not save you. You become a Christian only when something happens inside *you*.

Third, David's anointing did not depend upon Samuel, the prophet who poured the oil upon David's head. The proof of that is, after Samuel poured the oil on him, the prophet left. He did not stay to watch the Holy Spirit at his work in David's life; the Bible says, 'Samuel then went to Ramah' (1 Sam. 16:13).

Moreover, what God will do in your life will not depend upon the preacher who gives you the message. It is wonderful when I see people converted under my ministry and I watch them develop spiritually, but often people are converted at Westminster Chapel and then become members of another church and grow in grace there. Yet sometimes they visit us and I am encouraged to see that they have matured under someone else's ministry. This proves to me that it was not my rhetoric that led them to profess Christ but the work of the Holy Spirit. It is not what the preacher does but what *God* does that counts.

Fourth, David's anointing did not depend on him but

entirely on God's grace. The same is true for us. Paul said, 'For it is by grace you have been saved, through faith – and this not from yourselves, it is the gift of God . . .' (Eph. 2:8–9).

Perhaps you have not yet been converted because you doubt whether you are strong enough to persevere in the Christian life and say, 'I don't think I could hold out for long.' Well, if you were not truly converted you would be right; in fact, without the anointing of the Holy Spirit you would not last three days! But it is *God* who regenerates a person. And the grace that will save you is the grace that will change you and keep you.

I *know* I am going to heaven, but I am not trusting in my own efforts. I hope by the grace of God I will persevere in my Christian walk, but I am not depending on this; I could fall into sin tomorrow; no one is exempt from temptation. My assurance of salvation rests solely on the fact that Jesus paid my debt on the cross. And if you put your trust in him too, the Holy Spirit will plant 'the root from the stump of Jesse' in your heart.

5

The Danger of Feeling Good

1 Samuel 16:14–23

Someone once said that a Puritan is a person who fears that somebody, somewhere, may be feeling good. This is an unfair definition, but I know what he meant by it. I have seen some who are only happy when they are miserable, but *very* miserable if they see someone who is happy. Some people do not want you to take away their reason for complaining. This is why, before Jesus healed the invalid at the pool of Bethesda, he asked him, 'Do you *want* [my italics] to get well?' (John 5:6).

Feeling good is not necessarily bad or dangerous: God wants his children to feel good. Jesus said, 'Your Father has been *pleased* [my italics] to give you the kingdom' (Luke 12:32). Moreover, Paul tells us in Galatians 5:22, 'The fruit of the Spirit is love, joy, peace . . . '.

Saul felt good when he listened to David playing his harp. We read in 1 Samuel 16:23: 'Whenever the spirit from God came upon Saul, David would take his harp and play. Then relief would come to Saul; he would feel better, and the evil spirit would leave him.' However, it was bad for *Saul* to feel this way, and in this chapter I want to show you why.

Saul had disobeyed God and was unrepentant. If only he had asked God's forgiveness when Samuel came to him and said, 'Because you have rejected the word of the Lord, he has rejected you as king' (1 Sam. 15:23)! In the Bible we learn that often when God told someone, 'You are finished!' and that person repented, God changed his mind and forgave him. For example, we read in 1 Kings 21 that the prophet Elijah came to King Ahab, one of the most wicked kings in the history of Israel, and said, 'I have found you . . . because you have sold yourself to do evil in the eyes of the Lord. I am going to bring disaster on you' (v. 20). However, we read that Ahab repented:

> When Ahab heard these words, he tore his clothes, put on sackcloth and fasted. He lay in sackcloth and went around meekly.
> Then the word of the Lord came to Elijah the Tishbite: 'Have you noticed how Ahab has humbled himself before me? Because he has humbled himself, I will not bring this disaster in his day' (vv. 27–29).

God was moved by Ahab's remorse and forgave him.

The same was clear when God sent Jonah to Nineveh with this message: 'Forty more days and Nineveh will be overturned' (Jonah 3:4). Word soon reached the king, who repented in sackcloth and ashes and said:

> Let everyone call urgently on God. Let them give up their evil ways and their violence. Who knows? God may yet relent and with compassion turn from his fierce anger so that we will not perish' (Jonah 3:8–9).

Are you a backslider? Have you fallen into sin and despair, thinking, 'I am finished; my days are numbered, so it would be pointless for me to repent'? But God has not changed, and what was true in Old Testament times is true today: God will forgive you if you humble yourself and truly repent. One day a penitent David would throw himself on God's mercy and cry: 'The sacrifices of God are a broken spirit; a broken and contrite heart, O God, you will not despise' (Ps. 51:17). And when God sees *your* tears of repentance, his heart will be moved.

But Saul shed no tears; he dug in his heels. So we read in 1

Samuel 16:14, 'Now the Spirit of the Lord had departed from Saul, and an evil spirit from the Lord tormented him.' This shows that when we disobey God and justify our actions, we may hear strange voices, such not being the Holy Spirit, but their message will not bring peace.

Now when Saul was troubled by an evil spirit as a result of his disobedience, his attendants were certain they knew just the thing to cure him. So they went to the king with their well-meaning advice:

> 'See, an evil spirit from God is tormenting you. Let our lord command his servants here to search for someone who can play the harp. He will play when the evil spirit from God comes upon you, and you will feel better' (1 Sam. 16:15–16).

Saul was beset by those who had no real discernment about what he ought to do, but who, nevertheless, offered their advice. He trusted his attendants, but the best they could do was to advise him to find a musician to play him soothing music.

It is an awful thing to be surrounded by people you trust who offer bad advice. Perhaps you are not yet a Christian, or you are a backslider, and you are in trouble; maybe you are filled with anxiety and deeply depressed. Perhaps you have sinned by breaking up someone's marriage or perhaps you are 'living in sin' and your conscience is troubling you. Yet the only kind of advice you receive is 'Maybe you are taking life too seriously. You ought to relax and have a drink occasionally' or 'Look, you are tired and depressed; you need a holiday.' But seeking consolation in things that makes you feel good is dangerous, for such bad advice will lead you to deal only with the symptoms and never the cause of your problem. What you *really* need to do is to get right with God.

So encouraging King Saul to seek solace in music rather than seek God in repentance, was the worst thing his advisers could have done. The result was, that although Saul still wore the crown, he lost the anointing, the sense of God's Spirit upon him, and the day would come when he uttered what are possibly the saddest words in the Bible: 'God has turned away from me. He no longer answers me' (1 Sam. 28:15).

There are two things I want us to see in this chapter: (1) David entered Saul's service, and (2) the effect David had on Saul.

You may wonder how Saul knew about David. The answer is, one of his attendants went to him and said:

> 'I have seen a son of Jesse of Bethlehem who knows how to play the harp. He is a brave man and a warrior. He speaks well and is a fine-looking man. And the Lord is with him.'
>
> Then Saul sent messengers to Jesse and said, 'Send me your son David, who is with the sheep' (1 Sam. 16:18–19).

My point is, David did not approach Saul: people came to him.

Do you ever wonder if others will ever discover your gift? The way of the world is to advertise, so people become familiar with a name. In Hollywood they say, 'It doesn't matter what people say about you as long as they spell your name correctly.' But if you feel you need a high profile, remember, Jesus said, 'Whoever exalts himself will be humbled, and whoever humbles himself will be exalted' (Matt. 23:12). Do you really want to be exalted if God does not wish it? Surely not! If you want success at any cost, you are not Christ's disciple.

What, then, was the secret of David's success? I think we should note two things.

The first is, as we have seen, David did not advertise his talents. Interestingly, only *one* servant knew about David's talent. The same is true for you: it is not how many who know about you that counts; it is the right person, at the right time, in the right place, who sets things in motion, and only God can prompt someone to do that. When God is ready to use you, the world will find out about you, but *you* cannot instigate this.

The other reason for David's success was that the anointing of God was on him. I must tell you that whoever you are, however talented, your gift is useless to him without the anointing of the Holy Spirit. Perhaps God is keeping you in the background because you have a spiritual problem. If so, you need to see that he will not use you until, like David, you totally resign yourself to his sovereign will.

When Saul called David into his service, he played his harp in the sometimes threatening presence of the man who would become his enemy. Remember, when Samuel anointed David, Saul still wore the crown; it was a very dangerous thing for Samuel to do, but it was also dangerous for David. How do you suppose he felt when Saul summoned him to work at his court? Entering the king's service would be David's first test.

In some ways the anointing of the Holy Spirit can be daunting. If the Spirit of God comes upon you, he will suddenly summon you to service unlike anything you have ever dreamed of or planned, but Peter said we should not be amazed when we face trials:

> Dear friends, do not be surprised at the painful trial you are suffering, as though something strange were happening to you. But rejoice that you participate in the sufferings of Christ, so that you may be overjoyed when his glory is revealed (1 Pet. 4:12–13).

The very nature of the Christian witness means we should expect opposition, so do not think that if God anoints you, you will live in a state of perpetual ecstasy. Serving him may cost you dearly; it may thrust you right into the heart of Satan's territory. You may momentarily falter, saying, 'I can't do it.' But you *can do it*; God never elevates a person to the level of their incompetence, and, as surely as you have the anointing, he will lead you.

David must now do only one thing: to play that harp as

though he were playing for the Lord himself rather than for the king. Yet he must have been tempted to play his harp to please Saul. It is tempting when you are in the presence of powerful people to modify your gift accordingly. However, if you succumb to this impulse, you will fail, for you will grieve the Holy Spirit, who placed you where you are. You should seek to please God alone.

When David played his harp, the evil spirit would leave Saul for a while and he would feel good again. Nevertheless, feeling this way was bad for him, and, as I said earlier, good feelings can be dangerous. Let me explain why.

First, feelings can be so deceitful. For example, when we are in pain, we long for something that will take it away. Yet the ability to feel pain is a blessing because it signals something is wrong with our bodies, and it can be unwise to respond to pain by reaching for a powerful analgesic that will deaden it without first investigating its cause.

In a similar way, a troubled spirit can be a blessing, for that is the Holy Spirit's way of trying to reach you, so do not stifle your conscience and look for an escape. Indulging in alcohol, sex or drugs may give you a good feeling, but these do not deal with your real problems. If, however, you will listen to what God says through his word, you will come face to face with the truth about your condition. Hebrews 4:12 says:

> The word of God is living and active. Sharper than any double-edged sword, it penetrates even to dividing soul and spirit, joints and marrow; it judges the thoughts and attitudes of the heart.

So if God, like a master surgeon with his scalpel, takes his double-edged sword and begins to operate on you, although he does not use an anaesthetic and the experience is painful, thank him for it, for he will make you whole. David's music made Saul feel good, but it did not deal with his real need.

The second reason that feeling good is dangerous is that

good feelings diminish. This was the case with Saul. The Bible says, 'Whenever the spirit from God came upon Saul, David would take his harp and play. Then relief would come to Saul' (1 Sam. 16:23). Clearly, the good feeling Saul had did not last, and when David stopped playing, Saul would order him to start again.

When you run from God, you too will find that feelings of well-being are transient and you must repeat the activity that produced them. This is how people become addicted to drugs and alcohol. Feelings diminish, but Jesus promised to give lasting peace and joy (John 15:11).

Third, feeling good is dangerous because feelings are delicate and unreliable. We all have swings of mood, and our feelings are not trustworthy. We need to trust instead in what Jesus did for us when he died on the cross. His love for us does not waver, though our emotions change constantly. Satan loves to make us feel lonely, anxious and depressed, but he hates and fears the blood of Jesus. So when he tempts us to despair, we should plead that precious blood and say, 'Jesus died for me.' We must not depend on our feelings, but on this fact.

Fourth, good feelings can be dangerous because they prevent people from seeing their real need. Saul never knew why he felt better when David played his harp. However, he felt good because he was in the presence of a man anointed with the Holy Spirit.

When my wife Louise and I were in Miami, we happened to meet the founder of a well-known company. He invited me to his home and I would visit him there and pray with him. He enjoyed these meetings and would say, 'I feel so good when you are in my home!'

I would then ask him, 'Mr . . . , would you like to receive Jesus?'

'Well, I'm not ready to do that yet,' he would reply. 'But do come back; I feel so good when you are with me.'

Sometimes he would telephone me, inviting me to return,

and I would go to his house and pray with him again. His eyes would fill with tears and he would say, 'You make me feel so good.'

Sadly, I was unable to help him, and he is dead now. He was satisfied with a good feeling, as if everything was all right with his soul.

I will never forget preaching in Fort Lauderdale one evening and feeling the Holy Spirit coming on me in power as I spoke. In the congregation that night was an unconverted man whom we hoped would respond to the gospel. Now although he did not come forward at the altar call, I thought he was under great conviction and I could not wait to see him after the service. As he stood outside the church, I went up to him expectantly. He smiled broadly at me and said, 'I really liked your talk; it really made me feel really *good*.'

Oh no! It is so easy for a person to say he feels better when he is in the presence of the Holy Spirit. Yet what a pity if he is content with only a good feeling and goes to hell! As Jesus said, 'What good will it be for a man if he gains the whole world, yet forfeits his soul?' (Matt. 16:26).

If the Holy Spirit has convicted you of sin, it is better to feel bad now, for you can repent and seek God's forgiveness. Jesus loves you; he will pardon you and accept you. You can feel good in the *right* way if you will honour his word. Saul did not do this, but *you* can.

6

Anointed King – But Without A Crown

1 Samuel 17:1–26

One day David would become the greatest king Israel ever had. But that would not happen for a long time yet. Meanwhile, although David had the anointing, Saul had the crown.

Now instead of using the word 'crown' we could use the word 'vindication', a term meaning others believe you are right. I speak from experience when I say there is nothing more painful than not being vindicated, when, for example, you are falsely accused or when you see the truth yet you stand alone in your conviction. I know what it is to have family and close friends desert me; I *knew* that I was right, but no one else thought so. God could have vindicated me then, but I had to wait a long time for this to happen.

Perhaps you are waiting for vindication. You have the inner witness of the Holy Spirit that God is with you, but others question it and you long to be proved right. David longed for God to vindicate him; in Psalm 40:1 he said, 'I waited patiently for the Lord.'

Do you want the anointing? Have you been praying to be filled with the Holy Spirit? Perhaps you think that when you receive this blessing your Christian life will be easier. Yet when David was anointed and he was filled with the Holy Spirit, it was the beginning of the greatest time of testing he had ever experienced. So knowing it could begin the greatest period of trial you have ever faced, do you still want the anointing? Do you still want to be filled with the Spirit? For if you think for one moment that when you have the anointing everybody will say that you are right, then you are mistaken.

47

Possibly, nobody had a greater anointing of the Holy Spirit than Stephen, and before his fellow Jews stoned him to death, he spoke under the anointing probably like nobody had done since Peter had done on the Day of Pentecost (Acts 7:1–53), yet, as far as we know, Stephen had no converts at the time, and nobody was convinced that he was right. So do not think that if you have more of God everybody will fall at your feet and say, 'Of course, you are absolutely right!'

Now David was an Old Testament picture of Jesus, and we have a magnificent parallel between the two: David had the anointing without the crown, and so did Jesus; David had to wait years before he received the crown, and so did Jesus.

However, unlike David, Jesus was *born* a king. You may recall the Magi from the east asked Herod, 'Where is the one who has been born king of the Jews?' (Matt. 2:2). Jesus wore no crown, but he recognized his anointing, as Luke 4:16–21 clearly shows.

He went to Nazareth, where he had been brought up, and on the Sabbath day he went into the synagogue, as was his custom. And he stood up to read. The scroll of the prophet Isaiah was handed to him. Unrolling it, he found the place where it is written:

'The Spirit of the Lord is upon me,
   because he has anointed me
   to preach good news to the poor.
He has sent me to proclaim freedom for the prisoners
   and recovery of sight for the blind,
to release the oppressed,
   to proclaim the year of the Lord's favour.'

Then he rolled up the scroll, gave it back to the attendant and sat down. The eyes of everyone in the synagogue were fastened on him, and he began by saying to them, 'Today this scripture is fulfilled in your hearing.'

What wonderful news! You would have thought everybody would have clapped their hands and rejoiced, but, even before the service ended, they tried to kill him.

The nearest Jesus ever came to wearing a crown on earth was when the Roman soldiers pressed the crown of thorns onto his head before they crucified him (Matt. 27:27– 31). In fact, it was not until Jesus ascended to heaven that he was given the honour that had been due to him all along (Acts 2:33; Phil. 2:9).

But Jesus was never vindicated openly below. How did He deal with this? Paul uses an interesting expression when writing about Jesus in 1 Timothy 3:16. He says that Jesus was vindicated by the Spirit. I think this means two things.

Firstly, Jesus knew in his heart that he was vindicated because the Holy Spirit witnessed it to him. Similarly you may know the vindication of the Spirit. A situation can arise about which only God and you know the real truth. In such a situation you get your joy from knowing that God knows. Others will see it eventually, but for the present all that matters is that God knows.

Secondly, Jesus' kingship was acknowledged only by those, his disciples, who had been persuaded by the Spirit that Jesus was the king. Similarly, his disciples today proclaim that Jesus is king now. There will be a day when everybody will see that Jesus is king, but only those whose eyes are opened by the Holy Spirit see that he is king now.

But David is also a type of the Christian. We will see in subsequent chapters further aspects of this, but for now I want to focus on David as a type of the Christian as he was prepared for his meeting with Goliath. Goliath from Gath was a giant, he was nine feet six inches, the fear and dread of Israel. David saw Goliath when he went to give his brothers provisions from his father Jesse. He heard Goliath defying the armies of Israel. And he saw that all the soldiers of Israel were afraid. David was amazed that this was the case.

I want us to see three aspects of David's character at this

time. Remember he has the anointing but has not yet received the crown as his vindication.

The first aspect is this. When David left home *he was still respectful of his father*. David respected his father even although Jesse had thought that David was not suitable to be anointed by Samuel. When God calls you away from home, he wants you to investigate what he will do for you when you have severed the links. But he also wants you to show real respect for your parents, even if they are not Christians and may not approve of you.

The second aspect is this. *David wanted to be identified with his brothers and proved it by going right to where they were.* In a sense, all David needed to do to keep his father's orders was to give the provisions into the keeping of the officer in command of his brothers, and also ask the officer how they were. But David went right into the battle lines, risking his life.

David was like Jesus in this regard. Jesus is not ashamed to call us brethren. He comes to where we are and is right there with us. Jesus doesn't take us out of the fire, instead he gets into the fire with us. Perhaps, as a Christian you are going through one of the greatest trials of your life. If that is the case, remember that Jesus is with you.

If you try to protect yourself in the present because you have an anointing that indicates future significance, you are not behaving as a Christian should. David knew that the anointing was on him but that did not prevent him identifying himself with his brothers when the army was fighting the enemies of Israel. Let me tell you one of the principles concerning vindication. You try to preserve your life and you will lose it every time. If you try to protect yourself or your reputation by tiptoeing around places to make sure no one thinks ill of you, God will let you fall flat on your face.

The third aspect is this. *David was unafraid of Goliath, the enemy of Israel.* Goliath is a picture of Satan, the enemy of believers, who goes about as a roaring lion seeking whom he may devour. I would not be surprised if David knew right then that he was the one that was going to have to tackle Goliath, but instead of being afraid he began to ask the right questions. It may be that you know in your heart that God has called you for a special task. What you must do is involve yourself in the spiritual battle now and wait for God to publicly indicate that you have been given an anointing.

7

The Courage to be Yourself

1 Samuel 17:38–47

Are you allowing others to control your life? Are you afraid to do what you ought to do because of what others will think? The hardest thing in the world is to be yourself; it is always easier to adopt another as a role model, someone who appears to have 'got it right', and is thus more acceptable in the eyes of the world. Perhaps you think no one would like you if you were yourself, but nothing could be further from the truth. So in this chapter I want to challenge you to accept yourself as you are. The way to do this will become clear as we see how David prepared to tackle Goliath.

Standing more than 9 feet 6 inches tall, protected by heavy armour, Goliath was an awesome sight. He had challenged the armies of Israel to send out a champion to fight him, and declared the result of this encounter would determine the outcome of the battle (1 Sam. 17: 8–10). He struck terror into the hearts of Saul and the Israeli army, and no one dared to accept his challenge. But David could not believe that the Israelites could be intimidated by a man whom *he* could only see as an 'uncircumcised Philistine'. He decided *he* would be the one to tackle Goliath, and, finally, he persuaded the reluctant King Saul to allow him to do so (1 Sam. 17:37).

However, David immediately faced an unexpected test: the temptation not to be himself, for we read in verse 38:

> Then Saul dressed David in his own tunic. He put a coat of armour on him and a bronze helmet on his head.

Can you picture David, probably a teenager, weighed down with all this metal? He could not imagine himself tackling Goliath wearing Saul's cumbersome armour and wielding the heavy sword the king had also given him.

> 'I cannot go in these,' he said to Saul, 'because I am not used to them' (v. 39).

In effect, he was saying, 'This isn't me!'

No doubt David was *tempted* to do things Saul's way because he was grateful that he had allowed him to take up Goliath's challenge and wished to please him; moreover, out of respect for his position, he would not have wished to argue with the king.

Have you had a similar type of experience? Perhaps you can recall how indebted you felt to someone who did you a favour. Maybe, as in David's case, it was someone who was your superior, and you wanted to gain his approval by doing things in his way. In Romans 12:2, Paul warned Christians of adapting to ways of this world and said:

> Do not conform any longer to the pattern of this world, but be transformed by the renewing of your mind. Then you will be able to test and approve what God's will is – his good, pleasing and perfect will.

J.B. Phillips translated the first sentence of that verse like this: 'Don't let the world around you squeeze you into its own mould.'

David now faced a dilemma. Would he let Saul squeeze him into his mould? Until then, David had operated on a different level from those around him, who were so terrified of Goliath: he was filled with the Holy Spirit and motivated by a zeal for God, and he was *stunned* that the covenant people of God could think the way they were thinking.

It is a severe shock to every new Christian to discover how

worldly many professing Christians can be. At Westminster Chapel we find that when we lead people to the Lord, especially on the streets, where so many have no Christian background, they assume that all churches are alike and no matter which church they join, they will meet a minister who will be excited about their conversion. Yet to their dismay they find this is not always the case.

Moreover, they discover that not only do churches differ in their attitude to conversion but some tolerate practices that clearly contradict God's word. For example, I am appalled that some churches and denominations should let the world think that homosexual practice is only less than ideal and that being a practising gay and a clergyman is acceptable. That such a thing should happen in a church is unthinkable!

But sadly, today many Christians fail to protest about such practices because they are spiritually asleep. In the Parable of the Ten Virgins Jesus warned that this would happen in the last days. He said, 'The bridegroom was a long time in coming, and they all became drowsy and fell asleep' (Matt. 25:5).

Now three things are true when a person is asleep: (1) he is unaware he has been asleep until he wakes up; (2) he does things in his dreams that he would regard as inconceivable if he were wide awake, and (3) he does not like the sound of an alarm. So I expect few to appreciate it when I, as a minister in this country, am indignant that those who bear Christ's name and speak for him should stoop so low as to turn a blind eye to homosexual practices in the church. And when new Christians discover the church tolerates such practices, they are saddened and shocked, for they think *all* Christians share their excitement about the truths in the Bible.

David was in this kind of situation. He loved God and he believed his word, and he was shocked that God's people should cringe in fear when they heard Goliath blaspheming against God. As I said earlier, David was *stunned*. You see, he was operating at a *spiritual* level.

Are you facing a problem so grave that you are close to

despair? Perhaps you are looking in vain for a way out of your difficulties. If so, remember, God sometimes brings us to the place where there is nothing to do but to trust *him*. This was what God meant when he said, 'Not by might nor by power, but by my Spirit' (Zech. 4:6). It was also what Jesus meant when he said, 'With God all things are possible' (Matt. 19:26).

David had one underlying conviction: defeating Goliath was a *spiritual* matter and so he could say, 'The battle is the Lord's' (1 Sam. 17:47). The Israelites, the covenant people of God, were afraid because they were operating entirely at the natural, human level and had left God out of the situation. 'None of us stands a chance of killing Goliath,' they said fearfully, but no one brought *God* into the conversation. But David remembered God had told Abraham, 'I will bless those who bless you, and whoever curses you I will curse' (Gen. 12:3). So he said to himself, 'Goliath is cursing *us*! He is a dead man!' David saw the whole thing as *spiritual* warfare and he simply believed God's word.

This is what makes a person a Christian. He or she is someone who believes God's word and what it says about Jesus and the way to be saved. John Calvin taught that we may know that the Bible is the word of God through the inward testimony of the Holy Spirit, whom you receive when you become a Christian. And as you read God's word, the Holy Spirit will burn in your heart and he will convince you that the Bible is absolutely true.

David believed that, and while everyone around him was in a state of panic, he saw the truth, as a Spirit-filled person always does; he heard Goliath cursing God's covenant people and *knew* God would give him the victory over the giant.

However, David realized that if he wore Saul's armour, the Israelites would always see the victory as having a natural explanation and they would continue to keep God out; they needed to see the victory was *spiritual*.

Today we too need to see God working in a way that defies

natural explanation. Yet some will always try to explain things away, attributing events to natural causes. Some years ago I saw an interesting article in a national newspaper, offering an explanation of why David had been able to kill Goliath. The writer argued that Goliath probably suffered from a rare type of tumour of the pituitary gland that causes a variety of metabolic disturbances. One of these is *acromegaly*, a deformity characterized by the enlargement of the bones of the hands, feet and face, giving the impression of enormous stature. He said a quarter of those who suffer from acromegaly also have problems with their eyesight and lose their peripheral vision. So, the writer contended, David had probably attacked Goliath from one side, and as the giant could only see straight ahead, it would have been impossible for him to see a stone hurtling toward him from an angle. You see, some will always try to find a natural explanation for spiritual events.

David's decision about the way he would tackle Goliath was threefold: (1) to be true to his God, (2) to be true to those he represented, and (3) to be true to himself. This meant that he had to reject the well-meaning advice of those on his own side. It was a difficult thing to do, as I can testify. As a minister, I find that it is extremely hard to go against those who are for me; nevertheless, sometimes I have to say, 'I am sorry we cannot do that', for I know I have to be true to God, true to my congregation and true to myself.

But what does being true to yourself mean? I think it denotes four things.

First, you must be true to the revelation of God that the Holy Spirit has given you. My favourite line from Shakespeare is 'To thine own self be true'. God will *never* lead you to do anything that goes against your conscience. And when you become a Christian, for the first time in your life you will be true to yourself.

Second, you must be true to the gift God has given you. This means that you must function within the limitations of your gift. This was what David had to do when Saul dressed him in his heavy armour. You will remember he said, 'I cannot go in these . . . because I am not used to them.' So he took them off (v. 39). David was an expert with a sling, and he decided to use that and keep within the limits of his gift and talents. Some years ago a book was published called *The Peter Principle*. The writer argued that because someone is ambitious or is needed for a job no one else is prepared to tackle, he is promoted to the level of his incompetence, where he can no longer function with ease and becomes stressed. This often leads to high blood pressure and, sometimes, to a broken marriage and a nervous breakdown. Yet if he had remained at his previous job, all would have been well, but he exceeded his capabilities and was unable to manage.

As Christians, we too must come to accept the limitations of our ability and gifting. We all have our pride and like to think God can use us, and there is always a temptation to want to move ahead before we are ready. However, he may be saying to you, 'Be patient; don't ruin everything now for a rise in pay, or for more prestige or an easy way out. I need to prepare you for the task ahead. Wait! Your time will come.'

Third, you must be true to the way in which God has prepared you. David had to do that. When Saul dressed him in his armour, David said:

'Your servant has been keeping his father's sheep. When a lion or a bear came and carried off a sheep from the flock, I went after it, struck it and rescued the sheep from its mouth. When it turned on me, I seized it by its hair, struck it and killed it' (1 Sam. 17:34–35).

When the lion and the bear confronted him, David had no idea that the reason God allowed him to face such a dangerous and difficult situation was that he was preparing him then for his encounter with Goliath.

Perhaps you are going through a time of great trial now. However, if you keep your eyes on God, if you will wait on him, you will see this difficult period in your life as a time of preparation.

Fourth, to be true to yourself means to be true to methods with which you feel comfortable and which have stood the test of time. When David set out to defeat the enemy, he used the time-honoured method that had always been his source of support and comfort. So he refused to wear Saul's armour, but he took his familiar staff in his hand and began walking. He must have looked foolish, approaching a giant who was armed to the teeth. I can imagine his brothers saying, 'Well, there he goes, with his silly old staff!' Yet we see the reason for David's confidence in his staff when we read what he said about it in Psalm 23:1-4:

> The Lord is my shepherd, I shall not be in want.
>   He makes me lie down in green pastures,
> he leads me beside quiet waters,
>   he restores my soul.
> He guides me in paths of righteousness for his name's sake.
>   Even though I walk through the valley of the shadow of death,
> I will fear no evil,
>   for you are with me;
>   *your* rod and *your* staff, they comfort me [my italics].

You see, David's staff was *God's* staff; his rod was *God's* rod.

When God called Moses to lead the Israelites out of captivity in Egypt, Moses told God that he doubted if they would listen to him. But God replied by asking, 'What is in your hand?'

'A staff,' Moses replied.

'That will do,' God said (see Exod. 4:1–5).

This is what God is saying to you. He says, 'I have prepared you for service and I have given you a staff. This is enough! Trust in me.'

David had faith, so he laid down Saul's armour and began

walking away with his staff, trusting in what God would do for him. In Psalm 20:7 David put it like this:

'Some trust in chariots and some in horses,
but we trust in the name of the Lord our God.'

So David went out to face Goliath with his staff in his hand, true to the time-honoured method that had always been his comfort. He rejected the advice of those around him who would have weighed him down with Saul's armour. He put his trust in what God would do for him and kept his eyes on him.

And if you have decided to become a Christian, you too must refuse to listen to those who would weigh you down with useless advice, saying, 'Your salvation depends on what *you* do. You must *earn* it by good deeds, by joining a church and being baptized.' They are wrong. The Bible says that as far as your salvation is concerned, *only one thing matters*: you must place you trust in what Jesus has done for you. You must come empty-handed and say, 'Lord, I have nothing to offer you; please take me as I am.'

8

The Courage to Accept God's Way

1 Samuel 17:38–47

Are you thinking of becoming a Christian? Perhaps you are hesitating because you are troubled by so many doubts and wonder if you will manage? Maybe you say to yourself, 'I'm scared people will laugh at me. How can I defend myself against such attacks? How can *I* live the Christian life? I am not strong enough.' My answer is, you *will* have sufficient strength if you do things in God's way. That was what David did: he first discerned *how* God intended him to defeat Goliath, and then he did it in God's way. 'But what *is* God's way?' you may ask. Well, there are four things I want to show you about it.

First, I want you to see that God's way is the way of apparent foolishness.

To the Israeli army, David must have seemed like a complete fool: he had rejected the advice of the king and had refused to wear his armour, and he had ignored his brothers' scorn. Now, to cap it all, taking only his staff, his sling and five smooth stones from a nearby stream, this teenage boy was heading towards Goliath! People could not believe their eyes. Such arrogance, such folly!

The gospel seems utter folly to many. Paul said, 'The message of the cross is foolishness to those who are perishing, but to us who are being saved it is the power of God' (1 Cor. 1:18). You see, the only way to be certain you will go to heaven one day is to believe that God punished his own Son for your sins and that Jesus took *your* place on the cross. Now if you say, 'That is the most foolish thing I have ever heard', I reply,

'God's way *is* the way of apparent foolishness.' In the eyes of the world a Christian seems like a complete fool, as Paul, who had one of the greatest intellects in history, pointed out when he wrote, 'We are fools for Christ' (1 Cor. 4:10) and 'If any one of you thinks he is wise . . . he should become a "fool"' (1 Cor. 3:18).

The world is blind to the truth, but when we obey God and enter into a relationship with him, we begin to acquire discernment, as the writer of Psalm 111 said, 'The fear of the Lord is the beginning of wisdom' (v. 10). The world may indeed regard God's plan of salvation as 'foolishness', but as Paul said, 'The foolishness of God is wiser than man's wisdom, and the weakness of God is stronger than man's strength' (1 Cor. 1:25).

Second, I want you to see that God's way is the way of comparative loneliness.

We have seen that David set off for his encounter with the giant wearing no armour and carrying only a staff and a sling. One might have thought that David would have asked Saul to regroup his army, so they might march behind him and at least afford him *some* protection. But he faced the enemy alone because he *knew* that God had a plan and that God's way was right.

Have you decided God's way is right? If so, remember, God's way can be the way of comparative loneliness. Jesus calls you to follow him, even if nobody else does. You may be the only Christian in your group at college or in your workplace; you may be the only member of your family who is converted. You may even have to separate from a non-Christian boyfriend or girlfriend, for Jesus calls you to himself. *He* knew how lonely God's way can be, for his own disciples forsook him and fled, and he went to the cross alone (Mark 14:50).

Third, we see that God's way is by public example.

Everything that David did, he did publicly. Everyone watched him set out to tackle Goliath: his brothers, the king and the entire Israeli army all saw him.

Similarly, when we become Christians, Scripture teaches that we should be open about our faith and publicly confess Jesus as our Lord and Saviour (Rom. 10:9–10). You may exclaim in dismay, '*I* could never do a thing like that!' But you *can*, for Jesus promises that he will give you his Holy Spirit (Acts 1:8); he will fill you with such love for Jesus that you will *want* to tell others about him.

This was what the disciples discovered on the Day of Pentecost. During Jesus' ministry among them, they had been happy to follow him while he was performing miracles and while it seemed that one day everyone would acclaim him as the Messiah, but when he was arrested, they thought, 'This isn't the way we thought it would end!' and fled (Matt. 26:56); Peter even denied *knowing* Jesus (Matt. 26:69–75). But they found they were wrong: Jesus rose from the dead (Matt. 28), and after his ascension (Acts 1:1–10), the Holy Spirit came down and filled them with a new love for the Lord (Acts 2).

Furthermore, the Spirit gave them something that they had hoped for above all else – a second chance. You see, they were ashamed that they let Jesus down and longed for the day when they might have another opportunity to confess him.

When that day came, they unashamedly and boldly preached the gospel, enraging the members of the Sanhedrin (the Jewish supreme court). The Bible says, 'They called the disciples in and had them flogged. Then they ordered them not to speak in the name of Jesus' (Acts 5:40). But the more the authorities threatened them, the more the disciples' hearts began to leap within them. They looked at each other and exclaimed, 'This is wonderful!' Suffering shame is normally something we all avoid like the plague, but Acts 5:41 says, 'The apostles left the Sanhedrin, rejoicing because they had been counted worthy of suffering disgrace for the Name.' And when someone becomes a Christian, this is the way he or she feels too.

Fourth, God's way is the way of simplicity.

Saul's armour had been elegant, carefully honed and was

heavy; to the onlookers, it would have seemed much the best thing for David to wear as protection. But he took it off and set off to meet the giant with only his staff, his sling and five small pebbles to use as ammunition. They were amazed! But God loves to do things to surprise people. His ways often seem foolish in the eyes of the world, but as Paul said, 'The foolishness of God is wiser than man's wisdom, and the weakness of God is stronger than man's strength' (1 Cor. 1:25). David chose God's way – the way of simplicity.

Sadly, generally speaking, the church today has lost its way, because it no longer preaches the simple message of the gospel. Instead it relies on scholarship, fine architecture, beautiful buildings and clever sermons to impress people; this results in them thinking only one thing: they are saved by good works! Yet all they have to do to be saved is to trust in the blood that Jesus, the God-man, shed on the cross (John 3:16).

'But how can I be *sure* that this is God's way?' you may ask. I think there are five ways by which you may know.

First, you know you are being true to yourself. Your heart and your conscience will tell you that it is *right* to accept the gift of salvation and to confess Jesus Christ as your Lord and Saviour. Jesus will never ask you to violate your conscience.

Second, you know that it is God's way when you see he has prepared and equipped you to deal with your problem and the solution is close at hand. David knew that Saul's armour was not going to work: it was too large and too heavy. But years of practice perfecting his aim with his sling had prepared him for this day. He had it with him that day, for he took it wherever he went; moreover, ammunition was in the stream nearby. God had prepared and equipped David for the encounter with Goliath, and everything he needed to kill Goliath was readily available.

Have you been looking for the solution to your problems? Look no further, the answer is at hand, for God has prepared your heart to receive the gospel. Paul put it like this:

The word is near you; it is in your mouth and in your heart, that is, the word of faith we are proclaiming: That if you confess with your mouth, 'Jesus is Lord,' and believe in your heart that God raised him from the dead, you will be saved (Rom. 10:8–9).

Third, you will know for sure that it is God's way when the one who would destroy you scoffs at you.

As David moved toward Goliath, and the giant saw his opponent was probably a teenager, he felt deeply insulted. He had challenged the Israelites to pick a *man* to fight him, but here was a *youth* approaching; moreover, he was wearing no armour and not even carrying a sword. Goliath was outraged and responded by jeering at his opponent:

'Am I a dog, that you come at me with sticks?' And the Philistine cursed David by his gods. 'Come here,' he said, 'and I'll give your flesh to the birds of the air and the beasts of the field!' (1 Sam. 17:43–44).

Goliath is a picture of the devil, who would keep you blind and bound. In 2 Corinthians 4:4 Paul said, 'The god of this age has blinded the minds of unbelievers, so that they cannot see the light of the gospel of the glory of Christ, who is the image of God.' Satan wants to keep you in his grip and destroy you, and if you are thinking of becoming a Christian he will scoff, 'Don't be such a fool!' In fact, he will do everything in his power to stop you accepting salvation and confessing your faith in Jesus.

Fourth, you know it is God's way when you see your *only* hope lies in God's power to save.

David had now committed himself: he would be a fool if he did not go on because God had hemmed him in. But he had rejected Saul's armour and lacked a man's strength; Goliath was a giant, much more powerful than he was. David's *only* hope rested with what *God* would do for him. But he was confident that God would save him, so when Goliath roared, 'I'll give your flesh to the birds of the air and the beasts of the field!' David was undeterred and replied:

> 'You come against me with sword and spear and javelin, but I come against you in the name of the Lord Almighty, the God of the armies of Israel, whom you have defied' (1 Sam. 17:45).

He knew that *God's* power would determine the outcome of the encounter.

When you become a Christian, you will see God did it all. You will look back and see how God shaped your life by convicting you of sin and bringing you to your knees. You will realize there is no going back, for God has hemmed *you* in, and your hope of salvation rests solely on what Jesus did when he died on the cross for you.

Fifth, God's way means you can have assurance of the outcome in advance.

Do you know how David replied to Goliath's taunts and threats? He simply said:

> '*This day* [my italics] the Lord will hand you over to me' (v. 46).

Today! It can happen *now,* for I have authority to tell you that you can know *today* how God will deal with you on Judgment Day. Make no mistake: that day is coming. The writer to the Hebrews said, 'Man is destined to die once, and after that to face judgment' (Heb. 9:27).

Can you imagine how an offender feels when he is put on trial and stands before the judge? He must wonder nervously which judge will try his case, for some are known to be more lenient than others.

I had the thrill of leading my old friend Don Gurgiolo to Christ. He was once the captain of a fishing boat in the Florida Keys. Before he was converted, he was caught smuggling cocaine and arrested. However, he was thrilled when he discovered that the judge was a fellow Italian. 'He is bound to be lenient,' he thought. I went to his trial and watched as the judge sentenced him to 32 months in prison! The outcome was not the one he expected.

However, as I said, Christians may know in advance what the outcome of their trial at the Final Judgment will be. This is not arrogance: they simply believe God's word, which says:

> 'God so loved the world that he gave his one and only Son, that whoever believes in him shall not perish but have eternal life' (John 3:16).

To be certain of being acquitted on Judgment Day, all you have to do is to respond to the gospel. Maybe you are waiting for proof that you are doing the right thing in becoming a Christian. This is a grave mistake: God will not shake you by the shoulders and force you to be converted. We read in 1 Samuel 17:40 that '[David] approached the Philistine'. David moved toward Goliath because God *told* him to do this. Through his word, God has spoken to you. Will *you* make a move and respond to his offer of salvation?

9

Unmasking Satan's Lies

1 Samuel 17:38–47

Once you make the courageous decision to be true to yourself and accept God's way, you will meet opposition. In fact, every new Christian finds that he or she has a new enemy: the devil. Now if you have recently been converted, knowing something of Satan's character and his scheming ways will help you to anticipate his attacks and to avoid unnecessary trouble. So you will find David's encounter with Goliath instructive, for it shows us something of the way the devil operates, because, as we have seen, the giant is an Old Testament picture of Satan. The first thing you need to know is that the devil is a liar; that is his nature: he cannot *but* lie, as Jesus, speaking to unbelieving Jews, pointed out:

> 'You belong to your father, the devil, and you want to carry out your father's desire. He was a murderer from the beginning, not holding to the truth, for there is no truth in him. When he lies, he speaks his native language, for he is a liar and the father of lies' (John 8:44).

The first time we hear of Satan telling a lie was in the Garden of Eden after God told Adam:

> 'You are free to eat from any tree in the garden; but you must not eat from the tree of the knowledge of good and evil, for when you eat of it you will surely die' (Gen. 2:16–17).

Satan then appeared to Eve in the guise of a snake and said the very *opposite* of what God said:

'You will not surely die,' the serpent said to the woman. 'For God knows that when you eat of it your eyes will be opened, and you will be like God, knowing good and evil' (3:4).

That was the devil's first lie, and he has been lying ever since. The problem was, Eve believed Satan rather than God.

Next you need to know that not only is the devil a habitual liar but he has a curious way of coming alongside, making suggestions to so demoralize you that you give up all thought of defeating him. This was what Goliath tried to do as David approached him:

'Come here,' he said, 'and I'll give your flesh to the birds of the air and the beasts of the field!' (1 Sam. 17:44).

But David refused to believe the lies of the enemy.

Now you may ask, 'What kind of lies will Satan put to *me?*' Well, the devil commonly tries to deceive people by telling three huge untruths.

The first lie is, you will not suffer the consequences of your sin. Remember, the first lie the devil told Eve was 'You will not die.' Satan constantly tries to make you believe that you can sin with impunity. But the Bible warns, 'Do not be deceived: God cannot be mocked. A man reaps what he sows' (Gal. 6:7). You *will* reap the consequences of your sin! There is no way that you can sin and not be sorry eventually.

The second lie he uses only if you did not believe the first. He will say that your sins are too serious to be forgiven. 'Never believe', says the devil, 'that God can simply wash your sins away, and in any case it is too late for you; what you have done is unforgivable.' In fact, one of Satan's favourite tricks is to make someone think that he has committed the unpardonable sin, which is to deny the testimony of the Spirit (see Matt. 12:31), and keep him oppressed and despairing in the belief he has lost his salvation. But if you affirm that Jesus is God in the flesh, you have *not* blasphemed the Spirit! Satan is lying.

The third lie is, you can *earn* your salvation. Sadly, this is what most people believe today, even those who have been brought up in the church. This amazes me; one would expect non- churchgoers to say this, because, after all, they have not had the illumination of the Holy Spirit through preaching. But many who have been brought up in the church and have even been baptized still trust their good works will get them into heaven. They have believed Satan's lie and remain unconverted.

'All right,' someone might say. 'But how do I know that it is *Satan* who says these things?' Well, I will show you three ways of proving this. The first proof it is Satan's voice you hear is that the suggestion makes you afraid. Goliath was shouting across the valley and threatening the armies of Israel. His intention was to demoralize them by filling them with terror. In 1 Samuel 17:23–24 we read:

> Goliath . . . stepped out from his lines and shouted his usual defiance, and David heard it. When the Israelites saw the man, they all ran from him in great fear.

Satan's method is always to engender fear. I am not talking about the fear of God, which is a reverence and a holy awe that we have for him; I am talking about feelings of anxiety and dread. These feelings come from the devil. They *cannot* come from God, for the Bible says, 'God hath not given us the spirit of fear; but of power, and of love, and of a sound mind' (2 Tim. 1:7 AV).

The second proof is that the proposition the devil puts to you is unfair.

> Then the Philistine said, 'This day I defy the ranks of Israel! Give me a man and let us fight each other' (1 Sam. 17:10).

Goliath knew that Israel had no warrior as tall and as strong as he was. The devil is like that: he never plays fairly, so he will slyly suggest that you can appease God by your own efforts.

Now if Satan has made you think that your good works will save you, I want you to realize what you must do to satisfy God's justice. The God of the Bible is a holy God, who hates sin, and he demands *perfection* before anybody can enter heaven. You must be pure, clean and holy, sinless in your thoughts, in your words and deeds, 60 seconds a minute, 60 minutes an hour, 24 hours a day, 365 days of the year, all the days of your life. That is the *only* standard of righteousness that God accepts.

However, the devil wants you to believe that your good deeds and your church membership will be sufficient to earn your salvation. But remember, Satan is lying and being unfair. He wants you to think that so that you will never see the only way to be saved. The Bible says, 'The god of this age has blinded the minds of unbelievers, so that they cannot see the light of the gospel of the glory of Christ' (2 Cor. 4:4).

The third proof is that Satan suggests that it is too late so that you might as well give in to him. You will remember Goliath roared: 'Come here . . . and I will give your flesh to the birds of the air and the beasts of the field.' What do you suppose were his tactics here? Well, he was bluffing: he hoped that his bloodcurdling roar would so demoralize David that he would think he stood no chance against him.

This is a technique Satan uses frequently. Peter warned Christians to be on their guard against such tactics, saying, 'Be self-controlled and alert. Your enemy the devil prowls around like a roaring lion looking for someone to devour' (1 Pet. 5:8). The lion's roar petrifies its prey and makes it believe resistance is useless. The devil's strategy is similar: he roars to try to make you believe that you have already ruined your life and it is too late to repent.

But Jesus says, 'It is *not* too late.' As long as you affirm the Spirit's testimony about Jesus, I can tell you upon the authority of God's word that, should you be willing to confess

Jesus as God's Son, you have *not* committed the unpardonable sin; you have not committed any sin that he cannot forgive. Jesus offers forgiveness to the worst sinners on earth. In fact, he invites *all* those burdened by the power and guilt of their sin to come to him, saying, 'Come to me, all you who are weary and burdened' (Matt. 11:28). If this describes you, then you are the kind of person Jesus calls. He says, 'If you are like that, then *come*! No matter *how* bad you feel, *how* deep your sins, come to me; I will give you rest.' It is *not* too late; the Bible says, '*Now* is the time of God's favour, *now* is the day of salvation [my italics]' (2 Cor. 6:2).

Before I finish this chapter, I want us to see three more things about Satan that will help to prevent you falling for his tricks.

First, Satan knows you well.

The Bible tells us that Goliath looked at David and weighed him up:

> Meanwhile, the Philistine, with his shield-bearer in front of him, kept coming closer to David. He looked David over and saw that he was only a boy, ruddy and handsome, and he despised him (1 Sam. 17:41–42).

You see, when David obeyed God by moving towards the giant, he aroused Goliath's attention.

Similarly, when you begin to follow God, *you* arouse Satan's attention. Perhaps you have never been aware of the devil before. Today many people do not even believe that he exists. But Satan is delighted when someone says, 'I don't believe in a personal devil', for it proves to him that he has succeeded with them.

However, you will not be *truly* aware of the devil until you move in God's direction. Jonathan Edwards used to say, 'When the church is revived, so is the devil', and when you become a Christian, Satan will begin to attack you.

Let me give you two examples showing the way he

operates. Perhaps the Holy Spirit has convinced you that it is right to tithe and that God will bless you for doing this. But the first week, instead of receiving a blessing, you receive a bill from the Inland Revenue, or find your car breaks down and you face an unexpected expense. You see, Satan will do his best to make you believe that tithing is not for you. Or perhaps you decide to witness for the Lord on the streets, and you find that Satan will cause someone to swear at you or even threaten you with violence. He wants to dissuade you from testifying to others, to make you say, 'Well, that's the last time I try that!'

He will always oppose you once you try to walk in the light. And once David moved in a direction that threatened Goliath's interests, Goliath noticed him.

Moreover, he saw that David was but a youth. Now when a child is converted, Satan is threatened, and he will always react by causing others to mock the youngster's conversion. So we find older Christians smirking and expressing cynicism when a child confesses Jesus. Another of his tactics is to induce the church and its members to neglect the children. I cannot see how Christian parents can justify *not* bringing their little ones to church. I was converted when I was six years old, and I thank God that my parents made me go to church every time the door was open.

Goliath also noticed that David was 'ruddy and handsome'. Similarly today Satan wants the best of our young people. This is a generation, generally speaking, where many ungifted people who have no calling have entered the ministry, but had Satan not seized so many of the best minds, they would not be there. There was once a day in England when the best minds aspired not to the fields of science, literature or law, but to theology.

The second thing I want to show you is that Satan hates you. Look again at verse 42:

He looked David over and saw that he was only a boy, ruddy and handsome, *and he despised him* [my italics] (1 Sam. 17:42).

Have you any idea how much Satan hates you? He regards you with an icy hatred. He hates you because he wants to keep you blind and bound; he wants you to lose your soul and go to hell (2 Cor. 4:4). However, he will try to camouflage that hatred. He will try to lull you to sleep and make you think all is well; he will tempt you with the glitter of this world to keep you from following Jesus Christ. But once you become a Christian, you will discover just how deep his hostility is. His hatred for you will be so great, he will be unable to contain it. And when Goliath saw David, he roared:

'Am I a dog, that you come at me with sticks?' (v. 43).

Martin Luther used to say, 'The one thing that the devil can't take is ridicule'. You see, Satan is full of pride, and so was Goliath. He was enraged to see David, a mere youth, approaching him without armour, carrying only a staff and a sling. Verse 43 tells us of his reaction:

The Philistine cursed David by his gods (v. 43).

Like Goliath, Satan shows his hatred by the language he uses.

When you are converted, the Holy Spirit will give you a new vocabulary and you will not want to take God's name in vain or use obscenities. You see, when you are angry and feel like swearing, you mirror the hatred of the devil toward God. I remember hearing that a young lady who was converted during a service at Westminster Chapel exclaimed on the way home, 'Oh my God!' But the Holy Spirit checked her immediately, and she said later, 'I knew I couldn't talk like that any longer.'

The third thing I want you to see about Satan is his weakness. He only reacts when he is threatened:

'Come here,' [Goliath] said, 'and I'll give your flesh to the birds of the air and the beasts of the field' (v. 44).

Despite the fact Goliath saw his opponent was only a youth, he felt uneasy as David approached him, so he tried to make him afraid. Similarly, whenever Satan is stirred up, it is a sign you are doing something right, and he hopes that by making you afraid, you will back down. So when you are converted, he threatens, 'I will destroy you!' But he is lying. Remember, his tactics are to work through fear and lies. The truth is, when you become a Christian, Jesus will be with you and he will protect you. My father often used to quote this verse: 'The one who is in you is greater than the one who is in the world' (1 John 4:4). Satan cannot fulfil his promises or carry out his threats, but he lies to make you afraid, saying, 'You can't live the Christian life; you are too weak!' But by the grace of God and the help of the Holy Spirit you *can*.

Next you need to know that Satan always overreaches himself: it is a habit that he cannot break. So if you are a Christian, you may rest assured that whenever the devil attacks you it is because God is planning something bigger.

The classic example of this was when Jesus died on the cross. Satan was the architect of the plan to kill Jesus and he *thought* that he had won a great victory, but he went too far. Had he known that this was the very way God would bring about our salvation, he would never have done it, as Paul pointed out in 1 Corinthians 2:7–8:

We speak of God's secret wisdom, a wisdom that has been hidden and that God destined for our glory before time began. None of the rulers of this age understood it, for if they had, they would not have crucified the Lord of glory.

Up to the last minute the devil hoped that Jesus, nailed to the cross and suffering untold agony, would lose his temper with those who mockingly shouted, 'Come down from the cross;

if you are the Son of God! . . . He saved others, . . . but he cannot save himself!' (Matt. 27:40, 42).

But what if Jesus *had* responded to his tormentors? Had he done so, he would have sinned and Satan would have won. Yet it became clear that the devil had overreached himself when Jesus spoke in love, saying, 'Father, forgive them, for they do not know what they are doing' (Luke 23:34).

No matter what method Satan uses to attack you, if you have the love of Jesus in your heart, he will overreach himself. Goliath's lie was 'This day I will feed your flesh to the birds of the air and the beasts of the field!' But David defeated the giant, and similarly, Jesus defeated the devil when he died, still sinless, on the cross.

10

Out on a Limb for God

1 Samuel 17:38–47

When I was a boy, I always read the 'funny pages', as we called our comics in America. One of my favourite comic strips was called 'Mutt and Jeff.' I remember that in one story Jeff needed to trim his tree, so he climbed out onto a limb and sawed it off. Of course, he was foolishly sitting on the wrong side of the sawed branch and fell to the ground.

When you go out on a limb for God, though, unlike Jeff, you are not doing anything stupid, you may think there is a risk that you will fall and look foolish in the eyes of the world. That was the risk David took when he accepted Goliath's challenge and set off alone to tackle him.

Goliath cursed David by his gods and roared:

'Come here, and I'll give your flesh to the birds of the air and the beasts of the field!' (1 Sam. 17:44).

But David refused to be intimidated by these threats and replied:

'You come against me with sword and spear and javelin, but I come against you in the name of the Lord Almighty, the God of the armies of Israel, whom you have defied.' (v. 45).

David put his faith in *God's* power to defeat Goliath.

Having faith means you must go out on a limb for God, but you can be confident that the branch you sit on will *not* be sawn off, for the Bible says, 'The one who trusts in him will *never* [my italics] be put to shame' (Rom. 9:33; see also Ps. 25:3).

Now this chapter is relevant in three ways.
First, it will show what takes place in the mind of a person who hears the gospel. He has to decide whether he wants to become a Christian, and whether his faith means enough to him to confess Jesus publicly.

However, many people believe they do not need to be converted because they think they are Christians already. There are various reasons why they think like this. Some say, 'I am a Christian because I was born in a Christian nation.' Some say, 'I had a Christian upbringing; I went to church with my parents and I was baptized into the Christian faith, so I am all right.' Others say, 'Of course, I am a Christian. I do good to others and I lead a decent moral life.' However, they forget the followers of non-Christian religions, Hindus, Moslems, Buddhists and Sikhs, for example, also have high moral standards. So leading a moral life is not an infallible sign that one is a Christian. In fact, *none* of the things I have mentioned here make people Christians, as I hope you will see.

The second reason my message is relevant is that it shows what happens in the mind of a person whom God is preparing for leadership.

David was secretly anointed to be the future king, but first God had to prepare him for the task ahead. 'But', you may say, 'surely, David didn't *need* preparation: he had the anointing of the Holy Spirit. Was that not enough?' No. It is never enough preparation for leadership. You can be filled with the Holy Spirit but lack the technique, the temperament, the patience, the charisma and the ability to lead others.

The third reason this message is relevant is that I want you to see the nature of *true* faith. Do you have true faith? You may say, 'Certainly! I believe in God.' Well done! Yet Satan also believes in God and trembles (Jas. 2:19). I hope you will see that it is not enough simply to believe God exists.

You may ask, 'How do I k*now* if I have true faith?' I will show you six proofs by which you may tell.

The first proof of true faith is, one is aware of the devil's intentions.

David knew Goliath's intention was to destroy the Israelites. Goliath had roared, 'I defy the ranks of Israel!' (1 Sam. 17:10). But David also knew the Israelites were the people whom God had chosen from all the peoples of the earth and made his very own (Deut. 7:6). We see his deep conviction of this when we read his prayer in 2 Samuel 7:23:

> 'And who is like your people Israel— the one nation on earth that God went out to redeem as a people for himself, and to make a name for himself, and to perform great and awesome wonders by driving out nations and their gods from before your people, whom you redeemed from Egypt? You have established your people Israel as your very own for ever, and you, O Lord, have become their God.'

Psalm 147:20 sums it up perfectly: 'He has done this for *no other* nation [my italics].'

Now the Israelites, the covenant people of God, are a picture of the church, which the devil wants to destroy. Satan plans to bring the name of the church into such low repute that the world scoffs at it. He has had something of a victory, for the world has no respect for the church today.

Do you wonder what kind of weapons Satan is using? Well, let us see the kind of weapons Goliath had? David said, 'You come against me with sword and spear and javelin . . . ' (1 Sam. 17:45). In other words, Goliath's weapons were *carnal* weapons. Similarly, Satan tries to ensure the church uses non-spiritual weapons against him; he knows these will be completely ineffective.

One of his tricks is to persuade the church to leave the Holy Spirit out of its affairs. He knows the church cannot successfully wage warfare against him without the Spirit, for it is from the Holy Spirit that the church derives its power (see Acts 1:8). Another of his tactics is to distract the church from the work God gave it to do. This is a time when the church has resorted to involving itself with politics and social issues to keep it going. Now these are concerns that society *should* address, but it is not the role of the church to do so. The church's task is to evangelize (Matt. 28:19). Satan hates it when the church opposes him by moving in spiritual power, concentrating on the task God has given it to do.

Sadly, the church in general is unaware of Satan's tactics. As someone once remarked, 'If the Holy Spirit were completely withdrawn from the church today, 90 per cent of its work would continue as if nothing happened.' But faith has its eyes wide open to what the devil is planning.

However, one is conscious one is opposing Satan. Some years ago I went out on a limb in my ministry. I was not really frightened, although I knew I was heading for trouble and that repercussions would follow, for I knew that what I had to do would stir up Satan's hatred towards me. But I knew God would bring me through, because whenever someone puts one's ministry on the line for the sake of the gospel, God will protect him.

Similarly, when you become a Christian and publicly confess your faith, you will stir up Satan's hatred towards *you*; nevertheless, you must oppose him. David said to Goliath, 'I come against you.' Now the devil is one for whom you should have a healthy respect; do not take him lightly, but do not be *too* afraid: remember, he is a conquered foe. The Bible says, 'Resist the devil, and he will flee from you' (Jas. 4:7).

The second proof of true faith is, you operate in the strength of God's name.

Note that David said to the Philistine, 'I come against you in the name of the Lord Almighty . . .' (1 Sam. 17:45). Do you realize what it means when you say you are going in somebody's name? Let me explain by giving you an example. When Great Britain sends an ambassador to a foreign state, what he or she says is in the name of Her Majesty the Queen and they represent her government. David could challenge the mighty Goliath, for he went in God's name, and it was from *him* that he derived his authority. Similarly, when Christians act in faith, they operate in the strength of God's name and do what *he* wants done.

Sometimes this means one must operate supernaturally – beyond one's natural gift or natural ability. David was an expert with a sling and knew he could probably hit Goliath. Yet do you really think that he would risk his life by trusting in his own ability and in his own efforts? Not when tackling a giant more than nine feet six inches tall! He knew he needed to use *God's* strength. Remember the words of the prophet Zechariah: '"Not by might nor by power, *but by my Spirit*," says the Lord Almighty [my italics]' (Zech. 4:6). True faith does not rely on human efforts: it operates using *spiritual* weapons.

The third proof of true faith is, one identifies with those with whom God himself is pleased to be identified.

Let us look again at what David said to Goliath: 'I come against you in the name of the Lord Almighty, *the God of the armies of Israel* [my italics] . . . ' (v. 45). Knowing that God had set his affection upon Israel, David wanted to be identified with God's people.

God has a people in the world today: the church. And though it is filled with people who are weak, God loves it dearly.

Now the church has always been understood throughout its history as both visible and invisible. Let me explain. The *invisible* church is made up of all of those who have been washed by the blood Jesus shed on Calvary's cross. The invisible church is what matters primarily. Members of the invisible church are also part of the *visible* church, and we can see them as they attend services week by week at their local place of worship. The visible church, however, includes some who are not converted, because they think that simply being born into a Christian home, being baptized or confirmed, or producing good works makes them Christians. So it is possible to be part of the visible church and *not* be part of the invisible church.

However, when you become a Christian, and part of the invisible church, you will want to be a part of the visible church too. It is filled with people who are weak and sinful; no one in the church is perfect: we are all sinners and so often let our Lord down and need his forgiveness. But do not tell me you can love God and be detached from his body, the church, for faith identifies with those with whom God is pleased to be identified. The writer of Hebrews put it this way:

> Both the one who makes men holy and those who are made holy are of the same family. So Jesus is not ashamed to call them brothers. He says,
>
> 'I will declare your name to my brothers;
> in the presence of the congregation
> I will sing your praises' (Heb. 2:11–12).

In a word, faith is not ashamed of God's people, the church. Remember, David was so sure of God's love for Israel, he was not ashamed to be identified with the Israelites and to go out on a limb against Goliath.

The fourth proof of true faith is, one is indignant but, oddly enough, encouraged when God's name is dishonoured.

This statement seems something of a paradox, but I will explain it. What underpinned David's fearlessness with Goliath was that David knew that anybody who talked like Goliath did about God was doomed; this encouraged him. Yet he was also angry that Goliath should spew out such venom against the God of Israel and against God's people.

How do *you* feel when God's name is dishonoured? Perhaps you know what it is to use vile language and spout obscenities. But now you have professed Christ, do you feel concerned and uneasy about the language you use? True faith is indignant when it hears the name of God dishonoured, and when you check yourself, it shows that you are changing inwardly.

Let me tell you an interesting story. John Wesley, who lived in the eighteenth century, once went to preach in Newcastle and wrote in his journal, 'Never have I heard such open profanity and witnessed such extensive godlessness. This place is ripe for revival.' And God sent it! Many today, faced with bleak conditions, say, 'Oh this is awful! Whatever will happen next?' John Wesley looked for the place that seemed hopeless and looked for God to change the situation. Remember, true faith is indignant, but encouraged when God's name is dishonoured.

The fifth proof of true faith is, one is assured of the outcome before others know it.

The Christian knows two things about the future.

The first is that the day is coming when every person who ever lived will stand before God at the Final Judgment. It is a mysterious but undoubted truth in the Bible that there will be a general resurrection of the dead. Billions of people will rise from graves, from places where cremated ashes were scattered; the oceans will also give up their dead. The same God who created you will restore your body and transform it. John described the scene in his vision on the Isle of Patmos:

I saw a great white throne and him who was seated on it. . . . And I saw the dead, great and small, standing before the throne, and books were opened. Another book was opened, which is the book of life. The dead were judged according to what they had done as recorded in the books. The sea gave up the dead that were in it, and death and Hades gave up the dead that were in them, and each person was judged according to what he had done (Rev. 20:11–13).

You must give an account of how you have lived your life to the God of the Bible. You will have all the time you want to state your case. You will plead, 'Not guilty! In your name I have done many good deeds. I was kind to others; I lived a moral life; I went to church and put money in the collection bag; I gave generously, even when it hurt me financially to do so. Lord, you *must* remember that!'

God will reply, 'Yes, I remember that. Have you anything more to tell me?'

'Yes. Do you remember, two or three years ago when I was in trouble, I *prayed*?'

God will say, 'Yes, I remember. Is there anything more?'

'Well, what more do you want me to say?'

'Have you finished?'

Then, shaking with fear, you will begin to get the message and plead, 'Well, yes, but *please*, Lord, *please*!'

But God will say, 'I never knew you. Depart from me into everlasting punishment' (see Matt. 7:21–23; Matt. 25:46).

The second thing the Christian knows about the future is what the outcome will be for him or her on Judgment Day. Do you know what David told Goliath in verse 46?

'This day the Lord will hand you over to me.'

David could be totally confident when he told Goliath this. David *knew* that God would give him the victory.

It is not arrogance to be certain of the outcome: it is simple trust in God's own word. I *know* I will go to heaven when I die, not because I am a minister or because I have tried to live a godly life, but because Jesus died on the cross and paid my debt. I am going to heaven; *he* said so.

The sixth proof of true faith is, faith that it will be a testimony to both the church and the world.

David said in verse 47:

'All those gathered here will know that it is not with sword or spear that the Lord saves, for the battle is the Lord's . . . '.

In other words, David was telling Goliath, 'The Philistines will discover how God does things; the armies of Israel will discover this; e*verybody* will know.'

David knew that when he had killed Goliath the Philistines would be defeated and the armies of Israel would be encouraged. And when you are converted and publicly acknowledge Jesus as your Saviour, you will not please the world, but you *will* encourage the church. David said that *everyone* around him would know that the Lord saves. Show that you have true faith: go out on a limb for God and let everyone know you are his.

11

A Natural Explanation Defied

1 Samuel 17:42–49

What made David the greatest king that Israel ever had? What was the reason for his genius? Was it simply that he was a brilliant military and political leader, a gifted poet and a talented musician? Are these the only ways in which we are to understand him?

Something of his character is revealed when we remember that here was a person who was *stunned* that the Israelites were terrified of Goliath. David could not understand how an ungodly, insolent man could speak to the people of God as Goliath was doing and go unpunished. David was a person who had such faith in God's word that when he heard the giant roaring he said, 'Goliath is finished!' He remembered that long ago God had made a covenant with Abraham and had promised, 'I will bless those who bless you, and whoever curses you I will curse' (Gen 12:3). He knew God's promise held good for Abraham's descendants, the Israelites. David simply believed God's word, so he knew that Goliath stood no chance.

However, David knew that a *super*natural victory was needed, for if he killed Goliath with Saul's sword or spear, protected by the king's heavy armour, then the armies of Israel would see it as a victory that could be explained naturally. He realized the Israelites needed to see *God* at work. He was also determined that the Philistines should know there was a God in Israel. So David envisaged a victory that defied a natural explanation.

This is what is needed today. I long to see God at work in

such a way that the most sceptical person is compelled to see that God exists and he is moving in power. The world believes there is a *natural* explanation for Christianity, that it fulfils some deep emotional need within someone who is 'made that way'. They are wrong: conversion is not psychological, but something *God* does, and defies a natural explanation.

The church also needs to see God moving in power, for sadly, the state of Christianity now is much like the state of the Israeli army in David's time, when those who represented God – being filled with fear – did nothing to show there was a God in Israel.

Today, generally speaking, the church is hardly recognizable as the one Jesus began. Let me give you an example of how far it has moved from its origins.

Christians in this country today are mainly from the middle-classes. But a sign that the Messiah had come was that the gospel was preached to the *poor* (Isa. 61:1). And if you could see a video tape of those who followed Jesus around, you would see the poorest of the poor with him, hanging on to his every word, saying, 'He's my kind of man: he accepts me' (Mark 12:37 AV). Jesus was never embarrassed by the kind of people who wanted to be around him. But if that type of person were to walk inside the door of many churches today, people would look askance and ask, 'Whatever is that person doing *here*?'

But that is not all. We have reached the place where the church no longer sees conversion as a miracle of grace. (I speak generally because there are exceptions, and I thank God for them.) The only miracles in which some are interested are those of healing, the casting out of demons, or the giving of some dramatic prophecy. Now I am *not* against these things, but surely the greatest miracle of all is when the Holy Spirit takes hold of a person and turns him around, so he sees there *is* a God, and he realizes it is God alone who saves.

Goliath is also to be seen as a picture of the unbeliever. Are you a Goliath? If so, what will it take to bring about your fall? You may laugh at this, saying, 'That is the most flattering thing I have ever heard! But I am not a Goliath; I am not strong, and I am no threat to anyone!' But if you are not a Christian, you need a fall because you are defying God by rebelling against him, by your self -righteousness, and by your mockery of the church.

'Why *should* I respect the church?' you may ask. Now if you have been looking at the dearth of good leadership in the church, the lack of spiritual aptitude, or you have seen the ambiguous attitude of the church in general towards sin, some things you have said may have merit. However, I want to show three things in this connection.

First, Goliath had to answer God despite the condition of Israel's cowardly army.

Goliath felt no fear of God. Why should he? God's people were frightened – a poor testimony to the God whom they claimed to worship. So Goliath felt he could defy the armies of Israel with impunity. The behaviour of the Israeli army did *nothing* to put a fear of God in him; they were fearful and they were cowards, doing nothing to show they really believed there was a God in heaven.

As we have seen, the state of the church today is comparable to the Israeli army in David's day, and they are in retreat. Not only is attendance at an all-time low, but the church leaders, who have the ear of the media, often make the situation worse when they speak. The leadership is weak, and the church's stand on morality is so equivocal that many wink at sin.

Seeing this, few people have a fear of God. Nevertheless, they are still without excuse. Goliath would still have to answer to God *despite* the condition of Israel's cowardly army.

Second, Goliath would still have to answer to the truth for the truth's own sake, despite the fact few believed it.

Let us look at verse 45. David said:

'I come against you in the name of the Lord Almighty, the God of the armies of Israel, *whom you have defied* [my italics].'

The *truth* was, Goliath had defied God. David presented Goliath with the truth, and Goliath would *have* to answer to it.

Now Goliath came from Gath. We read, 'A champion named Goliath, who was from Gath, came out of the Philistine camp' (v. 4). There is an expression in the Bible, 'Tell it not in Gath' (2 Sam. 1:20; Mic. 1:10). Gath was the city that symbolized the whole Philistine nation, where the enemies of God's people were born and bred. David was horrified that the Philistines would hear about Israel's sad state. He did not want them to sneer at the state of Israel's cowardly armies. He wanted them to think they were numerous and powerful and were representing God.

But the armies of Israel had let God down, and today the church has let you down. I am embarrassed to have to admit that the modern church has largely departed from God's infallible word, the Bible, and we are at a low ebb spiritually. But church history, which began two thousand years ago, is like a line graph: it has its high and its low points. When it is at a low point, people say, 'The church is finished', but they are unaware that God has a way of restoring and reviving his people. Jesus said that the gates of Hades will not overcome his church (Matt. 16:18).

Perhaps more people are converted when the church moves in spiritual power, but if you are unconverted, it will not do for you to excuse yourself to God by pointing at the weakness of the church; neither its failings nor the apparent superiority of the enemies of the Christian faith will change the truth of eternity.

Think for a moment about eternity, the endless realm into which you enter when you die. You have a soul that is immortal, and when you stand before God it will not help your case to say, 'Ah, but this church leader said hell did not exist.'

Goliath defied the armies of Israel, but he still had to answer the truth for its own sake, though those who were supposedly on the side of truth had let him down.

Third, it was not a question of *whether* Goliath would fall, but *how* he would fall.

When David approached the giant and said, 'I come against you in the name of the Lord Almighty', I think Goliath knew in his heart of hearts that David was speaking the truth. Do you know what Goliath *should* have done? He should have fallen to his knees and cried, 'I surrender!' But he stuck to his guns and paid the penalty.

Moreover, it is not a question of whether *you* will fall but how. Let me explain.

Quoting from Psalm 118:22–23, Jesus said:

'Have you never read in the Scriptures:

"The stone the builders rejected
has become the capstone;
the Lord has done this,
and it is marvellous in our eyes"?

'Therefore I tell you that the kingdom of God will be taken away from you and given to a people who will produce its fruit. He who falls on this stone will be broken to pieces, but he on whom it falls will be crushed' (Matt. 21:42-44).

What was Jesus saying when he applied these prophetic verses to himself? Well, think of builders using various stones they have cut to size. One selects a stone, but on discovering that it does not seem to fit anywhere, he tosses it to one side. However, when the work is almost finished, the workers realize they need a capstone to fit an awkward shape in the most important place in the building. Then someone remembers the discarded stone and finds it. To everyone's delight, they discover that it fits the awkward space exactly, and the stone that the builders rejected is put in the key position.

Jesus is like that stone. The Bible says, 'He came to that which was his own, but his own did not receive him' (John

1:11). He was the answer to Israel's prayers, but the Pharisees said, 'We won't have him'; the Sadducees said, 'We can't stand him', and the chief priests said, 'He is a heretic.' So they all rejected him and nailed him to a cross. Yet three days later Jesus rose from the dead in triumph, and the one the Jewish leaders rejected was given the place of highest honour at the head of the Christian church.

But you will recall that Jesus also said, 'He who falls on this stone will be broken to pieces . . .'. He said this to illustrate a great truth: We can come in repentance and throw ourselves on him and be broken in spirit. Nothing is lovelier in God's eyes than a broken spirit, when a person who was once so haughty and arrogant finally says, 'I was wrong; I am sorry.' David himself would one day say in true remorse, 'A broken and contrite heart, O God, you will not despise' (Ps. 51:17).

Goliath could have said this. Recognizing that David came from God, he could have thrown himself on God's mercy. But he entertained no thoughts of repentance; he preferred to take his chances, which seemed so good; after all, the people of God were weak and David was little more than a youth. Yet what do you suppose happened?

> As the Philistine moved closer to attack him, David ran quickly towards the battle line to meet him. Reaching into his bag and taking out a stone, he slung it and struck the Philistine on the forehead. The stone sank into his forehead, and he fell face down on the ground.
>
> So David triumphed over the Philistine with a sling and a stone; without a sword in his hand he struck down the Philistine and killed him (1 Sam. 17:48-50).

The outcome of David's encounter with Goliath defied a natural explanation: *God* did it.

But let us look now at the whole of Matthew 21:44. Jesus said, 'He who falls on this stone will be broken to pieces, *but he on whom it falls will be crushed* [my italics].'

Do you remember the Parable of the Wedding Banquet? Jesus said that a certain king gave a wedding feast for his son:

> But when the king came in to see the guests, he noticed a man there who was not wearing wedding clothes. 'Friend,' he asked, 'how did you get in here without wedding clothes?'
> The man was speechless.
> Then the king told the attendants, 'Tie him hand and foot, and throw him outside, into the darkness, where there will be weeping and gnashing of teeth' (Matt. 22:11-13).

The parable illustrates God's gracious invitation to the marriage feast of his Son and his bride, the church; all those who repent and accept the gospel may come, for a change has taken place in their hearts. However, it also warns of the judgment awaiting those without the appropriate wedding clothes, those who reject God's offer of salvation.

Goliath stuck to his guns and he became a fool, but you still have a choice. Will you fall on Jesus and repent or will you wait for the day when you will stand before God and answer for your life? Remember, it is not a question of *whether* you will fall, but *how*.

12

When Your Hero Dies

1 Samuel 17:45–53

All of us, I suppose, have had our heroes. When I was a boy, my hero was a baseball player. Most people living in Kentucky supported the Cincinnati Redlegs, but for some reason I liked the New York Yankees, and my hero was the centrefielder, Joe DiMaggio. I almost worshipped him. Years later, after he retired from baseball, I went up to him and introduced myself. I was in my thirties at the time, but I acted like a fourteen-year-old, shook his hand and asked for his autograph. It was the greatest feeling!

I have also had *spiritual* heroes and so, perhaps, have you. However, sometimes our heroes die in our eyes. Why? Because, unexpectedly, they let us down and disappoint us, and we see they have feet of clay after all. So beware of making this mistake, for the more you admire a person, the greater your disappointment when he or she falls in your estimation. It is only a matter of time, because the best of God's saints have at least one flaw. As John Calvin said, 'In every saint there is something reprehensible.'

Now in this chapter, I want us to look at certain people who are Old Testament pictures that illustrate important truths.

First, I want to remind you that the Israelites are a picture of the church. In David's day Israel was not looking to God and, sadly, generally speaking, neither is the church now.

According to the New Testament, the church is a mixed company. As we saw in the previous chapter, the church is both visible *and* invisible, and not everybody who is part of the visible church is necessarily part of the invisible church.

Sadly, many believe that merely being members of a church guarantees they will go to heaven. Yet one can be a part of the visible church and remain unconverted.

Second, I want to show you that the Philistines are a picture of the millions in the world who oppose the church of God. In fact, the world hates no other body of people as much as it hates the church, especially when the church takes a stand for righteousness.

The Philistines were pinning their hopes on one person: their champion, Goliath. Yet what do you suppose happened when David killed Goliath? In 1 Samuel 17:51 we read this:

> When the Philistines saw that their hero was dead, they turned and ran.

Now if you are not a Christian, you are a part of the world and you also have a hero. (I will reveal his identity before the end of this chapter.) My question is, what will you do when your hero lets you down and you discover he has feet of clay?

Third, I want to remind you that David is an Old Testament picture of Jesus. At first, Israel seemed to have no hero, only a weak king. However, David was to become the hero they lacked.

We may see David as a picture of Jesus in two ways. First, the victory that he won, he won alone. And when Jesus shed his blood on the cross, he took our sins upon himself and *he alone* saved the world (Heb. 1:3 AV). The second way I want to show David as a picture of Jesus is this: the victory that he won was to save Israel, who mocked him and scoffed at the very thought of him taking on Goliath. Similarly, the victory Jesus won was to save a people who despised him and mocked him and make them his church.

When David expressed his amazement that God's people should fear an uncircumcised Philistine like Goliath, his brother Eliab was angry and jeered, 'I know how conceited you are and how wicked your heart is; you came down only to watch the battle' (1 Sam. 17:28). However, David was undeterred and went to King Saul to volunteer to take on Goliath himself. Saul thought David had no chance of defeating the Philistine: 'You are only a boy,' he said (v. 33). The Israeli army had no faith in him either, and I dare say that when we get to heaven, we will watch a video replay of David approaching Goliath and see his own side jeering at him, unaware that what he was to do would secure the future of Israel.

Two thousand years ago no one knew that when Jesus went to the cross he was securing the future of his church. Acts 4:11 says this of him:

> He is the stone you builders rejected,
>   which has become the capstone.

> Salvation is found in no one else, for there is no other name under heaven given to men by which we must be saved.

The people Jesus came to save rejected him. They watched his torment as he hung helplessly on the cross and mocked him, jeering: 'Let him come down now from the cross, and we will believe in him. He trusts in God. Let God rescue him now if he wants him, for he said, "I am the Son of God"' (Matt. 27:42-43).

Then suddenly, Jesus cried out in Aramaic, *'Eloi, Eloi, lama sabachthani?'* which means, 'My God, my God, why have you forsaken me?' (Matt. 27:46).

That was the moment when God vented his wrath on one person. We will never know what it was like for Jesus to suffer as he did. (One reason that hell is eternal is that it can never satisfy God's justice whereas Jesus' blood did.) To those who stood around the cross it seemed that when Jesus died, he was finished. They were not to know that through his death God was, in fact, reconciling the world to himself (2 Cor. 5:19); neither did they foresee that three days later Jesus would rise from the dead in triumph.

There is an analogy here regarding revival. Did you know that the church is always revived at its darkest hour, at an unexpected time, in a surprising way and through the most unlikely people? When the world thinks that the church is finished, God raises up those who think differently.

In the eyes of the Philistines God's people were finished. But at Israel's darkest hour God sent David to them, an unlikely person, a mere youth, who, in normal circumstances, would have no place at the battle front.

When David saw Goliath, he knew what he had to do. Moreover, he was willing to look foolish and to be mocked and laughed at, for he *knew* that God would deliver Goliath into his hands, so he boldly told the giant that he was finished:

> 'This day the Lord will hand you over to me, and I'll strike you down and cut off your head. . . the whole world will know that there is a God in Israel. All those gathered here will know that it is not by sword or spear that the Lord saves; for the battle is the Lord's' (1 Sam. 17:46-47).

Some say we are living in a *post*-Christian era, but they are wrong: we live in a *pre*-Christian era: a wave of glory is coming and we are on the brink of it. God has yet to reveal exactly how and when it will happen. However, when it comes, it will come suddenly and will defy a natural explanation.

After David killed Goliath, those who had laughed at him suddenly became wise to what had happened and surged forward to pursue the enemy. Verse 52 says:

> Then the men of Israel and Judah surged forward with a shout and pursued the Philistines to the entrance of Gath.

It is easy to condemn them, but we are all like that: we are all cowards and scoff at that which the world thinks is ridiculous. But Jesus knows how weak we are; the apostle Paul said, 'When we were still powerless, Christ died for the ungodly' (Rom. 5:6).

The Israelites had to admit that David was their hero after all. Similarly, years later, many of those who heard the Spirit-filled apostles preach on the Day of Pentecost had to admit *they* had been wrong to despise Jesus.

The Bible says, 'He came to that which was his own, but his own did not receive him' (John 1:11). The people of Israel had long looked forward to the coming of the Messiah. On the Day of Pentecost Peter proclaimed their Messiah had indeed come with these words:

'Men of Israel, listen to this: Jesus of Nazareth was a man accredited by God to you by miracles, wonders and signs, which God did among you through him, as you yourselves know. This man was handed over to you by God's set purpose and foreknowledge; and you, with the help of wicked men, put him to death by nailing him to the cross' (Acts 2:22-23).

The people Peter addressed were those who had so recently dismissed the claims of Jesus and had clamoured for his death, shouting, 'Crucify him! . . . Let his blood be on us and on our children!' (see Matt. 27:15-26). But when they heard Peter speak their hearts were 'cut to the quick' and they asked the apostles: 'Brothers, what shall we do?' (Acts 2:37). When they rejected Jesus, they had aligned themselves with the enemy; now they had to admit they were wrong.

Are you still on the enemy's side? Perhaps you have professed to be a Christian, but in your heart you know you are not. What good will your false profession of faith be when you stand at the Judgment?

However, many people make no pretence of being Christians: they are openly on Goliath's side. Have you sided with the Goliaths of this world? Have you scoffed at the church? Maybe you are one of those who have declared, 'The church is finished!' and you have lined up behind Goliath, saying, 'I am backing a certain winner!'

Let me give you some examples of modern Goliaths.

Secularism. Do you believe that the world has come of age and no longer needs to believe God exists? Do you think what you see in nature is all there is? The German philosopher Feuerbach said, 'You are what you eat.' He contended you do not have a soul: you are just matter. Perhaps you agree with him and believe that when you die, that is the end. You may think, 'Well, this life is all that there is, so I want to make the most of it.' Beware: this secular philosophy can lead to making materialism your god. This is one example of a modern Goliath.

Marxism. Have you been flirting with the philosophy of Karl Marx? He was the 'genius' that handed on a rationale that became known as 'Atheistic Communism', and although it has failed in Russia, in Eastern Europe and in China, there are foolish people who still think it will work in Western society.

Liberalism or modernism. I do *not* mean the political party of that name but those who criticize the Bible. In the nineteenth century certain scholars decided that the Bible was just a book written by human beings and should be criticized in the same way as the works of Shakespeare or Wordsworth, for instance. This philosophy quickly spread through the universities. I know many men who, when they were first students of theology, were told that the Bible is not a reliable book. 'There *are* some good things in it,' said their professors, 'and here and there one can find the word of God, but it is not infallible.' Many of these people gave up their faith. Have you refused to accept that the Bible is the infallible word of God? Is this your Goliath?

Evolutionary theory. This hypothesis has long been taught and accepted as though it were a proven fact. I will speak only briefly about this here, but I want to ask you this: Are you aware of the disillusionment that is setting in the scientific community regarding the theory of evolution? Now, increasingly, the most intelligent scientists are saying that this theory does not truly explain the origins of life. Moreover, if evolution is true, the Bible is not. Are you hiding behind the theory of evolution? Is this your Goliath?

Earlier I said that if you are not a Christian, you have a hero, and I promised to reveal his identity. Well, Goliath is an Old Testament picture of the devil, and if you are unconverted, then *Satan* is, in fact, your hero. What will you do when you see him fall?

On the Isle of Patmos the apostle John foresaw in his vision what Satan's supporters will do when, at the Final Judgment, they see their hero has fallen and they face God's wrath:

> I watched as he [Jesus] opened the sixth seal. There was a great earthquake. The sun turned black like sackcloth made of goat hair, the whole moon turned blood red, and the stars in the sky fell to earth, as late figs drop from a fig tree when shaken by a strong wind. The sky receded like a scroll rolling up, and every mountain and island was removed from its place.
>
> Then the kings of the earth, the princes, the generals, the rich, the mighty, and every slave and every free man hid in caves and among the rocks of the mountains. They called to the mountains and the rocks, 'Fall on us and hide us from the face of him who sits on the throne and from the wrath of the Lamb! For the great day of their wrath has come, and who can stand?' (Rev. 6:12-17).

What will you do when your hero finally falls before your eyes? You will run! You will try in vain to hide from God's anger. I urge you to 'flee from the coming wrath' (Matt. 3:7). Run from it *now* because if you try to do it later, it will be too late. It is not a question of *whether* you are going to see your hero fall; it is only a question of *when*.

The Bible says:

> When the Philistines saw that their hero was dead, they turned and ran. Then the men of Israel and Judah surged forward with a shout and pursued the Philistines to the entrance of Gath and to the gates of Ekron. Their dead were strewn along the Shaaraim road to Gath and Ekron (1 Sam. 17:51-52).

The Israelite armies had shown themselves to be weak and faithless, for none of them had dared to tackle Goliath. But when David defeated their enemy, they pitched in, realizing they were on the winning side.

If you have lined up behind Satan you will lose your soul, but even a weak Christian will go to heaven. Do you want to know why? Because they know Jesus Christ defeated the devil and paid the penalty for their sin on the cross and they have accepted his offer of salvation.

You will recall that many of those who heard Peter's sermon on the day of Pentecost, realized they had been wrong to reject Jesus, and, 'cut to the quick', they had asked, 'Brothers, what shall we do?' (Acts 2:37). Are you asking, 'What shall I do?' I will tell you. Admit that you are a sinner and change your allegiance. Shout, 'Satan, you are finished!' Put your trust in Jesus, and today *you* will be on the winning side!

13

Coping with Success

1 Samuel 17:54–18:9

Sometimes God allows a person to do something extraordinary at the beginning of his life to launch him into a career that will bring him world fame and be a great blessing to the world. When David killed Goliath, it was, in a sense, the greatest single thing that he ever did; never again would he do anything as spectacular, and, compared with this, his other feats in some ways seem relatively inconsequential.

David's victory over Goliath led to King Saul taking him into his service and further achievement. The Bible says:

> Whatever Saul sent him to do, David did it so successfully that Saul gave him a high rank in the army (1 Sam. 18:5).

This verse shows us three things: (1) David's initial success in killing Goliath did not happen by chance; (2) God continued to grant David success, and (3) God could trust David to handle it well.

Coping with success is not easy. My friend Joseph Tson once put it to me like this: 'Ninety-five per cent of us can handle failure, but only 5 per cent can handle success.' Now God is not against us being successful. In fact, the Bible says: 'Humble yourselves . . . under God's mighty hand, that he may *lift you up* in due time [my italics]' (1 Pet. 5:6). God wants to exalt us and he wants us to have success, but only to the degree we can cope with it. As Dr Martin Lloyd-Jones once said, 'The worst thing that can happen to a person is to succeed before he is ready.' And when we get to heaven, perhaps we will discover that God worked overtime to keep success from us to preserve us.

What was the secret of David's success? Well, I believe success came to David because he did not seek it. Let me explain.

You will recall that the royal household employed David to play the harp for Saul whenever 'an evil spirit from the Lord tormented him' (1 Sam. 16:14). Yet what do we discover?

> David went back and forth from Saul to tend his father's sheep at Bethlehem (1 Sam. 17:15).

Now you may say, 'Well, if they asked me to entertain the Queen at Buckingham Palace, you wouldn't catch me going back to the country to look after sheep.' However, David's attitude was different: he did not say, 'I have been anointed as the future king, so I need to stay at court and make a name for myself'; he returned to the pasture.

Now we may long to succeed and be recognized, but this teaches us that we must be patient and not try to elevate ourselves. Remember, Jesus said, 'Whoever exalts himself will be humbled, and whoever humbles himself will be exalted' (Matt. 23:12). If we are patient, God will find us when our time has come.

David waited for God to exalt him, and, when the time was right, God unexpectedly gave him an irresistible opportunity: the chance to tackle Goliath. However, David's motive was altruistic: he was not seeking fame, nor was he trying to prove himself; he was simply angry that an uncircumcised Philistine could speak as he did against God and against God's people and go unpunished.

The Bible tells us David's victory over the giant brought him swift recognition:

> As soon as David returned from killing the Philistine, Abner took him and brought him before Saul, with David still holding the Philistine's head.

'Whose son are you, young man?' Saul asked him.
David said, 'I am the son of your servant Jesse of Bethlehem'
(vv. 57-58).

David had succeeded, but he had waited for God's timing.

In this chapter I want us to see four reactions to David's
success that teach us (1) how to cope with our own success;
(2) how to cope with the success of others, and (3) how to
cope with the way others react to our success.

First, we see the reaction of one who becomes a friend and
stays a friend.

One of the most beautiful things in David's life was the
close friendship he enjoyed with Saul's son Jonathan. Yet it
is remarkable that the friendship should exist at all. You see,
Jonathan was himself a war hero and God had singularly used
him in the past. In 1 Samuel 14 is the thrilling story of how
Jonathan, accompanied only by his sword-bearer, won a
remarkable victory for Israel against the Philistines. So
Jonathan might so easily have felt slighted and jealous when
God chose David to kill Goliath; yet we see the opposite was
the case:

> Jonathan became one in spirit with David, and he loved him as
> himself. . . . Jonathan made a covenant with David because he
> loved him as himself. Jonathan took off the robe he was wearing
> and gave it to David, along with his tunic, and even his sword,
> his bow and his belt (1 Sam. 18:1, 3–4).

Envy is often a natural reaction when a new hero comes upon
the scene. I believe this was part of the problem that the
disciples had – Peter, James and John, in particular – when
Saul of Tarsus came out of the blue (see Acts 9:26). 'Who is
he? He is not one of us: he didn't follow Jesus. Why would
God choose *him*?' These are the kinds of thoughts that
probably troubled them at first.

This attitude is common today: many Christians cannot

cope with their jealousy when God brings in a new face. However, we must remember that he is sovereign and can act as he wills, and we must be so devoted to his honour that we affirm anyone he chooses. To speak against such a person is to touch God's anointed, a thing the Bible expressly forbids (1 Chron. 16:22).

A godly person does not feel threatened when God uses another, and Jonathan showed true godliness, for, seeing that David was God's choice, he immediately accepted him. It was the beginning of a great friendship.

Second, we see the reaction of Saul's army officers, who accepted David.

Let us look now at the whole of verse 5:

> Whatever Saul sent him to do, David did it so successfully that Saul gave him a high rank in the army. This pleased all the people, and Saul's officers as well (1 Sam. 18:5).

Now the latter could afford to be grateful, for none of them had dared to tackle Goliath; they owed everything to David.

However, there was a second reason that they welcomed David among them: the Authorized Version says that David 'behaved himself wisely' (v. 5). You see, when David was with them, he did not gloat about his victory over Goliath, nor did he chide them for their cowardice. He might so easily have said, 'You are just a bunch of weaklings!' But he refrained, and they loved him for his forbearance and graciousness. David's modesty proved he could cope with success, and his sensitivity showed he was prudent.

Third, we need to consider the reaction of a friend who becomes an enemy: I speak of Saul.

Can you think of anything sadder than a friend who turns against you? This experience can be alarming, for we speak more freely to our closest friends and, sometimes, may make certain unguarded comments, never dreaming that one day they would use these against us. However, we should remember it is a painful possibility that friends can suddenly turn on us.

I think we should be wary of trusting someone who tries to be too intimate at first acquaintance. I have been a minister for many years and my experience has been that those who rush in do not turn out to be true friends.

However, David did not see the warning signs when, almost immediately, the king became so friendly. Recognizing that he owed the continuing existence of his kingdom to David, and feeling that he was too young to pose any threat, initially, Saul could not bear to let him out of his sight. The Bible says:

> 'Saul kept David with him and did not let him return to his father's house' (1 Sam. 18:2).

Coping with another person's success is always easier if they are no threat to us. The great Charles Spurgeon was a most unusual man – a phenomenon. He preached to six thousand people every Sunday, and next day his sermons were cabled to New York and translations were sent all over the world. Yet are you aware that in his day other clergymen ridiculed him? The Calvinists called him an Arminian, and the Arminians called him a Calvinist. But the main reason for their hostility had nothing to do with his theology: they simply envied his achievements. Today ministers love him, for they are not overshadowed by his success. However, if Spurgeon were alive today, it would be a different story!

Fourth, we must consider the reaction of those who rejoiced at David's success from a distance: I speak of the reaction of the people.

Saul was pleased to have David with him until people made the young man a folk hero when the army returned from the battle against the Philistines. We read:

> The women came out from all the towns of Israel to meet King Saul with singing and dancing, with joyful songs and with tambourines and lutes. As they danced, they sang:

> 'Saul has slain his thousands,
> and David his tens of thousands' (1 Sam. 18:6-7).

People can be so tactless; they should have known that Saul could not cope with this.

> Saul was very angry; this refrain galled him. 'They have credited David with tens of thousands,' he thought, 'but me with only thousands. What more can he get but the kingdom?' And from that time on Saul kept a jealous eye on David (vv. 8-9).

Now do not be *too* hard on Saul; the question is, can you regard yourself objectively and detect your own envy of others? It denotes an unusual degree of objectivity or great spirituality when you realize *you* are jealous of someone.

How do these things apply to you?

Well, the greatest thing that can ever happen to you is that you accept salvation and become a Christian. And when you publicly confess Jesus as your Lord and Saviour, you are brought into the church. Here you will encounter four conditions of people: (1) there will be those who become lifelong, close friends; (2) there will be those who accept you as a friend, although they never become close; (3) there will be others, whom you never get to know well, who, nevertheless, will rejoice that you have confessed Christ, for such a thing always thrills the church; but (4) God may raise up in your life a friend who becomes an enemy.

I say this because I do not want you to have a false picture of the Christian life. Do not think that becoming a Christian will solve all your problems: the Christian life is difficult. In fact, Jesus put obstacles in the way of those who would follow him, saying, 'If anyone would come after me, he must deny himself and take up *his cross* and follow me [my italics]' (Matt. 16:24).

Bearing your cross means you will suffer persecution. First, you will experience persecution from the world. Do not think for a moment that your unconverted relatives and friends will be thrilled because you are a Christian. Moreover, your colleagues at work will think that you are out of your mind or that you have some emotional problem. 'You will sort this out in a few weeks,' they will say.

But, as I said earlier, you may also experience persecution from a fellow Christian, and this is harder to accept. I wish I could say that any church you join would be perfect; but such a church does not exist. Churches are filled with sinners (but sinners saved by grace), and, occasionally, you will encounter someone who, for some reason, is jealous of you and treats you unkindly. To a new Christian such small-minded behaviour comes as something of a shock, but you should remember that *you* will not be perfect either.

Jesus knew what it was to have people who envied his success. In fact, the Bible says that the Jews demanded the Romans crucify him because they were jealous of him (Matt. 27:18; Mark 15:10). So he knows and understands how you feel when others hurt you by their jealousy.

However, God gives you a thorn in the flesh with good reason: to keep you from becoming arrogant. He gave David a thorn in the flesh, namely, King Saul, to keep him humble. Perhaps David could not have coped with his success if he did not have to watch out for Saul. And when you become a Christian, you will find God has a way of keeping you humble too.

14

Coping with Deception

1 Samuel 18:6-30

Nobody likes being deceived, but learning that a friend has betrayed you is especially hard to bear. You feel angry with yourself for being so gullible and deeply hurt that someone you trusted could have turned against you.

Pain like that is probably without equal, as David could testify. Deeply wounded by the treachery of a friend, he wrote: 'His speech is smooth as butter, yet war is in his heart; his words are more soothing than oil, yet they are drawn swords' (Ps. 55:21).

What makes deception deception is that one is unaware it is happening at the time. However, certain Christians do receive warning that all is not well. One of the gifts of the Spirit Paul describes in 1 Corinthians 12 is the gift of 'distinguishing between spirits' (v. 10). Someone who has this gift has a measure of objective discernment: the ability to know better than most what is happening. Obviously David did not have this gift, for he was unaware that Saul was deceiving him.

Now when you are deceived, you believe a lie. A backslider believes Satan's lies. One lie that he believes is, he can get a little closer to the world without succumbing to its temptations; in fact, he thinks, he may be all the stronger for it.

In Genesis is the story of Lot, a relative of Abraham. When he left Abraham to go his separate way, Lot pitched his tent on the outskirts of Sodom, a notorious centre for homosexual practice (Gen. 13:12). He thought he was the exception to the rule and could mix with bad company without compromising his principles.

Some Christians think like Lot today and regard it as a sign of great spirituality to get close to the world without giving in. But great spirituality is the *opposite* of that: it is anticipating temptation and avoiding it. Indeed the reason Christians fall into sin is because they do not avoid temptation.

Backsliding begins when we listen to the devil, who is always out to deceive. Lying is Satan's earmark. As Jesus said, 'He is a liar and the father of all lies' (John 8:44). You will remember the devil lied from the beginning. We saw in an earlier chapter that Satan's first recorded lie was to Eve in the Garden of Eden, a lie that caused Adam and Eve to sin and brought about the fall of humanity (Gen. 3).

But deception is more difficult to detect if the person lying to us is a friend, or someone who is known for his godliness, or someone whose reputation is unimpeachable. Yet what if that person was also a king? Believing Saul was his friend, David trusted him completely, unaware that the king's feelings towards him had changed and that he had become insanely jealous.

Now God did not allow David to know what was happening then, and this made it difficult for him. He did not know that God had rejected Saul as king (see 1 Sam. 15:26) and Saul was operating on borrowed time, nor did he realize that the king no longer had presence of mind. Had he known these things, he would have been prepared for Saul's betrayal, but he had to learn the hard way that those we trust might turn on us and even seek to do us real harm.

Indeed soon Saul's jealousy turned to violent hatred:

> An evil spirit from God came forcefully upon Saul. He was prophesying in his house, while David was playing the harp, as he usually did. Saul had a spear in his hand and he hurled it, saying to himself, 'I'll pin David to the wall.' But David eluded him twice (vv. 10-11).

David escaped these attempts on his life, but he felt threatened, bewildered and trapped. 'What am I to do?' he probably thought. 'I don't understand why Saul has suddenly turned on me. Surely, the king is a man of God! But a godly man wouldn't act like this!'

One of life's most difficult lessons is that we must never place too much confidence in others. David would learn to put his trust in God alone, and later he could write, 'Some trust in chariots and some in horses, but we trust in the name of the Lord our God' (Ps. 20:7).

Determined to rid himself of David, Saul tried another tactic. He decided to give the young man command of more than a thousand troops (1 Sam. 18:13). 'David will be unable to handle this responsibility,' he thought. 'His inexperience will lead him to make mistakes and his men will turn against him. And when the people get to hear about that, they will no longer regard him as such a hero!'

But things did not work out the way Saul had planned: David was a good leader and won the trust and affection of his men. The Bible says:

> David led the troops in their campaigns. In everything he did he had great success, because the Lord was with him.
> When Saul saw how successful he was, he was afraid of him. But all Israel and Judah loved David, because he led them in their campaigns (1 Sam. 18:13-15).

David's increased popularity only served to fan the flames of Saul's jealousy, and he became increasingly desperate to rid himself of him.

Saul's next ploy was to offer the young man his daughter's hand in marriage.

> Saul said to David, 'Here is my elder daughter Merab. I will give her to you in marriage; only serve me bravely and fight the battles of the Lord.' For Saul said to himself, 'I will not raise a hand against him. Let the Philistines do that!' (v. 17).

115

Now for reasons that are not clear and need not concern us here, this marriage did not take place, and Saul gave Merab in marriage to another man (v. 19). However, the king learned his daughter Michal was in love with David:

> When they told Saul about it, he was pleased. 'I will give her to him,' he thought, 'so that she may be a snare to him and so that the hand of the Philistines may be against him' (v. 21).

What kind of father would do a thing like that! Every young woman looks forward to marrying the man of her dreams! But Saul cared nothing for his daughter's feelings and ruthlessly set out to use her to ensnare the man she loved.

Although we are not speaking of physical or sexual mistreatment here, I say this was a form of child abuse, for Saul planned to use his child for his own selfish ends.

However, he was not the only father in the Old Testament to be willing to sacrifice his child to achieve his purpose. Let us return to the story of Lot, who, you will remember, had pitched his tent on the outskirts of Sodom.

We read in Genesis 19 that two angels came to visit Lot, who welcomed them into his house and offered them hospitality (vv. 1-2). The Bible describes what happened next:

> Before they had gone to bed, all the men from every part of the city of Sodom – both young and old – surrounded the house. They called to Lot, 'Where are the men who came to you tonight? Bring them out to us so that we can have sex with them.'
>
> Lot went outside to meet them and shut the door behind him and said, 'No, my friends. Don't do this wicked thing. Look, I have two daughters who have never slept with a man. Let me bring them out to you, and you can do what you like with them' (vv. 4-8).

Can you imagine a father stooping so low! That the rape of Lot's daughters did not take place was only thanks to God's graciousness, for the two angels intervened and rescued the family from this situation (see Gen. 19:10-22).

Later, in different circumstances, Saul was preparing to sacrifice *his* daughter Michal. But first he had to persuade David to marry her:

Saul ordered his attendants: 'Speak to David privately and say, "Look, the king is pleased with you, and his attendants all like you; now become his son-in-law"' (1 Sam. 18:22).

I do not think that Saul's servants knew what he intended to do; they probably had no idea he was using them. However, someone who is out to deceive others, who commands much respect because of his exalted position, will always find people to carry out his wishes.

The devious king was appealing to David's pride. When Saul offered Merab, David said:

'Who am I, and what is my family or my father's clan in Israel, that I should become the king's son-in-law?' (1 Sam. 18:18).

His response to the prospect of marriage with Michal was similar:

'Do you think it is a small matter to become the king's son-in-law? I'm only a poor man and little known' (v. 23).

In other words, David said, 'I am not worthy of this honour.'

Saul sent his attendants back to David with this tempting message:

'The king wants no other price for the bride than a hundred Philistine foreskins, to take revenge on his enemies.' Saul's plan was to have David fall by the hands of the Philistines (v. 25).

The king had thought, 'Right. David wants a feeling of self-worth, so let's make him *think* he can acquire it. But his pride will lead him to his death, for the Philistines will kill him. Nevertheless, just in case he survives, I'll allow him such a short time to complete his task that he'll be bound to fail.

Then everyone will see he is not the great man they thought him to be. Whatever happens, I'll be rid of him. This time my plan is foolproof!'

Saul's appeal to David's pride was successful, and he set out on his mission, unaware of the king's deception.

Satan appeals to *our* pride when it comes to the question of salvation. You see, we instinctively want to feel that *we* have achieved something. So the devil plays upon these self-righteous feelings by trying to persuade us we can do the impossible and save ourselves by our good deeds. But God will not allow us to be converted by our own efforts or take the credit for our salvation. In Romans 4:2 Paul said, 'If, in fact, Abraham was justified by works, he had something to boast about – but not before God.' The God of the Bible is the God of glory, who said, 'I am the Lord; that is my name! I will not give my glory to another . . .'. (Isa. 42:8).

But David accomplished the task Saul had considered impossible. The Bible says:

> Before the allotted time elapsed, David and his men went out and killed two hundred Philistines. He brought their foreskins and presented the full number to the king so that he might become the king's son-in-law (1 Sam. 18:26-27).

You will have noted that not only did David complete his task 'before the allotted time elapsed' but he did *more* than the king had asked of him: Saul had asked only for *one* hundred foreskins, but he returned with *two* hundred. How can we explain David's success and his survival against all the odds? The answer is simple: *God* stepped in and overruled.

This is an illustration of salvation by grace alone. Paul said we cannot earn salvation: it is the free, unmerited gift of God. In Ephesians 2 he put it this way:

> Because of his great love for us, God, who is rich in mercy, made us alive with Christ even when we were dead in

transgressions – it is by grace you have been saved. And God raised us up with Christ and seated us with him in the heavenly realms in Christ Jesus, in order that in the coming ages he might show the incomparable riches of his grace, expressed in his kindness to us in Christ Jesus. For it is by grace you have been saved, through faith – and this not from yourselves, it is the gift of God – not by works, so that no-one can boast' (vv. 4-9).

If it were not for the fact that God overrules, none of us would ever become Christians. Perhaps you thought that someone becomes a Christian because he is predisposed to 'that sort of thing', and you say, 'I know Christianity turns some people on, but it's not my scene.' As I said, none of us would be converted if it were left to us. Paul says, 'Like the rest, we were by nature objects of wrath' (Eph. 2:3). In other words, we deserve punishment. But in his mercy God steps in to deliver us.

God intervened in Lot's situation and saved his life. You will recall he had grieved God when he chose to live near Sodom and had fallen into sin, yet God saved him, for just before he destroyed the city by fire, he snatched Lot from the burning (Gen. 19:12–29). Lot's rescue proves that God will forgive and restore the backslider who returns to him; in fact, in the New Testament Peter describes Lot as 'a righteous man' (2 Pet. 2:7).

Are you like Lot? Perhaps Satan has deceived you into believing that you could get close to the world and remain unscathed. You were in grave danger, but God has reached you in time, and he will bring you through.

But it is not only the backslider who believes Satan's lies. Perhaps you believe you can save yourself by your good deeds. If that is so, then Satan, who wants you to lose your soul, has deceived you too.

'But', you may ask, 'How can I believe that *God* will not deceive me if I turn to him?' Because Satan wants to destroy you, but God wants to save your life – not just your *soul,* but your life. God comes to you and says, 'I do not want you to live a life filled with chaos and despair. I want you to know the best way to live is *my* way, and I want you to spend eternity in heaven.'

15

Coping with a Broken Vow

1 Samuel 19:1–18

What is the difference between a vow and a promise? Well, when we make a promise we say, 'I *assure* you I will do this', but when we make a vow we say, 'I *swear* I will do it.' The crucial difference between a promise and a vow is that making a vow is more serious.

The Bible emphasizes the seriousness of a vow or an oath (sometimes the terms can be used interchangeably) and says:

> When a man makes a vow to the Lord or takes an oath to bind himself by a pledge, he must not break his word but must do everything he said (Num. 30:2).

> If you make a vow to the Lord your God, do not be slow to pay it, for the Lord your God will certainly demand it of you and you will be guilty of sin (Deut. 23:21).

> When you make a vow to God, do not delay in fulfilling it. He has no pleasure in fools; fulfil your vow. It is better not to vow than to make a vow and not fulfil it (Eccl. 5:4-5).

According to Jesus a simple promise is enough for the Christian. Jesus said: 'Do not swear at all: either by heaven, for it is God's throne; or by the earth, for it is his footstool; or by Jerusalem, for it is the city of the Great King' (Matt. 5:34). He meant you do not have to say, 'I *swear* I will do it', you simply say, 'I *will* do it.' To put it another way, a Christian's word should be as binding as his oath.

But occasionally even a Christian must swear to tell the

truth, in a court of law, for example. We should not be unwilling to do this; Jesus' point was, we should not have to do this with one another.

The purpose of an oath is to provide absolute assurance that a person is telling the truth, for we know people sometimes tell lies. (Psalm 58:3 says we lie from the time of our birth.) So when someone makes a vow, he will swear, as Hebrews 6:16 puts it, 'by the greater', to dispel any doubt in the mind of the other party that he is being truthful.

When a couple get married, they make solemn vows to each other. Sadly, today, in increasing numbers, people break these vows, leaving their partners disillusioned and often heartbroken.

In this chapter we will see that David had to cope with the pain of a broken vow. But first, let me remind you of the events leading to this.

David had become so popular in Israel that King Saul, inflamed with jealousy, grew increasingly determined to kill him. Twice he tried to pin David to the wall with his spear (1 Sam. 18:10-11), and then he sent him out on what he thought was an impossible mission, hoping the Philistines would kill him (1 Sam. 18:17-30). But all his efforts came to nothing, for God would not allow him to hurt David.

Now Saul decided to get his son Jonathan to do his dirty work for him and ordered him to kill David. But Jonathan, who was very fond of David, was horrified and went to warn his friend of Saul's murderous intentions. Having found David, he said:

> 'My father Saul is looking for a chance to kill you. Be on your guard tomorrow morning; go into hiding and stay there. I will go out and stand with my father in the field where you are. I'll speak to him about you and will tell you what I find out' (1 Sam. 19:2-3).

True to his word, Jonathan interceded on his friend's behalf, appealing to Saul's sense of justice:

Jonathan spoke well of David to Saul his father and said to him, 'Let not the king do wrong to his servant David; he has not wronged you, and what he has done has benefited you greatly. He took his life in his hands when he killed the Philistine. The Lord won a great victory for all Israel, and you saw it and were glad. Why then would you do wrong to an innocent man like David by killing him for no reason?' (1 Sam. 19:4-5).

Saul seemed then to come to his senses, for we read:

Saul listened to Jonathan and took this oath: 'As surely as the Lord lives, David will not be put to death.'
So Jonathan called David and told him the whole conversation . . . (vv. 6-7).

David felt he could trust such a serious vow as this, for not only was it made by a king to a king's son, but it was sworn in the name of God himself: 'As surely as the Lord lives . . .'. So he probably sighed with relief and said, 'That is great news!'

So Jonathan took him back to his father's court, and we read that 'David was with Saul as before' (v. 7). It was just like old times.

Then something happened to inflame Saul's jealousy again:

Once more war broke out, and David went out and fought the Philistines. He struck them with such force that they fled before him (v. 8).

Again David was a hero in the eyes of the people. This was too much for Saul:

An evil spirit from the Lord came upon Saul as he was sitting in his house with his spear in his hand. While David was playing the harp, Saul tried to pin him to the wall with his spear, but David eluded him as Saul drove the spear into the wall (vv. 9-10).

You see, Saul was able to keep his vow until he was faced with the same conditions as before. But when a person's heart is unchanged, evil remains deep within it.

Perhaps, in good faith, you once made a vow to God, but now you have let him down and you bear a heavy burden of guilt. You may say, 'I don't know what to do. I have asked God to forgive me, but I can't forgive myself. I *keep* letting him down. I can't trust myself any longer.' But God knows how you feel, and he will forgive you. Moreover, so you can forgive yourself, he will *show* you that you have changed by setting a test before you.

Joseph set such a test before his brothers.

You may remember they had been so jealous of Joseph that they sold him into slavery, thinking they had seen the last of him. But God had his hand on Joseph, and eventually, he was freed to become the Prime Minister of Egypt (see Gen. 39 – 41).

Joseph met up with his brothers again when they came to buy corn from Egypt during a famine. Over the years their hearts had changed and they had repented; nevertheless, they still bore a heavy burden of guilt.

They did not recognize Joseph, and, at that point, he did not make himself known to them. He had long ago forgiven them, but he wanted to test them to see if they had changed. So he sold them the corn and then ordered his silver cup to be put into Benjamin's sack. Unaware of this subterfuge, the brothers left for home, only to be pursued by Joseph's steward, stopped and accused of theft (Gen. 44).

When the steward found the cup, he announced that the guilty person would have to return to Egypt to become Joseph's slave but the others were free to return home. In this lay the test: the brothers had the opportunity to save themselves by leaving Benjamin to his fate; would they seize the opportunity to save their own skins? But they had truly repented of their actions towards Joseph and insisted on returning to Egypt with Benjamin.

The brothers passed Joseph's test with flying colours and learned that he had forgiven them and, what is more important, that *God* had forgiven them. Moreover, having resisted the opportunity to commit a similar sin, they knew they had changed and could forgive themselves.

John Newton was once discussing 1 Corinthians 15:10 with a friend. (The text says, 'By the grace of God I am what I am, and his grace to me was not without effect.') He looked across the table to where his companion sat and said, 'I am not what I *ought* to be, I am not what I *want* to be, I am not what I *hope* to be, but thank God I am not what I *used* to be.' You see, in his grace, God enables us to see the change in ourselves and we do not need to make another vow.

The trouble with Saul was that his contrition was not real. Moreover, he had become so dull of hearing that *he* no longer heard God speak and so was incapable of true remorse.

Hebrews 6:4 describes those whose hearts have become so cold that they are no longer capable of remorse:

It is impossible for those who have once been enlightened, who have tasted the heavenly gift, who have shared in the Holy Spirit, who have tasted the goodness of the word of God and the powers of the coming age, if they fall away, to be brought back to repentance, because to their loss they are crucifying the Son of God all over again and subjecting him to public disgrace.

When God speaks to you, it is important that you seize upon it immediately. I know of a man who said, 'For twenty years I went to church without ever being gripped by a sermon. I became so despondent about this that I thought I had committed the unpardonable sin. Then, one evening, as I listened to the minister's address, my heart was stirred. The message got home at last! I was overjoyed because at last I heard God speaking to me. That message from the Lord was more precious than gold!' So if you feel the Holy Spirit stirring your heart, fall to your knees and thank God that he is still speaking to you.

As I said earlier, Saul no longer heard God speaking to him, and, sadly, he could no longer be 'brought back to repentance'. When he threw his spear at David yet again (v. 10), the young man realized he would have to accept the fact that things would get no better and for the rest of his life he would have to cope with Saul's broken vow.

Sometimes we too must face up to reality and see that certain situations will never change. But if we can come to terms with this, we will find true peace.

I believe this story teaches us four things.

First, we see the human heart is frail and sinful.

No child has to be taught how to lie: it is the most natural thing in the world. People begin lying from the moment they can speak, and if God does not step into their hearts, they will continue to lie. So it is naïve to put too much confidence in another person.

Second, we learn that people in high places can disappoint us.

Now some believe that Saul was not really regenerate. Many years ago I took this view, but I have come to see that he was truly a child of God. However, it is frightening to think that someone can degenerate as much as Saul did. He let God's people down, for he continued to lead them despite the fact he no longer heard God's voice.

Like Saul then, some Christian ministers let God's people down today, for they too continue to lead a church although they are no longer in touch with God.

Third, we learn that God's people must sometimes endure unsatisfactory conditions.

One of the most loathsome things happening in the church today is the preaching of what some call 'the prosperity gospel': the teaching that God wants all Christians to prosper materially. This is the *opposite* of what Jesus taught. He said: 'If anyone would come after me, he must deny himself and take up his cross and follow me' (Matt. 16:24). Such a person may prosper as well, but not because it was guaranteed by God.

So do not expect life to be easy after your conversion. You may find the colleague at work who has treated you unkindly will be even meaner, and you may find people you trusted completely now break the promises and vows they once made to you. You see, when you become a Christian, *you* will change but others will not.

Fourth, we learn God will be with us and he will provide a means of escape.

In 1 Samuel 19:9–12 we read:

> While David was playing the harp, Saul tried to pin him to the wall with his spear, but David eluded him as Saul drove the spear into the wall. That night David made good his escape.
>
> Saul sent men to David's house to watch it and to kill him in the morning. But Michal, David's wife, warned him, 'If you don't run for your life tonight, tomorrow you'll be killed. So Michal let David down through a window, and he fled and escaped.

So David slipped away from Saul's presence, and that night he fled.

Paul said that God protects the Christian and opens a way of escape:

> No temptation has seized you except what is common to man. And God is faithful; he will not let you be tempted beyond what you can bear. But when you are tempted, he will also provide a way out so that you can stand up under it (1 Cor. 10:13).

God does not leave us to face our difficulties alone, nor does he send us a trial we cannot bear. Deuteronomy 33:25 says: 'Your strength will equal your days.'

The writer to the Hebrews says Jesus knows and understands our human frailty:

> We do not have a high priest who is unable to sympathise with our weaknesses, but we have one who has been tempted in every

way, just as we are – yet was without sin. Let us then approach the throne of grace with confidence, so that we may receive mercy and find grace to help us in our time of need (Heb. 4:15-16).

Jesus will not moralize because we are weak; he will come alongside and say, 'I understand.' He is the one person who will *never* let us down: he is faithful, 'a friend who sticks closer than a brother' (Prov. 18:24).

Do you know the hymn 'What a Friend We Have in Jesus'?

> What a friend we have in Jesus,
> All our sins and griefs to bear!
> What a privilege to carry
> Everything to God in prayer!

Its composer, Joseph Scriven, had been jilted by his fiancée, who left him for another man, leaving him broken-hearted. But handing his pain and grief to God, he wrote these wonderful words. The last verse says:

> Do thy friends despise, forsake thee?
> Take it to the Lord in prayer!
> In his arms He'll take and shield thee,
> Thou wilt find a solace there.

This great hymn has brought comfort to thousands. It is amazing how God can bring such good from a sad situation and turn despair into hope.

When you cope with a broken vow, you have a choice: you can become bitter or let God turn it into the best thing that has ever happened to you. God can take your heartbreak and pain and use it to mellow you and make you stronger and wiser. He can transform your situation and you can look forward to the wonderful future he has planned for you. In 1 Corinthians 2:9 Paul said: 'No eye has seen, no ear has heard, no mind has conceived what God has prepared for those who love him.'

What do you suppose kept David from despair? He could not return to his family home nor could he stay with his wife Michal for fear of Saul; so he went to Samuel, who had anointed him, knowing that he was a true man of God and would tell him what he should do (1 Sam. 19:18). God will always lead us to one of his trusted servants.

Perhaps you are in trouble. Well, I am God's minister and I will give you the best news you will ever hear: Jesus will accept you as you are. He understands your weaknesses, and if you turn to him in genuine repentance he will say, 'I forgive you.'

The Bible says that God makes vows and he also makes promises; both are unchangeable, for it is impossible for God to lie (see Heb 6:18). We have one of his promises in John 3:16: 'For God so loved the world that he gave his one and only Son, that whoever believes in him shall not perish but have eternal life.' His promise in Romans 10:9 is similar: 'If you confess with your mouth, "Jesus is Lord," and believe in your heart that God raised him from the dead, you will be saved.' We can trust God's word completely for he swears by himself, and, as Hebrews 6:13 reminds us, he can swear by none greater.

The God of the Bible is alive; he will not let you down. The Bible is his infallible word and he has promised, '*Never* will I leave you; *never* will I forsake you [my italics]' (Heb. 13:5). 'The one who trusts in him will never be put to shame' (Rom. 9:33).

16

Coping with Grace

1 Samuel 20

The great Charles Spurgeon once said, 'If I knew I had twenty-five years left to live, I'd spend twenty of those years in preparation.'

Is God preparing you for some great task? Perhaps you ask, 'Why doesn't God use me *now*?' But maybe God has a task for you so unusual that he needs to take time to prepare you so you will be fit for the work he will call you to do. The problem is, so many of us want to succeed before we are ready.

God ensured that would not happen to David. David would one day become the greatest king Israel would ever have, but he would owe his success, partly, to his thorough preparation.

In earlier chapters we saw David having to cope with jealousy, deception and with a broken vow, but now I want us to see him coping with grace.

What is grace? Well, one Christian philosopher defined it like this: 'Love that looks upward is adoration; love that looks across is affection; love that looks down is grace.' Grace is unmerited favour, receiving mercy we do not deserve.

That is what salvation is. It is a gift from God: we do not deserve it and we cannot earn it; all we can do is accept it. Paul said, 'For it is by grace you have been saved, through faith – and this not from yourselves, it is the gift of God – not by works, so that no-one can boast' (Eph. 2:8).

However, some find it difficult to cope with grace; they cannot accept that someone may do something for them out of sheer love and kindness and find it impossible to believe that God loves them. I remember talking to a man who said sadly, 'I have been seeking salvation for ten years now.' I learned he was influenced by *Pilgrim's Progress*, John Bunyan's famous book, which has done much good and (I would not have the courage to say this if Spurgeon had not said it first) much damage. Having read it, this man felt that he could not go straight to the cross, but he had to live bearing a heavy burden of guilt. He was unable to accept the truth: God loved him.

Sadly, many believe that we get to heaven not because of what *God* has done for us but because of what *we* do for him. They feel that they cannot accept the death of Jesus on the cross until they have proved they have turned from sin and qualify for grace. They are wrong: Jesus has done *everything* necessary for their salvation, and all they have to do is to believe that and trust him.

Backsliders, who have wandered away from God, also find it difficult to cope with grace. Deep down they know that God still loves them despite their sin and their failure, but they struggle to cope with such unmerited favour.

Why is coping with grace so difficult? Because we are all self-righteous by nature. If someone does something for us, we immediately want to return the favour so we can feel virtuous. This is why it is so easy to believe that our salvation depends on our good works.

In this chapter I want us to consider three people: (1) Jonathan, who showed great grace to David; (2) David, who had to learn to cope with Jonathan's kindness, and (3) Saul, who feared and hated David because of his increasing popularity.

The friendship between Jonathan and David is one of the most extraordinary stories in the Bible. In 1 Samuel 18:3 we read, 'Jonathan made a covenant with David because he loved him as himself.' I do not understand this, for Jonathan was the king's son, the heir apparent, and, next to the king, he was the one who had most to lose by David's continuing popularity with the people. Had we been in Jonathan's shoes, I dare say most of us would have sided with King Saul. But Jonathan did the opposite. In fact, he defended his friend before his father and was so persuasive that Saul swore an oath before God that he would not harm David (1 Sam. 19:4-6).

However, this reprieve was only temporary, and Saul, again filled with envy and hatred, soon broke his solemn vow and made another attempt on David's life, leaving the young man with no choice but to go on the run (1 Sam. 19:9-10).

Now you may recall that when David fled from Saul, he went to the prophet Samuel (1 Sam. 19:18). That was a good move. Yet now we find David fleeing *from* Samuel. In Chapter 20:1 we read that 'David fled from Naioth at Ramah and went to Jonathan . . . '. The reason for this is unclear. Some theologians believe that Samuel encouraged David to leave, knowing Saul had discovered his hiding place (1 Sam. 19:19). However, the great scholar A.W. Pink thinks David made a mistake in leaving Samuel and took a great risk in going to Jonathan. I will not take either side, but David was indeed fortunate that Jonathan cared deeply for him, and it was by the grace of God that this move turned out to be a blessing and not the cause of his downfall.

Have you ever taken a course of action so risky that, but for God's kindness, it might have been calamitous? Some of us have found the right marriage partner only because God was so gracious. When I met Louise, I immediately fell head over heels in love – a risky thing to do. But she was the right partner for me, and I thank God for this. Sometimes he allows us to go in a certain direction and everything turns out well.

When David went to find Jonathan, God was gracious to him. Nevertheless, David probably had some doubts about the wisdom of what he had done. Why should he trust Jonathan? After all, he was the son of the man who was out to kill him.

Many people do not realize just how much God loves them. You see, we all have *some* damaged emotions and, to varying degrees, have experienced hurt and rejection. Sadly, many have been hurt so badly that they find it hard to believe *anyone* can love them. Now when they become Christians and feel God's wonderful love, they are on top of the world for a while. However, when the initial euphoria passes, they come down to earth with a bump and ask, 'Does God *really* love me as much as the Bible says he does? No one else has ever loved me like that. I *want* to believe it! But is it *really* true?'

This was the question in David's mind: 'Jonathan, I know you *said* you love me; we made a covenant. But can I believe you?' However, the words remained unspoken, and David merely said, 'There is only a step between me and death' (1 Sam. 20:3). This was his way of asking, 'Do you really care as much as you said?' Here we see David's frailty, his humanity.

But then he did something that was indefensible: he involved Jonathan in a lie. This may give some weight to the view that David was wrong to go to Jonathan, for God does not lead us in such a way that we have to resort to untruths.

The story is this: David wanted to know if it was safe for him to return to Saul's household, so he said to Jonathan:

'Look, tomorrow is the New Moon festival, and I am supposed to dine with the king; but let me go and hide in the field until the evening of the day after tomorrow. If your father misses me at all, tell him, "David earnestly asked my permission to hurry to Bethlehem, his home town, because an annual sacrifice is being made there for his whole clan"' (1 Sam. 20:5-6).

Now that was a lie and it is indefensible.

Interestingly, the Bible never glosses over human weaknesses. We often read biographies of famous people, but they rarely give a balanced appraisal of a person's character. But the Bible tells the story like it is, and shows us here that, like ours, David's character was flawed.

In fact, what David did, put the friendship between him and Jonathan to the test. Jonathan might have been tempted to interrupt him, saying, 'Look here, David, we are friends, but in asking me to lie, you are pushing our friendship too far', but he refrained and allowed David to continue:

'If he says, "Very well," then your servant is safe. But if he loses his temper, you can be sure that he is determined to harm me. As for you, show kindness to your servant, for you have brought him into a covenant with you before the Lord. If I am guilty, then kill me yourself! Why hand me over to your father?' (vv. 7-8).

Obviously, David did not trust Jonathan completely. But Jonathan made it clear his love for David was genuine and had no strings attached.

Jonathan proved his love in four ways:

First, he gave David his word that he would not betray him. He replied:

'Never! . . . If I had the least inkling that my father was determined to harm you, wouldn't I tell you?' (v. 9).

God has given us *his* word: John 3:16 says, 'For God so loved the world that he gave his one and only Son, that whoever believes in him shall not perish but have eternal life.' All we need do is believe. Moreover, the promise is to '*whoever* believes . . . [my italics]'. No matter what our background is, what our politics are or how great our sin, if we turn to him in faith and repentance, God will save us. Jesus said, 'With God all things are possible' (Matt. 19:26).

Second, Jonathan proved his love by asking David to affirm *his* love for him:

And Jonathan made David reaffirm his oath out of love for him, because he loved him as he loved himself (1 Sam.20:17).

Now this is interesting. Jonathan could see that David was questioning his love, so he reassured him, saying, 'Look here, one day you will have the kingdom, so swear to me now that when that day comes, you will protect me.' In other words, he was showing David that he really believed in his great destiny.

Now when we become Christians, God assures us of *his* love by giving us a certain responsibility so we can see we matter to him. You see, he not only wants us to believe his word, but he wants us to know we have a future; he has an architectural blueprint for our lives and if we wait on him, he will reveal it (Jer. 29:11).

Third, Jonathan proved his love by his deeds. In private, unknown to David, Jonathan momentarily deflected Saul's wrath from David to himself.

The New Moon festival came and as the king sat down to eat, he noticed David's place was empty. He said nothing then, but the next day, noticing David was absent again, he asked Jonathan about it:

> 'Why hasn't the son of Jesse come to the meal, either yesterday or today?'
>
> Jonathan answered, 'David earnestly asked me for permission to go to Bethlehem. He said, "Let me go, because our family is observing a sacrifice in the town and my brother has ordered me to be there. If I have found favour in your eyes, let me go to see my brothers." That is why he has not come to the king's table.'
>
> Saul's anger flared up at Jonathan and he said to him, 'You son of a perverse and rebellious woman! Don't I know that you have sided with the son of Jesse to your own shame and to the shame of the mother who bore you?' (vv. 27-30).

In fact, Saul was so enraged that he took a javelin and threw it at Jonathan (v.33). This was a moment when the king turned his wrath on his son.

However, Saul's rage pales in comparison to God's anger when he punished his Son for our sins, which were transferred to Jesus when he was crucified. Paul said, 'God made him who had no sin to be sin for us' (2 Cor. 5:21). And as Isaiah had earlier prophesied, 'The Lord . . . laid on him the iniquity of us all' (Isa. 53:6). God hates sin with an indescribable hatred, and when Jesus hung on the cross, he turned his wrath on him.

Fourth, Jonathan proved his love because he kept his word. He arranged to give David a signal to let him know whether it was safe for him to stay at court and had said:

> 'The day after tomorrow, towards evening, go to the place where you hid when this trouble began, and wait by the stone Ezel. I will shoot three arrows to the side of it, as though I were shooting at a target. Then I will send a boy and say, "Go, find the arrows." If I say to him, "Look, the arrows are on this side of you; bring them here," then come, because, as surely as the Lord lives, you are safe; there is no danger. But if I say to the boy, "Look, the arrows are beyond you," then you must go, because the Lord has sent you away' (vv. 19-22).

David obeyed and hid behind the rock for what must have seemed to him like an eternity. Perhaps he began to wonder anxiously, 'Has Jonathan forgotten? Has he changed his mind? Maybe it is too much to expect him to go against his father's wishes.' Perhaps David even thought, 'God will never use me now. My situation is hopeless!'

However, then he heard distant voices. His heart pounded furiously, but he dare not look lest he be seen. He *thought* he heard Jonathan's voice, but he could not be sure. Suddenly, an arrow swished over his head and landed beyond the target. Two more arrows followed in quick succession, each following the same path. True to his word, Jonathan had sent a signal.

He heard Jonathan say clearly to his servant, 'Isn't the arrow beyond you?' Then he heard his friend shout to the boy, 'Hurry! Go quickly! Don't stop!' (vv. 37-38). The lad retrieved the arrows and left.

After the boy had gone, David got up from the south side of the stone and bowed down before Jonathan three times, with his face to the ground. Then they kissed each other and wept together – but David wept the most (v. 41).

David saw that he had a true friend – the kind of friend 'who sticks closer than a brother' (Prov. 18:24). Jonathan had proved that his was an unconditional, lasting love.

Through his word, this is the message God sends you. He says, 'My love for you is unconditional and everlasting. The blood my Son shed on the cross has satisfied my justice. All you have to do is to affirm that.' Paul said:

'The word is near you; it is in your mouth and in your heart,' that is the word of faith we are proclaiming: That if you confess with your mouth, 'Jesus is Lord,' and believe in your heart that God raised him from the dead, you will be saved (Rom. 10:8-9).

17

Coping Alone

1 Samuel 21

In this chapter we will see a dark side of David. Many people think that the only black marks against him were his adultery with Bathsheba and his sin against God when he numbered the people – events that took place at the height of his glory as king (see 2 Sam. 11 and 1 Chron. 21:1). Few realize that David sinned equally while God was preparing him for kingship. In fact, his wrongdoing then proved he needed this time of preparation.

Now some scholars believe David was wrong to leave Samuel at Naioth (1 Sam. 20:1). A.W. Pink believes this was the point where David went off the rails. This is something that I will not try to resolve here; however, by the time David reached the priest Ahimelech, to whom he fled after leaving Jonathan, he was clearly in trouble.

David's problem did not spring from loneliness, although he was probably a very lonely man, for a person can be lonely and cope in *God's* strength. David's mistake was to try to cope alone.

Perhaps, like me, you know the feeling of coping alone. David certainly experienced this, and although God did not leave him, David had no sense of his presence.

Now it is possible to be *in* God's will and, at the same time, *out* of his will. Jonah was like this. God told him to go to Nineveh and preach against it, but he ran away from the Lord and set sail for Tarshish instead (Jonah 1:1-3).

When God is preparing us for his service, he often gives us a lot of rope so we can see what it is like to cope without him. Perhaps *you* are challenging God, saying, 'I'm going to go my own way and see if you do anything about it!' Be careful! You will be surprised just how far God allows you to go before he steps in.

In this chapter we see David running scared. You will remember he fled to Samuel, and then he left him and went to Jonathan, arguably a questionable thing to do, but God overruled. Now we learn he went to Ahimelech the priest at Nob (1 Sam. 21:1). He did not seek God's guidance but ran from one person to another, vainly trying to cope alone, a man in God's will, yet outside his will.

However, God did not stop loving David; and, when *we* go off the rails, he does not stop loving us; nevertheless, he will remind us of what we are like when left to ourselves, and we should never underestimate the consequences of going our own way.

I want to show you three things from the story of David's encounter with Ahimelech.

First, we see the anxiety he brought to the priest. The Bible puts it like this:

> David went to Nob, to Ahimelech the priest. Ahimelech trembled when he met him . . .' (1 Sam. 21:1).

Here we see David as a picture of a backslider or a difficult church member whose behaviour causes great concern to his church, especially to his minister.

Second, we see that in this moment of desperation David lied to the priest.

> Ahimelech . . . asked, 'Why are you alone? Why is no-one with you?' (v. 1).

David had probably not anticipated this reaction to his arrival, so on the spur of the moment, he made up a story that sounded plausible and replied:

'The king charged me with a certain matter and said to me, "No-one is to know anything about your mission and your instructions"' (v. 2).

The priest had no option but to believe this.

A backslider finds it easy to lie. However, on Judgment Day everything will be revealed. Jesus said, 'There is nothing concealed that will not be disclosed, or hidden that will not be made known. What I tell you in the dark, speak in the daylight; what is whispered in your ear, proclaim from the roofs' (Matt. 10:26). If God does not deal with our sin now, he will deal with it at the Judgment; but the consequences will be far worse then.

It is marvellous when God deals with our sin in our lifetime. However, his chastening can be painful, as the wayward Jonah discovered when the great fish swallowed him. For three terrifying days and nights he remained in its belly, while he learned his lesson (Jonah 1–2).

Third, we learn that David took advantage of the priest. He asked him:

'Now then, what have you to hand? Give me five loaves of bread, or whatever you can find.'

But the priest answered David, 'I don't have any ordinary bread to hand; however, there is some consecrated bread here – provided the men have kept themselves from women.'

David replied, 'Indeed women have been kept from us, as usual whenever I set out. The men's things are holy even on missions that are not holy. How much more so today!'

So the priest gave him the consecrated bread . . .' (1 Sam. 21:3-6).

David knew that he was asking the priest to do something questionable, for under the Mosaic Law only the priest should eat this bread (Lev. 24:9).

Now I confess I do not understand this point clearly, because in Matthew 12 Jesus justifies Ahimelech for giving

David the bread (see vv. 1-8). I will not try to resolve the issue here; I simply want to point out that David's request put the priest on the spot. However, somebody who is out of God's will is very difficult and will sometimes try to compromise God's ministers.

What should David have done? Well, he should have done three things.

First, he should have been truthful.

At times we are all tempted to lie because we fear the consequences of being honest. However, the consequences of lying are far greater than they would be if one told the truth. Moreover, one lie often leads to another, and soon David had to lie again. As Mark Twain said, 'A liar needs a perfect memory; the honest man does not.' You see, a liar has to remember everything he said to cover himself. All David needed to do was to tell the truth.

The Bible tells us about others who lied and lived to be sorry. Abraham was one such person. Genesis 20 tells the story of how he lied about Sarah, saying she was not his wife but his sister. The Bible says, 'Then Abimelech king of Gerar sent for Sarah and took her' (v. 2). Had it not been for God's timely intervention warning the king in a dream not to touch Sarah but return her to her husband, Abraham would have lost her.

Many public figures have rued the day when they lied to cover up their wrongdoing. If President Nixon had told the truth about the Watergate affair, it would have been embarrassing for him, but he would not have been forced to leave office in disgrace. Moreover, Edward Kennedy could have run for President on a Democratic ticket had he been truthful about the tragedy at Chappaquiddick.

In Psalm 51:6 (a psalm that he wrote after repenting of his adultery with Bathsheba) David said: 'Surely you desire truth in the inner parts.' By then, he had learned the hard way that lying is a sin.

Second, David should have asked the priest to make a sacrifice of atonement for him.

Perhaps you dislike the idea of a religion based on the sacrificial shedding of blood, but it was *God's* idea. After Adam and Eve sinned in the garden, God made them coats of skins, a process that involves shedding the blood and symbolizes how heinous sin is (Gen. 3:21).

We can never atone for our own sins; turning over a new leaf may make us feel better but it cannot wash our sins away. The only way atonement can be made is through sacrifice. Now in the Old Testament the offering was an animal: a goat, a calf, a lamb, or even a bull. These offerings foreshadowed the sacrifice of Jesus, hailed by John the Baptist as 'the Lamb of God, who takes away the sin of the world' (John 1:29).

The Bible says, 'All have sinned and fall short of the glory of God' (Rom. 3:23). We do not have to go out and rob a bank, commit adultery or murder someone to be sinners. Greed, lust, envy and hatred are sins, and if we do not ask God to deal with these, they will drive us to despair.

Third, David should have asked Ahimelech for guidance.

God had given his priests authority to answer questions that could not otherwise be decided by using sacred stones called Urim and Thummim. These were kept in a bag worn on the high priest's chest (Deut. 33:8-11). The priest would put his hand into the bag and take out a stone. If he withdrew the Urim stone, the answer was 'No', but if he pulled out the Thummim stone, the answer was 'Yes'. Ahimelech had the authority to use this technique to make God's will plain to David.

The fourth thing I want to show you about David's encounter with Ahimelech is that David had lost the spiritual power he once possessed. I am almost embarrassed to reveal this side of David, but it proves how far one can backslide.

The Bible tells us he repeated his lie:

David asked Ahimelech, 'Don't you have a spear or sword here? I haven't brought my sword or any other weapon, because the king's business was urgent' (v. 8).

Could this be the man who had killed a lion and a bear (1 Sam. 17:34-37)? Could this be the man who triumphed over Goliath and 'without a sword in his hand . . . struck down the Philistine and killed him' (1 Sam. 17:50)? How sad that a man God had anointed and filled with his Spirit was now demanding a sword and resorting to something he once did not need!

Ahimelech was still anxious and confused, wondering, 'What's happening here? Something's not quite right. Things don't add up.' But having been put on the spot, he replied:

> 'The sword of Goliath, the Philistine, whom you killed in the Valley of Elah, is here; it is wrapped in a cloth behind the ephod. If you want it, take it; there is no sword here but that one.'
>
> David said, 'There is none like it; give it to me' (1 Sam. 21:9).

Here is proof he had become a backslider: the man who killed Goliath was demanding the giant's own sword.

Like David, are you doing something you once would not have dreamed of doing: trying to solve your problems by resorting to worldly methods?

The fifth thing that happened when David was coping alone was the saddest of all: he forfeited his testimony to the world.

Let us see how this came about. In verse 10 we read:

> That day David fled from Saul and went to Achish king of Gath.

David probably thought, 'No one will know me in Gath; I will be safe there', but he was wrong, for, as we see in verse 11, he was recognized:

> The servants of Achish said to him, 'Isn't this David, the king of the land? Isn't he the one they sing about in their dances?
>
> > "Saul has slain his thousands,
> > and David his tens of thousands"?'

David was unaware that his reputation had spread that far. You may say, 'I have no reputation to worry about. No one would give me a second thought.' But you may be mistaken: you never know *who* may be watching and admiring you.

David was dismayed. He thought he had found a refuge where no one would recognize him and take word of his whereabouts to Saul. He knew he had to do something quickly to get them to leave him alone:

> So he feigned insanity in their presence; and while he was in their hands he acted like a madman, making marks on the doors of the gate and letting saliva run down his beard' (v. 13).

The servants of King Achish had had a high opinion of David, but it would be a long time before they could look up to him again. He was now useless as a witness to God.

This was a shameful episode in David's life. But everything that happened to him then was God's wonderful way of letting him see what he was like when left to himself. God wanted David to see what *he* could do for him, and, finally, God overruled.

Like David, have *you* let God down and forfeited your testimony to the world? Perhaps you think sadly, 'He will never use me now.' But he *will*: God had not finished with David and he has not finished with you.

We have all backslidden and have let God down, but he loves us and he understands our human frailty. David himself penned some of the most tender words in Scripture: 'He knows how we are formed, he remembers that we are dust' (Ps. 103:14). David was to experience God's forgiveness, and in verse 12 he reminds us of God's grace and compassion: 'As far as the east is from the west, so far has he removed our transgressions from us.'

However, I have to add a sad footnote. David's encounter with Ahimelech had tragic consequences. You see, Doeg the

Edomite, a servant of Saul, overheard everything and could not wait to tell his master about it:

'I saw the son of Jesse come to Ahimelech . . . at Nob. Ahimelech enquired of the Lord for him and gave him provisions and the sword of Goliath the Philistine' (1 Sam. 22:9-10).

As he listened to Doeg's story, Saul became determined to take vengeance on Ahimelech for helping David and ordered Doeg to assassinate the priest and his entire family. The Bible says:

That day he [Doeg] killed eighty-five men who wore the linen ephod. He also put to the sword Nob, the town of the priests, with its men and women, its children and infants, and its cattle, donkeys and sheep (1 Sam. 22:18-19).

Only one man escaped the massacre. He was Abiathar, Ahimelech's son. He fled to join David and told him what had happened. David replied sadly:

'That day, when Doeg the Edomite was there, I knew he would be sure to tell Saul. I am responsible for the death of your father's whole family' (1 Sam. 22:22).

David realized he would have to live with this for the rest of his life. You see, God forgives sin, but the consequences of wrongdoing remain.

18

Coping with Stress

1 Samuel 22

In 1 Corinthians 10:11 Paul said, 'These things [i.e. things that happened to God's people in the Old Testament] happened to them as examples and were written down as warnings for us.' In other words, we can regard the characters in the Old Testament as historical pictures depicting the way God would have us live.

In this chapter we will see David as a picture of the Christian who, while being prepared for God's service, has to cope with stress.

Probably all God's people have to cope with stress at some period in their lives. The Bible is full of stories about people who, at times, had to cope under great pressure. Elijah, Moses, Job, Jacob and Jeremiah, are among the characters who come to mind. Coming to more modern times, I think of William Cowper, who had a tragic life and suffered intense mental anguish. From his pen came one of the greatest hymns ever written: 'God moves in a mysterious way, His wonders to perform', a reminder that God can bring great good from suffering.

Since Christian believers are not exempt from any of the stresses that affect everyone else, do not think that conversion will turn you instantly into a mature, emotionally stable person, especially if there is a psychological blueprint that anticipates emotional difficulties.

These often stem from childhood traumas and leave lasting scars. For instance, a child who has been sexually abused will possibly be affected for life. I remember once talking to a man who had heard me preach about homosexuality and AIDS. He admitted being a practising homosexual, but when I asked him, 'Why are you like this?', he eventually revealed that his earliest memory was that of a hand reaching into his crib. I need not spell out the rest.

However, often we cannot explain the reasons for our behaviour, for in the same way most of an iceberg is submerged and hidden from view, most of our experiences are hidden deep in our subconscious.

God could heal our damaged emotions and erase all harmful memories instantly, and sometimes he does so, usually as a result of much prayer. However, for reasons I do not understand, he does not usually do that at the time of conversion; moreover, he does not heal everyone.

Now this chapter is not a treatise on psychology, nor is it a psychoanalytic study of David. (I wish I were capable of that.) We do not know all the underlying reasons for David's stress, but we must remember that David had experienced a kind of insecurity hitherto unknown to him. As the youngest of seven children, his family might have overprotected him. Then, probably still a teenager, David was suddenly taken from his home to live among strangers in Saul's palace, where he soon became the object of the king's hostility and was forced to go on the run. Where was he to go? He was unable to go home, for that would be the first place Saul would look for him. Is it any wonder he felt stressed! Even the most stable character, who had the benefit of the most loving and careful upbringing, would find it difficult to cope under these conditions.

In great distress, David took refuge in the cave of Adullam. Here he could hide from Saul, and be alone, at least for a while. This was not wrong; even Jesus, the God-man, wanted to be alone sometimes.

Jesus knew what it was to experience intense stress. The Bible says that on the eve of his crucifixion his anguish was so great that 'his sweat was like drops of blood falling to the ground' (Luke 22:44). But having shared our pain, he understands our failings. Hebrews 4:15 says: 'We do not have a high priest who is unable to sympathise with our weaknesses, but we have one who has been tempted in every way, just as we are – yet was without sin.' So if you have a problem you cannot discuss with anyone, if you have a weakness, if you have been hurt in some way or damaged emotionally, tell Jesus; he will understand.

As I said earlier, we do not know all the reasons for David's suffering; nevertheless, some causes of his stress are obvious.

First, there was physical privation. We know that he had been hungry because he went to the priest Ahimelech and had asked for food (1 Sam. 21:3). It is also likely that, living rough and in constant fear of capture, David had difficulty sleeping and became increasingly exhausted.

For a while, David must also have endured a degree of financial stress. How was he to manage without any source of income? As we have seen, earlier he had been begging for food.

Coping while under financial pressure is very difficult. I speak from experience: I know what it is to be in debt and to dread the bills that arrive in the post.

David was also worried about his family. Knowing Saul was ruthless, and fearing that he would take revenge on his parents, David went to the king of Moab with this request:

'Would you let my father and mother come and stay with you until I learn what God will do for me?' So he left them with the king of Moab, and they stayed with him as long as David was in the stronghold ((1 Sam. 22:3-4).

Later, when he heard of the massacre at Nob (see 1 Sam. 22:11-19), he knew his fears for his parents' safety were justified.

There is no greater source of anxiety than concern for our loved ones. Parents worry about their children. 'Why are they like they are? Where did we go wrong? Could we have done more for them?' All parents ask themselves questions like these. And sometimes children worry about parents and wonder anxiously, 'Is Mum all right? Is Dad overdoing things?'

David was also under spiritual stress. However, before we look more closely at this, I want to explain that there are two kinds of spiritual stress: I call these 'pre-conversion stress' and 'post-conversion stress'.

Pre-conversion stress is a good thing. It happens when you begin to think about your soul. Perhaps you have accepted the theory of evolution and believed that we have descended from apes and death will be the end, so your philosophy has been 'eat, drink and be merry, for tomorrow we die'. Yet, for some reason, now you suddenly begin to question this and wonder, 'Why am I here? Why is there order in the universe? Is there a Creator after all?' You realize that you are more than a physical being: you have an immortal soul and someday you must stand before God and give an account of your life. This is pre-conversion stress – the fear of hell.

The greatest kindness a Christian can show you is to warn you that hell exists. I remember, some years ago, one of our church members gave a tract I had written called 'What is Christianity?' to a London taxi driver. He took it away and returned a week later, looking for me. Weeping in the back of his cab, he said, 'If this tract is true, I am going to hell.' I led him to the Lord and he was converted. As I said, pre-conversion stress is a good thing.

The same is true of post-conversion stress, because when people experience this, they begin to worry about their relationship with God.

When Christians fail to keep their eyes on Jesus, they become backsliders. It is difficult to reach such people, for they are 'filled with [their] own ways' (Prov. 14:14 AV). In fact, some have become so cold and dead that nothing moves them. So when an obvious backslider comes to me in the vestry of Westminster Chapel and says, 'I am worried about my spiritual state', I know that is a good sign. What worries me are those who never think about their spiritual condition.

As I said earlier, David suffered from spiritual stress. We have seen in an earlier chapter that at some point *he* had become a backslider. I will not repeat the proofs that he had stepped outside God's will here, but I want to remind you that David had not been calling on God as he should have done and God used stress to get his attention.

This is what he sometimes has to do with the Christian. I can give you five reasons why he does this.

(1) He may want us to slow down. Are you like me, living in the fast lane? I have to prepare four sermons each week, keep up correspondence, talk to people who ask to see me, give time to my family and keep up my devotional life. And these things are just the *tip* of the iceberg! So sometimes God allows me to meet a stressful situation to make me slow down or even to come to a stop.

(2) He wants to help us to recognize our limitations, and lest we have an inflated opinion of ourselves, he reminds us that we are fallible.

(3) Understanding what stress is like enables us to help others with this condition. It is so easy to be judgmental, but Jesus said, 'Do not judge, or you too will be judged' (Matt. 7:1). If we have had difficulty in coping with our own stress, never again should we be the ones who leap in to criticize another.

(4) God uses stress to mould you into the person he wants you to be. Dr Gaius Davis calls this 'creative stress'.

(5) God uses stress to drive us to himself. I sometimes call this 'external chastening'. However, God does not use this method of disciplining us immediately. He begins by using *internal* chastening, by speaking to us through

151

his word. But if we refuse to listen, he will get our attention by placing us in a difficult or unpleasant situation. This was the kind of chastening Jonah experienced in the belly of the great fish God sent to swallow him. Do you remember what happened then? 'From inside the fish Jonah prayed to the Lord his God' (Jonah 2:1). Jonah *prayed*! God finally had his attention.

Now at some point after David left King Achish of Gath to take refuge in the cave of Adullam, something happened to David and God got his attention. Although the Bible does not give us details, three things show us David had learned his lesson.

First, we see he was now listening to God. You will remember that fearing Saul would take revenge on his parents, David had asked the king of Moab to give them refuge. The way he phrased his request shows he had changed. He put it like this: 'Would you let my father and mother come and stay with you *until I learn what God will do for me* [my italics]?' In other words, he said, ' I will wait until I know what *God* wants me to do.' David had learned that never again should he make a move without clear guidance from God.

Second, we see his composure in the face of bad news. You may recall that having escaped from the massacre at Nob, Abiathar went to David and told him everything. Did you note David's reply? He said:

'Stay with me; don't be afraid; the man who is seeking your life is seeking mine also. You will be safe with me' (1 Sam. 22:23).

His calm response to such dreadful tidings shows he had learned not to panic.

Sometimes we all have to face bad news. Do you go to pieces then or, like David, do you remain calm because you are living in God's presence? The Bible says the man who fears the Lord 'will have no fear of bad news' (Ps. 112:7).

Third, we see that in his distress David turned to God. Are you aware that he wrote at least two psalms while he was in the cave of Adullam? In Psalm 57 David cried out for God's mercy:

'Have mercy on me, O God, have mercy on me,
    for in you my soul takes refuge.
I will take refuge in the shadow of your wings
    until the disaster has passed' (v. 1).

And in Psalm 142 again David implored the Lord to deliver him from his enemies:

'I cry aloud to the Lord;
    I lift up my voice to the Lord for mercy.
I pour out my complaint before him;
    before him I tell my trouble' (vv. 1–2).

Who would have known then that these psalms would form part of the canon of Scripture and would feed the church?

Do you remember that in an earlier chapter I told you how the broken-hearted Joseph Scriven wrote the hymn 'What a friend we have in Jesus' *after he was jilted by his fiancée*? This was creative stress. The Bible says, 'No eye has seen, no ear has heard, no mind has conceived what God has prepared for those who love him' (1 Cor. 2:9). And if you wait on him, he will turn your stress and pain into something glorious.

David learned some valuable lessons from his time of suffering.

He certainly learned to appreciate his family more. You will remember that there had been tensions between him and his brothers, who were jealous of him (see 1 Sam. 17:17–29). However, when they heard of David's troubles, they put their differences aside and went to the cave of Adullam to lend him support (1 Sam. 22:1). David must have greatly appreciated this.

Like David, when we work through stress, we appreciate those who love us in a new way.

David also learned to welcome people whom, in other circumstances, he would not have wished to call his friends. Verse 2 says:

> All those who were in distress or in debt or discontented gathered round him, and he became their leader.

Do you see what God was doing? He was turning David into a picture of Jesus. The Bible says of Jesus that 'the *common* people heard him gladly [my italics]' (Mark 12:37 av). Jesus said we should welcome the needy and people who have no social status and cannot do anything for us in return. In Luke 14 he put it like this:

> 'When you give a luncheon or dinner, do not invite your friends, your brothers or relatives, or your rich neighbours; if you do, they may invite you back and so you will be repaid. But when you give a banquet, invite the poor, the crippled, the lame, the blind, and you will be blessed. Although they cannot repay you, you will be repaid at the resurrection of the righteous' (vv. 12-14).

God sent poor and common people to join David, lest, when he became king, he forgot his humble origins. It was as if he were saying, 'Don't forget, David, I have chosen you from the sheep fields!' It was a lesson David learned well: time after time the Bible makes it clear that he never forgot he had been a simple shepherd (e.g. see Ps. 23).

And lest we pretend that *we* are special, God has a way of reminding us of our background.

When Paul wrote to the church at Corinth, he pointed out that not many of their converts were from an intellectual, influential, wealthy elite. He put it like this: 'Brothers, think of what you were when you were called. Not many of you were wise by human standards; not many were influential; not many were of noble birth' (1 Cor. 1:26). In other words, Paul said the church is mainly composed of ordinary people.

Perhaps you have felt too embarrassed to go to church because you come from a poor social background or you are ill-educated and poor. Maybe you feel you have nothing to offer God, for you are 'a nobody'. If so, remember that God chooses his church mainly from those whom the world would call 'nobodies'. In fact, he chooses the kinds of people who gathered around David in the cave of Adullam: 'All those who were in distress or in debt or discontented gathered round him . . . ', and David welcomed them. Jesus will welcome *you*. He understands how you feel and says, 'Come to me . . .' (Matt. 11:28).

19

Coping Away From Home

1 Samuel 23

'There's no place like home' the old song tells us. I think most of us would agree with this sentiment, and many of us know that being away from home can be a painful experience.

When we first came to England from America in 1973, our son T.R. was seven and our daughter Melissa was three. Those early days in a foreign country were difficult for us all, but it seemed then that we would be returning to America within three years. So I would bring the family together to pray and say, 'It won't be long now. We are going home!' Then, unexpectedly, we found ourselves committed to serving God in London. Many years have passed since then and our children have grown up, but sometimes I still dream of going home.

Perhaps David, hiding from Saul in the cave of Adullam, dreamed of the day he could go home. However, that option was now closed because that would be the first place Saul would look for him. In fact, his parents were no longer there for, as you will recall, David had arranged for them to take refuge with the Moabites (1 Sam. 22:3).

David was probably homesick, for nothing was like it was and he missed things that he had previously taken for granted. It seems likely that among the things he longed for was the water from the well at Bethlehem.

In 2 Samuel 23 is a passage that many Old Testament scholars believe describes David at this time:

> During harvest time, three of the thirty chief men came down to David at the cave of Adullam, while a band of Philistines was

encamped in the valley of Rephaim. At that time David was in the stronghold, and the Philistine garrison was at Bethlehem. David longed for water and said, 'Oh, that someone would get me a drink of water from the well near the gate of Bethlehem!' So the three mighty men broke through the Philistine lines, drew water from the well near the gate of Bethlehem and carried it back to David. But he refused to drink it; instead, he poured it out before the Lord (vv. 13-16).

I will not go into his reasons for wasting the water here; my point is that, like so many of us when we are away, David missed his home comforts.

Not only was David homesick but, as you will recall, he went off the rails. Now this was not necessarily because he was no longer living with his parents; nevertheless, when young people first leave home, they often find it hard to cope with their sudden freedom.

In the previous chapter we saw that David learned that he should never do anything without clear instructions from God. So now he waited patiently until he learned what God wanted him to do, and, eventually, God spoke to him through the prophet Gad:

The prophet Gad said to David, 'Do not stay in the stronghold. Go into the land of Judah.' So David left and went to the forest of Hereth (1 Sam. 22:5).

In Judah, he would be among his own tribe, but he was still unable to go home.

What is home? I suppose we could define it as the place where everything is familiar. Perhaps, having left home, you now find yourself in a different kind of church. Maybe you are anxious because you are to begin a new job. In fact, everything seems strange.

However, there are several ways in which God will help you cope with unfamiliar circumstances.

First, he will give you a new family.

He did this for David, as we see in 1 Samuel 22:1:

David left Gath and escaped to the cave of Adullam. When his brothers and his father's household heard about it, they went down to him there. All those who were in distress or in debt, or discontented gathered round him, and he became their leader.

Now, most of his companions were not related to him and were not the kind of people he was used to; nevertheless, he welcomed them; they were his new family and they were the ones who stood by him.

You will find your new family when you join a church. I do not know if we will ever live in America again, but Louise and I found a new family at Westminster Chapel. Many of our closest friends are among the congregation, and they are the ones who stand by us in times of need.

Second, God will help you by giving you a new sphere of service.

David heard that the Philistines were attacking Keilah, a small frontier town in Judah, and looting the threshing floors. This news angered him, for the threshing floors hinted at that which was sacred – the sacrifices foreshadowing the sacrifice of Jesus on the cross. He could not bear to think that uncircumcised Philistines would enter the town and destroy it. The Bible says:

> He enquired of the Lord, saying, 'Shall I go and attack these Philistines?'
> The Lord answered him, 'Go, attack the Philistines and save Keilah' (1 Sam. 23:2).

God sent David to Keilah because he needed him there.

You see, you do not have to be at home to protect God's interests, and nothing will make you feel more secure than discovering God needs you. This knowledge will fill that void of loneliness, and, if you become involved in the battle where God has placed you, you will feel at home.

In a sense, you cannot go home anyway. After I had been the minister at Westminster Chapel for a while, I took my family back to Kentucky for a visit. Not only had it been a long time since my last visit, but I wanted T.R. and Melissa to see my childhood home in Ashland. As I drove up the street where I had lived, I began to say, 'Look, *this* was the house where . . . '. Then I stopped. Could this *really* be my former home? Everything was different. There used to be a big cherry tree in the front garden, but someone had chopped it down. Moreover, someone had altered the front of the house. It did not look like my old home and this saddened me until I realized I could not go home: God had given me a new sphere of service in London, and he had said, 'Get involved where the battle is. *That* is where I have put you.'

For David, the field of battle was at Keilah. However, he now faced a new dilemma, for the very thought of fighting the Philistines sent panic into his men. Verse 3 reveals their reaction to this news:

> But David's men said to him, 'Here in Judah we are afraid. How much more, then, if we go to Keilah against the Philistine forces!'

David discovered his new family was flawed.

You too will find that the new family God gives you has its faults. But you should remember that no church is perfect: like all families, each has its warts and blemishes.

However, the reluctance of David's men to face the enemy posed a serious problem: he and his followers were no longer united. He had to defend *God's* interests, but his followers wanted to defend *their* interests, and, anxious to avoid trouble, they were loath to come out of hiding.

Sadly, churches do not speak with one voice, but divisions among God's people are harmful and prevent Christians from uniting against their true enemy, the devil, and distract them from preaching the gospel.

Let me give you an illustration. Some years ago a Christian paid the Post Office £50,000 to frank letters from London with the message 'Jesus is alive!'. For some reason this upset the leader of one church, who publicly criticized him for spreading the gospel message in this way. He reminded me of King Saul, who was almost as interested in getting rid of David as he was in fighting the Philistines!

However, finally, David united his men behind him and sought the Lord again:

> Once again David enquired of the Lord, and the Lord answered him, 'Go down to Keilah, for I am going to give the Philistines into your hand' (v. 4).

It was as if he were asking, 'Did you *really* say that we must fight the Philistines and save Keilah, Lord?' However, God's reply was the same.

Perhaps Jonah hoped God would change his mind about sending him to Nineveh. But after the great fish vomited him onto dry land, we read, 'The word of the Lord came to Jonah a *second* time . . . [my italics]'. God's message was unchanged: 'Go to the great city of Nineveh' (Jonah 2:10–3:2).

Maybe the Lord has told you to do something. Perhaps he wants you to break away from the world and adopt a lifestyle that honours his holy name. But you ask, 'Lord, did you *really* say that?' But God will not change his mind.

The third way God will help you to cope away from home is that he will answer your prayers.

He answered David's prayers, and David's new family rallied round him as he set off to save Keilah from the Philistines. The Bible says:

> So David and his men went to Keilah, fought the Philistines and carried off their livestock. He inflicted heavy losses on the Philistines and saved the people of Keilah' (1 Sam. 23:5).

Only a short while before, David's situation had seemed desperate: he had little money or food and he was not even sure how he was going to manage. Yet now he had cattle and food too; moreover, he had saved the inhabitants of Keilah.

Nothing helps cure homesickness more than answered prayer. Just pray, stand back and watch God at work and you will see your situation change.

However, David had to learn to go on with God despite bitter disappointment, for he had word that Saul had discovered his whereabouts. This was something he and his men had feared would happen once they left the safety of the cave of Adullam. So David again went to the Lord and said:

> 'O Lord, God of Israel, your servant has heard definitely that Saul plans to come to Keilah and destroy the town on account of me. . . . Will the citizens of Keilah surrender me to him?'
> 'The Lord said, "They will" ' (vv. 10, 12).

What a dreadful blow to think that the very people that David had saved were so ungrateful and were prepared to betray him to Saul!

When God gives you a new sphere of service, how will you cope with the shock if the people you are helping turn against you? Such an experience is painful at any time, but even more so when you are away from home. However, you will find what Peter said about persecution instructive:

> Dear friends, do not be surprised at the painful trial you are suffering, as though something strange were happening to you. But rejoice that you participate in the sufferings of Christ, so that you may be overjoyed when his glory is revealed. If you are insulted because of the name of Christ, you are blessed, for the Spirit of glory and of God rests on you (1 Pet. 4:12–14).

You see, if you can rejoice when people turn against you, you will know you have close fellowship with God, and no matter where he has placed you, you will be at home.

20

Coping with Depression

1 Samuel 23:7-18

Many psychologists see stress as the common denominator of all psychopathology, and say how one copes with anxiety determines whether it will lead to something more serious.

One reaction to stress is the onset of depression, a condition marked with feelings of worthlessness, dejection and worry. A depressed person becomes vulnerable to harmless threats and minor frustrations; he fears failure and feels inadequate, unworthy of love and respect and is often troubled by feelings of guilt over some trivial misdemeanour committed long ago.

We all know what it is to feel like this, but sometimes people become so severely affected by depression, they are unable to cope.

Now there are three general causes of depression. But as we consider these, we should note that often this condition cannot be attributed to any single cause and may result from a combination of these factors.

First, depression may stem from a physical or biological disorder. For example, exhaustion can lead to depression. A person may get overtired because the pressures of work are such that he feels unable to take time off to relax and he becomes tense, irritable and unable to sleep properly. Eventually something has to give, and depression sets in. Women are vulnerable to the kinds of depression men often fail to understand. Postnatal depression affects many women and can be very severe. Then, when they get older and their bodies lose oestrogen, some women experience menopausal depression.

Next we come to depression that results from psychological or emotional stress. Psychologists say that this often stems from damage inflicted in childhood, for example, when a person has experienced rejection or has been subjected to physical or sexual abuse. Such traumas sometimes cause a sudden breakdown later in life, triggered perhaps by the stress of a new job, a death in the family or financial pressures.

Now it is often said that Christians seem vulnerable to emotional stress. Indeed when faced with a depressed patient who confesses he is a Christian, some unconverted psychiatrists say Christianity is partly responsible for his condition. So why do so many Christians suffer from depression? It does not seem a good testimony to the world.

I think there are two explanations. First, Christians undergo the same kinds of experiences as everyone else. We all have damaged emotions and conversion does not necessarily deal with these, although God may relieve some of the pain and distress they cause. Second, unlike non-Christians, we have an enemy: the devil. The Bible tells us that unbelievers are no threat to Satan, for he has blinded them to their spiritual condition (2 Cor. 4:4). But when we are converted, we stir up Satan's hatred, and he will ruthlessly try to thwart God's plans. Of course, an unconverted psychiatrist would dismiss this as nonsense; nevertheless, we should remember the devil *is* at large and he can cause a depressive illness.

Third, we come to spiritual depression. Those who suffer from this condition feel that God has let them down or that they have let him down. God once seemed so close to them, but now he seems so far away that he seems almost like an enemy.

Since spiritual depression can have all the earmarks of that which is caused by physical or emotional stress, so symptomatically, one cannot always tell the difference. However, Christians can see their depression is spiritual in nature when they see tokens of God's blessings; then they realize that he still loves them and begin to feel better.

We are looking at a phase in David's life when God was preparing him for a great task. David often found this preparation painful, and he frequently experienced periods of spiritual depression. His depression is clearly evident at the beginning of Psalm 13, where he poured out his soul to God:

> How long, O Lord? Will you forget me for ever?
> How long will you hide your face from me?
> How long must I wrestle with my thoughts
> and every day have sorrow in my heart?
> How long will my enemy triumph over me? (vv. 1-2).

In this chapter we find David in a depressed state in the desert of Ziph. In 1 Samuel 23 we read:

> While David was at Horesh in the Desert of Ziph, he learned that Saul had come out to take his life. And Saul's son Jonathan went to David at Horesh and helped him to find strength in God.
> 'Don't be afraid,' he said. 'My father Saul will not lay a hand on you' (vv. 15-17).

How marvellous that God sent Jonathan to reassure David then!

We discover what precipitated David's depression in verse 7:

> Saul was told that David had gone to Keilah, and he said, 'God has handed him over to me, for David has imprisoned himself by entering a town with gates and bars.'

Saul, who had not heard from God for a long time, suddenly began to use religious language, and, for all I know, he had his hands in the air exclaiming, 'David is trapped in that walled city. Look what God has done for me!' News of what Saul was saying reached David soon after he had emerged from a period of stress. He had tasted blessing from God, and then, suddenly, he heard this and fell back.

This commonly happens as Christians emerge from depression: they may receive great blessing from God and feel on top of the world, believing their depression is cured; then something unpleasant happens and they have a sudden relapse.

David had thought that he had been coping with an enemy God had abandoned, but here was Saul praising God for delivering David into his hands. 'Oh, no!' David thought, baffled by the king's sudden piety, 'Saul sounds so confident. I must be opposing the man God wants. God will punish me for this. I am finished!' He had yet to learn that hypocrites can give the impression of godliness, when, in fact, the opposite is true.

However, then David did what *we* should do when we are depressed: he sought the Lord. The Bible says:

> When David learned that Saul was plotting against him, he said to Abiathar the priest, 'Bring the ephod' (v. 9).

The priest obeyed and David prayed for guidance, saying:

> 'O Lord, God of Israel, your servant has heard definitely that Saul plans to come to Keilah and destroy the town on account of me. Will the citizens of Keilah surrender me to him? Will Saul come down, as your servant has heard? O Lord, God of Israel, tell your servant.'
> And the Lord said, 'He will.'
> Again David asked, 'Will the citizens of Keilah surrender me and my men to Saul?
> And the Lord said, 'They will' (vv. 10-12).

This unwelcome news depressed David more.

Similarly, Christians may feel worse after seeking the Lord because they do not like what he tells them; it happens frequently.

However, all Christians who want to walk with God must expect to face persecution. In Acts 14:22 Paul and Barnabas put it like this: 'We must go through many hardships to enter the kingdom of God.' But Paul contended that we should regard suffering for Christ as a privilege, saying: 'For *it has been granted to you* on behalf of Christ not only to believe on him, but also to suffer for him . . . [my italics]' (Phil. 1:29). And in 1 Thessalonians 3:3 he said no one should be 'unsettled by these trials'.

Sadly, sometimes this suffering is at the hand of another Christian, and this is particularly hard to bear. If the world is against you, you can cope, but when your enemy is a highly respected church member, who talks piously about God, you think, 'How could this happen to me? I don't want to oppose someone as godly as that!' But the Lord may show you that the situation will worsen before it improves.

When you are depressed, you sometimes see no hope of recovery and find it difficult to understand what is happening. David could not fully appreciate all that was happening to him then, but he discovered that 'weeping may remain for a night, but rejoicing comes in the morning' (Ps. 30:5). And you too will recover; then you will look back and see clearly what David came to see.

First, he saw God had given him a mediator.

God sent a priest to be at David's side. You will recall that Abiathar survived the massacre of the priests at Nob and fled to join David (1 Sam. 22:20). Now David had his own priest to represent him before God.

God has given us a mediator: Jesus, his own Son. When Jesus came to earth and died on the cross, he stepped between us and a holy God and paid the penalty for our sin. Today the risen and ascended Jesus is at God's right hand interceding for us. Through him, and *only* through him, we have access to God (1 Tim. 2:5; Heb. 7:25).

Now not only did a priest act as a mediator, he also revealed God's will. You will remember that when Abiathar fled from Saul, he took the ephod with him (1 Sam. 23:6), and through this David learnt what God wanted him to do (v. 9).

When you become a Christian, Jesus will reveal God's will for you. He may tell you to do things that you find difficult and unpleasant and you must deny yourself and say 'No' to a lifestyle that is not pleasing to God. Consequently your old companions may treat you with hostility and suspicion, but Jesus will never desert you, and if you keep your eyes firmly fixed on him, he will guide you along the way. This was what David discovered when he asked for God's guidance about Keilah.

Second, he realized God had given him two signs that he was with *him* and not with Saul.

The first of these signs was that God communed with him. When David asked, 'Will the citizens of Keilah surrender me to him? Will Saul come down, as your servant has heard?' God replied, 'He will' (1 Sam. 23:11). David did not like what he heard; nevertheless, God was talking to him, and that was a *strong* hint he was on his side.

I remember once hearing a preacher say, 'God often gives hints rather than directions.' You see, if you have an enemy who is also a Christian, God cannot say, 'I am with you and against him', because that person is his child too and he is still dealing with him. However, he will encourage you by giving you strong hints that he is with you.

The other hint God gave David to show he was with him was his refusal to allow Saul to harm him. Verse 14 says:

> David stayed in the desert strongholds and in the hills of the Desert of Ziph. Day after day Saul searched for him, but God did not give David into his hands.

Remember, Saul had boasted, 'Look what God has done for me! He has delivered David right into my hands.' But Saul had deceived himself, for even with all the resources available to him, he could not find David. David came to see that day after day God had protected him. In Psalm 27 David wrote of God's unfailing love, saying:

The Lord is my light and my salvation—
whom shall I fear?
The Lord is the stronghold of my life—
of whom shall I be afraid?
When evil men advance against me to devour my flesh,
  when my enemies and my foes attack me,
  they will stumble and fall' (vv. 1–2).

God protected David, and he will protect you. In the words of the prophet Zechariah, he will be 'a wall of fire' around *you* (Zech. 2:5).

Third, he saw that God had sent a special friend to encourage him.

When Jonathan came to David, he said nothing new, but he gave David the reassurance he so badly needed: 'Don't be afraid,' Jonathan said, 'My father Saul will not lay a hand on you' (1 Sam. 23:17).

Just when you need it most, God will send a special friend to support you. I speak from experience.

Many years ago, when I was going through what was then the greatest trial of my life, I received an unexpected letter from New Guinea, giving me badly needed reassurance from Arthur Blessitt. We barely knew one another at the time, but he said he suddenly felt God was calling him to write to me. His words of encouragement arrived on the day I needed them most.

We all need one or two special friends. You may say, 'I don't have anyone.' But the Bible says, 'A man that hath friends must show himself friendly' (Prov. 18:24 AV). So get to know people in the church; *they* are your real family, and God will give you one or two friends among them who will be special. The writer of Hebrews wisely says, 'Let us not give up meeting together, as some are in the habit of doing, but let us encourage one another . . .' (Heb. 10:25).

If you are depressed, remember God will provide all you need: he promises (1) provision by the blood of Christ; (2) preservation by the overruling grace of God, and (3) Christian fellowship. In fact, he can use depression to help you discover these truths.

When David began Psalm 13 he was in despair, yet he ended this psalm with an outpouring of praise, saying:

> I trust in your unfailing love;
> my heart rejoices in your salvation.
> I will sing to the Lord,
> for he has been good to me (vv.5-6).

The God who freed David from his despair will set you free too; then, like David, you will praise God, saying, 'I will sing to the Lord, for he has been good to me.'

21

Coping with Betrayal

Have you ever had to cope with betrayal? Has someone you trusted let you down? David experienced that, and, perhaps he was thinking of someone involved in the incident that we are to study now when he wrote: 'Even my close friend, whom I trusted, he who shared my bread, has lifted up his heel against me' (Ps. 41:9). And when Judas betrayed *him*, Jesus applied this verse to himself (John 13:18).

Now if God is to use you, eventually, *you* will need to experience the pain of betrayal, because it will humble you, it will mellow you, and it will enable you to encourage others in a similar situation. Yet, I suppose, we are never quite prepared for the shock when close friends turn against us.

David had experienced betrayal before. You may remember that Saul broke his vow concerning him (1 Sam. 19), and then the people of Keilah decided to hand him over to his enemy (1 Sam. 23). Now he was to be betrayed yet again.

After he left Keilah, David fled to Ziph, a region in the Judaean desert. One would have thought the people there would have felt honoured to have him among them, but they quickly realized they had more to gain by aligning themselves with Saul.

Sometimes God puts people in our paths whom we take for granted and even treat coldly, seeing no advantage in cultivating their acquaintance. However, this attitude is contrary to the teaching of the Bible, for Jesus said:

> 'When you give a luncheon or dinner, do not invite your friends, your brothers or relatives, or your rich neighbours; if you do, they may invite you back and so you will be repaid. But when

you give a banquet, invite the poor, the crippled, the lame, the blind, and you will be blessed. Although they cannot repay you, you will be repaid at the resurrection of the righteous' (Luke 14:12-14).

Let me tell you about my friend Arthur Blessitt.

Some years ago Arthur built a wooden cross, 12 feet high and weighing about 90 pounds, and stood it in his coffee shop in Sunset Strip, California. One day God told him to carry the cross around the world as a witness. Arthur has now walked across many countries, carrying the cross and sharing the gospel. He was once awarded the Sinai Peace Medal, and the night before he crossed into Egypt he stayed in Prime Minister Begin's home in Israel.

However, he does not always receive a warm welcome. He once told me of an incident that happened as he walked across Canada:

'One night I decided to stop in a certain town, and, as I always do, I went to a church to ask if they would allow me to leave the cross there overnight. You see, there's always a danger it will become a target for vandals. I wasn't asking for a bed for the night; I intended to sleep rough, as I often do. But the minister refused. I was not surprised: a church will often turn me away, but if I go to an inn, the landlord will be only too glad to help. So I went to the local pub then and asked the landlord if *he* would keep it safe for me. "Sure!" he said, "Bring it in."

'Later, someone from the church who had overheard my conversation with the minister came to find me. "I am so sorry," he said, "but we didn't know who you were at the time."

'" It's OK," I said. "Don't worry." What else could I say? But deep down, I didn't feel it was all right. It shouldn't have mattered *who* I was.'

His story reminds me of Hebrews 13:2, which says, 'Do not forget to entertain strangers, for by so doing some people have entertained angels without knowing it.'

When Jesus came, the Jews refused to accept *him*. They did not believe he was God's promised Messiah; Jesus simply did not fit their concept of the Messiah and, accusing him of blasphemy, they rejected him. Moreover, when they managed to nail him to a cross, they were convinced they had been right. You see, they could not conceive that God would allow the Messiah to end his life in such ignominy. As Isaiah had prophesied, they 'considered him stricken by God, smitten by him, and afflicted' (Isa. 53:4). In fact, they saw him as accursed, for the Bible says, 'Anyone who is hung on a tree is under God's curse' (Deut 21:23). Little did they know that, by rejecting Jesus, they rejected the one who would become the head of God's church. Acts 4:11 says of him, 'This is the stone which was set at nought of you builders, which is become the head of the corner' (AV). The Jews had made a terrible error.

The Ziphites also made a grave mistake, for they too rejected the man God had chosen to lead them. In 1 Samuel 23:19 we read:

> The Ziphites went up to Saul at Gibeah and said, 'Is not David hiding among us in the strongholds at Horesh, on the hill of Hakilah, south of Jeshimon?'

This verse shows that David obviously felt welcome among these people and trusted them completely. However, we should remember that sometimes people can seem warm and friendly and give no hint they are about to knife us in the back. And I suspect that, seeing their smiling faces, David had no inkling of what was about to happen.

W*hy* did they betray David? The answer is, because they saw a chance to be regarded as heroes and to curry favour with the king. They were not interested in Saul's vendetta with David, nor did they care that he might lose his life: they thought only of themselves.

Judas Iscariot's reasons for betraying Jesus were purely selfish too, as we see in Matthew 26:14-15:

> Then one of the Twelve – the one called Judas Iscariot – went
> to the chief priests and asked, 'What are you willing to give me
> if I hand him over to you?' So they counted out for him thirty
> silver coins.

When the opportunity arose of making some money, Judas
seized it.

Judas was obviously not a true believer. John 12:1–8 tells
us that when Mary took a jar of expensive perfume and poured
it on Jesus' feet and wiped them with her hair, he complained
loudly about the expense, saying:

> 'Why wasn't this perfume sold and the money given to the poor?
> It was worth a year's wages.' He did not say this because he
> cared about the poor but because he was a thief; as keeper of the
> money bag, he used to help himself to what was put into it (vv.
> 5–6).

This was rather a hypocritical reaction from someone who
was a thief!

However, I do find it hard to understand why Jesus chose
Judas to be one of his disciples in the first place, for he knew
Judas would betray him. Speaking to his disciples, Jesus said
in John 6:70:

> 'Have I not chosen you, the Twelve? Yet one of you is a devil!'
> (He meant Judas, the son of Simon Iscariot, who, though one of
> the Twelve, was later to betray him.)

Perhaps he chose Judas as a sober reminder that not everybody
who makes a profession of faith is a genuine believer. Some
just like keeping company with God's people but there will
come a time when their hypocrisy will surface.

I think another reason that Judas betrayed Jesus was he
was tired of being on a collision course with the Sanhedrin,
the supreme council in Jerusalem. How much better to become
a hero and gain favour with them! 'Not only can I make some

money out of this,' he probably thought, 'but if I align myself with the authorities, it will make up for three wasted years!'

Judas had heard all Jesus' sermons and had become so familiar with him that he was no longer interested in anything he had to say. He did not believe Jesus was anyone special.

Certainly nothing about Jesus' appearance led anyone to believe he was special. Isaiah said of Jesus, 'He grew up . . . like a tender shoot, and like a root out of dry ground. He had no beauty or majesty to attract us to him, nothing in his appearance that we should desire him' (Isa. 53:2). Jesus looked like anybody else. In fact, so ordinary was his appearance that the Jews asked Judas to give them a sign identifying Jesus lest they arrest the wrong man (Mark 14:44).

I suspect the Ziphites looked at David and asked one another, 'Who is this man? What is so special about him? He is very ordinary', and seeing no advantage in aligning themselves with him, they decided to hand him over to the king. Such selfishness is the essence of betrayal.

However, selfishness blurs one's discernment. Had the Ziphites been truly spiritual, they would have recognized that David was a man of God. But like Judas, they were unable to see beyond the physical. David seemed to be no match for Saul. His original band of four hundred men had grown to six hundred, but they were poorly equipped, and, compared to the size of Saul's army, his was a meagre force. But David was operating on a *spiritual* level, and the outcome of his struggle would not depend on human resources or on conventional weapons.

Paul recognized that the battle was spiritual. Describing the kinds of weapons we have as Christians, he said :

Though we live in the world, we do not wage war as the world does. The weapons we fight with are not the weapons of the world. On the contrary, they have divine power to demolish strongholds (2 Cor. 10:3–4).

When preaching, it is sometimes tempting to appeal to people's carnal minds and make Jesus more attractive, in the hope that they will be converted. But this would be wrong: God does not save people in ways one might expect; he saves them by revealing the truth about the cross. That was why Paul said when he went to Corinth (a city that had many intellectuals and influential people among its population): 'I am determined to know nothing among you save Jesus Christ and him crucified' (1 Cor. 2:2). He resisted the temptation to appeal to their intellects and water down the gospel.

I was once asked to preach the gospel to the Parliamentary Christian Fellowship. When I arrived at the flat, where the meeting was to be held, I discovered that about a hundred people, some of them household names, had gathered to hear me speak. 'Please make your talk gentle, Dr Kendall,' said the person who had invited me to speak.

'Make it gentle!' I thought. 'Oh dear! How can I do that?'

Well, I preached for about thirty-five minutes, and my talk was as gentle as I could make it. But when I finished there was an awful silence; then people tiptoed out 'What have I done!' I thought. 'What have I done!'. I turned to the organizer and said, 'Look, that's as gentle as I have ever been.' I could see what he was thinking: 'What must he be like when he is *not* gentle!' But I did not know any other way to put the message across. You see, if you preach the gospel, you will almost certainly cause offence.

Now you will remember the carnally minded Ziphites had decided to ingratiate themselves with Saul and tell him where he could find David. As they had hoped, the king was delighted with the information and said:

'The Lord bless you for your concern for me' (1 Sam. 23:21).

They would have felt foolish if Saul had brushed them aside, but his obvious delight and his pious language boosted their spirits, for it confirmed that what they had done was right.

When Judas Iscariot betrayed Jesus, the chief priests were 'delighted' too (Luke 22:5). That made Judas feel better. He would have been embarrassed if they had been uninterested in the information he was so keen to sell.

However, sometimes, traitors are asked to do more than they had planned.

Saul had not yet finished with the Ziphites, for he continued like this:

'Go and make further preparation. Find out where David usually goes and who has seen him there. They tell me he is very crafty. Find out about all the hiding-places he uses and come back to me with definite information. Then I will go with you; if he is in the area, I will track him down among all the clans of Judah' (1 Sam. 23:22–23).

You see Saul probably wanted to test the Ziphites' loyalty to him, so he gave them more to do.

When Judas went to the priests to betray Jesus, perhaps he hoped that all he would have to do was to tell them where they could find him. But they did not let him off so lightly. 'You must accompany us when we arrest Jesus,' they said. 'You must point him out to us.' (see Mark 14:44).

Here the analogy between the Ziphites' treachery against David and Judas' treachery against Jesus breaks down.

The Ziphites treachery eventually came to nothing. This was what happened:

As Saul and his forces were closing in on David and his men to capture them, a messenger came to Saul saying, 'Come quickly! The Philistines are raiding the land.' Then Saul broke off his pursuit of David and went to meet the Philistines. . . . And David went up from there and lived in the strongholds of En Gedi (vv. 26–29).

God diverted Saul's attention and David was spared. The Ziphites had made fools of themselves.

However, Judas' treachery succeeded, for the Jews arrested Jesus, tried him and condemned him to death.

Now Judas soon realized he had made a terrible mistake:

> When Judas, who had betrayed him, saw that Jesus was condemned, he was seized with remorse and returned the thirty silver coins to the chief priests and elders. 'I have sinned,' he said, 'for I have betrayed innocent blood.'
>
> 'What is that to us?' they replied. 'That's your responsibility.'
>
> So Judas threw the money into the temple and left. Then he went away and hanged himself' (Matt. 27:3–5).

Jesus said, 'Woe to that man who betrays the Son of Man! It would be better for him if he had not been born' (Mark 14:21). This verse is one of the strongest affirmations of eternal punishment in the Bible, so do not let anybody tell you that death is the end, for you have an immortal soul.

But God used Judas' act of betrayal to save the world. Had you stood at the foot of the cross, you would have seen no evidence that God was at work, yet everything that happened was part of his predetermined plan. Hundreds of years earlier Isaiah had foreseen the crucifixion and had prophesied: 'He was stricken by God, smitten by him, and afflicted . . . . It was the Lord's will to crush him and cause him to suffer' (Isa. 53:4, 10). And Peter said of Jesus: 'This man was handed over to you *by God's set purpose and foreknowledge*, and you, with the help of wicked men, put him to death by nailing him to the cross [my italics]' (Acts 2:23). As Paul wrote in his letter to the Romans: '[God] did not spare his own Son, but gave him up for us all' (Rom. 8:32).

22

A Tender Conscience

1 Samuel 24:1–7

Someone has said that the difference between religion and Christianity is who initiates what you do. People initiate religion, and everything that happens has a natural explanation. Christianity is the opposite of that: Christianity begins with God, and everything that happens defies a natural explanation.

Jesus used an analogy to show that regeneration is something God does. Comparing conversion to birth, he said, 'You must be born again' (John 3:7). None of us initiated our own birth, and none of us can initiate our new birth. We may have begged for mercy, crying, 'Lord, save me!' but we did this only because *God* had begun something within us. In James 1:18 we read, 'He chose to give us birth through the word of truth . . .'. In other words, we are converted only because God steps in.

Moreover, our conversion is *totally* of God. You see, we are not saved by our works but by what Jesus did for us on the cross. Paul said, 'To the man who does not work but trusts God who justifies the wicked, his faith is credited as righteousness' (Rom. 4:5). Followers of natural religion say it is what *you* do that counts, but Christians know they are justified only because of what *God* does.

David knew it is God alone who saves; nevertheless, he was tempted to do the unthinkable and save himself. Let us see how this came about.

The Bible says:

> After Saul returned from pursuing the Philistines, he was told, 'David is in the Desert of En Gedi.' So Saul took three thousand

chosen men from all Israel and set out to look for David and his men near the Crags of the Wild Goats.

He came to the sheep pens along the way; a cave was there, and Saul went in to relieve himself. David and his men were far back in the cave. The men said, 'This is the very day the Lord spoke of when he said to you, "I will give your enemy into your hands for you to deal with as you wish."' Then David crept up unnoticed and cut off a corner of Saul's robe (1 Sam. 24:1–4).

I will not enter the debate about whether this was a serious transgression, but I must point out that had David done more than damage the king's robe, he would *certainly* have sinned against God. As it was, he was immediately conscience-stricken, for he knew that he had come close to competing with something that is God's prerogative alone. God says, 'It is *mine* to avenge; *I* will repay [my italics]' (Heb. 10:30).

When someone hurts us, it may be tempting to take matters into our own hands and get even or clear our names, but God says, 'No, don't you dare! Leave it to me. I will deal with this.'

I want to show you four things from this story.

First, a leader must rise above his zealous followers. You will recall that when David's supporters discovered King Saul was in the cave where they were hiding, they said to David: 'This is the day the Lord spoke of when he said to you, "I will give your enemy into your hands for you to deal with as you wish."' In other words, they wanted David to kill Saul.

Now I want to show you something that is very interesting. In 1 Samuel 23:7 we read that when Saul heard that David had gone to Keilah, Saul said excitedly, '*God* has handed him over to me . . . [my italics]'. Now we see that David's followers said, '*God* has delivered Saul into your hands.' In effect, both sides claimed God was on their side. Now who was right? Well, both parties had been too hasty and had jumped to the wrong conclusion: God had not delivered David into Saul's hands; in fact, God protected him; and he had not delivered

Saul into David's hands now, for *he* would deal with Saul in his own good time.

The lesson for Christian leaders here is that we must beware of our followers getting too excited and, if necessary, we must reprove them.

We learn in 1 Samuel 24:5 that David rebuked his men, saying:

> 'The Lord forbid that I should do such a thing to my master, the Lord's anointed, or lift my hand against him, for he is the anointed of the Lord.'

A rebuke may sting, but, when deserved, it is a blessing. The kindest thing Joseph Tson ever did for me was to rebuke me. He hurt me deeply, but it was one of the greatest messages that I have heard: 'R.T., you must totally forgive them.' As Proverbs 27:6 says, 'Wounds from a friend can be trusted.'

It is a great test of their fidelity to God when ministers rebuke their followers. It is something they find very difficult to do, because they are grateful for their support and the last thing they want to do is to offend them. Nevertheless, a rebuke is sometimes necessary.

When we started the Pilot Lights group, some of its members went out onto the streets to witness and in their enthusiasm put Jesus stickers on all the windows of the stores on Victoria Street. That was embarrassing enough, but then I received a letter from Westminster Abbey complaining that they had infiltrated their literature by sticking our tracts with theirs inside the Abbey. I had to write a letter of apology and gently admonish the offenders. They were my followers, but they were getting me into trouble and I had to stop it.

Second, you must refuse a 'salvation' that can be naturally explained. David could have saved his life by killing Saul then. Here was the perfect opportunity to get rid of his enemy and become king; it would have been so easy. But David knew that if he succumbed to that temptation, not only would he have it on his conscience for the rest of his life but he would have done it in his own strength. So wisely, he stayed his hand.

Are you trying to save yourself? Perhaps you are pinning your hopes of salvation on your good deeds and high moral standards or on your baptism and regular church attendance. If so, you are confusing Christianity with religion; these things have a natural explanation, because they are things you do. We cannot initiate our new birth. Christianity is *totally* of God: it is he alone who saves.

Third, I want to show you that when you walk in the light, the Holy Spirit reveals sins that otherwise go unnoticed. The Bible says: 'David was conscience-stricken for having cut off a corner of his robe.'

Some might say, 'I don't understand why he felt like that. If it had been up to me, I would have ruined Saul's robe completely. Probably I would have gone further and killed him.'

But when you are walking in the light things will bother you that do not trouble others. You see, 'walking in the light' means being constantly open to the direction of the Holy Spirit and doing whatever he tells you to do. You may still fall into sin, but when you do wrong, like David, you will feel ashamed.

I know exactly how David felt when he cut off a corner of Saul's robe. I know what it is to be concerned about things that others would brush aside, thinking they were of little consequence.

Many years ago I said something to Luis Palau that I regretted almost immediately. It was not something terribly bad, and many would not have given it a second thought, but I could not get it out of my mind. Four years later I was invited to speak at Spring Harvest. When I arrived, the organizers said, 'Luis Palau is speaking tonight and he wants you to sit next to him on the platform.' I realized then that God had given me a chance to apologize. I did so after the service, and Luis replied, 'Thank you, R.T. You needn't have said that for my sake, but I know God wanted you to do it.' God was so good to give me the opportunity to put things right. It is wonderful to have a clear conscience.

Fourth, and chiefly, I want you to see why a tender conscience is so important. Well, if your heart is not sensitive, you will not hear God speak. To me, the most important thing in the world is to hear God's voice. I do not want to become spiritually deaf, and I know that if I try to justify my wrongdoing, my conscience will begin to grow hard.

Perhaps you can remember being gripped by God's word, but now you say, 'Oh, I've heard all that before!' Why are you not gripped now? It is because you did not obey then. For when you ignore God's voice, you become dull of hearing, according to Hebrews 5:11 (AV). This is why Scripture warns, 'Today, if you hear his voice, do not harden your hearts' (Heb. 4:7). So if you can still hear God's voice, however faintly, act at once. Do not take the chance that you will hear him speak again; the Bible says, 'My Spirit will not contend with man for ever' (Gen. 6:3).

It is wonderful to hear God speak. It is only when you hear his voice that you can be saved, for salvation comes only from God. So if your conscience troubles you, and things bother you that never bothered you before, the Holy Spirit is speaking to you. Keep a tender conscience and obey him now.

23

Why Listen to an Imperfect Preacher?

1 Samuel 24:8–22

What is a hero? I think a hero is someone who does something unusual in terms of self-discipline and keeps quiet about it. You may recall that David had a chance to be a hero. It happened when Saul entered a cave, unaware that he and his men were hiding further back in the darkness. David refrained from killing his enemy, but he crept up beside him and cut off a part of his robe. Afterwards he felt ashamed; nevertheless, when Saul left the cave, he could not resist telling him what he had done:

> Then David went out of the cave and called out to Saul, 'My lord the king!' When Saul looked behind him, David bowed down and prostrated himself with his face to the ground. He said to Saul, 'Why do you listen when men say, "David is bent on harming you"? This day you have seen with your own eyes how the Lord gave you into my hands in the cave. Some urged me to kill you, but I spared you; I said, "I will not lift my hand against my master, because he is the Lord's anointed"' (1 Sam. 24:8–10).

Now I think that David should have confessed what he had done to God, but he should not have even let Saul know that he was there. In other words, David had the chance to be a hero, but missed it.

God wants each of us to become heroes, committed to the tasks he has given us to do, without feeling the need to seek public recognition. I believe that at the judgment seat of Christ we will discover the *real* champions of the Christian faith are not the Billy Grahams or the Arthur Blessitts of this world but those who prayed for evangelists like them.

When Joshua and his men fought the Amalekites, Moses, Aaron and Hur climbed to the top of a hill to intercede with God for them. Whenever Moses held up his hands, the Israelites prevailed, but when his arms grew tired and he lowered them the Amalekites gained the upper hand. So Aaron and Hur held up Moses' hands until sunset, when the Israelites won the battle. Aaron and Hur were the real heroes that day, not Moses or Joshua and his men (Exod. 17:10-13).

God wanted David to have the qualities and strength of character that would fit him for kingship. Clearly David was not yet ready for this task and would need further preparation, for although he had spared Saul's life he could not resist the temptation to let him know that he had him at his mercy.

Perhaps you wonder why God does not allow you to gain promotion or achieve some particular ambition. The truth is, he knows you are not yet ready. God does us a favour when he withholds certain things from us, for he knows that our characters need refining. God's delay then was for David's sake.

How much better if David had said nothing to Saul. He gained no advantage by telling him what he had done: it did not change the king's attitude towards him because Saul already knew that David was not seeking to harm him. All that happened was that Saul manipulated David into swearing an unnecessary oath, for when he heard David call, Saul looked behind him and asked:

> 'Is that your voice, David my son?' And he wept aloud. 'You are more righteous than I,' he said. 'You have treated me well, but I have treated you badly. You have just now told me of the good you did to me; the Lord gave me into your hands, but you did not kill me. When a man finds his enemy, does he let him get away unharmed? May the Lord reward you well for the way you treated me today. I know that you will surely be king and

that the kingdom of Israel will be established in your hands. Now swear to me by the Lord that you will not cut off my descendants or wipe out my name from my father's family.'

So David gave his oath to Saul (1 Sam. 24:16-22).

David's confession did nothing to further his cause. Saul wept and affirmed David's righteousness but his heart remained hard. And if we read the rest of verse 22, we will see the *proof* nothing had changed. 'Then Saul returned home, but David and his men went up to the stronghold.'

I want to show you three things from this episode in David's life.

First, God gave Saul another chance to get right with him despite David's imperfection. The Bible says, 'We have this treasure [the light of the gospel] in jars of clay to show that this all-surpassing power is from God and not from us' (2 Cor. 4:7). What does that mean? Well, it means that God will use me as a minister though I am imperfect. *David* was an imperfect man, and, although he himself was not yet ready for kingship, what he told Saul was true. Saul had done some foolish things and his relationship with God was in a sorry state, but he refused every chance he was given to get right with God. I am imperfect but what I am saying is true, and the onus is on those who hear me to get right with God.

Second, one day Saul would wish with all his heart that he had availed himself of this chance to repent. Perhaps people have warned you repeatedly of the consequences of disobeying God and rejecting the gospel. Maybe you take the gospel message for granted and think wearily, 'I have heard it all before!' However, one day you will look back and say, 'If only I could turn the clock back! Now it's too late.'

Saul knew that everything David said was true, but he rejected the chance to get right with God and was without excuse.

Third, this incident is a preview of the judgment seat of Christ. What do we mean by 'the judgment seat of Christ'?

What does the Bible say about it? Well, in Romans 14:10-12 Paul said:

> You, then, why do you judge your brother? Or why do you look down on your brother? For we will all stand before God's judgment seat. It is written:
>
> > "'As surely as I live," says the Lord,
> > "Every knee will bow before me;
> > every tongue will confess to God.'"
>
> So then, each of us will give an account of himself to God.

Paul returned to the theme of judgment in 2 Corinthians 5:10:

> For we must all appear before the judgment seat of Christ, that each one may receive what is due to him for the things done while in the body, whether good or bad.

In his vision on Patmos John had a preview of what would happen on judgment day. Describing what he saw in this vision, he said:

> 'The sea gave up the dead that were in it, and death and Hades gave up the dead that were in them, and each person was judged according to what he had done' (Rev. 20:13).

This day will dawn very soon, and we can never say that God did not warn us about it. You may ask, 'What about those who have never heard the gospel?' I answer, there is no hope for them that I know of, but God is just and may judge them by a different standard. However, those who *have* heard the gospel are accountable for their response to it.

I want to show you now how the encounter between David and Saul typifies what will happen at the judgment seat of Christ.

First, we see that when Saul heard David's voice, he prostrated himself on the ground (1 Sam. 24:8). When Jesus returns we will all bow down to Jesus and confess him as Lord. '"As surely as I live," says the Lord, "Every knee will bow before me; every tongue will confess to God"' (Rom. 14:11). But this will not save us, because God requires we acknowledge Jesus in *faith*, and faith will not be possible then. Our only hope of salvation is to confess him now.

The second thing we see is Saul was confronted with the obvious. Similarly, everything that happens at the judgment seat of Christ will simply be a review of the truth. Think of a guilty prisoner on trial: he knows the evidence against him is true; nevertheless, he may be amazed that the police have uncovered so much. In a sense, our only surprise at the judgment will be that our lives were recorded in such detail. But at the judgement seat of Christ it will all be revealed.

If you are not a Christian, at the judgment, perhaps for the first time in your life, you will weep openly when you have to acknowledge your folly. You will not only weep but, according to the Authorized Version of the Bible, you will *wail* in your anguish and despair. No one likes others to see them cry, but all the peer pressure that influenced you in the past will have vanished.

Third, we see Saul was listening to the one he wanted to kill. Today the same anti-God spirit remains. The unconverted hate Jesus; they would like to be rid of him. However, on judgment day everyone will face him and hear him speak. In Revelation 1:7 John said, 'Every eye will see him, even those who pierced him.' This verse refers not only to those who hammered in the nails that fastened Jesus to the cross but to us all, because, as sinners, we all put him there.

Fourth, we see that Saul had to affirm David's righteousness (1 Sam. 24:17). It is often hard to understand why God allows bad things to happen, and many people hate him. But you must affirm his righteousness in faith now, because on that final day you will *see* that he is righteous. Then you will cry in despair, 'Oh, I didn't know! I am sorry. God, Help me!' But it will be too late.

If you are truly converted, when you meet adversity, you are able to hold onto the Lord, and through the power of the Holy Spirit you will see that God is perfect in all his ways (see Ps. 18:30).

Fifth, we see that at last Saul showed concern for his family. In Luke 16 we read the parable of the rich man and Lazarus. The latter went to heaven but the rich man went to hell. However, he kept hoping that somehow he could escape, and he begged Abraham to help him:

> 'Father Abraham, have pity on me and send Lazarus to dip the tip of his finger in water and cool my tongue, because I am in agony in this fire.' But Abraham replied, 'Son, . . . between us and you a great chasm has been fixed, so that those who want to go from here to you cannot, nor can anyone cross over from there to us.'
>
> He answered, 'Then I beg you, father, send Lazarus to my father's house, for I have five brothers. Let him warn them, so that they will not also come to this place of torment.'
>
> Abraham replied, 'They have Moses and the Prophets; let them listen to them.'
>
> 'No, father Abraham,' he said, 'but if someone from the dead goes to them, they will repent.'
>
> He said to him, 'If they do not listen to Moses and the Prophets, they will not be convinced even if someone rises from the dead' (vv. 24, 25-31).

The Roman Catholic Church holds the doctrine of purgatory. The idea is that, even if a person is in purgatory for millions of years, eventually he or she will get out. However, I must respectfully point out that this teaching is unbiblical: hell is eternal and those who are lost are lost forever.

Today many people think the Bible is out of date and irrelevant; they do not believe hell exists, nor would they believe it even if someone came back from the dead to testify to the truth. But the only way we can be saved is through faith.

Finally, this story teaches us that we ought to recognize a good thing when we see it. David was imperfect, but Saul recognized that what he said was true, and all he had to do was repent. He acted as if he were sorry, but had his remorse been real David would have known it; however, he could see Saul was still determined to kill him. God gave Saul another chance, but he failed to take advantage of it and would have to take the consequences.

I am imperfect, but I am telling you the truth. Jesus said, 'You will know the truth, and the truth will set you free' (John 8:32). The truth is, on the cross Jesus paid the penalty for our sin. What then should you do when you recognize a good thing? Simply say, 'Lord, I'm sorry' and mean it. God has given *you* another chance to get right with him. How will you respond?

24

Letting God Do What He Does Best

1 Samuel 25

We have all had mentors who were special to us, people we trusted, who could be relied upon to give wise advice, and, even if we did not telephone them every day, we had the security of knowing they were there. However, there comes a day when God calls them home and we are alone.

This happened to David. In 1 Samuel 25:1 we read:

> Now Samuel died, and all Israel assembled and mourned for him; and they buried him at his home in Ramah.

Samuel's death meant that David would no longer have the support of a man who was very important to him, for it was he who had anointed David as the future king of Israel, and David knew he could always turn to him for advice. But Samuel died, and David could look only to his God.

After Samuel's death David and his men moved into the Desert of Maon. The Bible tells us that a descendant of Caleb lived here:

> A certain man in Maon, who had property there at Carmel, was very wealthy. He had a thousand goats and three thousand sheep, which he was shearing in Carmel. His name was Nabal . . . (vv. 2-3).

Clearly Nabal was a wealthy man and had considerable influence within the community. Theologically speaking, we would say he was blessed with common grace.

What is common grace? It is God's goodness to all humanity. This is *not* the grace that saves, but God's goodness to everyone. For example, God may have blessed you with a satisfying job, with a good marriage partner, with a comfortable home or with riches. Perhaps you protest, 'I have worked hard for what I have!' But others have worked as hard as you, yet they do not all have what you have. 'Well,' you may reply, 'I am pretty clever.' But others are equally as clever as you, yet they do not all have what you have. All good things in life come from God, and, like Nabal, you have received a good measure of his common grace.

David had been very good to Nabal and had protected his flocks (see v. 7). Now he thought, 'Perhaps Nabal will do *me* a favour.' So he sent ten young men to Nabal with this message:

> 'I hear that it is sheep-shearing time. When your shepherds were with us, we did not ill-treat them, and the whole time they were at Carmel nothing of theirs was missing. . . . Therefore be favourable towards my young men, since we come at a festive time. Please give your servants and your son David whatever you can find for them' (vv. 7-8).

A reasonable request one would think.

However, Nabal's response was churlish:

> Nabal answered David's servants, 'Who is this David? Who is this son of Jesse? Many servants are breaking away from their masters these days. Why should I take my bread and water, and the meat I have slaughtered for my shearers, and give it to men coming from who knows where?' (vv. 10-11).

When David's men returned and told him what Nabal had said, he lost his temper and decided to take immediate revenge:

> David said to his men, 'Put on your swords!' So they put on their swords, and David put on his. About four hundred men went up with David, while two hundred stayed with the supplies (v. 13).

They were on their way, seeking vengeance.

Nabal was wrong, but David was also wrong to try to avenge himself. God said, 'It is *mine* to avenge; *I* will repay [my italics]' (Heb. 10:30). So if someone has mistreated you, do not lift a finger: let God deal with that person. But David decided that *he* was going to deal with Nabal.

Now a key element in the story is that one of Nabal's servants secretly went to Nabal's wife Abigail and told her what had happened (1 Sam. 25:14-17). The Bible describes Abigail as 'an intelligent and beautiful woman' (v. 3). She was, by any standards, a woman with extraordinary qualities, and, without telling Nabal, she intervened to prevent a tragedy.

The Bible says:

Abigail lost no time. She took two hundred loaves of bread, two skins of wine, five dressed sheep, five seahs of roasted grain, a hundred cakes of raisins and two hundred cakes of pressed figs, and loaded them on donkeys. Then she told her servants, 'Go on ahead; I'll follow you.' But she did not tell her husband Nabal (vv. 18-19).

She met David in a mountain ravine and began to intercede for her husband:

When Abigail saw David, she quickly got off her donkey and bowed down before David with her face to the ground. She fell at his feet and said: 'My lord, let the blame be on me alone. Please let your servant speak to you; hear what your servant has to say. May my lord pay no attention to that wicked man Nabal. He is just like his name – his name is Fool, and folly goes with him. But as for me, your servant, I did not see the men my master sent.

'Now since the Lord has kept you, my master, from bloodshed and from avenging yourself with your own hands, as surely as the Lord lives and as you live, may your enemies and all who intend to harm my master be like Nabal. And let this gift, which your servant has brought to my master, be given to the men who follow you. Please forgive your servant's offence, for the Lord will certainly make a lasting dynasty for my master, because he fights the Lord's battles' (vv. 23-28).

I can only call Abigail a picture of Jesus, who intervened to prevent us from being eternally lost.

She kept David from doing something that he would regret for the rest of his life, and, when he came to his senses, he thanked her.

David said to Abigail, 'Praise be to the Lord, the God of Israel, who has sent you today to meet me. May you be blessed for your good judgment and for keeping me from bloodshed this day and from avenging myself with my own hands' (vv. 32-33).

Then Abigail went home, intending to tell her husband what had happened. However, when she arrived, she discovered that Nabal was having a banquet and he was very drunk. So she decided to say nothing to him until the next morning: it was useless to waste words on someone in that condition.

Then in the morning, when Nabal was sober, his wife told him all these things, and his heart failed him and he became like a stone. About ten days later, the Lord struck Nabal and he died (vv. 37-38).

David recognized he had met a remarkable woman, and, after Nabal's death, he sent for Abigail and made her his wife (vv. 40-42).

What does this story teach us?

First, we learn that sometimes a woman has to differ with her husband. Now you may ask, 'Why do you say that?' Well, one reason is, if she is saved and he is not, she must obey God; however, she must also try to be the best wife in the world in hope that her husband will be influenced by her witness and come to Christ.

Let me give you an illustration. Many years ago I was the pastor of a church in Fort Lauderdale, and among my congregation was a lady who wanted to get closer to God. But one day she said to me, 'My husband won't come to church, and he wants me to stay at home too. What shall I do?'

'Well,' I said, 'I think you should tell him that you want to get closer to God and you want to be more involved in the life of the church. However, if your husband still insists on you staying at home, then do so. But I want you to be the best wife he could wish for.'

She took my advice, and in less than six weeks her husband came to church with her. Later he said, 'I realized that whatever was changing her *had* to be right. So I decided to come and see what it was for myself. Now, I want to become a Christian too.'

However, this approach does not *always* work. And in Matthew 10:34-36 Jesus warned his followers to expect bitter opposition from those who were dearest to them:

> 'Do not suppose that I have come to bring peace to the earth. I did not come to bring peace, but a sword. For I have come to turn
> '"a man against his father, a daughter against her mother, a daughter-in-law against her mother-in-law – a man's enemies will be the members of his own household."'

So sometimes when only one partner in a marriage is converted, it causes conflict.

The name 'Nabal' means 'fool', and Nabal was certainly a very foolish man. Yet Abigail was not only trying to spare David from bloodshed, she was trying to save her husband's life. In other words, she was being a good wife.

The second thing we learn from this story is that your testimony may be instrumental in another person's conversion. In this story an unnamed witness changed everything. In verse

14 we read that one of Nabal's servants went to Abigail and explained what David's messengers had wanted from her husband (1 Sam. 25:14-17). It was as a direct result of his action that Abigail intervened.

You never know the good you do by witnessing to others. They may never know your name; nevertheless, they may be converted because of your testimony. One man who was converted through the witness of one of the Pilot Lights on the street told me, 'I have looked for that person in church for the last three years, but I have never seen him again. I just want to thank him for bringing me to Christ.'

I think heaven will be full of Christians who received no recognition for doing God's will on earth. If you are one such person, something that ought to encourage you is to remember the judgment seat of Christ. Paul said: 'We must all appear before the judgment seat of Christ, that each one may receive what is due to him for the things done while in the body, whether good or bad' (2 Cor. 5:10). On that final day God will open the records, dispense true justice and reward Christians according to their faithfulness. Perhaps you feel that, compared to the great evangelists, you are of little account. But maybe you have been one who, unseen and unknown, has prayed for others. The Billy Grahams of this world, the Arthur Blessitts and other Christians who enjoy a high profile here may take second place to some who were simply faithful. I find that so exciting and so encouraging.

The third thing we learn from this story is that one day God will remind everybody of an event they thought insignificant at the time. You will recall that in the morning, when Nabal was sober, Abigail reminded him of the incident between him and David's men and told him of what she had done to avert a tragedy. Suddenly, his face fell and he realized that this was the moment that had determined his future. Too late, he remembered his contemptuous response: 'Who is this David? Who is this son of Jesse?'

John 6:42 tells us that the Jews made a similar, dismissive

response to Jesus and said, 'Is this not Jesus, the son of Joseph, whose father and mother we know?'

Speaking of the final judgment, Jesus revealed the destination of those who scorn him and his followers:

> Then he [the King] will say . . . 'Depart from me, you who are cursed, into the eternal fire prepared for the devil and his angels. For I was hungry and you gave me nothing to eat, I was thirsty and you gave me nothing to drink, I was a stranger and you did not invite me in, I needed clothes and you did not clothe me, I was sick and in prison and you did not look after me.'
>
> They also will answer, 'Lord, when did we see you hungry or thirsty or a stranger or needing clothes or sick or in prison, and did not help you?'
>
> He will reply, 'I tell you the truth, whatever you did not do for one of the least of these, you did not do for me' (Matt. 25:41–45).

Thousands will remember the Westminster Chapel Pilot Light ministry then, although few people take us seriously now. I recall one man saying to Louise, 'Well, I see your husband has his slaves out on the streets again!'

You may not be taking this message too seriously, but this passage of Scripture shows us that everybody will recall something they once thought unimportant.

Abigail said to Nabal, 'Do you realize that David was coming to *kill* you, and would have done so had I not stopped him?' When Nabal heard that his heart died within him. He only lived ten more days, and during that time he was 'like a stone'. This shows a person can live on for a while but have no further chance to get right with God, because his heart is dead. So if you feel the slightest whisper of the Holy Spirit, act *now*.

One incident is forever engraved on my mind. I was fifteen years old when it happened. One day Dr W.M. Tidwell, an evangelist, came to speak to our Sunday school. ' R.T.,' he said, 'Would you help me with an illustration, please? I am going to preach on the parable of the man who had no wedding garment [Matt. 22:1–14], and I would like you to take his role. Would you kindly sit on the platform and allow some people to tie you up and carry you out of the back of the church?'

'Certainly, Dr Tidwell,' I replied.

Dr Tidwell preached with great power and there was an unusual presence of God in the service. In church that day was a sixteen-year-old girl named Patsy, whom I knew well. Although she came from a devout Christian home, she had developed into a rebellious teenager. That morning she sat in the back row, and, as the men carried me out of the church, she sniggered. At the altar call several people went forward and were converted, but old Dr Tidwell was not satisfied and said, 'I cannot end this service yet. Somebody here this morning is receiving their *last* call.'

That was a bold statement, but this man was eighty years old, a veteran who discerned the ways of God. He added, 'I will not have it on my conscience that I have closed the service.' Everybody sat and waited but nothing happened, and eventually they left the church.

The next evening, after I had finished my newspaper round, I went home and was greeted by my mother, who said, 'Have you heard about Patsy?'

'No. What's happened to her?'

'You don't know? Oh, it's awful! A couple of hours ago, as she was on her way home from school, a car mounted the pavement and smashed into her. She was killed instantly.'

The only thing we could think about was that twenty-eight hours earlier Dr Tidwell had said, 'Somebody is receiving their *last* call.'

A fourth thing this story teaches us is that a person can have a godly heritage and still be lost. Nabal was one such person. He was descended from Caleb, an Old Testament hero and a man who had great faith (see Num. 13; Deut. 1:34–36). In fact, the author of 1 Samuel thought Nabal's ancestry so prestigious that he put it on record (1 Sam. 25:3). Caleb was a truly godly man, but Nabal was lost.

Nabal knew who David was. Remember, he said, 'Who is this David? Who is this Son of Jesse?' You may have been born in a Christian home and know who Jesus is; you may even be a church member, and, like Nabal, God may have blessed you materially, but unless you accept Jesus as your Saviour, you can never enter heaven.

My fifth, and final, point is that God will deal with those who mistreat us if we leave it entirely to him.

Now one can say that God does *everything* perfectly, but if I had to name one thing that he has given more attention to than anything else it would be justice. God is for the underdog: he loves to vindicate someone others have mistreated. He does not like it when people hurt you, but if you lose your temper and try to take revenge, he does not like that either. Remember, God said, 'It is mine to avenge; I will repay.' In fact, if you decide to avenge yourself, he will simply take his hands off and say, 'All right! Y*ou* handle it.'

God is the most maligned individual in history. People hate him and do not understand his ways. Every Saturday, when we go out to evangelize, we hear the same angry question: 'If he is a God of love, why does he allow bad things to happen?' But he knows that people think ill of him, and he will have the last word, for the day is coming when he will clear his name. Furthermore, he will vindicate those who have waited for him to act. Occasionally, he *will* vindicate us in our lifetime, but he does not promise to do this. But vindication is what *he* does best, and you must leave the timing to him.

David was bent on revenge, but Abigail intervened, and, in his kindness, God kept David from taking vengeance on Nabal. God wanted David to see what *he* would do, and he dealt with Nabal without his help, but David could never take any credit for it.

We cannot take any credit for our salvation. In fact, God hates it when people think their good works will save them. He decided to save humanity in such a way that no one could ever brag about it, so he came into the world himself in the person of Jesus Christ and paid the penalty for our sin himself. We owe our salvation entirely to his grace. Paul put it like this: 'For it is by grace you have been saved, through faith – and this not from yourselves, it is the gift of God – not by works, so that no-one can boast' (Eph. 2:8).

25

Why Does God Allow Evil to Continue?

1 Samuel 26:7–26

People often ask Christians, 'Since God is all-powerful, all-holy, all-wise and all-merciful, why does he allow evil to continue?' It is one of the most difficult questions anyone can pose, for evil is the *opposite* of what God is: he is holy. In his prayer the prophet Habakkuk said, 'Your eyes are too pure to look on evil' (Hab. 1:13).

Note, I am not dealing with the question 'Why did God allow evil to *enter* the world?' No one can answer that, and I would not dare to try to do so; however, I will try to answer the question 'Why does God allow evil to continue?'

Let us consider this deep philosophical problem in the light of 1 Samuel 26.

In this chapter we will see that David had a perfect opportunity to kill Saul and hasten the moment of his own accession to the throne, but he preferred to honour God by waiting on his timing. And, in turn, one day God would honour David for not taking revenge, for, under David's leadership, God would make Israel a powerful and influential nation in the Middle East; moreover David's name would be exalted beyond his wildest dreams.

This story is about a secret mission that would take David into the heart of his enemy's camp, a formidable task requiring great courage. The expedition was necessary because David felt the time had come to prove once and for all that he and King Saul were totally different in character. The Bible says:

David . . . asked Ahimelech the Hittite and Abishai son of Zeruiah, Joab's brother, 'Who will go down into the camp with me to Saul?' (1 Sam. 26:6).

Abishai volunteered immediately, and the two men made their way to Saul's camp.

Their first task was to get past the outer circle of the men on guard. They succeeded, and then, stepping silently and carefully, they worked their way into the very heart of this huge encampment. Not one soldier stirred as they stealthily made their way to the very spot where the king lay sleeping on the warm sand.

Seeing a chance to rid David of his enemy, Abishai whispered:

'Today God has given your enemy into your hands. Now let me pin him to the ground with one thrust of my spear; I won't strike him twice' (v. 8).

But David refused to take advantage of the situation and replied:

'As surely as the Lord lives,' he said, 'the Lord himself will strike him; either his time will come and he will die, or he will go into battle and perish. But the Lord forbid that I should lay a hand on the Lord's anointed' (1 Sam. 26:10–11).

So Abishai stayed his hand.

Nevertheless, David wanted Saul and his men to know he had been there:

So David took the spear and water jug near Saul's head, and they left. No-one saw or knew about it, nor did anyone wake up. They were all sleeping, because the Lord had put them into a deep sleep (v. 12).

Then the two men slipped out of Saul's camp. The mission was a total triumph.

The analogy is this: David must have felt greatly tempted to bring his trial to an end then, and Jesus must have been greatly tempted to end his agony on the cross.

Luke describes the scene at the crucifixion:

> The people stood watching, and the rulers even sneered at him. They said, 'He saved others; let him save himself if he is the Christ of God, the Chosen One'.
>
> The soldiers also came up and mocked him. They offered him wine vinegar and said, 'If you are the king of the Jews, save yourself' (Luke 23:35–36).

Jesus had the power to do just that.

So if you ask, 'Could God stop evil in the world?' the answer is 'Yes'. And if you ask, 'Could Jesus have come down from the cross?' again the answer is 'Yes'. We are talking about the Son of God, the Creator of the world, of whom John said:

> In the beginning was the Word [Jesus], and the Word was with God, and the Word was God. He was with God in the beginning.
>
> Through him all things were made; without him nothing was made that has been made. . . .
>
> The Word became flesh and made his dwelling among us (John 1:1-3, 14).

While Jesus was on this earth, he proved his divine power by performing great miracles: he fed the five thousand with the loaves and the fish (Matt. 14:13-21); he enabled Peter to walk on water, as he himself did (Matt. 14:22-32); he raised Lazarus from the dead (John 11:1-44), and he calmed the storm simply by commanding the wind to cease (Luke 8:22-25). So Jesus could easily have come down from the cross, but had he done so, he would not have carried out God's plan to save the world.

Now you may say, 'Well, surely Jesus could have waited a few minutes, and then, having done everything necessary to save humanity, he could have come down from the cross.'

But Jesus needed to show that he had *died*, and then he needed to rise from the dead. 'Well,' you may reply, 'couldn't he have died and then returned to life while the soldiers were there to witness it?' No, because God had planned to save the world in a certain way. So although Jesus had the power to vindicate himself and take revenge on those who crucified him, he allowed evil to continue.

Although Jesus is God in the flesh, by becoming man as though he were not God, he became subject to his Father. Jesus said: 'The Son can do nothing by himself; he can do only what he sees his Father doing, because whatever the Father does the Son also does' (John 5:19). And in verse 30 he added: 'I seek not to please myself but him who sent me.' In other words, he did what his *Father* wanted.

You could say that Jesus was a man who had double vision, because he saw everything around him, but at the same time he kept his eyes on his Father and did nothing without his permission. He might have been tempted to come down from the cross, but his Father said, 'No'. Perhaps, inwardly, Jesus reasoned with him and said, 'Father, *surely*, we can stop the evil and defeat the devil now?' Still God said, 'No'.

So Jesus died and, *humanly speaking*, made it impossible for anyone to believe on him. It was as though he was trying to deter anyone who thought he was the Messiah. Dying on a cross was the most shameful death imaginable; it was the way criminals, people regarded as the dregs of society, were executed. How could such an end possibly honour God? 'Jesus is a weakling,' the Jews thought. 'He is not the Messiah. God would never have allowed the Messiah to end up on a cross!' However, Jesus died to make *faith* possible, and God wants us to honour his Son by believing his word.

Jesus is all-powerful: he created the universe and he *could* get your attention immediately in the way that he will get it when he returns to the earth. Revelation 1:7 describes the Second Coming like this:

Look, he is coming with the clouds,
    and every eye will see him,
even those who pierced him;
    and all the peoples of the earth will
mourn because of him.

If you do not listen to God now, he will get your full attention then, and you will say, 'You are God! You are powerful!' But it will be too late, because you will be affirming Jesus only because you see the obvious.

God seeks a people who will believe his word and honour his Son in *faith*. Have you ever said to someone, 'Won't you just *believe* me? Do I have to prove everything to you?' God wants us to believe in *his* integrity, so he chose to save the world in a way that requires faith in what Jesus did on the cross.

You may exclaim, 'That's a foolish idea!' Paul would be the first to agree. He said, 'We preach Christ crucified: a stumbling-block to Jews and foolishness to Gentiles' (1 Cor. 1:23). God said, 'I want to save the world, but *I* will choose the way to do it', and he chose to save people through the preaching of the gospel.

Now some will scoff when they hear the gospel, but when the Holy Spirit deals with us, we realize that it is true: Jesus is God's Son and he became our substitute. You see, God knows we can never live the kind of life that he requires, a life of perfect holiness in thought, word and deed, but this is where his love comes in. Jesus lived a perfect life and *he* took the blame for our sins and satisfied God's justice (2 Cor. 5:21; Isa. 53:6). And God did not destroy the devil two thousand years ago; he let evil continue a little longer so we could be saved.

David could have ended Saul's tyranny by killing him as he slept, but he had faith that *God* would deal with Saul. Moreover, he committed his zealous followers to have faith in a sovereign God. This is amazing! Abishai, who loved

David, said, 'Let me kill him.' But David said, 'No. Let *God* deal with him.' David taught Abishai a lesson: God is sovereign and he would vindicate David. David's followers would respect and admire him for that.

Jesus teaches his followers a similar lesson: God is sovereign and we must leave him to vindicate us in his own way. And when I think how the crucified Jesus refused to vindicate himself but said, 'Father, forgive them, for they do not know what they are doing' (Luke 23:34), I see in him a love that is matchless and I want to follow him.

However, you will recall that David wanted Saul to know that although he had him at his mercy, he had spared him, so 'he took the spear and water jug near Saul's head'. Saul and his men were unaware of what David was doing because God put them into a deep sleep.

When Jesus died on the cross, the devil was unaware of what God was doing. In fact, he thought he had won a great victory, for he was the architect of Jesus death: he had persuaded Judas Iscariot to betray Jesus and had caused wicked men to crucify him. But Satan always overreaches himself; he did not know that this was how God had planned to save the world all along. In 1 Corinthians 2:7-8 Paul says:

> We speak of God's secret wisdom, a wisdom that has been hidden and that God destined for our glory before time began. None of the rulers of this age understood it, for if they had, they would not have crucified the Lord of glory.

David's men, then, would learn the nature of true faith and would discover that God had a plan and he would vindicate David.

Saul's men also learnt a lesson that night, for they realized later that David could have destroyed them had he wished to do so. The Bible says:

David crossed over to the other side and stood on the top of the hill some distance away; there was a wide space between them. He called out to the army and to Abner son of Ner [Saul's bodyguard], 'Aren't you going to answer me, Abner?'

Abner replied, 'Who are you who calls to the king?'

David said, 'You're a man, aren't you? And who is like you in Israel? Why didn't you guard your lord the king? Someone came to destroy your lord the king. . . . Look around you. Where are the king's spear and water jug that were near his head?' (1 Sam. 26:13–16).

Abner saw only too clearly what David could have done. Furthermore, *all* Saul's followers would hear the king say to David:

'I have sinned. Come back, David my son. Because you considered my life precious today, I will not try to harm you again. Surely I have acted like a fool and have erred greatly' (v. 21).

Everyone now could see David's integrity, and, if they were wise, they would have realized that Saul had deceived them and crossed over to David's side.

God wanted David to refrain from killing Saul, so David might have a greater victory. And he did not want Jesus to come down from the cross or destroy the devil then, because he wanted his Son to have a *far greater* victory. You see, through Jesus' death and resurrection, God will bring 'many sons to glory' (Heb. 2:10), and Romans 8:29 says: 'For those God foreknew he also predestined to be conformed to the likeness of his Son, that he might be the firstborn among *many* brothers [my italics].'

The great Charles Spurgeon had an interesting theory. He maintained that since the Bible says that 'in everything [Christ] should have the supremacy' (Col. 1:18), there will be more people in heaven than in hell. But the Bible also says, 'Small is the gate and narrow the road that leads to life, and only a few find it' (Matt. 7:14), so it seems that few will be saved. Yet Spurgeon argued that there would be more people in heaven than in hell because he believed all babies go to heaven. That being true, when you think of the millions of abortions in the last few years, we are talking about a great many people. Therefore, had Jesus come down from the cross or destroyed the devil then, no people would have been saved.

In due time God would honour David for not taking revenge on Saul, for David would become the greatest king Israel would ever have. However, no one acknowledged David as king then, and David's decision to spare Saul postponed his vindication.

Similarly, Jesus was the unrecognized king of the Jews. Pilate, the Roman governor who sentenced him to death, put a placard on the cross, saying, 'THIS IS JESUS, THE KING OF THE JEWS' (Matt. 27:37). He meant to mock but, unknowingly, he had written the truth.

Jesus could have ended his suffering on the cross at any moment, but he resisted temptation and carried out his Father's plan to save humanity. This means that Jesus has to wait until he is openly vindicated. However, one day God will publicly honour his Son, and Jesus will be proclaimed 'King of kings and Lord of lords' (Rev. 17:14, 19:16). When he returns to this earth, millions will acknowledge him as king, not just the few people who watched his crucifixion outside the walls of Jerusalem. But for this to happen evil has to continue.

For us, the waiting period means a prolongation of grace, giving time for more people to be born and to be converted.

Now you may ask, 'What about the people who won't be saved?' Well, I have to tell you that Saul's men continued following him, realizing that they had been deceived, and only had themselves to blame for their predicament. For when David shouted to Abner across the valley and said, 'Look around you. Where are the king's spear and water jug that were near his head?' they could see (1) David was truly a man of God, and (2) their king was wicked. So by choosing to follow Saul, they condemned themselves. They could have crossed the line and joined David.

The analogy is, by nature we are all on the devil's side and he has deceived us. The Bible says, 'The god of this age has blinded the minds of unbelievers, so that they cannot see the light of the gospel of the glory of Christ' (2 Cor. 4:4). However, when the Holy Spirit shows us that Satan has deceived us, we too have a choice: we can either stay on his side or cross over to God's side by coming in repentance to the foot of the cross.

God wants you to be one of those who, when Jesus comes again, will not be ashamed. When Jesus returns to the earth, there will be two kinds of people: those who are ashamed and those who are unashamed (see 1 John 2:28). The former will be those who chose to stay on the devil's side, while the latter will be those who committed their lives to Jesus Christ. We are still living in the period of grace, a time when God allows evil to continue, but it is because he wants you to be saved and Jesus to have the greater glory.

26

Are Christians Perfect?

1 Samuel 27:1–28

Are Christians perfect? I deal with this subject for two reasons.

First, I want you to understand the very nature of the gospel. Our good deeds and good intentions cannot save us. God is holy, and, if we are to avoid eternal condemnation, we must attain perfect righteousness. However, sin taints everything we do, so our salvation depends entirely upon the righteousness of another: God's Son Jesus Christ, who lived a sinless life. When he died on the cross, all our sins were transferred to him and his righteousness was transferred to us (2 Cor. 5:21). David was a man after God's own heart (1 Sam. 13:14), yet he was not perfect; he will go to heaven, but only because of the righteousness of another.

Second, I share these thoughts with you because I want to encourage you.

There are three kinds of Christians. First, there is the weak Christian who asks, 'Can I *really* be a Christian when I am like I am?' Then there is the backslider who asks, 'Can I *still* be a Christian in the light of what I have done?' And third, there is the strong Christian, although probably he or she has known times of weakness or even times of backsliding.

Now you may ask, 'Can a backslider lose his salvation?' No. The adage 'Once saved, always saved' is true. Moreover, God will forgive and restore the sinner who turns in repentance to him (1 John 1:9).

In this chapter we see David as a backslider, living among the enemies of God's people. Many people think that David's adultery with Bathsheba (2 Sam. 11) marks the lowest point in his life. However, I agree with A.W. Pink and Charles Spurgeon, who said that *this* was the time when David sank as low as he would ever get.

This was not the first time David left the rails. In an earlier chapter we saw how he got into trouble by making decisions without checking that they were in line with God's will. But David repented and decided never again to make a move without first consulting the Lord (see 1 Sam. 22:3).

For a long time all was well. First, we saw how David saved Keilah (1 Sam. 23:1–5). Then we had a picture of a tender conscience when he spared Saul's life and regretted damaging even a corner of his robe in (1 Sam. 24:5). Next we saw how David obeyed God by not taking revenge on Nabal (1 Sam. 25), and then we saw how he spared Saul's life yet again (1 Sam. 26). These were the high points in David's spiritual life.

But in this chapter we will see David sinking to a very low ebb indeed. No child of God is exempt from imperfection, and now David repeated his earlier mistake and again stepped outside God's will. The Bible says:

> David thought to himself, 'One of these days I shall be destroyed by the hand of Saul. The best thing I can do is to escape to the land of the Philistines. Then Saul will give up searching for me anywhere in Israel, and I will slip out of his hand' (1 Sam. 27:1).

Having given free rein to his imagination, David did the unthinkable and returned to Achish, king of Gath and identified himself with Israel's enemy, an act tantamount to treason. Once David had been so glad to get away from Achish that he had feigned madness (1 Sam. 21:10–15). Now you would think he would have felt so embarrassed about this charade that he would not want to face the king again. However, as Charles Spurgeon said, 'If left to unbelief, one will fall into the same sin'.

How did he get into this situation? Well, Spurgeon made four observations about this.

First, he pointed out that David was human, so sometimes he fell into sin. All human beings are weak and sinful. That is why we should never put too much confidence in another person. When I discover that somebody looks up to me, I am afraid because I could let him down (although I pray that I would not). So resist the temptation to look up to another Christian, for eventually he or she will disappoint you. Look only to Jesus Christ, who is perfect: he will *never* fail you. David spoke wisely when he said, 'It is better to take refuge in the Lord than to trust in man. It is better to take refuge in the Lord than to trust in princes' (Ps. 118:8–9).

Second, Spurgeon pointed out that David had experienced a long period of trial. This being the case, we should not judge David too harshly. How would you like it if a king, with all the resources of the nation at his disposal, was hunting you down because he regarded you as a threat? David thought his trial would never end and had cried, 'How long, O Lord? Will you forget me for ever? How long will you hide your face from me?' (Ps. 13:1). Now, at the end of his tether, he cried, 'Lord, I can't stand it any longer!' As Spurgeon put it in his quaint nineteenth-century language: 'A perpetuity of tribulation is very hard to bear', and, if you had experienced such a long ordeal, you might have done the same thing.

Third, Spurgeon pointed out that David had passed through a period of 'great excitement of mind'. You may remember that one moonlit night David and Abishai tiptoed into Saul's camp and took away his spear and water jug to prove to Saul that they could have killed him (1 Sam. 26). The mission was a total triumph, but perhaps David was feeling so good about this that he was basking in glory.

The devil can use a moment like that. On Mount Carmel the prophet Elijah had one of the most spectacular victories recorded in Scripture (1 Kgs. 18:16–46). However, Satan got in, and only a few days later Elijah was so filled with fear that he pleaded, 'I have had enough, Lord. . . .Take my life' (1 Kgs. 19:4).

How easy it is for a person who has had a great spiritual victory to become the object of a satanic attack! So if you are feeling good now, be on your guard: the devil hates you feeling like this and, if he can, he will catch you unawares and bring you to a low ebb. This was what he did to David, who was so thrilled about his triumph over Saul.

Fourth, Spurgeon observed that David failed to pray about his situation. In fact, David's folly was to forget God and listen to the enemy. Remember, he had been complimented by none other than Saul himself. In 1 Samuel 26:25 Saul said to David, 'May you be blessed, my son David; you will do great things and surely triumph.' Perhaps Saul's flattery went to his head. The devil will do anything to make us over-confident and will think nothing of using flattery as a weapon against us. However, sadly, we often fail to see what Satan is doing and, before we know it, like David, we start to backslide.

Let me describe the stages of backsliding.

Stage One: *The mind.* Backsliding begins when you allow your imagination to control you. David thought, 'One of these days I shall be destroyed by the hand of Saul' (1 Sam. 27:1). He was wrong. Was this the same David who had confronted Goliath saying, 'You come against me with sword and spear and javelin, but I come against you in the name of the Lord Almighty' (1 Sam. 17:45)?

Can you recall a time when you had faith like that? Can you remember when you could hardly wait to get to church and you loved to pray and read your Bible? But then, perhaps, you allowed your imagination to take over and fell prey to deceptive fantasies and fears. Backsliding begins in the mind.

Stage Two: *The mouth.* Next you voice your evil thoughts and succumb to temptation.

This was what David did. Look at 1 Samuel 27:5:

Then David said to Achish. 'If I have found favour in your eyes, let a place be assigned to me in one of the country towns, that I may live there.'

However, you can often resist temptation simply by keeping your mouth shut. In Matthew 5:27–28 Jesus said:

'You have heard that it was said, "Do not commit adultery." But I tell you that anyone who looks at a woman lustfully has already committed adultery with her in his heart."'

At that stage the adulterous thoughts are only in the mind. But do you know what often happens? The person who is having these sinful thoughts lets the object of his lust know what he is thinking. Now the situation is under control until the moment he speaks. That is when the devil *really* gets in. This is true not only of adultery but also of other kinds of sin: sexual sin, greed and jealousy, for example.

James warned Christians about the destructive potential of the tongue, saying:

The tongue is a small part of the body, but it makes great boasts. Consider what a great forest is set on fire by a small spark. The tongue is also a fire, a world of evil among the parts of the body. It corrupts the whole person, sets the whole course of his life on fire, and is itself set on fire by hell' (Jas. 3:5–6).

Now until the moment David gave them voice, his thoughts were under control, but as soon as he spoke, the devil took advantage of the situation.

Stage Three: *Minimizing the danger.* David reasoned like this: 'All I want to do is to live in Gath; then Saul will forget about me and I will be safe.' In other words, he downplayed the problem by rationalizing. So be careful you do not find your own solution to your difficulties and fail to consult God, because if you rationalize and minimize the problem, you will make matters worse.

Stage Four: *Misplacement.* Look at 1 Sam. 27:6–7:

So on that day Achish gave him Ziklag, . . . David lived in Philistine
territory for a year and four months.

David was now in a foreign country and had done the
unthinkable: he had joined the forces with none other than the
king of Gath. There was a legendary expression in Israel: 'Tell
it not in Gath.' Let me explain the significance of this phrase
by asking a question. Are there certain people whom you hope
will never hear what you have done? Maybe you do not want
your parents, your best friend or your marriage partner to
discover it, and you say, 'Whoever else hears about this, don't
tell *them*!' Well, the Israelites felt that way about Gath; they
did not want the people there to learn of any of Israel's
failings. But now they really had something to crow about, for
an Israeli hero had actually joined forces with them.

Speaking of the spiritually unfaithful, James said: 'You
adulterous people, don't you know that friendship with the
world is hatred towards God? Anyone who chooses to be a
friend of the world becomes an enemy of God' (Jas. 4:4).

Because he did not renew his faith through prayer, David
gave way to unbelief. The result was that he became a man of
war. No one will doubt that David was a military genius, but
fighting became a way of life to him and he dealt with the
enemy ruthlessly. The Bible says:

Whenever David attacked an area, he did not leave a man or
woman alive, but took sheep and cattle, donkeys and camels, and
clothes (1 Sam. 27:9).

Both Spurgeon and A.W. Pink believe that the blood David
shed then was the reason God would not allow him to build the
temple later, for in 1 Chronicles 22:7–8 David said to
Solomon:

'My son, I had it in my heart to build a house for the Name of the Lord my God. But this word of the Lord came to me: "You have shed much blood and have fought many wars. You are not to build a house for my Name, because you have shed much blood on the earth in my sight."'

I think this is a warning to us all. In Galatians 6:7 Paul said, 'Do not be deceived: God cannot be mocked. A man reaps what he sows.'

Stage Five: *Misery*. The stages of backsliding may seem insignificant but they lead to wretchedness. Remember in 1 Samuel 27:12 Achish said '[David] will be my servant for *ever* [my italics]', and later he told David, 'You must understand that you and your men will accompany me in the army. . . . I will make you my bodyguard *for life* [my italics]' (1 Sam. 28:1–2). Do you know what this means? Once sin grips you, it will not easily let you go.

However, we have a merciful God, and his is a love that will not let us go. In fact, Jeremiah said that God is *married* to the backslider (Jer. 3:14). David had become willing to commit overt treason against Israel, but, despite David's unfaithfulness, God prevented him from doing so.

You may think that you are in great trouble now, but God has kept you from worse danger; he has reached you just in time. Perhaps you feel sin will not let you go, but neither will God let you go. If you are a backslider and you know God has been dealing with you, you can have a real victory. Make a clean break. Come out of hiding and show the world that you are turning your back upon your sinful way of life. God will accept the backslider who returns to him in true repentance.

27

The Sheer Grace of God

1 Samuel 29

Have you ever stopped to consider just how much you have to be thankful for? I hope that before you reach the end of this chapter you will have a fresh, but sobering, awareness of how good God is to us all.

I want now to look at a shameful episode in David's life and contrast it with what happened to Saul. I will not deal with Saul's visit to the witch of Endor in detail, but I will refer to it.

Saul was panic-stricken because his enemies were planning a massive attack on Israel. The Bible says:

> In those days the Philistines gathered their forces to fight against Israel. . . . The Philistines assembled and came and set up camp at Shunem, while Saul gathered all the Israelites and set up camp at Gilboa. When Saul saw the Philistine army, he was afraid; terror filled his heart (1 Sam. 28:1, 4–5).

Since God was no longer speaking to him (see v. 6), in desperation, Saul turned to a witch. He had made witchcraft illegal, but he knew of one who was still functioning at Endor, and, now a nervous wreck, he consulted her.

Also a pitiful sight was Israel's *future* king, for David was now at the lowest spiritual ebb of his life. However, God had not finished with him, and the way God dealt with David then clearly shows his goodness and grace towards his people.

Now the interesting thing about the Bible is that, when talking of the people of God, it tells the *whole* story and does not hide their wickedness and shame. Here the Bible depicts

David as he really was, a child of God who was often weak and sinful.

In 1 Samuel 29 we find the culmination of David's sixteen-month stay with Achish, king of the Philistines, Israel's avowed enemies. The Bible says:

> As the Philistine rulers marched with their units of hundreds and thousands, David and his men were marching at the rear with Achish (1 Sam. 29:2).

David was not only willing to fight with the Philistines but was willing to take up arms against his own people in the forthcoming battle. Had the Israelites known about this, they would not have allowed him to ascend the throne. But God did not allow them to know everything about their future king.

Moreover, God graciously intervened and prevented David from actually committing this act of treachery. This was what happened:

> The commanders of the Philistines asked, 'What about these Hebrews?'
>
> Achish replied, 'Is this not David, who was an officer of Saul king of Israel? He has already been with me for over a year, and from the day he left Saul until now, I have found no fault in him.
>
> But the Philistine commanders were angry with him and said, 'Send the man back, that he may return to the place you assigned him. He must not go with us into battle, or he will turn against us during the fighting. How better could he regain his master's favour than by taking the heads of our own men? (vv. 3–4).

Outvoted, King Achish asked David to leave. God would not allow David to fight against Israel.

However, far from being grateful that God had stepped in to save him from ruin, David protested and said to Achish:

'But what have I done? . . . What have you found against your servant from the day I came to you until now? Why can't I go and fight against the enemies of my lord the king?' (v. 8).

With these words, he affirmed his allegiance to the enemy.

Both Saul and David were in a sorry state. Here was Saul consulting a witch and David preparing to betray his country.

Both men were hypocrites. Despite having made witchcraft illegal, Saul had consulted a witch and had asked her to raise up the spirit of Samuel, while David had become willing to fight against Israel. But when he became king he did not say to his future subjects, 'Look, before you crown me, there is something you ought to know about me.' This was something he would always keep from them.

It is easy to condemn such hypocrisy, but would you like people to know everything about you? Do you have a skeleton in your cupboard, a carefully guarded secret, and you pray nobody will ever discover it, because if the truth came out you would be finished?

I want to ask you an even more pertinent question: would you have committed a serious sin had not circumstances prevented you? To dispel any feelings of uneasiness, perhaps you rationalized and said, 'Well, what else *can* I do? God will understand.' Perhaps David's reasoning was similar and he said, 'Saul wants to kill me, so God won't blame me for attacking him. It's self-defence!' People often try to justify their actions like this.

In an earlier chapter I told you how Abraham's nephew Lot pitched his tents near Sodom, a town notorious for its homosexual practices (Gen. 13:12). Lot felt that he was strong enough to live close to the world without succumbing to its temptations. Yet when men from the city surrounded his house and demanded that his two angelic visitors go out and have sex with them, Lot offered them his virgin daughters instead (Gen. 19:8). Surely this was the worst thing any father could do! But he had reached the point at which that perversion seemed less evil than it otherwise would have been. As it happened, Lot was spared from committing this sin simply because the men were homosexuals and wanted the two angels. Now in the New Testament Peter calls Lot 'righteous' (2 Pet. 2:7). This tells us that God uses the principle of *grace* to deal with his people.

Grace is God's unmerited favour, when he deals with us as though we were righteous. God sent his Son into the world to die on a cross to bear our sins. Jesus was our substitute, and when we repent of our sin and plead the blood that he shed his righteousness is imputed to us (2 Cor. 5:21). This has *nothing* to do with our works; it is sheer *grace*. The same principle applies throughout the Bible, so in Old Testament times, people were saved by anticipating the death of Jesus on the cross.

God showed his grace to Jonah when Jonah ran from him and boarded a ship bound for Tarshish. You will recall a great storm blew up that seemed likely to sink the ship and the mariners said, 'Come, let us cast lots to find out who is responsible for this calamity. They cast lots and the lot fell on Jonah' (Jonah 1:7). Jonah was found out, but he could never take any credit for that: *God* was at work.

David also experienced that grace, for, as we have seen, God intervened and prevented him from actually fighting against his own people. However, he was willing to do this, so he sinned.

In the Sermon on the Mount Jesus said that sin begins in the mind. He put it like this:

> 'You have heard that it was said, "Do not commit adultery." But I tell you that anyone who looks at a woman lustfully has already committed adultery with her in his heart' (Matt. 5:27–28).

'Well,' someone may say, 'if *lusting* is committing adultery, I have already sinned in my mind, so I might as well go ahead and do it.' But the devil can use a scripture like that. Jesus was saying that we sin if we entertain such evil thoughts in our minds. However, this is not the same thing as actually committing the sin.

If God has kept you from committing such a sin, did you come *close* to committing it? God has a way of showing us what is in our hearts. When Jesus said, 'I have much more to say to you, more than you can now bear' (John 16:12), he was referring not only to the truth of the gospel but also to our sinful nature. Discovering the truth about ourselves is like peeling away the layers of an onion, and, little by little, God shows us our sinful condition.

Most of us want to think well of ourselves and regard ourselves naïvely. When we hear of what someone else has done, we often think, 'Isn't that awful! I would never do something like that.' Yet we forget we are all made of the same clay, and, given the same circumstances, but for the grace of God, we would do the same thing. If you say, 'That is nonsense!' then you are self-righteous and need to discover that the sheer grace of God has kept you from becoming a sex maniac, a murderer or an Adolf Hitler.

I believe Saul was a child of God. This opinion shocks many who cannot believe that a regenerate person could act as Saul did, but when Samuel appeared to Saul, he said, 'Tomorrow you and your sons will be with me' (1 Sam. 28:19). That is the equivalent of being in what Jesus called 'paradise'– a place of bliss, where the saved are with the Lord (Luke 23:43). I believe Saul is an example of a person who is saved as one 'escaping through the flames' (1 Cor. 3:15) and you will see him in heaven, but I do not think he will have what Peter called 'a rich welcome' (2 Pet. 1:11).

However, if David had died then, I do not think he would have merited 'a rich welcome' either. I do not know what his entrance into heaven will be like, but he recognized God had dealt with him graciously, and in Psalm 103:10 he said, 'He does not treat us as our sins deserve or repay us according to our iniquities.'

If we received our just deserts, we would be eternally lost, and, even if God simply disciplined us for every sin we have committed, we could never lift up our heads. But God is gracious and selective in the way he deals with his children, and I never cease to be amazed at his goodness and mercy.

What had Saul done to deserve God's mercy when Samuel promised, 'Tomorrow you will be with me'? The answer is, nothing: it was sheer grace. And who would become Saul's successor? Eventually, it would be David. What had David done to deserve that? The answer is, nothing: again, it was sheer grace.

We have done *nothing* to deserve salvation and can take no credit for it. Read 1 Corinthians 4:7: 'For who makes you different from anyone else? What do you have that you did not receive? And if you did receive it, why do you boast as though you did not?' Read Titus 2:11: 'For the grace of God that brings salvation has appeared to all men.' We are saved entirely by the grace of God.

In his final moments Saul consulted a witch, but God graciously saved him. Moreover, in his grace God not only prevented David from committing treason but he also kept that information from being widely known. And in his grace God has kept others from knowing everything about you.

'Well,' you may say, 'if we are saved by the grace of God, then I guess I am saved.' No. Paul said, 'It is by grace you have been saved, *through faith* . . . [my italics]' (Eph. 2:8). In Romans 3:25 he put it like this: 'God presented [Jesus] as a sacrifice of atonement, *through faith in his blood* [my italics].' This means that you must come to the place that you exercise faith. You must admit that you are a sinner and cannot save yourself and recognize that Jesus, the God-man, paid your debt on the cross.

You may now say, 'Well, does that mean that once I am saved I can live as I please?' No. Those who are governed by the principle of grace are subject to God's discipline (or chastening). Hebrews 12:6 says, 'The Lord disciplines those he loves, and he punishes everyone he accepts as a son.'

There are three levels of chastening: (1) internal chastening, (2) external chastening, and (3) terminal chastening. Internal chastening happens when you receive a warning from the Holy Spirit. If you hear him speak fall on your face and thank God, for that is the best way to have your problem dealt with. External chastening happens if you fail to heed the Spirit's warning and God steps in. This was the kind of chastening Jonah received when he ran away from God and was swallowed by the great fish. However, if God still cannot get your attention, you will experience terminal chastening. Then God will give you no further opportunity to repent, and you *may* die prematurely.

Saul experienced this kind of chastening, and in 1 Corinthians 11 Paul spoke of some Christians whom God had called home because of the irreverent way in which they celebrated the Lord's Supper (v. 30).

Now Christians who experience terminal chastening do *not* lose their salvation. However, they will not receive a rich welcome in heaven and, according to 1 Corinthians 3:15, they are saved as those 'escaping through the flames'.

28

Living on the Edge of Despair

1 Samuel 30:1–8

Have you ever been in a situation so desperate that you felt it was impossible for things to get worse, but then they did? David had known many dark periods in his life: he had had to cope with loneliness, with Saul's jealousy, with deception, with a broken vow, with stress, with depression and betrayal. But now came the darkest hour of all, when he was on the edge of despair.

Until now, as well as times of suffering, there had been bright spots in his life. God had given him a following, and, when he took refuge in the cave of Adullam, the force of four hundred men who joined him there soon grew to six hundred. David had the support of two wives, and, best of all, he had communion with God. All these things had now vanished: David's men, once so fiercely loyal, had become disillusioned with him; his wives had been abducted, and he no longer had the sense of God's presence. In fact, he had reached rock bottom.

Let us see how this came about.

You will recall that God had always protected David from Saul. However, instead of continuing to trust in God, David had foolishly sought political asylum with King Achish, a Philistine and the avowed enemy of Israel (1 Sam. 27). Achish thought highly of David, but his officers distrusted him, and when David set out with Achish to attack Israel, they demanded that the king send him back (1 Sam. 29:4–5). David realized he had no future with the Philistines and must leave. But where was he to go? He could not return to Achish, and he believed that ahead of him in Israel was Saul, who also distrusted him and sought to kill him.

Do you know what it is to be in a situation where nobody trusts you completely? I remember that when I left my old denomination for theological reasons, so many no longer trusted me to preach. Some Baptist churches invited me to speak, but they did not trust me completely because I had not been brought up in the Baptist tradition. Those were very discouraging years. I had to sell vacuum cleaners to make a living, and my family resented my lifestyle. Being a door-to-door vacuum cleaner salesman is not what makes for being a proud father. I seemed to have no future. Like David, I was in no-man's-land.

David and his men returned to Ziklag in the southern part of Israel, where their wives and children were living. But, as they approached the town, they were shocked to see wisps of grey smoke rising from piles of ashes where their homes had once stood. The Bible says:

> The Amalekites had raided the Negev and Ziklag. They had attacked Ziklag and burned it, and had taken captive the women and all who were in [Ziklag], both young and old. They killed none of them, but carried them off as they went on their way (1 Sam. 30:1–2).

Despair overwhelmed the Israeli troops as the truth sank in. We read:

> David and his men wept aloud until they had no strength left to weep (v. 4).

Do you know what it is like to have close friends, who once supported you loyally, turn against you? That was what happened to David then. For the first time, David's six hundred men turned their anger on him and began to mutter among themselves. 'If David were *really* a man of God, this couldn't happen,' they said. 'This is his fault. Let's get rid of him!' News of what they intended to do soon reached David's ears, and the Bible says:

> David was greatly distressed because the men were talking of stoning him; each one was bitter in spirit because of his sons and daughters (v. 6).

His situation was desperate.

However, David's most serious problem was not the disaffection of his men, but that until then he felt he had done nothing wrong. He had not seemed bothered that he had been living under the protection of Israel's enemy. In fact, as you will recall, when Achish said, 'You have to leave', David had begged the king to let him stay and join the Philistines in attacking Israel (1 Sam. 29:8), and had God not intervened, David would have ruined his chances of becoming king.

Would David ever come to his senses? He had lost friends; he had lost his following; he had lost the family and, most importantly, he had lost faith: he seemed to have no future. However, *God* was at the bottom of everything that happened. You see, once David had decided, 'Never again will I do anything without first asking God' (see 1 Sam. 22:3), but his resolve was short-lived and now he was paying dearly for it. God needed to get his attention and removed everything that David had been leaning on so he would turn to him once more.

Sometimes God has to take extreme measures to make us listen to him. Initially he speaks to us through his word, as through a preacher or through a hymn. However, if we turn a deaf ear, he has other ways of getting our attention and he may bring us to rock bottom, where our only hope is to call upon his name. But when we renew our trust in him, God will say, 'Why didn't you seek me earlier? That was all I wanted you to do.'

At last, David realized there was only one to whom he could turn. And in one of the most wonderful verses in the Bible we read:

David found strength in the Lord his God (1 Sam. 30:6).

Then God intervened and everything changed. We read:

> David recovered everything the Amalekites had taken, including his two wives. Nothing was missing: young or old, boy or girl, plunder or anything else they had taken. David brought everything back (vv. 18–19).

God gave David a marvellous victory. We can sum up everything that happened to David before he 'found strength in the Lord his God' in the word 'chastening'. God disciplines his children (Rev. 3:19), and if you have wandered away from him, he will say, 'You are not listening to me!' and begin to deal with you. He can be severe. For example, he may take your health away temporarily or cause you to lose your job; he may even put you into a position where you have nobody to turn to but him. This was how he disciplined David.

David had become a friend of the world and this displeased God. James 4:4 says: 'You adulterous people, don't you know that friendship with the world is hatred towards God? Anyone who chooses to be a friend of the world becomes an enemy of God.' So if you are a Christian and you align yourself with the enemy of the church, you force God to treat you as an adversary. This was exactly what happened when David went to live among the Philistines, the enemies of God's people.

Now I want to show you *how* David 'found strength in the Lord'. Although I cannot be 100 per cent certain, I believe he did four things.

First, I think David reflected on how God had led him thus far. I suspect he thought about the way God had protected him when he was a shepherd and wild animals had attacked his flock (see 1 Sam. 17:34–37). Then he probably remembered that God delivered him from Goliath (1 Sam. 17:40–50) and had repeatedly delivered him from the hand of King Saul and he said, 'All I have to do is to put my trust in the Lord again.'

Do you recall the time when you knew God had his hand on

you and kept you from harm? You may say, 'Well a lot has happened since then. I haven't been living for the Lord as I ought to have done; I think God has abandoned me now.' You are wrong: God *is* with you; he does not mock you. You have hope.

Second, I think David realized that, although his followers were panicking and blaming him for their predicament, trusting God meant that he should keep his head. He might have reasoned like this: 'God has given me a destiny: I am the future king of Israel. But if I sink now, I am not fit for kingship.'

Perhaps God has chosen you for a task that no one can do but you. Is he trying to get your attention? Is he testing your mettle? God was right in choosing you, but you justify his choice by the way you react in times of trial. Do you despair, indulge in self-pity or become angry with God, or do you find your strength to overcome in him alone?

Third, I believe David remembered how gracious God is. David probably realized how long he had been in the crossfire of men's personal priorities. Saul had put himself first; Achish had put his commanders first, and David's own followers had put their wives and families first. But David knew that God loved him with an unselfish, everlasting love.

One day David would describe God's compassionate and loving nature like this:

> The Lord is compassionate and gracious,
>   slow to anger, abounding in love.
> He will not always accuse,
>   nor will he harbour his anger for ever;
> he does not treat us as our sins deserve
>   or repay us according to our iniquities (Ps. 103:8–10).

If God dealt with us as our sins deserved, we could not even lift our heads. Some day he will summon us to stand before him at the final judgment. But if we put our faith in what Jesus did on the cross, we will have nothing to fear, for God freely forgives all those who turn to him in repentance.

David knew that although he had sinned, God would forgive him and accept him as he was, and in Psalm 103 he also wrote:

> As far as the east is from the west,
>   so far has he removed our transgressions from us.
> As a father has compassion on his children,
>   so the Lord has compassion on those who fear him;
> for he knows how we are formed,
>   he remembers that we are dust (vv. 12–14).

Perhaps you think, 'If I were God, I would have nothing to do with a person like me!' But God loves us like we are, with all our frailty and human weaknesses, and he accepts us as we are. Paul said, 'While we were still sinners, Christ died for us' (Rom. 5:8).

Jesus died for *everyone*. John 3:16 says: 'For God so loved the world that he gave his one and only Son, that *whoever* believes in him shall not perish but have eternal life [my italics].' Grasping this is important, because if you doubt the universal calling of the gospel, Satan will do his best to discourage you by whispering, 'How do you know he died for *you*?' Martin Luther once said: 'I am so glad that God said he "so loved the world, . . . that *whosoever* believeth should not perish", because even if God had said that he loved Martin Luther, that if Martin Luther believed Martin Luther would not perish, I would be afraid he was referring to *another* Martin Luther.' You may feel that you are the most unworthy person that ever lived, but God says, 'Come to me; I will forgive you' (see Matt. 11:28 and 1 John 1:9).

Fourth, I think David found strength in God, because not only did he repent of his wrongdoing but he also promised anew that never again would he leave God out of his life. He realized that God wanted *all* his attention and had brought him to the place where he had no one to whom he could turn but him.

Today this same God says, 'I want *your* attention. I want *all* of you.' He loves you so much that not only did he send his Son to die for you on a cross, but he brings you to the place where you depend on him alone. His love is truly wonderful.

When we hit rock bottom, we hit the Rock. When we touch *him*, things begin to happen and work together for good.

29

How to Turn Defeat into Victory

1 Samuel 30:6–20

At what was undoubtedly the darkest hour of his life thus far, David was unaware that sometime earlier Saul had consulted a witch and she had raised the spirit of Samuel (1 Sam. 28:4-25). Had David known that the prophet had given Saul twenty-four hours to live, he would not have been so desperate. But David believed he was in no-man's-land: King Achish had asked him to leave because his army commanders distrusted him (1 Sam. 29:1-11), and he thought he could not return to Israel for fear of Saul.

You will recall that after the Philistines rejected them, David and his men returned to Ziklag, the little town Achish had given them. Their hearts were heavy enough, but nothing prepared them for the scene of devastation when they entered the town: where their houses had once stood were piles of grey, smoking ashes, and the ruined town was deserted. Then the terrible truth sank in: the Amalekites had sacked Ziklag and taken their wives and children captive. This was more than they could bear. The Bible says, 'David and his men wept aloud until they had no strength left to weep' (1 Sam. 30:4).

Once David's men had been fiercely loyal. When they joined him in the cave of Adullam, they believed that he was a man of integrity, the man *God* had chosen to lead them and thought that Saul's persecution of him was grossly unfair. However, now they saw the disaster at Ziklag as God's judgment on David. 'If David were truly a man of God,' they argued, 'this would not have happened.' Bitter and disillusioned, they talked of stoning him (v. 6).

Now it would help us understand their attitude, if we know something about the Hebraic way of thinking. The Hebrews of old assumed that any kind of adversity or tragedy was a sign of God's judgment. This was why, when Job lost all of his possessions, his so-called friends said that his suffering was punishment for wrongdoing (e.g. see Job 8:4).

Six hundred years before Jesus was born, Isaiah described the reaction of the Jews to the crucifixion and said, 'We considered him stricken by God' (Isa. 53:4). You see, to them, it was inconceivable that God would allow the Messiah to be crucified. Had Jesus been the Messiah, they reasoned, God would have intervened. And when that did not happen, they were convinced the crucifixion was God's judgment on him.

One of the greatest prophets in the Old Testament was Elijah. In Zarephath, where Elijah was ministering, there was a widow who believed in Elijah until one day disaster struck. The Bible puts it like this:

> The son of the woman who owned the house became ill. He grew worse and worse, and finally stopped breathing. She said to Elijah, 'What do you have against me, man of God? Did you come to remind me of my sin and kill my son? (1 Kgs. 17:17-18).

When trouble came, this woman turned against the prophet.

Nothing is more discouraging than to have someone who trusted you completely suddenly doubt you. Moses, Elijah and David all experienced this.

However, Rudyard Kipling, in his famous poem 'If–' said the ability to survive such experiences is proof of a person's maturity.

> If you can keep your head when all about you
> Are losing theirs and blaming it on you;
> If you can trust yourself when all men doubt you,
> But make allowance for their doubting too . . .
> You'll be a man, my son!

In 1 Corinthians 13:11 Paul pointed out that Christians should become spiritually mature, and, drawing upon his own experience, said: 'When I was a child, I talked like a child, I thought like a child, I reasoned like a child. When I became a man, I put childish ways behind me.'

Perhaps God is saying to you, 'I want you to grow up and become responsible for your actions, but don't become demoralized. Find out what my purpose is for you. I will *never* leave you. Fight back!'

David's final phase of preparation for kingship would lead *him* to maturity. In 1 Samuel 30:6 we read this:

> David found strength in the Lord his God.

The Authorised Version says, 'David encouraged himself in the Lord his God.' He had received no encouragement from Achish. He had received no encouragement from Saul, and sadly, now he received no encouragement from his six hundred men. David had lost all human support. Yet, strange as it may seem, it was probably the best thing that could have happened to him then.

When disaster strikes, you may not understand it at the time, but on reflection you will realize that God allowed it to happen so that you would depend upon him alone. David was speaking from experience when he said in Psalm 118:8: 'It is better to take refuge in the Lord than to trust in man.'

Once I said to an old and trusted friend, 'Everyone in whom I have put too much faith eventually has disappointed me, but *you* never have, and I know you never will.' However, within four months of that conversation, when I was undergoing the worst trial of my life and desperately needed his support, he deserted me. The one person whom I believed would never disappoint me did.

God is a jealous lover (Zech. 8:2): he wants our undivided attention, so sometimes he will send a trial that leaves us with no choice but to turn to him. Then we can do what David did and turn defeat into victory.

You may recall that there are various levels of chastening. *Internal* chastening comes when God speaks to us through preaching or through his word. But if we refuse to listen, we will experience *external* chastening, when God uses external factors to act on us. For example, we may suffer a financial setback or a period of ill health, or something so awful happens that we cry, 'Lord, did you *have* to do that to me?'

God will then reply, 'Well, I didn't want to, but it was the only way to get your attention.'

Sometimes God uses a calamity in our lives to drive us to him.

One of the most thrilling moments of my life, was when I led Don Gurgiolo to Christ. I was preaching in Islamorada, Florida. Before the service the host pastor said, 'There will be a fishing captain here tonight.'

'Who?' I asked.

'Don Gurgiolo.'

'Are you serious?' I said. 'He is the man who taught me how to bonefish. He's going to be here tonight?'

'Yes. But he doesn't bonefish any more; he is a captain of a big boat and he fishes for marlin and sailfish and that sort of thing now.'

After the service Don invited me to go out on his boat later that week. Meanwhile I learned he had become a cocaine dealer, but the FBI had caught him and he was awaiting trial.

I led him to Christ on the boat. I knew his conversion was genuine, but when people in the Keys heard about it, they said cynically, 'Don's only turned to God because he hopes it will save him from a prison sentence.' Well, I think he probably *did* hope he would not have to go to jail, but he was sentenced to three years. However, he emerged from prison a stronger Christian than one could ever have imagined. He continued to serve the Lord in the Keys, and he told everyone that his predicament brought him to Christ. In the autumn of 1999 God called Don home to be with the Lord. He died a victorious Christian himself.

Perhaps you are in great trouble now and you wonder, 'Why is this happening to *me*? Other people do far worse things than I do and get away with it.' I can tell you why this happens. The Bible says, 'The Lord disciplines those he loves, and he punishes everyone he accepts as a son' (Heb. 12:6). God does not treat everyone like this, however. He tends to ignore those who are destined for hell, but says, 'Those whom I love I rebuke and discipline' (Rev. 3:19). God brought you to this situation because he loves you and he wants you to turn to him. The psalmist said:

Why are you downcast, O my soul?
Why so disturbed within me?
Put your hope in God,
for I will yet praise him (Ps. 42:5).

When we put our trust in God, he will transform a seemingly hopeless situation.

David experienced God's chastening and reached the brink of despair. However, when he put his faith in God, David turned disaster into triumph. And no matter how desperate your situation, you too can turn defeat into victory.

I think you can do so by taking three steps.

Step one is internal: it is something that happens in your heart. To take this step you must stop blaming everybody else for your predicament and face the truth about yourself: you are a sinner and you must get right with God.

The wonderful thing is that God freely forgives. Perhaps you feel ashamed and say, 'I have asked God to forgive me before; I can't ask him again.' Yes, you *can*; that is what he wants. 'But I have let him down so often,' you may reply. Yes, but God knows how weak you are. The Bible says, 'For he knows how we are formed, he remembers that we are dust' (Ps 103:14). You may say, 'If only I could believe that God *really* loves me.' God replies, 'I *do* love you and I will forgive you. Just come back to me.'

Step two is external. David did something that was public, and in 1 Samuel 30:7 we read:

> David said to Abiathar the priest, the son of Ahimelech, 'Bring me the ephod.'

You may recall that the ephod was God's way of giving guidance to his people then. The ephod was a little pouch worn on the high priest's chest containing two stones: the Urim and Thummim. The priest would reach his hand into the bag and take out a stone. If he withdrew the Thummim stone, God's answer was 'Yes' and if he withdrew the Urim stone, God's answer was 'No'.

If only David had done this sooner and asked if it was God's will for him to live among the Philistines, he would have spared himself from so much pain! But I believe the reason he did not do it then was that he had already made up his mind and had no intention of changing his plans.

Today we have the Bible to guide us. However, we often fail to consult God's word because, like David, we have already decided what to do and are stubborn. But if only we turned to God's word and allowed him to direct our steps, we would be spared from so much trouble and needless guilt!

But David did not want to repeat his earlier mistake and ignore God, and we read:

> Abiathar brought [the ephod] to him, and David enquired of the Lord, 'Shall I pursue this raiding party? Will I overtake them?' (1 Sam. 30:7-8)

David showed considerable courage in turning to the priest, because it allowed his followers to see his vulnerability. You see, if the priest had said, 'God says, "Do not pursue the Amalekites",' they would never recover what they had lost and would have been even more convinced that David was not a man of God. On the other hand, if God's answer was

'Yes, pursue your enemies', and they were unable to find them, they would blame David for that. But David publicly demonstrated his faith and asked Abiathar to find out what God wanted them to do. So the priest reached his hand into the ephod and withdrew the Thummim stone.

> 'Pursue them,' he answered. 'You will certainly overtake them and succeed in the rescue' (v. 8).

The third step needed to turn defeat into victory is to remain open to God's own unexpected way of bringing success.

Little did David and his men know when they saw a man lying, half-dead, in a field that *he* would be instrumental in saving them. We read:

> They found an Egyptian in a field and brought him to David. They gave him water to drink and food to eat – part of a cake of pressed figs and two cakes of raisins. He ate and was revived, for he had not eaten any food or drunk any water for three days and three nights.
>
> David asked him, 'To whom do you belong, and where do you come from?'
>
> He said, 'I am an Egyptian, the slave of an Amalekite. My master abandoned me when I became ill three days ago. We raided the Negev of the Kerethites and the territory belonging to Judah and the Negev of Caleb. And we burned Ziklag.'
>
> David asked him, 'Can you lead me down to this raiding party?'
>
> He answered, 'Swear to me before God that you will not kill me or hand me over to my master, and I will take you down to them' (vv. 11-15).

An Egyptian was the *last* person to whom a Hebrew would turn for help. Nevertheless, he was the instrument God chose to use to give them their victory.

True to his word, the Egyptian led them down to the place where the Amalekites were celebrating the success of their raid. The Bible says:

> David fought them from dusk until the evening of the next day ....
> David recovered everything the Amalekites had taken, including
> his two wives. Nothing was missing: young or old, boy or girl,
> plunder or anything else they had taken. David brought everything
> back (vv. 17-19).

Within the space of twenty-four hours their situation was
transformed because they were open to the unexpected way
God sometimes acts.

The way God has chosen to save humanity may surprise
you. Perhaps you have said, 'The *last* thing I will do is to pin
my hopes of salvation on blood that was shed on a cross.'
This may indeed seem strange; nevertheless, the *only* way
you can be saved is to believe in what Jesus did for you at
Calvary (Acts 4:12).

When you become open to God, he will meet your need in
a most surprising way and turn *your* defeat into victory.
However, first, you must recognize you have sinned against
him, and then ask him to forgive you and to take control of
your life.

30

Too Grateful Not To Forgive

1 Samuel 30:16–25

Are you on the brink of disaster? Do you face a bleak future? Do not despair; Jesus says, 'Come to me, all you who are weary and burdened, and I will give you rest' (Matt. 11:28). He will accept you as you are. 'Leave the future to me; see what I can do,' he says. 'With God all things are possible' (Matt. 19:26).

David could testify to the truth of that, for within the space of forty-eight hours God turned total tragedy in his life to total triumph. You will recall that, having been sent away by the Philistines, David and his men had returned to Ziklag, where they had lived, to find it a smoking, deserted ruin; the Amalekites had raided the town and seized their families and everything they possessed. This bitter blow was too much for David's men and they spoke of stoning him.

This was undoubtedly the darkest hour of David's life thus far, but in 1 Samuel 30:6 we read: 'David found strength in the Lord his God'; then he asked the priest to bring out the ephod so he could find out what God wanted him to do. The answer came: 'Pursue them [the Amalekites]. . . . You will certainly overtake them and succeed in the rescue' (v. 8). David's men then united behind him, and they pursued their enemy and recovered everything they had taken (vv. 16-20).

The Bible says:

> Nothing was missing: young or old, boy or girl, plunder or anything else they had taken. David brought everything back. He took all the flocks and herds, and his men drove them ahead of the other livestock, saying, 'This is David's plunder' (vv. 19-20).

However, at this point, I must explain that some of David's six hundred followers did not take part in the battle against the Amalekites. The Bible says:

> David and the six hundred men with him came to the Besor Ravine, where some stayed behind, for two hundred men were too exhausted to cross the ravine. But David and four hundred men continued the pursuit (1 Sam. 30:9-10).

But after defeating the Amalekites, David returned to the Besor Ravine and discovered he faced a new set of problems, for an undercurrent of discontent ran through the troops who had fought with him. Having taken all the risks, they wanted to exclude the men who had remained behind with the supplies from sharing the spoils and lost no time in voicing their resentment, saying:

> 'Because they did not go out with us, we will not share with them the plunder we recovered. However, each man may take his wife and children and go' (v. 22).

David had another crisis on his hands.

The Authorized Version calls the troublemakers 'men of Belial' (v. 22). Belial was a biblical nickname for the devil, and here was Satan, trying to spoil the successful outcome of the battle by making trouble.

But whenever God gives a great victory, the devil moves in. Jonathan Edwards used to say, 'When the church is revived, so is the devil.' So when the revival that we pray for comes, do not think everything will be easy: Satan will get in. In fact, whenever a church experiences great blessing, the devil often tries to make trouble by playing upon someone's jealousy of another. Satan knows it is easy to attack Christians in this way, and they often fail to see what he is doing, for, although we can readily spot envy in someone else, we rarely detect it in ourselves.

Do you know the Parable of the Workers in the Vineyard? Jesus told this story in Matthew 20:1-16:

The kingdom of heaven is like a landowner who went out early in the morning to hire men to work in his vineyard. He agreed to pay them a denarius for the day and sent them into his vineyard.

About the third hour he went out and saw others standing in the market-place doing nothing. He told them, 'You also go and work in my vineyard, and I will pay you whatever is right.' So they went.

He went out again about the sixth hour and the ninth hour and did the same thing. About the eleventh hour he went out and found still others standing around. He asked them, 'Why have you been standing here all day long doing nothing?'

'Because no-one has hired us,' they answered.

He said to them, 'You also go and work in my vineyard.'

When evening came, the owner of the vineyard said to his foreman, 'Call the workers and pay them their wages, beginning with the last ones hired and going on to the first.'

The workers who were hired about the eleventh hour came and each received a denarius. So when those came who were hired first, they expected to receive more. But each one of them also received a denarius. When they received it, they began to grumble against the landowner.

'These men who were hired last worked only one hour,' they said, 'and you have made them equal to us who have borne the burden of the work and the heat of the day.'

But he answered one of them, 'Friend, I am not being unfair to you. Didn't you agree to work for a denarius? Take your pay and go. I want to give the man who was hired last the same as I gave you. Don't I have the right to do what I want with my own money? Or are you envious because I am generous?'

So the last will be first, and the first will be last.

This parable shows that some people cannot bear others getting something they do not seem to deserve.

No one *deserves* to go to heaven. We are saved only because of what someone else has done for us: Jesus, God's Son, died on a cross and paid our debt. My simple trust in what he did at Calvary is my assurance of salvation.

Since he is saved only by the grace of God, theoretically, a person can become a Christian seconds before death, although he may have lived a vile life. Henry VIII is notorious for his many wives, his adulterous affairs and his murderous acts, yet it is said that, as the king lay on his deathbed, unable to speak, the cardinal who was with him said, 'Your Majesty, if all is well with your soul, just grip my hand.' After a moment the king firmly squeezed his hand, and shortly after this he died.

The four hundred men who fought the Amalekites with David ought to have been thrilled that God had restored their wives and children to them instead of carping about their exhausted comrades who had stayed to guard the supplies. But David wisely silenced the dispute like this:

> 'No, my brothers, you must not do that with what the Lord has given us. He has protected us and handed over to us the forces that came against us. . . . The share of the man who stayed with the supplies is to be the same as that of him who went down to the battle. All shall share alike' (1 Sam. 30:23-24).

David was too grateful *not* to forgive. He was thankful not only for the sudden and incredible victory but also because God had restored his credibility in the eyes of his men. Above all, he could see his future was now as bright as ever, despite the questionable way he himself had been living for the previous sixteen months.

Are you bitter about something? Maybe someone has hurt you and you say, 'I can never forgive that person for what he did to me.' I have met people who are so resentful that poison spews out from their mouths as soon as they start to speak. I have even heard some say, 'I would rather go to *hell*, than forgive him!' But if you allow hatred to consume you, it is *you* who are in the greatest bondage. Your hatred is your way of trying to punish the other person, but all you are doing is destroying yourself. The bitterness that gnaws you will put wrinkles on your face, raise your blood pressure to dangerous levels, affect your heart or give you arthritis. Note, I am not saying that these diseases are always caused by hatred; nevertheless, this sin *can* cause them.

Why did David decide to share the spoils equally? Was *he* not annoyed with those two hundred men who had stayed behind? Perhaps he was, but I think he made that decision because he was so grateful for the merciful way in which God had treated *him*. He had been foolish: without consulting God, he had chosen to live with the enemies of his people, and had God not found him out he would have fought against them.

Have you noticed how some people seem to get away with everything? However, when God does not deal with a person's sins in this life, it is an ominous hint that he will deal with them at the final judgment. So it is marvellous when God finds us out.

Moreover, God has a way of protecting us while he deals with us. He may let others discover our flaws up to a point, but not totally. Had David fought against Israel or if word had got back to his fellow Hebrews that he had been willing to do so he could never have ascended the throne. Yet not only did God graciously prevent David from fighting against his own people but he concealed this fact from them.

David recognized how merciful God is; and in Psalm 103 he wrote: 'He does not treat us as our sins deserve or repay us according to our iniquities' (v. 10). Nevertheless, I think David was shaken to the core when his men turned against him; and so he turned to God and asked, 'Lord, are *you* still with me?' That was the moment he 'found strength in the Lord his God' and received God's forgiveness.

Knowing *God* has forgiven us is wonderful, because *he* is the one who matters. When others hold a grudge against us, we are saddened, but we realize that it is they who have the problem.

David's situation had seemed hopeless: his troops had turned against him; he could not go back to Achish nor could he return to Israel. God was the only one to whom he could turn for help then. But David was so ashamed; he knew he did not *deserve* God's mercy and could plead only the blood of the sacrificial system, which foreshadowed the sacrifice of Jesus.

It is wonderful how God gives his people a second chance. Remember, Jonah refused to obey God and go to Nineveh (Jonah 1:1–2). However, we read, 'Then the word of the Lord came to Jonah a *second* time [my italics]' (Jonah 3:1). God offers you another chance too. You may say, 'But I have made such a mess of my life! My situation is hopeless!' But God says, 'Let *me* handle it; I can do *anything*.' God loves problems that other people cannot deal with, and, if he takes your case, he may solve your problems immediately or he may take a little time, but he *will* succeed.

Remembering how graciously God had dealt with him, David thought, 'If *I* did not receive the punishment I so richly deserved, why should these two hundred soldiers be punished simply because they were exhausted?' So when the others said, 'We refuse to share the spoils with those weaklings!' David said, 'Stop it! Everyone will share alike.'

When we are tempted to judge others, we too should remember how graciously God deals with us. In his Sermon on the Mount Jesus said:

> 'Do not judge, or you too will be judged. For in the same way you judge others, you will be judged, and with the measure you use, it will be measured to you.
>
> 'Why do you look at the speck of sawdust in your brother's eye and pay no attention to the plank in your own eye? How can you say to your brother, "Let me take the speck out of your eye," when all the time there is a plank in your own eye?' (Matt. 7:1–4).

But it is not easy to forgive someone who has let us down. 'How do I do it?' you may ask. Well, first, remember God has forgiven your sins, and, if you do not believe they are all that bad, I ask you this: How would you like him to flash all your thoughts and deeds on a big screen for everyone to see?

Next, ask the Holy Spirit to show you what you are capable of doing. If he answers your prayer, you will be horrified. When I see the capability of my own heart to sin and how God spared me, I am appalled. And if I judged others, knowing what God has done for me, I would be a hypocrite. Jesus said we are not to judge self-righteously. He put it like this:

'You hypocrite, first take the plank out of your own eye, and then you will see clearly to remove the speck from your brother's eye' (v. 5).

David resisted the temptation to be judgmental and handled the situation wisely. He discreetly pointed out to his troops that the two hundred men who were left behind had guarded the supplies (1 Sam. 30:24). This point would not have been lost on those who had taken part in the battle, and they probably said to one another, 'If we had had to carry the supplies with us, we would have had to go much more slowly. Perhaps the others did us a favour.'

However, maybe those two hundred men *were* ashamed that they had not fought with their comrades, but David graciously allowed them to save face.

Perhaps you feel ashamed. Maybe you have let somebody down. But this may be God's way of accomplishing a greater victory. When Joseph forgave his brothers he said, 'God sent me ahead of you to . . . save your lives by a great deliverance' (Gen. 45:7). Joseph was gracious in forgiving his brothers and allowed them to save face. I marvel that God, in his kindness, always allows us to avoid the humiliation we deserve. Surely when God has been so good to us, we can be gracious to others!

31

God's Sleeves Rolled Up

2 Samuel 1:2-4

Do you ever complain that God is slow in answering your prayers? If we are honest, I think we would all admit to having cried, 'Lord, *why* don't you answer my prayer? *When* will you come to my rescue?'

Nothing is more encouraging than to discover that the characters in the Bible were ordinary human beings, who had the same kinds of feelings and questions as we have. Like us, they longed for God to answer their prayers, and the cry 'O Lord, how long?' is a strain running throughout the Bible (e.g. see Isa. 6:11; Dan. 12:6-7; Rev. 6:9-10).

'O Lord, how long?' was David's cry too, and in Psalm 6:3 he wrote:

'My soul is in anguish. How long, O Lord, how long?'

And in Psalm 13:1-2 he begged God again to deliver him from his enemy and said:

'How long, O Lord? Will you forget me for ever?
How long will you hide your face from me?
How long must I wrestle with my thoughts
and every day have sorrow in my heart?
How long will my enemy triumph over me?'

God often seems slow to act; however, there comes a time when he *does* step in. For hundreds of years the prophets cried, 'How long, O Lord, will it be before you send us the promised Messiah?' But when the time was right, God fulfilled his promise. Galatians 4:4-5 put it like this: 'When the time had fully come, God sent his Son, born of a woman, born under law, to redeem those under law, that we might receive the full rights of sons.'

We may think that God is not listening to our prayers, but I believe that he is looking forward to the moment when he can sit down with each of us and explain everything. Then he will tell us why he allowed certain things to happen to us and why he waited so long before he rolled up his sleeves, saying, 'Enough is enough!'

In this chapter I want us to see that God is never too early or too late: his timing is always perfect.

We need to consider this from three viewpoints. First, we need to see it from the viewpoint of the person who is hurting. I suppose most of us can identify with someone who cries in anguish, 'Lord, how long?' Second, we need to consider God's timing from the viewpoint of the one who inflicts the pain. No one wants to be identified with someone like that, but we must remember that sometimes *we* are the ones who hurt others. And third, we need to see it from the viewpoint of the one who is hurt most: God himself.

People often shake their fists at God, shouting, 'I *hate* him for allowing this to happen!' Unfortunately, the Greek view of God, often called 'the impassivity of God', has crept into Christian circles, and many think that God has no feelings, but they are wrong. Often people do not realize God *has* to allow bad things to happen and what is at work is, in fact, his integrity and love.

Now we will look at three characters who can be set alongside these points of view. First, there is David, who expressed his pain when he wrote in the Psalms, 'O Lord, how long?' Next there is Saul, who was responsible for David's trial, and, third, there is God himself, whose honour was at stake.

Remember, God never wanted Israel to have a king. In 1 Samuel 8:6–7 we read this:

When they said, 'Give us a king to lead us,' this displeased Samuel; so he prayed to the Lord. And the Lord told him: 'Listen to all that the people are saying to you; it is not you they have rejected, but they have rejected me as their king.'

And in 1 Samuel 8:22 we read:

The Lord answered, 'Listen to them and give them a king.'

The kingship was not God's idea, but he let the people have their own way, and for a while all was well. But the time would come when, for the sake of his honour, he would have to show his people they should never have asked for a king.

God often has to consider several factors when deciding when is the right time to intervene. You may wonder why God did not act when David cried in great distress, 'O Lord, how long?' but has it occurred to you that perhaps he was being patient with *Saul*?

Maybe someone has hurt you and you ask God, 'Why do you let him get away with this, Lord? Why don't you step in? Why don't you judge him?' But perhaps God is saying, 'I can't do it yet; I have to be patient with this person: I am still dealing with him.' Have you ever considered how patient God is with you? We read in Psalm 103:8: 'The Lord is compassionate and gracious, slow to anger'.

However, as I said earlier, the time comes when God does step in, but he will do it only when the time is right. You may think you can use emotional blackmail or shake your fist at him and he will say, 'Oh dear! I don't want you to be upset with me; I will do what you ask straight away.' But, as James says, 'God cannot be tempted by evil' (Jas. 1:13) and 'The wrath of man worketh not the righteousness of God' (Jas. 1:20 av). In other words, you can do nothing to *force* God to act. Yet when the Sauls of this world obviously won't repent and the Davids of this world cannot go further, God rolls up his sleeves and becomes involved.

The time had now come when David had to move on. But where could he go? He and his men could no longer stay in Ziklag because it was in Philistine territory. On the brink of despair, David *thought* he would have to return to Israel and resume his life as a fugitive. But God saw David could no longer cope with those conditions and finally intervened to spare him from further harassment.

God knows how much we can bear. In 1 Corinthians 10:13: Paul said, 'No temptation has seized you except what is common to man. And God is faithful; he will not let you be tempted [or tested] beyond what you can bear.' So the time comes when God says, 'I know you can't take it any more' and intervenes.

God's timing is perfect. And just when David thought he was going to have to start running again from Saul, a visitor arrived. The Bible says:

> On the third day a man arrived from Saul's camp, with his clothes torn and with dust on his head. When he came to David, he fell to the ground to pay him honour.
> 'Where have you come from?' David asked him.
> He answered, 'I have escaped from the Israelite camp.'
> 'What happened?' David asked. 'Tell me.'
> He said, 'The men fled from the battle. Many of them fell and died. And Saul and his son Jonathan are dead' (2 Sam. 1:2-4).

This was the moment when David realized that at last God had stepped in to judge his enemy.

Now you may say, 'Saul committed suicide; you can't say that was *God's* doing.' But we *know* that God intervened because he said, 'In my anger I gave you a king, and in my wrath I took him away' (Hos. 13:11).

God had given Saul many opportunities to seek his forgiveness. For example, twice David refrained from vindicating himself, and each time Saul had a chance to repent (see 1 Sam. 24 and 1 Sam. 26). Saul *acted* as if he were sorry, but only for a while and he always hardened his heart again, so finally God withdrew his grace and left him to himself. Then Saul had to admit, 'God has turned away from me. He no longer answers me' (1 Sam. 28:15). This was God's judgment on the king.

The worst kind of judgment that God could ever bestow on you is to leave you to yourself. Who knows what that will mean! It may not happen immediately, but one day your end will be as tragic as Saul's was. Although you may not commit suicide, as Saul did, something even worse could happen to you. Paul warned, 'Do not be deceived: God cannot be mocked. A man reaps what he sows' (Gal. 6:7).

The Bible says that God ultimately punishes sin in two ways.

First, he created hell. Now hell was God's idea, not mine. If God turned to me and asked, 'How would you like to punish sin, R.T.?' I would come up with several different ideas but I would never think of hell. Hell is the most offensive notion that man has ever encountered. I don't understand it, but I am God's ambassador and I have no right to give my own opinion; I am simply telling you what the Bible teaches. However, those whom God will send to hell will *know* they are receiving their just deserts, for he is incapable of error. In Psalm 18:30 David said, 'As for God, his way is perfect', and in Psalm 145:17 he said, 'The Lord is righteous in all his ways.'

The second way in which God punishes sin is through the cross. God sent his Son into the world, and at Calvary Jesus shed his blood and became the object of God's wrath. He bore all our sins, paid our debt and satisfied God's justice. Just before he died Jesus said, 'It is finished.' (John 19:30). Now that is the English translation of the Greek word *tetelestai*, the colloquial expression used in the ancient market place meaning 'paid in full'.

These two methods are the *only* ways in which God ultimately deals with sin. Note, it is not a question of *whether* he deals with our sin: it is a question of *how* he deals with it. One day, God will roll up his sleeves and bring those who have rejected his Son to judgment.

The surprising thing was that when David heard about Saul's death, he wept. He undoubtedly felt some relief that the nightmare was over, but he wept because then he was given to feel what God feels. It will give God no pleasure when he says on that final day, 'Depart from me, you who are cursed, into the eternal fire prepared for the devil and his angels' (Matt. 25:41). He says this will grieve him: 'I take no pleasure in the death of the wicked' (Ezek. 33:11).

But remember, God said, 'My Spirit will not contend with man for ever' (Gen. 6:3) and Paul said, 'Now is the time of God's favour, now is the day of salvation' (2 Cor. 6:2). So if you hear the Holy Spirit speaking, act now. God was so patient with Saul, but, as we have seen, the time came when God withdrew his grace from him and brought him to judgment. Saul's end was so pitiful, but *yours* does not have to be like that.

32

When Problems Are Not Over

2 Samuel 1

In September 1970 my wife, T.R. and Missie, who was only three weeks old then, left Fort Lauderdale for Nashville, Tennessee, where I was to return to university to take my BA degree. 'If I get that,' I thought, 'I will never feel discontented again.' Soon after I gained my BA I had an opportunity to go to the Southern Baptist Theological Seminary in Kentucky. I was delighted and said, 'When I get my degree in theology, I will be content.' But before long I was invited to work on a master's degree at the University of Louisville. 'If I get that', I said, 'I will *know* that I have arrived.' At the same time I received an invitation from Oxford to study for the D.Phil., and I thought, 'If I succeed in getting this, I will be set up for life.'

Have you ever said, 'If I could fulfil *this* dream, nothing will ever upset me again' or 'If I could only solve *this* problem, I *know* that I would be happy'? David once felt that way. He had a problem: an enemy who was dedicated to his demise, and he longed for God to end Saul's tyranny. No doubt David thought, 'If only I could resolve my problem with Saul, I could live a normal life. Nothing could ever bother me quite so much again.'

In some of his psalms he cried out to God, begging him to end his trial. Let me quote from Psalm 57, which he wrote while hiding from Saul in the cave of Adullam:

Have mercy on me, O God,
    have mercy on me,
for in you my soul takes refuge.
    I will take refuge in the shadow of your wings

> until the disaster has passed.
> I cry out to God Most High,
> to God, who fulfils his purpose for me.
> He sends from heaven and saves me,
> rebuking those who hotly pursue me (vv. 1-3).

And in Psalm 59, which he wrote after Saul sent assassins to watch his house, he said:

> Deliver me from my enemies, O God;
> protect me from those who rise up against me.
> Deliver me from evildoers
> and save me from bloodthirsty men.
> See how they lie in wait for me!
> Fierce men conspire against me
> for no offence or sin of mine, O Lord.
> I have done no wrong, yet they are
> ready to attack me
> Arise to help me; look on my plight! (vv. 1-4).

Year after year David prayed that God would deal with his enemy. He thought, 'If only this problem were out of the way, I could live happily. Nothing would ever bother me so much again.'

Now in 2 Samuel 1:17-20 we read this:

> David took up this lament concerning Saul and his son Jonathan, and ordered that the men of Judah be taught this lament of the bow:

> Your glory, O Israel, lies slain on your heights.
> How the mighty have fallen!
> Tell it not in Gath,
> proclaim it not on the streets of Ashkelon,
> lest the daughters of the Philistines be glad,
> lest the daughters of the uncircumcised rejoice.

This is part of a great lamentation, written with tremendous intensity and melancholy.

Now had someone shown David these words two years

earlier and said, 'This is what you will be saying soon', he would probably have replied, 'I find that hard to believe. It seems as if my troubles with Saul will *never* come to an end.' But finally God did intervene and brought vengeance upon Saul (1 Sam. 31). David's mortal enemy had gone and the kingship was at hand.

However, David immediately encountered new problems, for the house of Saul opposed the idea of him becoming king (2 Sam. 2). His troubles were not over.

Still, as you have undoubtedly discovered, when one set of troubles end, others begin. But the Bible says that God's people must expect times of trial. Jesus said, 'In this world you will have trouble' (John 16:33), and both James and Peter said Christians should welcome hardship. James wrote:

> Consider it pure joy, my brothers, whenever you face trials of many kinds (Jas.1: 2).

And Peter said:

> In this [the coming salvation when Jesus returns] you greatly rejoice, though now for a little while you may have had to suffer grief in all kinds of trials. These have come so that your faith – of greater worth than gold, which perishes even though refined by fire – may be proved genuine and may result in praise, glory and honour when Jesus Christ is revealed (1 Pet. 1:6-7).

Sadly, many preachers today stress the so-called prosperity gospel, which teaches that when people become Christians, they should always prosper materially, and promise more than the Bible *ever* pledges to deliver. Jesus did not try to get converts by promising them a prosperous future on earth: he put obstacles in the way of would-be disciples. We need to see the Christian faith from its proper perspective: Christianity is about our *eternal* destiny, and, as the Bible says, in this life we must expect hardship.

Suffering may take on a different form from one person to

another, but God knows the kinds of experiences we need, and every trial is tailor-made for our background, personality, calling and purpose. For example, some may experience financial problems, some may have to cope with a physical disability, while others may experience loneliness or the frustration of constantly having to deal with a difficult person.

But *nothing* happens to the Christian without God's permission, and I find it a great comfort that he is the author of every trial that comes my way: he knows how much I can bear and he is always with me (see Heb. 13:5). In fact, the promise of God's presence is one of the fringe benefits of Christianity.

Now when we become Christians we can expect two things: (1) heaven to come, and (2) heaven below. It is certain that every Christian will go to heaven one day, but what about heaven below? Well, God encourages us by giving us a taste of heaven here on earth, but our joys are mingled with trials. However, we should remember that we may serve God best in times of trouble; Jesus did his greatest work on the cross.

I think that, when Saul died, David made two false assumptions.

First, I think that he felt that when his problem with Saul ended, life would go smoothly. But when a messenger came bearing news of Saul's death, David learnt that Jonathan, his dearest friend, had been killed too.

Perhaps you can recall waiting patiently for some good news, only to discover when it arrived that something else had happened and cast a long shadow over everything.

I believe the second false assumption David made was that there was little wrong with him.

Like David then, many people think, 'Well, deep down, I am not all *that* bad', and they assume God will reward them accordingly. Often people set out to manipulate God and try to phrase their requests in a way that would make it difficult for him to say 'No'. For example, they may say, 'Lord, if you help me to get this job, I will do *this* for you' or 'If I get a lot of money, I will give some of it to you.' This implies, of course, that if the new job does not materialize or if the money does not come, they are not obliged to do anything for God!

Many of us ask God for things as though we deserved his favour and he *ought* to answer us, yet, despite our failings, God is so good. There is a lot wrong with us, but he wants to put it right and bring us into a close relationship with him.

When we began the Pilot Lights and went out to evangelize on the London streets, at first, my wife Louise was reluctant to take part. However, one day she said, 'R.T., I am going to be a Pilot Light today.' She was rather nervous; nevertheless, she stood bravely outside St James's Park Tube Station, offering tracts to passers-by. Half an hour passed, and then a young man wearing a Che Guevara tee shirt approached her and said, 'What have you got there?'

'Would you like one of these little pamphlets?' she said by way of reply.

'What is it?' he asked.

'It explains how you can become a Christian.'

He looked at her and tears filled his eyes. 'I am an atheist, a Marxist in fact,' he said. 'But five minutes ago I went into a church and I prayed, "God if you *are* there, please let me meet somebody today who believes in you."'

Maybe that young man would not want anybody to know that he had prayed like that, but God graciously answered and gave him an opportunity to turn to him in repentance.

David was entering a new phase of repentance and godliness. His heart was changed and he had a fresh concern for the honour of God's name. He had long wanted God to deal with his enemy, but when God finally intervened, David wept and, as you will recall, he said:

Tell it not in Gath,
    proclaim it not on the streets of Ashkelon,
lest the daughters of the Philistines be glad,
    lest the daughters of the uncircumcised rejoice (2 Sam. 1:20).

David did not want God's enemies to gloat over the death of the leader of God's people.

God wants to give you a love for him like that. In fact, one proof that a person is right with God is that he or she cares about God's reputation. When Christians fall into sin, it gives the enemy a chance to rejoice. In America people laughed about the downfall of Jim and Tammy Baker and Jimmy Swaggart. Sadly Christians joined the world in laughing and gossiping about them. We ought to hang our heads in shame that such things could happen.

David's relief that his troubles with Saul had ended was mixed with sorrow, and he would encounter more problems before he could become king of all Israel.

However, as we have seen, when one set of troubles subsides, new ones replace them. You may ask, 'Why does God allow this to happen?' Well, I think he has two reasons. First, we all grow best when we experience some suffering. Jesus is more real to me in times of pain, but when everything goes smoothly, I coast along, and then God says, 'R.T., I don't have your attention now, do I?' Second, God allows us to face frequent trials because he does not want us to become too attached to this earth. He wants us to set our sights on our *eternal* destination. Tragically, however, many will go through this life with all its sorrows and *still* miss heaven.

33

Why So Many Churches and Religions?

2 Samuel 2:4

Quoting Psalm 8:6, the writer to the Hebrews said that God '"put everything under his feet"'. Then, applying these words to Jesus, he added, 'In putting everything under him, God left nothing that is not subject to him. Yet at present we do not see everything subject to him' (Heb. 2:8). Two thousand years have passed since Jesus tasted 'death for everyone' (v. 9), yet today more cults, sects and denominations exist than ever before. Why? And why do so few involve themselves in true Christianity?

Let us consider these questions in the light of 2 Samuel 2, where once again we see David as a picture of Jesus.

After Samuel secretly anointed him, David waited many years to be crowned king. Finally, the day he had longed for arrived. The Bible describes his accession to the throne like this:

> The men of Judah came to Hebron and there they anointed David king over the house of Judah (2 Sam. 2:4).

Like me, you may regard this with a sense of anticlimax. The Bible simply states that they anointed David as king and does not even describe his coronation. Most disappointing of all, we learn that only *one* of the twelve tribes of Israel, the tribe of Judah, acknowledged David as king. Verses 8 and 9 reveal the reason:

> Abner son of Ner, the commander of Saul's army, had taken Ish-Bosheth son of Saul and brought him over to Mahanaim. He made him king over . . . all Israel.

Knowing Ish-Bosheth was a weak man, and selfishly intending to retain power in Israel, Abner had set him up as king and refused to bow down to David.

David's first act as king of Judah was to send a message to the men of Jabesh-Gilead, thanking them for rescuing the bodies of Saul and his sons from the Philistines and giving them an honourable burial (see 1 Sam. 31:11-13). He put it like this:

> 'The Lord bless you for showing this kindness to Saul your master by burying him. May the Lord now show you kindness and faithfulness, and I too will show you the same favour because you have done this' (2 Sam. 2:5–6).

It was an offer of total forgiveness intended to reach the whole of Israel. However, the Israelites treated this message with contempt and rejected the man whom God had chosen to be their king. Only relatively few, the tribe of Judah, acknowledged him.

One thousand years later once again most of the Jews refused to accept the person whom God had chosen to rule over them. Galatians 4:4 says: 'When the time had fully come, God sent his Son, born of a woman, born under law, to redeem those under law, that we might receive the full rights of sons.' Finally, the Messiah, the hope of Israel, was born. Love personified, he healed the sick, raised the dead and proclaimed a message of forgiveness. But despite all this, they rejected him. Read Mark 15:6-10, 12-13:

> Now it was the custom at the Feast to release a prisoner whom the people requested. A man called Barabbas was in prison with the insurrectionists who had committed murder in the uprising. The crowd came up and asked Pilate to do for them what he usually did.
>
> 'Do you want me to release to you the king of the Jews?' asked Pilate. . . . But the chief priests stirred up the crowd to have Pilate release Barabbas instead.

'What shall I do, then, with the one you call the king of the Jews?' Pilate asked them.

'Crucify him!' they shouted.

As John said, 'He came to that which was his own, but his own did not receive him' (John 1:11). The Jews had waited hundreds of years for the promised Messiah, but when he came, they killed him.

Happily, the story does not end there. On the third day Jesus rose from the dead and appeared to a few people: first to Mary Magdalene, and then to the eleven remaining disciples and later to others (at one point five hundred people saw him). In Acts 1:3 Luke says:

> After his suffering, he showed himself to these men and gave many convincing proofs that he was alive. He appeared to them over a period of forty days and spoke about the kingdom of God.

Then Jesus ascended to heaven. There, his Father gave him the honour that had been due to him all along and enthroned him at his right hand, a position showing Jesus' sovereign authority (Mark 16:19; Eph. 1:20; Heb. 1:3).

On the day of Pentecost Peter, preaching under the power of the Holy Spirit, proclaimed Jesus as God's Messiah, the king of the Jews. He put it like this:

> 'Therefore let all Israel be assured of this: God has made this Jesus, whom you crucified, both Lord and Christ' (Acts 2:36).

Peter then relayed King Jesus' first message to the whole of Israel:

> 'Repent and be baptised, every one of you, in the name of Jesus Christ for the forgiveness of your sins' (v. 38).

Jesus' message was one of total forgiveness. Around three thousand of those who heard it that day believed (v. 41), but most treated it with contempt.

Another character enters David's story now, a man by the name of Joab. Joab and Abner had two things in common: (1) each commanded the army of his leader, and (2) each was related to his hero, for Joab was David's nephew and Abner was Saul's cousin. The two men decided to meet:

Abner son of Ner, together with the men of Ish-Bosheth son of Saul, left Mahanaim and went to Gibeon. Joab son of Zeruiah and David's men went out and met them at the pool of Gibeon. One group sat down on one side of the pool and one group on the other side (2 Sam. 2:12-13).

The encounter began like a peace conference at Geneva, but then Joab and Abner decided to settle their differences by holding a cruel contest. They each selected twelve young men to represent them and ordered them to fight hand to hand while the others looked on. All twenty-four men died in the ruthless combat, and then a full-scale battle erupted. The Bible says:

The battle that day was very fierce, and Abner and the men of Israel were defeated by David's men (v. 17).

Hundreds of young warriors died needlessly, but neither Abner nor Joab gained an advantage. The only result of this battle was that there was more confusion than before.

Looking at the global situation at the beginning of the third millennium, we see more confusion, more churches and religions, than ever before and we wonder why. I believe we will find the story of the meeting between Joab and Abner instructive.

Joab was on David's side, but he had no authorization from David to act as he did and the result was confusion and conflict. Here Joab is a picture of religious people who purport to represent Christianity but negotiate with those who show contempt for the work of Christ and give conflicting messages that do not come from him. This results in new religions and new cults springing up almost every week.

Tragically, there have always been those who have acted

without authorization from Jesus, but who *appeared* to be on the right side and *claimed* they were speaking for him. This has resulted in confusion, conflict and, sadly, even bloodshed. In fact, all kinds of atrocities stain the history of the church. The Inquisition in the Middle Ages, when millions were tortured and killed in the name of religion, is just one case in point.

Many claiming to speak for God try to preach a social 'gospel'. Seeing so many people in need, it is easy for church ministers to fall into this trap, but the Bible clearly says their task is to lead men and women to Christ (Matt. 28:19-20). Those who profess Christianity but ignore the Great Commission may *think* they are speaking for Jesus, but they act without his authority.

I am doing everything within my power to reach those few who will be converted. You may ask, 'Why do you say 'few'?' Because in Matthew 7:13-14 Jesus said: 'Enter through the narrow gate. For wide is the gate and broad is the road that leads to destruction, and many enter through it. But small is the gate and narrow the road that leads to life, and only a few find it.'

Note, Jesus said that *many* embark upon the way that 'leads to destruction'. Those who did not acknowledge David as king eventually were killed, including Abner himself.

Like David, Jesus will establish his authority in two stages. Few people acknowledge his sovereign authority now, but this will change when he returns to the earth. Describing his vision of the Second Coming, John said:

I saw heaven standing open and there before me was a white horse, whose rider is called Faithful and True. With justice he judges and makes war. His eyes are like blazing fire, and on his head are many crowns. He has a name written on him that no-one knows but himself. He is dressed in a robe dipped in blood, and his name is the Word of God. . . . On his robe and on his thigh he has this name written:

KING OF KINGS AND LORD OF LORDS (Rev. 19:11-16).

The day is coming when 'at the name of Jesus every knee [shall] bow . . . and every tongue confess that Jesus Christ is Lord, to the glory of God the Father' (Phil. 2:10-11).

However, God planned that only those who believe his word will be saved. John 3:16 (the verse Martin Luther once called 'the Bible in a nutshell') says: 'For God so loved the world that he gave his one and only Son, that whoever *believes* in him shall not perish but have eternal life [my italics].'

You see, God wants people to believe him. You know that nothing dignifies you more than when someone says, 'I believe you.' God wants us to trust *his* word (Hab. 2:4; 1 Cor. 1:21). You may say, 'I will believe the gospel when I *see* it's true.' That is not *faith.* The Bible says, 'Faith is being sure of what we hope for and certain of what we do not see' (Heb. 11:1). It is the gift of God, imparted by the inner testimony of the Holy Spirit (Heb. 12:2; Rom. 8:16).

I recall once missing my train to South Wales and having to take a later one. Now since I do not believe in accidents, I wondered, 'Why did I miss my train? God is up to something! I think he wants me to witness to a particular person on *this* train. But to whom, I wonder?' At first, I thought it was the guard, so I witnessed to her and she said, 'I know who you are. You are Dr Kendall of Westminster Chapel. I have heard you preach.'

I thought, 'Well, it's not you; you are already a Christian.' I looked at the lady across the table. 'It's you!' I thought. 'God wants me to talk to you.' I spoke to her and gave her a tract. She accepted it politely, but immediately put it down and started reading a magazine. Then a man sitting nearby looked at me and smiled. I thought, '*You* are the man.' I was right. We began to talk. He told me he was an engineer from Cardiff and was unconverted. He listened as I witnessed to him, and he was clearly shaken by the gospel. Now he had had little exposure to the gospel previously, but within half an hour the Holy Spirit stirred his heart.

This is how we become Christians. The Bible says that

when the gospel is preached, the Holy Spirit goes to work in the hearts and minds of those who hear (John 16:8). My friend Henry Mahan put it like this: 'When the gospel is preached, it will save some and condemn others, but it will accomplish God's purpose.'

However, the Bible says, 'The god of this age has blinded the minds of unbelievers, so that they cannot see the light of the gospel of the glory of Christ' (2 Cor. 4:4). Satan plays upon our feelings of self-righteousness. Everyone is self-righteous by nature. Proof of this is the fact that all religions, except true Christianity, have one thing in common: they all teach that salvation depends on our good works. Christianity alone teaches that our salvation comes through the efforts of another. Jesus died on the cross, paid our debt, and all we have to do is to trust what he did for us.

Because of a kinship with their respective heroes, Joab and Abner thought they were safe and would escape judgment. Like them, many pin their hopes on family ties, thinking that because they have been born into a Christian family, they will be saved. They are mistaken: those who are saved are those who acknowledge Jesus Christ as their Saviour and Lord.

34

Losing the Gold

2 Samuel 2:3

At the 1988 Olympics in Seoul, a Canadian athlete who won the 100 metres in world record time was suddenly stripped of his title and banned for life after failing a drug test following the race. The so-called fastest man in the world had tested positively for an anabolic steroid. This substance is said to increase muscle bulk and power and, as far as competitive sports are concerned, is classed as an illegal drug. Only a few hours earlier this famous athlete had been awarded a gold medal and recognized as a world hero. But now, having been publicly disgraced, he slipped quietly out of Seoul in the middle of the night, boarded an aeroplane for Toronto, and was later discovered in hiding, embarrassed and ashamed.

In this chapter we will look at two Bible characters who also lost the gold: Abner, who had commanded King Saul's army, and Joab, who commanded David's forces.

Had Abner acknowledged David as king of Israel, he would have been a hero. He knew the Israelites wanted David to rule over them and that God had sworn on oath that David should be the king (Ps. 89:3-4), but in a selfish attempt to cling to power, Abner rejected David and set up Saul's weak son Ish-Bosheth as king instead.

Joab could also have been a hero had he waited for David's orders. However, he bore a grudge against Abner for killing his brother Asahel, and was seeking vengeance (see 2 Sam. 2:18-23). But God says, 'It is *mine* to avenge; *I* will repay [my italics]' (Heb. 10:30). If only Joab had let God do what God does best! Now some theologians think that a second reason Joab opposed Abner was that he did not want another powerful general to be equal to him under David's kingship; however, the Bible is silent about this. What we *do* know, however, is that Joab took things into his own hands and murdered Abner and, as a result, suffered the grossest kind of embarrassment and shame.

This was what happened.

The time came when the relationship between Abner and Ish-Bosheth broke down (see 2 Sam. 2:1–16). Ish-Bosheth accused Abner of having an affair with one of his father's concubines, a charge that so enraged Abner that he decided to defect to David. Ish-Bosheth's days as king of Israel were now numbered.

An extraordinary series of events followed:

> Abner conferred with the elders of Israel and said, 'For some time you have wanted to make David your king. Now do it! For the Lord promised David, "By my servant David I will rescue my people Israel from the hand of the Philistines and from the hand of all their enemies."'
>
> Abner also spoke to the Benjamites in person (2 Sam. 3:17-19).

Then, to David's surprise, Abner called on him and, without revealing his reason for his change of heart, offered to make a deal with him.

> When Abner, who had twenty men with him, came to David at Hebron, David prepared a feast for him and his men. Then Abner said to David, 'Let me go at once and assemble all Israel for my lord the king, so that they may make a compact with you, and that you may rule over all that your heart desires' (vv. 20-21).

Joab was not in the area then, but when he returned and discovered that David and Abner had made a covenant, he was furious. The Bible says:

> Joab went to the king and said, 'What have you done? Look, Abner came to you. Why did you let him go? Now he is gone! You know

Abner son of Ner; he came to deceive you and observe your movements and find out everything you are doing' (2 Sam. 3:24-25).

Without waiting for a reply, Joab stormed out, determined to sort out the matter himself. Read verses 26 and 27:

Joab then left David and sent messengers after Abner, and they brought him back from the well of Sirah. But David did not know it. Now when Abner returned to Hebron, Joab took him aside into the gateway, as though to speak with him privately. And there, to avenge the blood of his brother Asahel, Joab stabbed him in the stomach, and he died.

Now at Abner's funeral two things were apparent to the Israelites. First, they saw that the rumours that David had engineered the death of Abner were obviously untrue. Indeed David publicly humiliated Joab for killing Abner.

David said to Joab and all the people with him, 'Tear your clothes and put on sackcloth and walk in mourning in front of Abner' (v. 31).

Second, they realized that David's conduct was above reproach and he was a man of integrity, while Joab had acted despicably.

Joab lost the gold. You see, when others hurt us and treat us unjustly, although we may not realize it, we are close to God's heart. He *wants* to vindicate us; he is always for the underdog, but we must let him handle things. He says, 'Vindication is what I do best. Leave it to me.' However, God's timing is always perfect, so he may not act immediately. But Joab couldn't wait; he was a fool.

David's vindication in the eyes of the people at Abner's funeral and the revelation that Joab's character was flawed illustrate two important aspects of the final judgment.

First, the day is coming when God will publicly vindicate his Son. Let me remind you of what John said when God gave him a preview of the Second Coming:

> Look, he is coming with the clouds,
>   and every eye will see him,
> even those who pierced him;
>   and all the peoples of the earth will
> mourn because of him (Rev. 1:7).

Those who rejected Jesus will see that he is God's Son, and then they will face the final judgment.

God has ordained that the judge will be none other than Jesus. Acts 17:30-31 puts it like this: 'God . . . commands all people everywhere to repent. For he has set a day when he will judge the world with justice by the man he has appointed. He has given proof of this to all men by raising him from the dead.' This coheres with what Jesus himself said in John 12:48: 'There is a judge for the one who rejects me and does not accept my words; that very word which I spoke will condemn him at the last day.'

On that final day everyone will acknowledge Jesus and own him as Lord. Read Romans 14:11:

It is written:

'As surely as I live,' says the Lord,
    'Every knee will bow before me;
every tongue will confess to God. '

But for those who did not accept him as their Lord and Saviour in their lifetime, it will be too late.

Second, on that day God will not only reveal the truth about his Son, he will also reveal the truth about us. Jesus said: 'There is nothing concealed that will not be disclosed, or hidden that will not be made known' (Matt. 10:26). I find Christians get very nervous about this verse, for none of us likes the thought of others knowing what we are really like.

The Bible also teaches that some, but not all, Christians will receive a reward. Taking his illustration from the ancient Olympic Games, Paul said:

Do you not know that in a race all the runners run, but only one gets the prize. Run in such a way as to get the prize. Everyone who competes in the games goes into strict training. They do it to get a crown that will not last; but we do it to get a crown that will last for ever. Therefore I do not run like a man running aimlessly; I do not fight like a man beating the air. No, I beat my body and make it my slave so that after I have preached to others, I myself will not be disqualified for the prize (1 Cor. 9: 24-27).

In essence, Paul was saying that he did not know then if *he* would receive a reward. Notice how he put it: 'All the runners run, but only one gets the prize'. Only *one* person receives the gold medal.

However, there are many contests in the Olympics: basketball, tennis, boxing, weight-lifting and athletics, to name but a few. Similarly, in the Christian life there are many types of calling: God needs preachers, evangelists and missionaries it is true, but he also needs people to work in the background: he needs volunteers to clean the church perhaps or to work in the office and in the book room. There are many tasks, and if you are faithful to your calling, you will win the gold.

Finally, let me draw your attention to three lessons we can learn from 2 Samuel 3.

Lesson One: God often fulfils his purposes in an unexpected way. In Romans 11:33 Paul said, 'Oh, the depth of the riches of the wisdom and knowledge of God! How unsearchable his judgments, and his paths beyond tracing out!' God will get his way eventually, although *how* he will do it is usually a total mystery until the moment he unveils his plans.

David knew God had promised to make him king over all Israel, but many years later he was still waiting for God to keep his word. What an anticlimax it was for him when at last he became king and only one tribe acknowledged him! But, as I said earlier, when God promised David he would become king of Israel, he bound himself by an oath, and whatever God promises, he will do, for it is impossible for him to lie (Heb. 6:18).

Abner began an affair with one of Saul's concubines, and God used that event to make David king of Israel (see 2 Sam. 3:7-21). Who would have guessed that God would use something like that to achieve his purpose?

Lesson Two: There are two main ways in which we can lose the gold: (1) through sexual sin or (2) through pride. Pride caused Joab to lose the gold medal, and both pride and sexual sin caused Abner to forfeit his.

One thing competitive sports has taught us is that drugs stay in the body for a long time, and many athletes have discovered to their cost that traces of a forbidden substance will show up in a test later. And unless you repent, sooner or later, your sins will come to light and you will have to pay the penalty for them. Galatians 6:7 warns, 'Do not be deceived: God cannot be mocked. A man reaps what he sows.'

First, let us consider sexual sin. God says, 'I want you to live cleanly.' So if you are sleeping with your girlfriend or your boyfriend or if you are having an affair with someone who is married, stop. God hates sex outside marriage. You may try to justify your behaviour by saying, 'But this is different; we are deeply in love'. If this is your excuse, heed God's warning: it is *sin* and you will pay dearly for it.

How many major figures in the world today been been disgraced when a secret affair became public knowledge? For example, few doubt that, had it not been for the Chappaquiddick scandal, Edward Kennedy would have been elected president. And, doubtless, you can think of certain TV evangelists who have made fools of themselves over illicit sexual encounters and lost the gold.

When David met Abner and made an agreement with him, he had one condition, as we see in 2 Samuel 3:13:

> 'Good,' said David. 'I will make an agreement with you. But I demand one thing of you; Do not come into my presence unless you bring Michal daughter of Saul when you come to see me.'

Michal was David's wife, but when he was hiding from her father, Saul had given her to Paltiel son of Laish (1 Sam. 25:44). She should not have agreed to this, and Paltiel should not have married her: he knew she belonged to David. However, he was heartbroken when Ish-Bosheth gave orders that Michal was to return to David. The Bible says:

> Her husband . . . went with her, weeping behind her all the way to Bahurim (2 Sam. 3:16).

If you are on the point of becoming a Christian, you too may weep bitterly when you realize that you must give up somebody who is not yours. Sadly, for this reason alone many refuse to yield to Christ.

Now let us consider the sin of pride. As I said earlier, both Joab and Abner were affected by this sin, for Joab set himself above his king by acting without his authority, while Abner had a long history of rebellion against David.

Perhaps you feel it is beneath you to accept the idea that Jesus died for you on the cross. But you would be foolish to let your pride stand in the way, for your good deeds can never match the standard of righteousness God requires. He has decreed in his word that the *only* way we can be saved is to accept that Jesus is our substitute. He lived a perfect life and paid the penalty for our sin, and when we believe, all that he was and all he did is imputed to us (2 Cor. 5:21; Rom. 4:8).

Lesson Three: God is no respecter of persons. Joab was on the right side. In fact, he was on David's side all along, so I am sure that David found it hard publicly to humiliate his friend and the commander of his army.

You may say, '*I* am on the right side: I believe in God, I believe in the church, I believe in morality and doing good. Moreover, my parents were Christians; they made sure I was baptized and took me to church, so it follows that I am a Christian too.' If you think this way, let me remind you of what Jesus said in Matthew 7:22-23:

Many will say to me on that day, 'Lord, Lord, did we not prophesy in your name, and in your name drive out demons and perform many miracles?' Then I will tell them plainly, 'I never knew you. Away from me, you evildoers!'

Remember, God is no respecter of persons and no matter how exalted or how lowly your social status, when you stand before him at the judgment you will have one hope: that you believed his word.

Abner finally accepted David as king, but he did not live long enough to enjoy the benefits, for God took his life. Abner lost the gold. However, *you* can win it, but first you must acknowledge Jesus as your Saviour and King.

35

Vindication – Always Bitter-sweet

2 Samuel 4:1–5:2

The summer of 1956 when I was forced to break with my old denomination was the most painful era I had ever experienced. I lost friends and experienced great opposition from my family, who did not understand that God had shown me things that he had not revealed to them. I could not make them see the truths that were so obvious to me, and I longed for God to vindicate me.

This experience was but the beginning, for since then I have needed God to vindicate me several times, and he has sometimes done so. But I have learnt something born out in Scripture: vindication does not make us totally happy and it is almost always bitter-sweet.

I suspect that at some time in their lives everyone yearns to be vindicated, but we must not take matters into our own hands, for God says, 'It is *mine* to avenge; *I* will repay [my italics]' (Heb. 10:30). In fact, he regards this as so important that he repeatedly says in his word, 'Let *me* do that' (see Deut. 32:35; Ps. 94:1; Rom. 12:19). 'If you insist on getting involved, I will just step back and let you get on with it.' So do not even *think* of trying to clear your own name, for you will only postpone the day it happens.

In earlier chapters we have seen that David longed for God to vindicate him. Read his prayer in Psalm 7:

Arise, O Lord, in your anger;
    rise up against the rage of my enemies.
Awake, my God; decree justice. . . .

Judge me, O Lord, according to my righteousness,
according to my integrity, O Most High.
O righteous God,
who searches minds and hearts,
bring to an end the violence of the wicked
and make the righteous secure (vv. 6, 8).

In fact, around a quarter of the psalms, either directly or
indirectly, refer to vindication, because David wrote many of
them while he was running from Saul. No one longed for
vindication more than he did, and he often begged God to
clear his name (e.g. see Pss. 13, 57, 59).

As we do today, he sometimes imagined how wonderful
vindication would be and how he would praise God when it
came. Read Psalm 7:17:

I will give thanks to the Lord because
of his righteousness
and will sing praise to the name of
the Lord Most High.

You will recall he needed God to clear his name for two
reasons: (1) because Saul had spread a lot of lies about him,
and (2) because he longed for the Israelites to acknowledge
his right to be king. Yet when vindication finally came, David
found it bitter-sweet.

One reason vindication is bitter-sweet is that it often comes
in stages. The first stage is enough for us to say, 'I believe
God has vindicated me.' Yet soon we begin to realize that he
has not yet vindicated us *totally*.

The day came when David *was* enthroned, but only as king
of Judah. In a sense, this *was* a fulfilment of God's word, but
it was only a partial vindication, for eleven of the twelve tribes
of Israel refused to acknowledge him. In fact, another seven
years passed before all the Israelites recognized his integrity
and crowned him king (see 2 Sam. 3:6-21).

Do you know what it is to wait a long time for vindication?
Perhaps someone has lied about you at work or at school or at

your church – sadly, this can happen – and after a few days you say, 'Lord, how long must I put up with this? Please do something.' Yet what if you have to wait a year, or even longer, before God acts?

Now we see a development concerning David's vindication. After Abner's death many realized that David was the wave of the future and would inevitably become king of Israel. Two men saw a way of using this situation to their advantage. This was what happened:

> Now Recab and Baanah, the sons of Rimmon the Beerothite, set out for the house of Ish-Bosheth, and they arrived there in the heat of the day while he was taking his noonday rest. They went into the inner part of the house as if to get some wheat, and they stabbed him in the stomach. Then Recab and his brother Baanah slipped away.
>
> They had gone into the house while he was lying on the bed in his bedroom. After they stabbed and killed him, they cut off his head. Taking it with them, they travelled all night by way of the Arabah. They brought the head of Ish-Bosheth to David at Hebron and said to the king, 'Here is the head of Ish-Bosheth son of Saul, your enemy, who tried to take your life. This day the Lord has avenged my lord the king against Saul and his offspring' (2 Sam. 4:5-8).

They waited, certain that David would be delighted and reward them well, but he was horrified by their deed and said:

> 'As surely as the Lord lives, who has delivered me out of all trouble, when a man told me, "Saul is dead," and thought he was bringing good news, I seized him and put him to death in Ziklag. That was the reward I gave him for his news! How much more – when wicked men have killed an innocent man in his own house and on his own bed – should I not now demand his blood from your hand and rid the earth of you!'

So David gave an order to his men and they killed them (vv. 9-12).

David's vindication was tinged with sadness.

I want to show you three more reasons why vindication is bitter-sweet.

The first reason is, we must wait for vindication long enough for other things to become more important. When we are hurt, initially, we may be obsessed with clearing our names, but while this is the case, the chances are that God will say, 'You are not ready for vindication yet.' But when we put things into perspective other things will become more important, and he will say, 'I think you can cope with it now.' However, since it no longer matters as much, it will not be as sweet as we once anticipated.

David waited for twenty years for vindication after Samuel anointed him as king. What did he do while he waited? He focused on other things and when vindication finally came, he was no longer as passionate about it as he had been at first.

It was not until 1979 that my father said, 'Son, I can see now that God had his hand on you the whole time. I am so proud of you.' Twenty-three years had passed since the day he had written the date in his Bible. During those years I got on with the work God had given me to do and vindication became less important to me, so when it came it was no longer as sweet as I first envisaged.

The second reason vindication is bitter-sweet is that the person who hurt you may be shown in a bad light, but his downfall will sadden you. You will have reached the point where you have totally forgiven him.

Now if you say, 'I can never forgive him. I want him to suffer for the pain he has caused me', you are not saying, 'I want vindication', you are saying, 'I want *vengeance*'. This bitter spirit will cause God to postpone your vindication.

In fact, if you harbour a grudge, it is because you do not fully recognize what Jesus did for you on the cross, and you think that the sin of the one who hurt you is worse than yours. You may exclaim, 'But it is!' You are wrong, and if you ever see God in his purity and holiness, you will see things about yourself that will horrify you.

Before you can become a Christian, you must recognize that you are a sinner. The Bible says, 'All have sinned and fall short of the glory of God' (Rom. 3:23). Jesus said, 'When he [the Holy Spirit] comes, he will convict the world of guilt in regard to sin' (John 16:8). So when the Holy Spirit begins to stir your heart, you will see that your greed, your lust, your jealousy are wrong. Moreover, you will realize that your hatred for the person who hurt you is as heinous in God's eyes as his sin against you so you are in no position to point the finger at another. In the Sermon on the Mount Jesus put it like this:

> 'Do not judge, or you too will be judged. For in the same way as you judge others, you will be judged, and with the measure you use, it will be measured to you.
>
> Why do you look at the speck of sawdust in your brother's eye and pay no attention to the plank in your own eye?' (Matt. 7:1-3).

Do you recall the phrase in the Lord's prayer, 'Forgive us our debts, as we also have forgiven our debtors' (Matt. 6:12)? You cannot say that, and mean it, until you experience God's forgiveness, but when you do, you will be so grateful that you will *want* to forgive others.

David freely forgave those who had rejected him as king and proved it by his refusal to rejoice in Ish-Bosheth's downfall and by his refusal to dignify his murderers. It was only then that God vindicated David and the Israelites invited him to rule over them.

The Bible describes the event like this:

> All of the tribes of Israel came to David at Hebron and said, 'We are your own flesh and blood. In the past, while Saul was king over us, you were the one who led Israel on their military campaigns. And the Lord said to you, "You shall shepherd my people Israel, and you shall become their ruler"' (2 Sam. 5:1-2).

David received them without bitterness. Seven years had passed since they received his message offering forgiveness and reconciliation, but he did *not* say, 'It's about time you accepted me!' Realizing that the Israelites were embarrassed that they had waited so long before acknowledging him, he allowed them to save face and accepted them.

This illustrates the way in which God forgives us and allows us to avoid humiliation. He says, 'I know you have taken a long time to come to me, but it is all right, I forgive you totally.'

How can God forgive so freely, so completely? It was not easy for him; in fact, there was only one way in which he could do it: he himself became human. Read John 1:14: 'The Word became flesh and made his dwelling among us.' Jesus did not deserve to die: he lived a perfect life, but on the cross, he became 'sin for us' (2 Cor. 5:21) and paid our penalty. When God punished his Son for our sin, it was the hardest thing he ever did. But Jesus' blood satisfied God's justice and procured our salvation.

The third reason vindication is bitter-sweet is that although you will find it difficult you must be prepared to elevate principle above personal obligation. Had David been guided by a personal obligation when those two men brought him the head of Ish-Bosheth, he would have said, 'I am indebted to you!' and rewarded them. This was the reaction they expected, but the king had them executed.

At the final judgment many will try to impress God with their good deeds. Jesus said, 'Many will say to me on that day, "Lord, Lord, did we not prophesy in your name, and in your name drive out demons and perform many miracles?"' (Matt. 7:22). However, Jesus will elevate principle above personal obligation and say, 'I never knew you. Away from me, you evil-doers!' (v. 23). However, this will grieve him, for in the Bible he says, 'I take no pleasure in the death of the wicked' (Ezek. 33:11).

Recab and Baanah tried to impress David by a deed which they saw as good but which he saw as repugnant. Are you trying to get in God's good books? If you are trusting in your morality or in your good deeds, or your church membership

286

to get you into heaven remember, God sees our works as vile (Isa. 64:6). You must abandon all hope in them.

Ish-Bosheth's assassins showed that they did not know David at all. Similarly, at the judgment those who have faith in their own righteousness will show they do not know God, for his eyes are 'too pure to look on evil' (Hab. 1:13). Those who know him know the only way they can enter heaven is by accepting what Jesus did for them on Calvary's cross.

36

The Eternal City

2 Samuel 5:6–16

Rome is often called the Eternal City, but this honour belongs to Jerusalem, for when this world ends there will be a *new* Jerusalem, a city that will exist throughout eternity. That city is my future home. I have not seen it, but I have heard from one who has. He was none other than John, one of the twelve disciples, who described his sneak preview of the eternal city like this:

> I saw a new heaven and a new earth, for the first heaven and the first earth had passed away, and there was no longer any sea. I saw the Holy City, the new Jerusalem, coming down out of heaven from God, prepared as a bride beautifully dressed for her husband. And I heard a loud voice from the throne saying, 'Now the dwelling of God is with men, and he will live with them. They will be his people, and God himself will be with them and be their God. He will wipe every tear from their eyes. There will be no more death or mourning or crying or pain, for the old order of things has passed away.'

He who was seated on the throne said, 'I am making everything new!' (Rev. 21:1-5).

Then, as if anticipating that somebody would exclaim, 'That's too good to be true!' John added:

> 'Write this down, for these words are trustworthy and true' (v. 5).

In this chapter we will see how King David carried out his first political and military strategy after being anointed king of Israel. You may remember that for more than seven years after Saul died, David was simply king of Judah. Then, his headquarters were in Hebron, but when he became king over all Israel, he realized it would be a good political move to move his court to Jerusalem. He had two reasons: (1) Jerusalem was more central, and (2) the move would reassure his subjects that he would be impartial and not favour the Judaeans.

Jerusalem is an ancient city that dates from at least 1,700 BC. We first read about it in Genesis 14:18, a verse that says, 'Melchizedek king of Salem [later called Jerusalem] brought out bread and wine. He was priest of God Most High.'

God had promised to give Jerusalem to his people (see Zech. 3:2; cf. Zech. 1:14). However, this formidable, spectacular city was inhabited by the Jebusites, who had remained there even after Joshua led the Israelites into the land of Canaan (see Josh. 15:63; Jdg. 1:21). The Israelites had never brought Jerusalem into subjection and regarded it as unconquerable. But David could not bear the thought of Jerusalem remaining in the possession of God's enemies.

Before we become Christians, we are God's enemies. Do you know why? Well, Paul explained it to the Ephesians like this:

> As for you, you were dead in your trespasses and sins, in which you used to live when you followed the ways of this world and of the ruler of the kingdom of the air, the spirit who is now at work in those who are disobedient. All of us also lived among them at one time, gratifying the cravings of our sinful nature and following its desires and thoughts. Like the rest, we were by nature objects of wrath (Eph. 2:1-3).

Paul was saying that everyone is born spiritually dead. This is why unconverted people despise anything that is holy and bristle with hostility at the thought of Jesus' sacrifice on the cross. They *think* they are free, but the devil has them under his control and they are merely his puppets.

Paul continued like this:

But because of his great love for us, God, who is rich in mercy, made us alive with Christ even when we were dead in transgressions – it is by grace you have been saved. And God raised us up with Christ and seated us with him in the heavenly realms in Christ Jesus, in order that in the coming ages he might show the incomparable riches of his grace expressed in his kindness to us in Christ Jesus (vv. 4-7).

That means that *God* conquered those of us who are now his people. You see, we would *never* turn to him of our own volition: conversions are the work of his sovereign grace.

David always had Jerusalem in mind because it is only eight miles from Bethlehem, where he grew up. And looking at the seemingly unassailable fortress in the distance, no doubt he often thought, 'Jerusalem is in the heart of the land that belongs to us by God's promise; it should be *ours*' and dreamed of capturing the city for God. Now the time had come and he had sufficient troops to make an assault, for Israel finally came over to him, bringing 341,000 fighting men to join his forces.

Now I want to show you four things about Jerusalem then. First, Jerusalem was a *closed* city. The Bible says:

The king and his men marched to Jerusalem to attack the Jebusites, who lived there. The Jebusites said to David, 'You will not get in here; even the blind and the lame can ward you off.' They thought, 'David cannot get in here' (2 Sam. 5:6).

However, David was determined to subdue the city and make it his own.

Are you aware that God has his eye on you from the foundation of the world and you are living on his earth, unconquered? Are you aware that God loves you so much that he wants to subdue you and make you his very own? You may reply, 'Yes, I know that. But that would mean submitting to God's authority; I want to be free. So if I became a Christian, I would be really miserable.' That is exactly what the devil wants you to think! In fact, you will not know *real* joy or freedom until you surrender totally to God.

Jerusalem seemed impregnable. Previous attempts to capture the city had failed, but they had been made from without. David knew something of the topography of the city and remembered that the Gihon spring rose under the city and had been tapped by a tunnel driven through solid rock. The water ran through the tunnel into a large underground pool, which was connected to the surface by a vertical forty-foot shaft into which people could lower their buckets to draw up the cold, clear water. He realized that if he were to make a successful assault on Jerusalem, he would have to enter the city by this underground aqueduct and take it from within.

But whom could he send on this secret, dangerous mission? David decided to set his men a challenge and in 1 Chronicles 11:6 we read:

> David had said, 'Whoever leads the attack on the Jebusites will become commander-in chief.'
>
> Joab son of Zeruiah went up first, and so he received the command.

You will recall that Joab had once commanded David's army but had fallen into disgrace for killing Abner. Joab saw this as an opportunity to redeem himself in David's eyes.

Are you like Joab? Do you feel that you are a failure and long for a sense of self-worth? Well, the way to achieve this is to do exactly what God wants and get right with him. Sometimes the hardest thing in the world is to say, 'I'm sorry; I was wrong.' But the peace that will follow your confession is worth more than gold and will bring you joy.

Second, Jerusalem was a *conquered* city. Wading through waist-high water, Joab and others who followed his lead succeeded in getting into the city and captured it.

Perhaps you consider yourself impregnable and no one has ever reached you. But God knows your vulnerability, and by the power of his Holy Spirit he will suddenly break through your defences.

This was what he did with Saul of Tarsus, who later became the apostle Paul. Saul was on his way to Damascus to kill Christians, and if anybody looked invincible, it was he. However, in his heart a battle was taking place, and God said, 'It's hard for you to kick against the pricks, isn't it, Saul?' (see Acts 9:5 AV). Then, suddenly, Saul's resistance crumbled and he surrendered.

After David conquered Jerusalem, people gave it many nicknames: they called it 'the City of David', 'the royal city' and 'Zion', but it also retained its true name.

Names are important. We are all pleased when somebody remembers ours. God calls his children by name. Read Isaiah 43:1:

> But now, this is what the Lord says –
>> he who created you, O Jacob,
> he who formed you, O Israel.
>> 'Fear not, for I have redeemed you;
> I have summoned you by name;
>> you are mine.'

You will keep the name your parents gave you, even in eternity. At the judgment there will be a roll call; listen carefully for your name will be called. John said:

> I saw a great white throne and him who was seated on it. Earth and sky fled from his presence, and there was no place for them. And I saw the dead, great and small, standing before the throne, and books were opened. Another book was opened, which is the book of life. . . . If anyone's name was not found written in the book of life, he was thrown into the lake of fire (Rev. 20:11-12, 15).

However, if your name *is* read out from the book of life, you will be entitled to live in the new Jerusalem: your eternal home.

Third, Jerusalem is God's *chosen* city. In 2 Chronicles 6:6

God said, 'I have chosen Jerusalem for my Name to be there', and in Psalm 132:13 we read: 'For the Lord has chosen Zion, he has desired it for his dwelling; "This is my resting place for ever and ever; here I will sit enthroned, for I have desired it."'

Everyone who becomes a Christian has been chosen. Jesus said to his disciples, 'You did not choose me, but *I chose you* [my italics]' (John 15:16). However, the Bible also says, 'Whoever is thirsty, let him come; and whoever wishes, let him take the free gift of the water of life' (Rev. 22:17). Let me tell you an old story that beautifully illustrates this teaching:

> A Christian died and went to heaven. Outside the beautiful, pearly gates of the new Jerusalem, he saw this notice: 'Whosoever will, may come.' He entered through the gates into heaven and looked back. To his surprise he saw a notice pinned to the *inside* of the gates and read the words 'Those who have entered were chosen before the creation of the world' (see Eph. 1:4).

Jerusalem was a chosen city. God has chosen you. Do not resist him.

Fourth, Jerusalem was, and is, a *coveted* city.

Over the last three thousand years, no other city in the world has experienced more turmoil and fighting and has been more coveted. This is still the case, for today Moslems Jews and Christians all claim Jerusalem belongs to them.

Did you know *you* are coveted? The devil does not want you to turn to his arch-enemy Jesus Christ and acknowledge him as your Lord and Saviour. Satan covets you for himself. But remember, his final destination is hell (Rev. 20:10), and he wants to take you with him. Do not let him destroy you: surrender your life into God's keeping.

37

The Sound of Victory at Hand

2 Samuel 5:24

I think 2 Samuel 5:24 is one of the most extraordinary verses in the Old Testament:

> 'As soon as you hear the sound of marching in the tops of the balsam trees, move quickly, because that will mean the Lord has gone out in front of you to strike the Philistine army.'

Something good was about to happen: the Israelites could hear the sound of victory.

David was now king of all Israel and had taken the city of Jerusalem. However, no sooner had he done that than the Philistines attacked him.

I want to show you six things this story teaches us.

First, an attack of the enemy will follow every major achievement in the Christian life. When you become a Christian you gain a new enemy, or rather, to put it more accurately, you see the surfacing of an old enemy, for Satan has *always* been against you. However, you would not have realized this previously because before your conversion you were blind to your spiritual condition (see 2 Cor. 4:4). In fact, the devil does not even want you to believe he exists, and when you become a child of God, his rage knows no bounds.

The Philistines were Israel's old enemies and when David became king of Israel they returned to the attack:

> When the Philistines heard that David had been anointed king over Israel, they went up in full force to search for him . . . (2 Sam. 5:17).

In view of the fact that King Achish had once given David political asylum and he had been at one with them for a while (see 1 Sam. 27), you might have thought that the Philistines would leave their former ally alone. However, once David fulfilled God's purpose, Israel's old enemy turned on him.

This hints at what happens to the backslider. You see, when a Christian listens to the devil and justifies his sin, Satan leaves him alone because he has him just where he wants him. But when the backslider turns back to God and resists temptation, the devil will attack because he wants him to stay in his grip.

Second, this story teaches us that all our encounters with Satan must be defensive. You must *never* take the initiative and attack the devil because you are no match for him. However, if you wait for him to attack you, you will discover he is always resistible. As James said, 'Resist the devil, and he will flee from you' (Jas. 4:7).

In Acts 16 Luke describes an amazing incident that bears out this teaching. He said:

> Once when we were going to the place of prayer, we were met by a slave girl who had a spirit by which she predicted the future. She earned a great deal of money for her owners by fortune-telling. This girl followed Paul and the rest of us, shouting, 'These men are servants of the Most High God, who are telling you the way to be saved.' She kept this up for many days. Finally Paul became so troubled that he turned round and said to the spirit, 'In the name of Jesus Christ I command you to come out of her!' At that moment the spirit left her (vv. 16-18).

One of the most important passages on spiritual warfare is Ephesians 6:10-18, and the emphasis is on defence, not on offence. Take the offensive and you will be out of your depth; but when Satan attacks all you are required to do is 'STAND'.

Once the devil attacks, then, like Paul, you can defeat him, but always wait for *him* to take the offensive. In 2 Samuel 5 we learn it was the Philistines who initiated the battle.

Third, the story teaches us that when Satan attacks we

should drop to our knees. This was what David did. Verse 19 says:

> David enquired of the Lord, 'Shall I go and attack the Philistines? Will you hand them over to me?'

The Lord answered him, 'Go, for I will surely hand the Philistines over to you.'

David had learned the hard way never again to make a major decision without asking God, and when he learned the Philistines were preparing to attack, he turned to the Lord.

Perhaps you think, 'Who am I to talk to God? He won't listen to me.' But he will. As the hymn writer William Cowper said:

> Satan trembles when he sees
> The weakest saint upon his knees.

The devil regards the praying Christian as a great threat.

Fourth, we learn that we must ensure that the credit for our success goes to God. David attributed his victory to God. Look at verse 20:

> So David went to Baal Perazim, and there he defeated them. He said, 'As waters break out, *the Lord* has broken out against my enemies before me [my italics].

When we talk about resisting Satan, does it mean then that we sit back and leave everything to the Lord? No. Oliver Cromwell once summed up what our attitude should be like: 'Trust in God and keep your powder dry.' Yet when the victory comes, it should never cross our minds to take any credit for it. Like David, we should say, 'Look what *God* has done for me!' and then thank him.

Fifth, we learn that when something idolatrous is brought under the sovereign rule of Christ, it must be destroyed. Read verse 21:

> The Philistines abandoned their idols there, and David and his men carried them off.

In fact, the Authorized Version of the Bible says, 'David and his men burned them.' I speak of things to do with witchcraft and astrology. Perhaps you have dabbled with these and tried to justify yourself by saying, 'I'm sure that sometimes God works through such things.' No. *Anything* to do with the occult is of the devil, so take all your astrology books and burn them, and if you have a charm bracelet or any good luck charms, destroy them.

Sixth, we learn that Satan will return to the attack. Look at verse 22:

> Once more the Philistines came up and spread out in the Valley of Rephaim.

After you have defeated him, the devil will leave you in peace for a while, but he *will* return. Describing Jesus temptation, Luke says, 'When the devil had finished all this tempting, he left him *until an opportune time* [my italics]' (Luke 4:13). Remember, in this life you will not see the end of the war, only a series of victories.

However, Satan *is* a defeated foe and his time is running out. Revelation 20:10 describes his end like this: 'The devil ...was thrown into the lake of burning sulphur, where the beast and the false prophet had been thrown. They will be tormented day and night for ever and ever.' Did you know that hell was created for the devil and his angels? (see Matt. 25:41). Satan knows his end, but he wants to take as many as he can to hell with him; that is why he tries to keep people blinded to their need of Jesus Christ.

When the Philistines tried again to gain the upper hand, David prayed once more, and God told him to adopt a different strategy. The Bible says:

So David enquired of the Lord, and he answered, 'Do not go straight up, but circle round behind them and attack them in front of the balsam trees' (v. 23).

Now as long as you allow Satan to keep defeating you, you will not *need* to adopt new tactics, but once you have had a real victory, God will give you a new plan.

Let me show you four things about the new strategy God gave to David.

First, it was a strategy of surprise. You may ask, 'How can I take the devil by surprise? Surely he sees everything I am doing?' Yes, but Satan cannot read *God's* mind, so follow his instructions and you will be safe. If you keep your eyes on Jesus and do as he says, you will always outwit the devil.

Satan did not know what God was planning when he sent his Son into the world. He believed *he* was the architect of the plan to crucify Jesus, and when wicked men nailed the Saviour to a cross, he thought he had excelled himself. But Paul knew the plan originated in *God's* mind and said:

> We speak of God's secret wisdom, a wisdom that has been hidden and that God destined for our glory before time began. None of the rulers of this age understood it, for if they had, they would not have crucified the Lord of glory' (1 Cor. 2:7-8).

The devil did not realize that this was how God had decided to save the world. Here we see the success of God's strategy: he took his enemy by surprise.

If you are not yet a Christian, you can take Satan by surprise by accepting God's gift of salvation. When you plead the blood of Christ, Satan's dominion over you will be broken.

Second, this new strategy was the strategy of sound. Let us look again at what God said:

> 'As soon as you hear the sound of marching in the tops of the balsam trees, move quickly, because that will mean the Lord has gone out in front of you to strike the Philistine army.'

This sound means three things: (1) waiting, (2) listening, and (3) obeying.

First, you must *wait*. Do not move until you hear the sound. Before his ascension Jesus said to the disciples, 'Stay in the city [Jerusalem] until you have been clothed with power from on high' (Luke 24:49). Acts 2:1-2 tells us what happened then: 'When the day of Pentecost came, they were all together in one place. Suddenly a sound like the blowing of a violent wind came from heaven and filled the whole house where they were sitting.' What had the disciples been waiting for? They had waited for the *sound*, for clear instructions. And today God says to you, 'Wait for the sound.'

You may say, 'That is the silliest thing I have ever heard!' But the Bible says, 'There is a way that seems right to a man, but in the end it leads to death' (Prov. 14:12). So when God gives orders to wait, do as he says; you would be foolish to move until you have instructions from him.

Second, you must *listen*. Paul said, 'Faith comes from hearing the message, and the message is heard through the word of Christ' (Rom. 10:17). In Revelation 3:20 Jesus said, 'Here I am! I stand at the door and knock. If anyone hears my voice and opens the door, I will come in and eat with him, and he with me.' However, you cannot open the door until you hear his voice. In Jerusalem the disciples had to wait until they heard the sound.

Third, you must *obey*. Note how the Bible puts it: 'As soon as you hear the sound of marching in the tops of the balsam trees, *move quickly* [my italics].'

Luke tells us that when Jesus saw Zacchaeus in the sycamore tree he said, 'Zacchaeus, come down immediately. I must stay at your house today.' Then we read, 'So he came down *at once* and welcomed him gladly [my italics]' (Luke 19:6). In other words, Zacchaeus came running. So if God is speaking to you, act at once; you may never hear him speak again, for he said, 'My spirit will not contend with man for ever' (Gen. 6:3).

Third, it was the strategy of the supernatural. The sound came from the tops of the trees, which were out of reach. It had nothing to do with the troops on the ground: it came from God. This was what Jesus meant when he said, 'The wind blows wherever it pleases. You hear its sound, but you cannot tell where it comes from or where it is going. So it is with everyone born of the Spirit' (John 3:8). In other words, you cannot manipulate the Holy Spirit nor can you command him to speak to you. When a person becomes a Christian, it is because of what *God* does. Jesus said, 'No-one can come to me unless the Father who sent me draws him' (John 6:44).

How nervous the Israelites must have felt as they waited for God. They could see the Philistine army, but they could not move until they heard 'the sound of marching in the tops of the balsam trees'. How foolish they would have been had they done so, for then they would have been acting in their own strength.

Are you trusting your own efforts to get into heaven? God has a strategy to save you, but you must not attempt to upstage him. The only way you can be saved is to acknowledge that on the cross *Jesus* did everything necessary for your salvation. He said, '*I* am the way and the truth and the life. No-one comes to the Father *except through me* [my italics]' (John 14:6).

The Israeli army did things in God's way and defeated their enemy. The Bible says:

> So David did as the Lord commanded him, and he struck down the Philistines all the way from Gibeon to Gezer (v. 25).

And if you have heard God speak to you, you have heard the sound of victory. Move quickly.

38

Afraid of God

2 Samuel 6:1–11

Do you think a person should be afraid of God? In 2 Samuel 6:9, we are told that David was afraid of the Lord. David said, 'How can the ark of the Lord ever come to me?', after the anger of God was revealed against Uzzah for trying to steady the ark of the covenant as it was being taken by cart to Jerusalem. You may find this surprising but it is actually a sign that David had become submissive. Two verses previously, the author says that David was angry with God. Martin Luther said that we must know God as an enemy before we can know him as a friend.

Many people imagine that God is only a God of love. Of course, it is a wonderful truth to know that God loves you so much that he sent Jesus to die on the cross for your sins. But we are not to forget that there is also the wrath of God against our sin. As John the Baptist said in his preaching, we are to flee from the wrath to come.

So far in our studies in the life of David, Israel's greatest king, we have seen how he first established himself as the *political* leader when he united Israel and made Jerusalem the capital. Then we saw how David established himself as a *military* leader not only by conquering Jerusalem but by defeating the Philistines and other enemies of Israel. In this episode, when David attempted to bring the ark of the covenant to Jerusalem, he attempted to show himself as a *spiritual* leader as well.

The ark of the covenant had a notable role in Israel's history. In a real sense it symbolised the presence of God with his people. But by the time David becomes king of Israel, probably very few in Israel even knew what the ark was or where the ark was. It is amazing how a nation that had such a spiritual heritage, that had Moses and Joshua as its leaders, could sink so low. But that is the state of Britain and America at the present time. As nations, we have become more pagan than many countries in the third world to where we used to send missionaries with the gospel.

The ark was at the house of Abinadab. King Saul had not paid attention to it. In the previous generation the people of Beth-shemesh treated the ark as a curiosity item.

> But God struck down some of the men of Beth Shemesh, putting seventy of them to death because they had looked into the ark of the Lord. The people mourned because of the heavy blow the Lord had dealt them, and the men of Beth Shemesh asked, 'Who can stand in the presence of the Lord, this holy God? To whom will the ark go up from here?'
>
> Then they sent messengers to the people of Kiriath Jearim, saying, 'The Philistines have returned the ark of the Lord. Come down and take it up to your place.' So the men of Kiriath Jearim came and took up the ark of the Lord. They took it to Abinadab's house on the hill and consecrated Eleazar his son to guard the ark of the Lord (1 Sam. 6:19–7:1).

The book of Numbers (4:15) teaches no-one should touch the ark. But the people of Beth-shemesh had tried to look into the ark and seventy men had been killed by divine judgment. The ark had lain dormant for fifty years and a generation emerged that did not know God.

David wanted to restore the honour of God's name. He realised that the ark would symbolize the gracious but awesome presence of God to a nation that was devoid of spiritual leadership. David had the best of intentions and he was so excited about bringing the ark of God to where it could be prominent. He also arranged for thirty thousand Israelites to come together to worship God.

> David again brought together out of Israel chosen men, thirty thousand in all. He and all his men set out from Baalah of Judah to bring up from there the ark of God, which is called by the Name, the name of the Lord Almighty, who is enthroned between the cherubim that are on the ark. They set the ark of God on a new cart and brought it from the house of Abinadab, which was on the hill. Uzzah and Ahio, sons of Abinadab, were guiding the new cart with the ark of God on it, and Ahio was walking in front of it. David and the whole house of Israel were celebrating with all their might before the Lord, with songs and with harps, lyres, tambourines, sistrums and cymbals (2 Sam. 6:1-5).

The problem was that even David forgot God's own instructions about how to transport the ark. Instead of being carried by Levites it was put on a cart drawn by oxen.

On the way to Jerusalem, the ark shook, because the oxen stumbled, and a man by the name of Uzzah put his hand on the ark of God to steady it. It seemed a harmless thing to do, but it was a wrong action: 'The Lord's anger burned against Uzzah because of his irreverent act; therefore God struck him down and he died there beside the ark of God' (v.7). Uzzah fell dead because he ignored the clear and explicit edict never to touch the ark. (We need to remember that, as far as God is concerned, his glory means more to him than anything else.)

We can imagine the shrieks and the screams of the people, for this sudden drastic event startled them all. At first David was distraught and angry. What had started out as a wonderful day of celebration left him with a feeling of awe and bewilderment. Yet it was something that God did. So, I ask the question, what was God saying to Israel and to David by this act of judgment? I would suggest three things.

First, God was saying that his word does not change. Numbers 4:15 makes it very clear that only the sons of Kohath should carry the ark. God's word does not change and this is a very elementary lesson that we need to always remember.

Secondly, God was saying that he is no respecter of persons. David was the king of Israel. But God would not bend the rules even for his king. God will not change his word to suit your background.

Thirdly, David learned that God is not primarily interested in *who* is worshipping him or how *many* are worshipping him. What concerns God is *how* he is being worshipped.

So when you come in contact with the real God, you may be angry at first. But your anger should give way to fear.

39

Finding Your Friends

2 Samuel 6:12–23

King David had always wanted to bring the ark to Jerusalem because it symbolized God's glory, and theologians tell us that when he finally achieved this, he was so thrilled that he penned Psalms 15, 22, 24, 29, 30, 132 and 141.

David had tried to move the ark to Jerusalem before, but he did not carry out the ritual according to God's instructions (see Num. 4:5-20; 7:1-9), and a man by the name of Uzzah, who reached out to steady the ark, was struck dead on the spot. Contrite and afraid, the Israelites left the ark in the house of Obed-Edom, where it remained for the next three months (2 Sam. 6:1-11).

However, now David said, 'Let's try it again.' So in 2 Samuel 6:12 we read:

> David went down and brought up the ark of God from the house of Obed-Edom to the City of David with rejoicing.

This time he was careful to ensure the ark was moved in the way God had instructed. Nevertheless, the Israelites who bore the ark on their shoulders were cautious and took six steps forward to see what would happen. All was well, and David stopped to give thanks. The Bible says:

> When those who were carrying the ark of the Lord had taken six steps, he sacrificed a bull and a fattened calf. David, wearing a linen ephod, danced before the Lord with all his might, while he and the entire house of Israel brought up the ark of the Lord with shouts and the sound of trumpets (vv. 13-15).

Overjoyed, David saw that this time the ark *would* reach Jerusalem.

However, David's happiness was marred by the reaction of one very close to him. The person who chose not to share his joy was none other than his wife Michal. As rightful queen of Israel, she should have been at her husband's side as he led the ark into the city, but she refused to have any part in the proceedings. The Bible describes her attitude like this:

> As the ark of the Lord was entering the City of David, Michal daughter of Saul watched from a window. And when she saw King David leaping and dancing before the Lord, she despised him in her heart (v. 16).

When you experience the thrill of becoming a Christian, you will want to share your joy with your family and friends. But sadly, you may find that, far from being excited by your news, they will resent it and even exclaim, 'You must be mad!'

People said much the same thing about Jesus and his followers. His own family said, 'He is out of his mind' (Mark 3:21). Others said of the 120 people filled with the Holy Spirit on the day of Pentecost, 'They have had too much wine' (Acts 2:13). And later Festus shouted to Paul, who was then a prisoner on trial before him, 'You are out of your mind, Paul! Your great learning is driving you insane' (Acts 26:24).

We all like people to approve of us, especially those we love perhaps, but when we are converted, we discover that discipleship is costly. However, we should remember that Jesus expects his followers to put their love for him above their love for their family. Read what he said in Luke 14:

> 'If anyone comes to me and does not hate [the word 'hate' here in the Greek means 'to love less'] his father and mother, his wife and children, his brothers and sisters – yes, even his own life – he cannot be my disciple' (v. 26).

When God struck Uzzah dead, David was angry, but then he lowered his voice and became afraid. This is a typical reaction from someone in whom the Spirit of God is working. I regard it as an excellent sign when I hear that my sermon has provoked an angry response from someone in my congregation because this shows that the Holy Spirit is getting through to that person.

I remember that some years ago a young nurse was brought by friends to Westminster Chapel on an evening when I preached on God's wrath and the final judgment. After the service the young lady remained in her seat, speechless. The people who brought her asked kindly, 'Would you like to come back with us for a cup of coffee?' She made no reply. Ten minutes passed, and then they put their arms around her and asked, 'Are you all right?'

'I didn't think anybody believed in anything like that these days. Please take me home. I'll never come back to this church again!' she replied.

Nevertheless, during the week the young lady telephoned her friends and said, 'I think I *will* go again to hear that man preach.' She came, and that Sunday she was converted.

You cannot upstage God's word. Perhaps you say, 'If God exists, I want to find him' and so you begin to read the Bible. But in its pages you may discover things that you dislike, and the more you read, the angrier you may get. However, this is a sign the Holy Spirit is dealing with you, and it is only a matter of time before you realize that God's word is true and the *only* way you can be saved is in the way he has ordained.

You may think that if you are seeking God and you are *trying* to go in the right direction by leading a moral life and going to church, it will be all right, but you are mistaken. God says, 'The only way to be converted is to believe in what my Son did for you on the cross.'

David could never forget that someone died for his previous error. Uzzah paid the price and became the object of God's wrath, yet *David* was the one who organized the moving of the ark; *he* was the one who deserved to die. Years before when the ark was desecrated, God killed thousands (1 Sam. 6:19). But this time one man paid the penalty and the rest were spared. In this respect, Uzzah is an Old Testament picture of Jesus, who was punished for our sin on the cross.

So when David made a second attempt to move the ark, he did it in the way God had ordained and, as we have seen, all was well.

Moreover, as the joyful procession made its way into Jerusalem, David discovered who his real friends were. Michal reveals their identity. The Bible says:

> When David returned home to bless his household, Michal daughter of Saul came out to meet him and said, 'How the king of Israel has distinguished himself today, disrobing in the sight of the slave girls of his servants as any vulgar fellow would (v. 20).

Now Michal liked three things about David: his prestige, his power and his position and was outraged that he should forget his dignity and strip down to a linen tunic in public and rejoice with slave girls. But David did not want his elaborate royal robes to draw attention to *him*: he wanted the worshippers to focus their attention on God. Moreover, he knew that beneath his royal trappings he was just like everybody else and in God's sight we are all equal.

I come from a church born in revival. The Church of the Nazarene began in America in 1908. Its members had little education and no wealth or influence, yet they had a treasure beyond price: they had the glory of God. The founder of the movement was a man by the name of Phineas Bresee. In his last days he visited various churches with this message: 'Keep the glory down!' He knew that if the Nazarenes lost that, they were finished. You see, they had the glory, but nothing else.

The early Nazarene church was the fastest-growing denomination in the United States. Do you know why? Because revival power was present in their services, people would go to church to mock, but come out converted.

One characteristic of revival is that people cease to be self-conscious. You see, the more you have of God, the less conscious you are of how you look and feel. Many would love to raise their hands in the air as they worship but feel inhibited. However, when the revival comes, Christians will cease to care what others think: God will be all that matters. David got so carried away that he found himself dancing and leaping – a picture of a person caught up in revival worship.

Michal, however, is a picture of a person who *resents* revival. When the Welsh revival was at its height, many – including some Christians, sadly – jeered and scoffed. So when revival comes do not think everyone will clap their hands exclaiming, 'Isn't this wonderful!' They will say, 'Those people are fanatics!' and mock.

Note Michal chose to sulk indoors, watching from a window. 'I am certainly not going to make a fool of myself by going outside to join those people,' she thought. And when she saw her husband getting carried away, 'she despised him in her heart'. (Note, Michal paid a heavy price for her contempt, for verse 23 tells us that she 'had no children to the day of her death'.)

As soon as David came in, Michal told him just what she thought of his unrestrained behaviour. Undoubtedly, she expected him to reply, 'Oh, I see what you mean. I have made a fool of myself, haven't I? The slave girls got in on the act with their tambourines and we got excited. I am sorry, Michal.' But to her chagrin, David said:

> 'It was before the Lord, who chose me rather than your father or anyone from his house when he appointed me ruler over the Lord's people Israel – I will celebrate before the Lord. I will become even more undignified than this, and I will be humiliated in my own eyes. But by those slave girls you spoke of, I will be held in honour.'

In other words, David said, 'These are my kinds of people.' They were his *real* friends and he embraced them.

I want to show you four things about these slave girls.

First, they were *common*. They had no prestige or power, only a heart for God.

Earlier I said that when the Church of the Nazarene began, its members were poor and uneducated. But did you know that every great movement of the Spirit started among people who had no wealth or influence? The Bible tells us why. Writing to the church at Corinth, Paul said:

> Brothers, think of what you were when you were called. Not many of you were wise by human standards; not many were influential; not many were of noble birth. But God chose the foolish things of the world to shame the wise; God chose the weak things of the world to shame the strong. He chose the lowly things of this world and the despised things – and the things that are not – to nullify the things that are, *so that no-one may boast before him* [my italics] (1 Cor. 1:26-29).

Second, they were *chosen*. You see, those slave girls were the Lord's. They were also David's true friends, the friends *God* had chosen for him.

Over the years I have discovered my best friends have been those whom God chose for me. Before I learnt this lesson, when I enjoyed a person's company, I would try to cultivate his friendship, but finally I would discover that if God was not in the relationship it would not work. My best friends have been those where God has said, 'Hey! *These* are the people who are your true friends.'

Third, the slave girls were *categorized*. Michal called them 'slave girls'. (The twentieth–century equivalent would be working-class girls perhaps.) Michal was a snob and thought such people beneath David.

Often those who hate what you stand for will try to humiliate you and come up with a name intended to be derogatory. Did you know that the term 'Christian' was first used in derision? The disciples were following what was then simply called 'the way', but their opponents thought, 'Let's come up with something that will really make them look foolish.'

'I know,' someone said. 'Let's call them Christians.'

This was why Peter said, 'If you suffer as a Christian, do not be ashamed' (1 Pet. 4:16).

In the seventeenth century they called Christians 'Puritans' because the Puritans said the Reformation had not gone far enough. Do you know what they used to call the Nazarenes? 'Noisyrenes' or 'Holy Rollers'. People will often give you an unwelcome nickname and so distance themselves from you.

Hebrews 2:11 says: 'Both the one who makes men holy and those who are made holy are of the same family. So Jesus is not ashamed to call them brothers.' And although some will be embarrassed if you get carried away and tell everyone he is your Lord and Saviour, Jesus will not be ashamed of you. In fact, he said: 'Whoever acknowledges me before men, I will also acknowledge him before my Father in heaven' (Matt. 10:32).

Fourth, the slave girls were *cherished*. David cherished them.

Many people do their best to forget their background and try to sound sophisticated, always aiming to be seen with the 'right' people, but David never forgot that God had taken him from the sheep pens (Ps. 78:70), so he took off his royal robes and danced with the slave girls, unashamed.

In Luke 14 Jesus said we should find friends who will identify with our new love, people who will rejoice in the things we rejoice in, who are unashamed of the glory. In Luke 14 he put it like this:

> 'When you give a luncheon or dinner, do not invite your friends, your brothers or relatives, or your rich neighbours; if you do, they may invite you back and so you will be repaid. But when you give a banquet, invite the poor, the crippled, the lame, the blind, and you will be blessed. Although they cannot repay you, you will be repaid at the resurrection of the righteous' (vv. 12–14).

God says, 'These people are your real family; they are your friends. Don't despise them or be ashamed of them; cherish them.'

40

Coping with an Unfulfilled Dream

2 Samuel 7

Dreams fall into one of two categories: (1) those that *may* one day be fulfilled, and (2) those that can *never* be fulfilled.

David was now at the high-water mark of his life and riding on a crest of glory, for not only had he become king of Israel but he had captured Jerusalem and taken the ark of God into the city. Yet he said, 'It is not enough. I want to build a temple for God and place the ark inside.' However, this was one dream that God would *not* allow him to fulfil.

Now 2 Samuel 7 tells us a lot about David. For instance, we see he was an ambitious man, perhaps overambitious. He was the type of person who was utterly miserable unless he had a goal before him. David was rather like Alexander the Great, who wept because there were no more worlds to conquer. And now David exclaimed, 'I have had the greatest idea ever!' Let us see how the Bible puts it:

> After the king was settled in his palace and the Lord had given him rest from all his enemies around him, he said to Nathan the prophet, 'Here I am, living in a palace of cedar, while the ark of God remains in a tent' (2 Sam. 7:1–2).

These verses reveal both David's love for God and his respect for Nathan, God's prophet. Most national leaders feel threatened by a true prophet, but not David.

This chapter also tells us a lot about Nathan. For instance, from his response to David's idea we learn that he had great respect for the king:

Nathan replied to the king, 'Whatever you have in mind, go ahead and do it, for the Lord is with you' (v. 3).

We also learn that Nathan had a close relationship with God, for we read:

That night the word of the Lord came unto Nathan, saying:
'Go and tell my servant David, "This is what the Lord says: Are you the one to build me a house to dwell in?"' (vv. 4-5).

Christian leaders including those with prophetic gifts often find it very hard to admit their mistakes. However, they should take a leaf out of Nathan's book, for he proved that his love for God was greater than his respect for David and had the courage to go back to the king and say, 'When I told you to go ahead and build the temple, I was wrong.'

This chapter also tells us a lot about God. For instance, it reminds us that he is omniscient and speaks through his prophets. We also see that he does not let his obedient servants go for very long without pointing out their mistakes to them. God did not want David to build a temple for him, and through Nathan he said to David:

'I have not dwelt in a house from the day I brought the Israelites up out of Egypt to this day. I have been moving from place to place with a tent as my dwelling. Wherever I have moved with all the Israelites, did I ever say to any of their rulers whom I commanded to shepherd my people Israel, "Why have you not built me a house of cedar?"' (vv. 6-7).

God has a mind of his own and is particular about the manner in which we should worship him.

I believe this story teaches us four things about the way in which God wants us to worship him.

First, we learn that God will not allow anyone to patronize him. Having been left in peace by his enemies, David thought, 'What can I do now? There must be something. Ah, yes! Here

I am, living in a palace, while God himself lives in a tent. That's not right.' It was as though David were saying, 'I feel sorry for God; I'll help him out.'

Have you ever tried to patronize God? Many religious people believe that our salvation depends on what *we* do. So they think, 'It's Remembrance Sunday, so I will do my bit for God and go to church. And when the collection plate comes around, I'll make a generous donation. He will be pleased about that.' It is as if they are saying, 'Poor God! *Someone* must lend a helping hand.' But God says, 'Hey! Don't feel sorry for me.'

God had a similar message for David. David thought he would welcome his idea and say gratefully, 'Thank you, David. No one else has thought of building a temple for me.' But God refused to allow David to patronize him.

David had begun taking it for granted that he could do things that would impress God. However, he had forgotten an important truth: God is sovereign and has a will of his own. He is the same God who once said to Moses, 'I will have mercy on whom I will have mercy, and I will have compassion on whom I will have compassion' (Exod. 33:19).

So if you are thinking of trying to do God a favour, forget it; the God of the Bible requires that when you come to him, you humbly ask him for mercy.

Second, we learn that God's interests are those that will preserve the church. In verse 10 God put it like this:

> 'I will provide a place for my people Israel [Israel is an Old Testament picture of the church].'

David was thinking only of the present, of a temple that was visible, and though building a temple for God was a very noble idea, deep down he knew that he was really thinking more of himself than of God.

Moreover, David knew that God had preserved him from his enemies, but he began to think that God had done it for *his* sake, when, in fact, God had protected him for the sake of the *church*. God was looking beyond the present generation; he was looking forward, to the birth of the Messiah, for Jesus would be born of the house and lineage of David.

Third, we learn that God wants us to be willing to do nothing*: he wants to do something for us instead.*

Coping with a shattered dream is always hard, and David must have been deeply disappointed to learn from Nathan that God would never allow him to build the temple.

David could have ignored God and gone ahead with his plans, but had he done that, he would have been a fool.

It is always foolish to ignore God's word. Perhaps you have refused to accept the gospel and say, 'Something so simple is beneath me, I'm afraid.' However, you reject it at your peril.

Verse 18 tells us how David responded to the news Nathan brought. We read:

'Then King David went in and sat before the Lord . . .'.

The military strategist, the great warrior, *sat*, coming to terms with the fact that God wanted him to do nothing.

Maybe you have thought that to get a ticket to heaven, you always have to be doing something to please God. But God does not want us to do anything to save ourselves. He says, '*Be still*, and know that I am God [my italics]' (Ps. 46:10).

Interestingly, this chapter *begins* with David wanting to do something for God, but it *ends* with God saying, 'I'll do something for *you*.' For the 'Lord himself will establish a house for you' (2 Sam. 7:11).

For many years the big lie in religious circles has been 'You get to heaven because of what *you* do for God.' But the Bible says, 'You get to heaven only because of what *God* has done for you.'

If you were to stand before God and he were to ask you, 'Why should I let you into heaven?' how would you respond?

Perhaps you would say, 'Well, Lord, I have lived a good life; I attended church regularly and was baptized, and, of course, you will remember how generously I gave when the collection plate was passed around.'

Jesus said that at the last judgment many will remind God of the favours they did for him, but to no avail. He put it like this:

> Many will say to me on that day, 'Lord, Lord, did we not prophesy in your name, and in your name drive out demons and perform many miracles?' Then I will tell them plainly, 'I never knew you. Away from me, you evildoers!' (Matt. 7:22-23).

The only way to get to heaven is to recognize that your good deeds can never match the standard of righteousness that God requires, for they are all tinged by selfishness and corruption. As the prophet Jeremiah said, 'The heart is deceitful above all things and beyond cure' (Jer. 17:9). You must accept that God has done something for you: he has provided a substitute, one who did things perfectly: Jesus Christ, the God-man. Jesus said, 'Do not think that I have come to abolish the Law or the Prophets; I have not come to abolish them but to fulfil them' (Matt. 5:17). And he *did* fulfil the Law by living a sinless life and by an obedient death. All *you* have to do is own him as your Saviour.

Many people think it arrogant when Christians say, 'I *know* I am going to heaven.' Of course, if our entrance into heaven depended on our works, they would be right. But we know we will go to heaven, not because of what *we* have done for God, but because of what *he* has done for us.

Fourth, we learn that God decides what our goals and achievements will be. God set three *new* goals before David.

First, God said, 'Be grateful for what I have done for you already.' Look at 2 Samuel 7:8-9:

> 'Now then, tell my servant David, "This is what the Lord Almighty says: I took you from the pasture and from following the flock to

be ruler over my people Israel. I have been with you wherever you have gone, and I have cut off all your enemies from before you.'"

Perhaps you are grieving because there are no more worlds for you to conquer. But God says, 'Stop! Just sit still and be thankful for what I have already done for you.' When was the last time you paused to thank him for his goodness to you?

Second, God said, 'Be grateful for what I will do through you for others.' He put it like this:

'Now I will make your name great, like the names of the greatest men of the earth. And I will provide a place for my people Israel and will plant them so that they can have a home of their own and no longer be disturbed. Wicked people shall not oppress them any more . . .' (vv. 9–10).

In other words God told David, 'I will use you and your achievements to bless my people throughout history.' God knew the temple would be but a temporary monument. Solomon built the temple, but later it was destroyed. The Israelites rebuilt it, but again it was torn down. So what David wanted most would not have lasted for long. God wanted him to have a *permanent* memorial and said, 'David, *this* will be your legacy. Listen.'

'Your house and your kingdom shall endure for ever before me; your throne shall be established for ever' (v. 16).

Third, God said, 'Accept what I have decided with dignity.' Then he tested David to see how much he *really* loved him. Would David still serve him if he did not allow him to fulfil his dream?

God asks, 'How much do *you* love me? Will you continue to serve me if I withhold the thing you long for? Will you accept my decision with dignity?'

David responded to the news Nathan brought him by offering up a prayer of complete acceptance:

Then King David went in and sat before the Lord, and he said: 'Who am I, O Sovereign Lord, and what is my family, that you have brought me this far?

And as if this were not enough in your sight, O Sovereign Lord, you have also spoken about the future of the house of your servant. Is this your usual way of dealing with man, O Sovereign Lord?'...

How great you are, O Sovereign Lord! There is no-one like you, and there is no God but you, as we have heard with our own ears.... O Sovereign Lord, you are God! Your words are trustworthy, and you have given this good promise to your servant. Now be pleased to bless the house of your servant, that it may continue for ever in your sight; for you, O Sovereign Lord, have spoken, and with your blessing the house of your servant will be blessed for ever... ' (vv. 18–19, 22, 28–29).

David accepted God's decision with dignity and welcomed God's new goals for him. That made him great and ensured his name was recorded on the pages of history.

41

How to Seize the Moment of Real Glory

2 Samuel 7:18–29

In 2 Samuel 8 we see David at the height of his glory, as a military tactician, a political leader and as a great man of God. Look at verse 6, for example:

> [David] put garrisons in the Aramean kingdom of Damascus, and the Arameans became subject to him and brought tribute. The Lord gave David victory everywhere he went.

Now look at verse 14:

> He put garrisons throughout Edom, and all the Edomites became subject to David. The Lord gave David victory everywhere he went.

In fact, 2 Samuel 8 speaks of one victory after another, as David defeated nation after nation and expanded Israel's territory to its outer limit. The writer of 2 Samuel could undoubtedly have written another twenty chapters describing Israel's conquests in detail, but he mainly confined himself to listing them. You see, they became predictable, something the Israelites could take for granted.

Never again would Israel have such a comparable era, and never again would it have a king like David. Yet the writer of 2 Samuel makes it clear that this success meant little to David. If you look at your Bible, you will see he gives David's prayer in 2 Samuel 7 and the description of David's victories in 2 Samuel 8 roughly the same amount of space, although David's prayer lasted for only a few minutes while the victories were won over several years (see 2 Sam. 8:1).

What made David's prayer so significant? Well, it was during those few minutes when David waited on God and accepted one of his greatest disappointments with dignity that he experienced his moment of true glory.

I came to England in 1973 to study for the D.Phil. at Oxford. My thesis was to be on John Owen. My dream was to become an expert on this Puritan theologian. However, one day my supervisor came to me and said, 'We don't want you to continue with this study. We believe that you have a different thesis ahead of you.' Devastated, I telephoned Louise and said, 'I am coming home; I have bad news.' By the time I reached the house I had such a splitting headache that I went to bed, unable to accept that I could not fulfil my dream.

In those days I used to walk down Broad Street and gaze at the Sheldonian Theatre, where they award the degrees, dreaming of my moment of glory. When the day I had longed for finally dawned, I took my seat in the Sheldonian and waited as, one after another, students collected their awards. Soon they called my name and I went up to the Vice-Chancellor, received my degree, bowed and shook his hand. I wanted the moment to last forever, but my part in the proceedings lasted all of four seconds, and I thought, 'Is this it?' However, that was not my moment of true glory; that had come two years earlier when I finally accepted that God did not want me to write a thesis on John Owen.

We do not know how keenly David felt his disappointment when he learnt that God would not allow him to build the temple or how long he struggled to come to terms with this. We only know that he came to the point where he accepted God's will with humility and with gratitude. The Bible says:

> Then King David went in and sat before the Lord, and he said:
> 'Who am I, O Sovereign Lord, and what is my family, that you have brought me this far?' (2 Sam. 7:18).

This was his moment of true glory and the beginning of the era when he accomplished great things for God.

God has a task for you. However, you will not discover what it is until you commit yourself to him. You may turn out to be a great preacher; you may do things that will turn the world upside down and hear people say, 'What a great Christian!' However, your moment of true glory will be the moment you say, 'Yes, Lord' and submit to his will by welcoming him into your heart.

After David complied with God's will, he began to accomplish things effortlessly. But the victories described in 2 Samuel 8 meant nothing to him in comparison to his dream of building a temple for God. But the fact that he did not allow his achievements to go to his head meant God could trust him.

I have lived long enough to treasure my greatest disappointments, and I have seen that God has always acted in my best interests and had something greater in mind for me, and I am so thankful. So when your dreams are shattered, lower your voice and wait. See what God will do for *you.*

If you accept disappointments with grace and dignity, you will not regard success as so important as you once did. You will do things with ease because God will be in charge. You see, when you receive Jesus Christ as Saviour, you also receive him as Lord. He will take control of your life and all you have to do is to follow him. You will be like a shop with a sign on the door saying 'Under New Management.' Moreover, your obedience will mean God will trust you with success, as he did David.

I think that David's success depended on his accepting five truths.

First, David accepted his insignificance. Look again at 2 Samuel 7:18: 'Then King David went in and sat before the Lord, and he said, "Who am I, O Sovereign Lord, and what is my family?"' David was king and perhaps he had begun to think more highly of himself than he ought. Now he began to get things in perspective and thought, 'Who am I? I am unworthy of God's favour.'

Sometimes people think they are so important that God should come to them on bended knee and beg them to accept him. But when the Holy Spirit begins to deal with them, they kneel before God and humbly ask, 'Who am I, Lord, that you should notice me?'

Second, David accepted the fact that this present life is not all there is. Let me remind you of what God said to David in verse 12:

> 'When your days are over and you rest with your fathers, I will raise up your offspring to succeed you . . . '.

God reminded David that someday he would die and enter eternity.

When you enter eternity, you enter a timeless realm. Eternity is an everlasting *now*. The final line of 'Amazing Grace' describes eternity in heaven like this:

> When we've been there ten thousand years,
>   Bright shining as the sun,
> We've no less days to sing God's praise
>   Than when we first began.

It is a sobering thought that hell is also endless.

David had been taking himself and his ambitions so seriously, so God reminded him of his mortality. And when we have a vision of eternity, we too will see this life in its true perspective. Then our ambitions will no longer seem important: the only thing that will matter is what God wants.

Third, David accepted that he was God's servant. In fact, in three successive verses this was how he described himself in his prayer (vv. 19, 20, 21). Yet previously, albeit unconsciously, David had wanted God to serve *him*.

Sadly, today many Christians selfishly try to manipulate

God to further their own ambitions. Never think that you can become a Christian in order to use God. A Christian must regard himself or herself as God's servant.

The marvellous thing is that when you accept that you are in God's service, you will not take failure personally. Had David lost the battles described in 2 Samuel 8, he would not have felt he was a failure, because he would have known he had obeyed God. God does not ask us to be a success, he simply says, '*Follow* me [my italics]' (see John 1:43). David came to that place where he simply said, 'Yes, Lord'.

Fourth, David worshipped God. Look at 2 Samuel 7:22:

'How great you are, O Sovereign Lord! There is no-one like you, and there is no God but you, as we have heard with our own ears.'

Perhaps you feel angry with God for withholding something from you, but when you get right with him, you will come to the place where you say, 'Lord, your way is best' and worship him.

Furthermore, the Christian not only worships God but he loves him for being who he is. Has anyone ever told you, 'I love you just like you are'? It is the highest compliment one person can pay another. God loves you just like you are, and when you come to know him, you will love *him* for himself.

Fifth, David accepted the fact that God would do something for him. The chapter begins with David planning to build a house for God, but it ends with David accepting that God would build a house for him instead.

God does not want you to do anything for *him*; he wants to do something for *you*: he wants you to accept his gift of eternal life. But first you must recognize that you do not *deserve* to go to heaven; God hates self-righteousness. Like David, you must sit before him and humbly say, 'Who am I?' and accept that Jesus has done everything for you and then accept him as your Lord and Saviour.

The Bible says, 'No eye has seen, no ear has heard, no

mind has conceived what God has prepared for those who love him' (1 Cor. 2:9). When you become a Christian, he will take control of your life. You will not know exactly what he has planned for you, but however great your future in his service, remember, your moment of true glory will be the moment you say, 'Yes, Lord.'

42

Why Is God for the Underdog?

2 Samuel 9

If you spend eternity in heaven, you will always be aware that you are there only because, in his kindness, God came to your rescue.

The story of David's kindness to Mephibosheth is possibly the most amazing and accurate illustration of God's grace to sinful humanity in the Bible. It began when King David suddenly asked:

> 'Is there anyone still left of the house of Saul to whom I can show kindness for Jonathan's sake?' (v. 1).

Here we see David as a picture of God.

God seeks to be kind. The question is, to whom or to what does God look? Does he shower his grace on fallen angels or on the animal kingdom, for instance? No. God looks to the family that has offended him most, to fallen humanity.

Now if David had reacted in the way people normally do, he would have resented the family of the man who had hounded him for so long. But he refused to bear a grudge and sought to show Saul's relatives kindness.

There was indeed a member of Saul's house left. The Bible says:

> Now there was a servant of Saul's household named Ziba. They called him to appear before David, and the king said to him, 'Are you Ziba?'
>
> 'Your servant,' he replied.
>
> The king asked, 'Is there no-one still left of the house of Saul to whom I can show God's kindness?'

Ziba answered the king, 'There is still a son of Jonathan; he is crippled in both feet.'

'Where is he?' the king asked.

Ziba answered, 'He is at the house of Makir son of Ammiel in Lo Debar.'

So King David had him brought from Lo Debar, from the house of Makir son of Ammiel (vv. 2-5).

His name was Mephibosheth, who had been disabled by a terrible accident when a child (see 2 Sam. 4:4).

After the death of Saul and his father Jonathan Mephibosheth disappeared from public view. Unable to earn a living when he grew to adulthood, he lived in abject poverty in a remote and desolate spot called Lo Debar. He thought he was of no account and that everyone had forgotten about him. He never dreamt that one day he would hear messengers say, 'King David has summoned you.'

Are you like Mephibosheth? Do you feel unworthy of notice? If so, remember that God looks for a particular type of person: he seeks those who do not expect to be blessed and have nothing to offer him. Through the prophet Isaiah, he said, 'I revealed myself to those who did not ask for me; I was found by those who did not seek me' (Isa. 65:1).

What could Mephibosheth do to repay King David for his kindness? Nothing. You see, that is the way God is: he loves to do something for someone who can never return the favour, so he singles out the kind of person others reject. The Bible makes it clear that God is for the underdog. Read what Jesus said in Luke 14:

'When you give a luncheon or dinner, do not invite your friends, your brothers or relatives, or your rich neighbours; if you do, they may invite you back and so you will be repaid. But when you give a banquet, invite the poor, the crippled, the lame, the blind, and you will be blessed. Although they cannot repay you, you will be repaid at the resurrection of the righteous' (vv. 12-14).

Perhaps you are at the bottom of the social hierarchy and no one is interested in you. Perhaps you feel inferior because you have been poorly educated or have been the victim of racial prejudice. Perhaps you have financial or emotional difficulties or problems related to drink, drugs or sex and say, 'I am no use to anyone. God does not want a person like me.' You are wrong: you are just the kind of person Jesus came to seek.

It concerns me that the church today in Britain has become largely a middle-class phenomenon, for Jesus looked largely to the poor for his following. And if churches do not set out to attract the kind of people who gathered around him, there is something wrong. Indeed when revival comes, I will not be surprised if it bypasses all the respectable social structures of our age and attracts the poor and underprivileged.

Have you noticed that any new work of the Spirit often begins among the poor? You may recall that is the way in which Methodism began; that is the way in which my old denomination, the Nazarenes, sprang up in America and that is why God honoured the Salvation Army. But sadly, what often happens is that the next generation forgets the pit from which it was dug and tries to impress people. Do any of these movements preach with the same zeal for the unconverted today? We always seem to 'get above our raising', as we say in Kentucky and forget that God seeks to show kindness to the underdog.

How does God demonstrate his kindness? Well, he does it by the manner of his seeking and calling. He begins with a *general* call. Note the words 'Is there *anyone* still left? [my italics]'. This coheres with John 3:16, which says, 'For God so loved the world that he gave his one and only Son, that *whoever* believes in him shall not perish but have eternal life [my italics].'

However, Jesus said, 'Many are invited, but few are chosen' (Matt. 22:14). So the general call becomes a *specific* call. It begins with *whoever*, but then it is narrowed down to *those who are willing*. God says, 'Whoever is thirsty, let him come; and *whoever wishes*, let him take the free gift of the water of life [my italics]' (Rev. 22:17).

Maybe you ask, 'What about those people who are not poor and underprivileged; is there hope for them?' You will find the answer in the Bible, for when Paul wrote to the church at Corinth, he said:

> Brothers, think of what you were when you were called. Not many of you were wise by human standards; not many were influential; not many were of noble birth. But God chose the foolish things of the world to shame the wise; God chose the weak things of the world to shame the strong. He chose the lowly things of this world, the despised things – and the things that are not – to nullify the things that are (1 Cor. 1:26-28).

Note that Paul says that *not many* privileged people are called, implying that *some* are. But as far as the Bible is concerned, they are exceptions. However, if they repent and go to God empty-handed, pleading only the merit of Jesus' blood, he will save them.

Another thing you need to see about the manner of God's calling is, God saves sinners for the sake of the one he loves.

Remember David said, 'Is there anyone still left of the house of Saul to whom I may show kindness *for Jonathan's sake*? [my italics]'. The reason underlying his enquiry was that he wished to keep the covenant he had made with Jonathan. Let me remind you of this:

> [Jonathan said to David:] 'Do not ever cut off your kindness from my family – not even when the Lord has cut off every one of David's enemies from the face of the earth.'
>
> So Jonathan made a covenant with the house of David . . . . And Jonathan made David reaffirm his oath out of love for him, because he loved him as he loved himself (1 Sam. 20: 15-17).

So Mephibosheth sat at the king's table, knowing that David

was gracious to him for Jonathan's sake.

Jesus Christ is the Son of God. God confirmed their relationship to him at Jesus' baptism, when he said, 'This is my Son, whom I love; with him I am well pleased' (Matt. 3:17). But despite his love for his Son, God gave him up 'that whoever believes in him shall not perish but have eternal life.'

In fact, God made a covenant with his Son. These were the terms: Jesus would become our substitute and live a sinless life, keeping the whole law in thought, in word and deed, the Ten Commandments, the civil law, the moral law and the ceremonial law. Then he would die on the cross, and with his blood satisfy the justice of God. God then promised that whoever repented of their sins and owned Jesus as their Lord and Saviour would enter heaven. Jesus perfectly fulfilled the terms of the covenant and God keeps his promise.

Another thing I want to show you concerning the calling of God is, God seeks until he finds.

Remember, when David asked, 'Is there no-one still left of the house of Saul to whom I can show God's kindness?' no one had the slightest idea. So David must have ordered his servants to make a nationwide search. Eventually, Ziba a former servant of Saul came forward and said, 'There is still a son of Jonathan; he is crippled in both feet.'

'Where is he?' David asked.

'He is at the house of Makir son of Ammiel in Lo Debar,' Ziba replied.

Then David said, 'Well, go after him. Bring him to me.'

God seeks until he finds. How? He draws men and women to him by the power of the Holy Spirit. Jesus said, 'No-one can come to me unless the Father who sent me, draws him' (John 6:44). David invited Mephibosheth to come to him. But he could not walk; he had to be carried the fifty miles to David's court.

God invites you to come to him, but you cannot move of your own accord. You see, salvation is the work of the Holy Spirit; you can never take any credit for your conversion.

When Mephibosheth heard that the king had sent for him, he was terrified. The Bible says:

> When Mephibosheth son of Jonathan, the son of Saul, came to David, he bowed down to pay him honour (2 Sam. 9:6).

The Authorized Version of the Bible says that Mephibosheth 'fell on his face, and did reverence'.

When you first hear the gospel you may say, 'Well that was an interesting sermon; I'll give it some thought.' But you are not ready to accept salvation until you recognize that God is angry with your sin and if you died in your present state you would go the hell. Then filled with fear, you will cry, 'Is there *any* hope for me? Lord, save me!' That is the way the Holy Spirit leads us.

What did David do then?

> David said, 'Mephibosheth!'
>   'Your servant,' he replied.
>   'Don't be afraid,' David said to him . . .' (vv. 6-7).

In other words, the king put Mephibosheth's mind at ease. That is what God does when a sinner turns to him in repentance. No matter how great his sins, God freely forgives saying, 'Though your sins are like scarlet, they shall be as white as snow' (Isa. 1:18). God then gives two things to the underdog he has rescued.

First, he gives a promise. Read what David said to Mephibosheth:

> 'I will surely show you kindness for the sake of your father Jonathan. I will restore to you all the land that belonged to your grandfather Saul, and you will always eat at my table' (v. 7).

Mephibosheth did not expect this honour and did not deserve it; nevertheless, it was his from then on.

Second, God makes provision. David provided for Mephibosheth's needs. The Bible says:

> Then the king summoned Ziba, Saul's servant, and said to him, ' I have given your master's grandson everything that belonged to Saul and his family. You and your sons and your servants are to farm the land for him and bring in the crops, so that your master's grandson may be provided for. And Mephibosheth, grandson of your master, will always eat at my table' (vv. 9-10).

So Ziba, the servant, had care for Mephibosheth from then on.

When you become a Christian, God will take care of you. Jesus has promised that he will *never* desert you (Heb. 13:5), and Philippians 4:19 says, 'My God will meet all your needs according to his glorious riches in Christ Jesus.' By that, I do not mean that he will supply all your *wants*; for instance he may not give you designer clothes or a luxury car, but he will supply your *needs*, and you will know the joy of being in his presence.

The British sometimes say of a person, 'He was born to privilege.' And in the United Kingdom, if you are born to privilege, you are virtually assured of success.

Now I come from the hills of Kentucky. Do you know what our slogan was? 'Thank goodness for Arkansas!' You see, in the days when the USA had only forty-eight states Kentucky was almost at the bottom of the list as far as educational standards were concerned, but Arkansas was at the very bottom, and we loved them! You can tell from this how the rest of America feels about Kentucky.

However, I grew up knowing that even the Kentuckians looked down on me. You see, the Church of the Nazarenes was a very strict denomination and my parents would not allow me to go to the movies or to the dances at my high school. My fellow pupils mocked and called me a 'Noisyrene' or a 'Holy Roller'. But I developed a prayer life, and, even as a fifteen year old boy, I would pray for about two hours daily, because God made me see something that I want you to see: *I was born to privilege*. Peter put it like this: 'You are a chosen people, a royal priesthood, a holy nation, a people belonging to God, that you may declare the praises of him who called you out of darkness into his wonderful light' (1 Pet. 2:9). God gives his children dignity.

And for the first time in his life Mephibosheth was given dignity. What was his reaction to David's kindness? Look at verse 8:

> Mephibosheth bowed down and said, 'What is your servant that you should notice a dead dog like me?'

Mephibosheth was grateful.

God seeks to show his kindness to the 'dead dog' to those who know they have nothing to offer him in return for his favour, and he says, 'Come and dine at my table.' How can you thank him? By living the holy life into which he has called you (2 Tim. 1:9).

43

Rejecting Kindness – How Serious Is It?

2 Samuel 10

There comes a time when God's ministers must make the consequences of rejecting salvation clear. The Bible says, 'The soul that sinneth, it shall die' (Ezek. 18:4 AV). We should take this warning seriously, for none of us know how long we have left to live, and after we die it will be too late to repent. The Bible says, '*Now* is the time of God's favour, *now* is the day of salvation [my italics]' (2 Cor. 6:2).

We are looking at a period in David's life when he wanted to show kindness to others. In the previous chapter we saw his kindness to Mephibosheth. Now we see how he turned to the Ammonites, who were ancient enemies of Israel. This is what the Bible says:

> In the course of time, the king of the Ammonites died, and his son Hanun succeeded him as king. David thought, 'I will show kindness to Hanun son of Nahash, just as his father showed kindness to me.' So David sent a delegation to express his sympathy to Hanun concerning his father (2 Sam. 10:1-2).

David simply wanted to show the new king of the Ammonites that he cared.

We can sum up the gospel message in two words: *God cares*. In fact, he cares so much that he sent his Son into the world to die on a cross for our sins so those who believe may have eternal life (see John 3:16).

What was Hanun's initial reaction to David's kindness? Sadly, we will never know, for before he got a chance to say what he thought, the princes of Ammon intervened, afraid that he would be touched by David's sympathy. This was what they said:

> 'Do you think David is honouring your father by sending men to you to express sympathy? Hasn't David sent them to you to explore the city and spy it out and overthrow it?' (v. 3).

Swayed by this argument, Hanun rejected David's kindness. This was very sad, because I have a feeling that, initially, the king may have been moved by the message of condolence, but he did not get a chance to say so.

Sometimes when someone is listening to the gospel in church, an unconverted friend sitting beside him will think, 'I hope so-and-so is not taking this in.' So he will nudge his companion and whisper, 'You don't *believe* this rubbish, do you?' Not wanting to admit he feels moved, the other will reply, 'No, of course not.' Sadly, it is not only teenagers who give in to peer pressure; it can happen at any age.

Let us look more closely at the way in which the Ammonites rejected David's kindness.

First, we see the princes of Ammon distorted the truth. Remember, they said, 'Do you think David is honouring your father by sending men to you to express sympathy? Hasn't David sent them to you to explore the city and spy it out and overthrow it?' Thus they succeeded in making Hanun suspicious.

Satan always tries to fuel our suspicions. In fact, he tries to get in at the earliest possible moment. You will recall that almost immediately after Jesus was born, King Herod tried to kill him (see Matt. 2). And when the devil sees a work of the Holy Spirit beginning in your heart, he will step in and try to blind you to the truth.

You may ask, 'What is it that he doesn't want me to see?' Well, the devil wants to keep three things hidden from you.

The first thing Satan tries to hide from you is *Jesus' great compassion*. Most people react to our weaknesses by moralizing. (Sadly, Christians often forget the pit from which they were dug and are among the worst offenders. So fix your eyes on Jesus alone.) The writer to the Hebrews reminds us that Jesus knows what it is like to be tested. He put it like this: 'We do not have a high priest who is unable to sympathise with our weaknesses, but we have one who has been tempted in every way, just as we are – yet was without sin' (Heb. 4:15).

We all have failings. Perhaps you have an emotional weakness: maybe you cry easily or are over-sensitive; maybe you are quick to lose your temper; maybe you have a sexual weakness and people are put off by your sexual proclivity. But no matter what your problems are, Jesus says, 'I understand and I care.' Satan does not want you to believe that.

The second thing Satan tries to hide from you is that you can have *the comfort of knowing that God has forgiven all your sins.* We are all sinners (Rom. 3:23). You do not have to commit a serious sin like adultery or murder to be a sinner. Sin is lust, sin is hate, sin is greed. Do you know how many sins it takes to keep you out of heaven? *One.* One sin will ruin your hope of eternal life. But in his kindness God says, 'I will wash your sins away completely and forget about them' (Isa. 1:18; Jer. 31:34).

The next thing Satan tries to hide from you is that *Jesus Christ was your substitute.* He did everything for you that you could not do for yourself. He lived a sinless life (2 Cor. 5:21; Heb. 4:15), paid your debt on the cross and satisfied God's justice. And when you put your trust in his Son, God says, 'I will not judge you by your deeds, but by his.' That is sheer kindness.

Next we see that the Ammonites looked at David's message with hatred and expressed it by humiliating his messengers. The Bible says:

> So Hanun seized David's men, shaved off half of each man's beard, cut off their garments in the middle at the buttocks, and sent them away' (v. 4).

The Ammonites knew that the Israelites wore their long robes with dignity and the Levitical Law forbade men to clip the edges of their beards (see Lev. 19:27), so the indignities they inflicted on David's messengers were designed to show their contempt not only for them but also for God himself.

News of what had happened soon reached David:

> When David was told about this, he sent messengers to meet the men, for they were greatly humiliated. The king said, 'Stay at Jericho till your beards have grown, and then come back' (v. 5).

David ensured his messengers would be spared further humiliation.

Christians are human and when people insult us, we feel wounded. I speak from experience. It is hurtful when someone comes to me in the vestry of Westminster Chapel and is spiteful. It is hurtful when we go onto the streets to witness and people swear at us. However, we know that they are not directing their anger at us personally but at God. He has a way of preserving his servants.

How did David react when he heard how the Ammonites rejected his kindness and abused his servants? Well, he had to pass judgment. I want to show you *how* he did this, for it illustrates the way in which God judges those who reject his kindness.

First, we see David made a silent judgment. The Ammonites were unaware of what David was thinking when he heard that they had rejected his kindness. Moreover, they suffered no pangs of conscience.

Those who reject the gospel feel equally untroubled. They hear no crash of thunder to strike terror into their hearts as they walk out of church: they feel nothing. And for the moment, God keeps his thoughts to himself.

We also see David made a suspended judgment. David decided to wait before taking action, giving the Ammonites time to repent.

God waits, and, in his kindness, he often gives sinners more than one opportunity to respond to the gospel. But those who hear God speak once should not take for granted that they will hear him again. The Bible says, 'Today, if you hear his voice, do not harden your hearts' (Heb. 3:7–8). '*Now* is the time of God's favour, *now* is the day of salvation [my italics]' (2 Cor. 6:2).

Next, we see David made a strategic judgment. David decided to wait and see what else the Ammonites might do.

What did the Ammonites do? Verse 6 tells us they suddenly realized the enormity of the insult they had offered David. The writer of 2 Samuel put it like this:

> . . . the Ammonites realised that they had become an offence to David's nostrils . . . .

In other words, they thought, 'What have we done!' What a pity they did not think along these lines sooner. However, they showed no sign of remorse. Instead, they dug their heels in. Moreover, they turned to other nations for support. Let us look at the whole of verse 6:

> When the Ammonites realised that they had become an offence to David's nostrils, they hired twenty thousand Aramean foot soldiers from Beth Rehob and Zobah, as well as the king of Maacah with a thousand men, and also twelve thousand men from Tob.

People seek outside help for one reason: they are insecure. What the Ammonites *ought* to have done was apologize to David. If they had gone to him on bended knee and said, 'We are truly sorry', I am sure that David would have said, 'I forgive you.' However, they chose to make things worse for themselves.

If you are unconverted, God waits to see what you will do when you suddenly realize you are a sinner and have angered him. Perhaps you too will dig your heels in and make your situation worse by enlisting others to support you in some kind of campaign of hatred towards him. However, if you are wise, you will thank him for his forbearance and seek his forgiveness.

At this point I want to make these observations:

• Those who reject God's kindness, do so to their shame.

• Those who reject his kindness, do so at their peril. It is foolish to fight God. You may think God is very angry when you shake your fist at him, but God does not lose his temper. Remember, time is on his side.

• Those who reject the gospel will never know the benefits that could have been theirs. Sadly, the Ammonites would never know the advantages of aligning themselves with the people of God. Moreover, they would never know the security of having God himself on their side.

What was David's reaction to the Ammonites defiance? Well, he told his people to prepare for battle. We read:

> On hearing this, David sent Joab out with the entire army of fighting men. . . . Joab saw that there were battle lines in front of him and behind him; so he selected some of the best troops in Israel and deployed them against the Arameans. He put the rest of the men under the command of Abishai his brother and deployed them against the Ammonites (vv. 7, 9–10).

Tertullian, one of the early church fathers, once said, 'The blood of the martyrs is the seed of the church.' Persecution has never wiped out God's people, and the Israelites did not panic when they learnt that massive enemy forces were uniting against them; instead they took heart from their commander's faith in a just and righteous God, for Joab had encouraged them like this:

'Be strong and let us fight bravely for our people and the cities of our God. The Lord will do what is good in his sight' (v. 12).

Joab had not always been a good role model, but God had severely disciplined him and he had changed (see 2 Sam. 3:22–39).

Maybe you have not been a model Christian, but God has disciplined you and brought you to the place where you can encourage your fellow Christians and say, 'Be strong . . . . The Lord will do what is good in his sight.'

Trusting in this sovereign God, the Israelites prepared to attack. The Bible says:

Then Joab and the troops with him advanced to fight the Arameans, and they fled before him. When the Ammonites saw that the Arameans were fleeing, they fled before Abishai and went inside the city. So Joab returned from fighting the Ammonites and came to Jerusalem (vv. 13–14).

God came to Israel's rescue and their enemies were scattered. *No one* can fight God and win.

Finally, we see David made a *solemn* judgment. The enemy regrouped and David himself became involved. We read:

When David was told of this, he gathered all Israel, crossed the Jordan and went to Helam. The Arameans formed their battle lines to meet David and fought against him. But they fled before Israel . . . . When all the kings who were vassals of Hadadezer saw that they had been defeated by Israel, they made peace with the Israelites and became subject to them (vv. 17–19).

This is an illustration of how it will be on the last day. Now, Jesus sends his servants to do the work, but eventually he himself will return to the earth and become involved. In Revelation 1:7 John said:

> Look, he is coming with the clouds,
>   and every eye will see him,
> even those who pierced him;
>   and all the peoples of the earth will
>   mourn because of him.

Too late, people will bitterly regret rejecting God's kindness and will face a solemn judgment.

44

Watergate 1000 BC

2 Samuel 11

One day a man who had everything got up from an afternoon nap, walked out on the balcony of his luxurious home, and happened to notice a beautiful woman washing herself in her own courtyard nearby. Although this man had a number of wives and concubines to satisfy his sexual needs, this particular woman's physical appearance seized him like he had never been seized before. He felt he had to have her, no matter the cost. Lust and passion consumed him.

These words refer to David, the man after God's own heart. He was a man who knew God better than most people of his day, a man who was the object of God's singular mercy. David was sitting on top of the world.

Yet, in this case the sin of adultery became compounded with the sin of murder. David had sufficient warnings not to commit this sin. For one thing David knew that the word of God forbad adultery. David also should have respected Uriah's devotion to him. But he disregarded God's law, he disregarded Uriah's loyalty, he disregarded Uriah's feelings, and perhaps he disregarded Bathsheba's feelings.

David had a plan. He tried to cover the sin by arranging for Uriah to sleep with his wife. But Uriah had a scrupulous conscience and he couldn't bring himself to have a holiday with his wife when Joab and all his fellow soldiers were in the heat of the battle (2 Sam. 11:6-12). Then David adopts plan B which involved him arranging for Uriah to get drunk, figuring that with a little drink in him Uriah will forget about his fellow soldiers and will spend time with his wife. But this plan does not work either (v. 13), so David comes up with plan C. Joab is told to put Uriah right in the hottest part of the battle and then back off from him so that he may die (vv. 14-17). It is awful what a person will do to cover up sin.

In this chapter I want to discuss David's temptation. Sin is never committed without temptation preceding it. There is an important difference between temptation and sin. Although some feel guilty because of their temptations, it is not a sin to be tempted. What then can be said about David's temptation?

First, I would have to call it a *providential temptation*. What I mean is that circumstances so easily fall into place. I am not referring here to the providence of God, but to providential aspects of situations which appear to encourage particular responses. With regard to David and Bathsheba I will mention two aspects.

First, David happened to notice her. If she had taken her bath half an hour earlier, when he was still asleep, he would not have seen her. Many times I have counselled individuals who have fallen into sin and often they imagined that circumstances indicated their actions were correct. Things fell into place and coalesced in such a way that they thought God was behind it. When Eve in the garden of Eden partook of the forbidden fruit, she did so because it was pleasant to her sight. It seemed so appropriate to eat it.

The second providence was that her husband happened to be away from home for a few months. David knew how long Uriah would be at the battlefront. I suppose Bathsheba could justify it by saying she was lonely. Perhaps she was flattered that the king would want her, or perhaps she rationalized it by saying it would be wrong to refuse him.

Not only was the situation a providential temptation, it was also a *provocative* temptation. The temptation occurred when David saw a beautiful woman washing herself. It was both a sensual temptation and a sudden temptation. The sight of her was provocative to David and it could be that Bathsheba knew exactly what she was doing when she chose to bathe in view of where the king might see her.

Thirdly, it was also a *physical* temptation. Sex is a physical need. It is so easy to rationalize about our physical needs. Eve saw that the fruit was good to eat, and since God had made her with an appetite, it would not be wrong to eat the fruit. In the same way people today rationalize adultery.

Fourthly, it was a *permitted* temptation. God let it happen. While I am not glad that David fell into sin, I am so glad it is recorded in scripture. I am sure God wanted us to see that it was a man after God's own heart that fell into this kind of sin. The account is recorded as an example to us to remember that when David fell, God did not give him any special privilege. David had to suffer. Remember this, God is no respecter of persons.

But the fact that it was permitted by God does not mean that it was caused by God. James reminds us, 'Let no man say, when he is tempted, I am tempted of God.' There is a real danger of some believers assuming that, because they have asked God to guide their lives, certain temptations indicate what God wants them to do. God never tempts anyone to do a wrong action. Rather, temptation comes from our own inner evil desires.

Fifthly, this temptation was a *preventable* temptation. If David, as the leader of his people, had been where he should have been, at the battle, then this temptation would not have occurred. Because David chose to stay at home in his palace, he started off the chain of events which resulted in this temptation. Instead of fighting he became idle. One of the most effective ways to avoid succumbing to temptation is to be involved in obeying the Lord's commands, particularly those that involve witnessing for him. When we have that kind of commitment to the Lord, we are less likely to fall into temptation.

Sixthly, David's temptation was a *perilous* temptation. There is nothing so scandalous as sexual sin. I am named after Dr. R.T. Williams, a general superintendent in the Church of the Nazarene. When R.T. Williams would ordain young men into the ministry, he used to warn them of two dangers in the ministry – women and money. We know that the media has had a field day with the sex scandals involving some TV evangelists in America.

Yet God's grace shines through despite David's fall. In Matthew 1:6, the text says this: 'David was the father of Solomon, whose mother had been Uriah's wife.' This is how God dealt with it all. It was through Bathsheba that the Messiah was born. God can take the worst kind of sin and the greatest possible scandal and the most wicked kind of cover-up and bring about his purpose. That may encourage any readers who may be in deep sin and who think there is no way out.

The cover-up brought David down. It was Watergate 1000 BC. Yet all things work together for good to them that love God, to them who are the called according to his purpose.

45

Proof That You Are a Christian (Part One)

2 Samuel 12:1–24

Are you a Christian? This question is important, for no one should simply assume that he is. Millions mistakenly believe they are going to heaven because of their good deeds or because they were brought up in a Christian home or because they go to church and have been baptized. Sadly, these people have been deceived, and if they die in this condition they will go to hell.

There is a verse in the Old Testament that says, 'You may be sure that your sin will find you out' (Num. 32:23). This means that if you have ever committed a sin it is only a matter of time before it will be exposed. Now if you are a Christian, God will confront you with your sin in *this* life, while there is still time to repent. However, if you die unconverted, he will expose your sin at the final judgment, but then it will be too late. Never think that you can get right with God *after* you die; this is one of the devil's lies.

The question is, how long does it take you to realize that you have sinned? I think a measure of our spirituality is the speed at which we see that we have grieved God and come to repentance. Some of us take years to get to this point, some take weeks, but some take only seconds. If we can reduce the interval to seconds, we can often check ourselves and avoid grieving the Holy Spirit.

In Chapter 1 we saw that after King David committed adultery with Bathsheba and made her pregnant he murdered her husband Uriah in a desperate attempt to cover it up. The way was then clear for David to marry her. The Bible says:

When Uriah's wife heard that her husband was dead, she mourned for him. After the time of mourning was over, David had her brought to his house, and she became his wife and bore him a son (2 Sam. 11:26–27).

But verse 27 ends on a disquieting note, for it says:

The thing David had done displeased the Lord.

However, David felt no remorse. He was unaware of God's anger; he felt nothing: no thunderbolt came from heaven to strike fear into his heart. This is an example of the silent anger of the Lord.

In fact, two years went by before David realized that he had grieved the Holy Spirit, and even then God had to send the prophet Nathan to confront him with his sin (2 Sam. 12:1).

Now you may say, 'I can't understand why it took David two years to see that he had sinned. Surely, he would have realized it straightaway! After all, he knew the Law and the Ten Commandments backwards.' Well, it was because the most blatant sin is often the most blinding. You see, the conscious mind has a defence mechanism that screens out information that it would find too painful to deal with. Psychologists call this 'repression'. David repressed his guilt then, although his sin was obvious to everyone else.

We are all sinners (Rom. 3:23). As Isaiah said, 'We all, like sheep, have gone astray; each of us has turned to his own way' (Isa. 53:6). However, we need someone else to help us see this. The Bible says, 'God was pleased through the foolishness of what was preached to save those who believe' (1 Cor. 1:21). Now you may say, 'But how do I know that I can trust the preacher? How can I be certain that his message comes from God?' Well, let us look at Nathan, for he was a true man of God.

First, Nathan shows us that a true man of God is a person who is objective and will confront people with their sin. You may remember that David once told Nathan, 'I want to build a temple for the Lord' and Nathan replied, 'I like that idea. Go ahead. The Lord is with you.' But that night God came to him and said, 'You were wrong. You must return to the king and tell him that he is *not* to build a temple for me.' Nathan obeyed without hesitation, showing that he was governed by a concern to do God's will and not by his friendship for David (see 2 Sam. 7:1-17). Now, Nathan obeyed God by confronting David with his sin.

Second, Nathan shows us that a true man of God is concerned with God's honour and glory. Read what Nathan said to David in verse 14:

'By doing this you have made the enemies of the Lord show utter contempt.'

Nathan was grieved that even God's enemies had heard what the king had done and had scoffed about it.

When God's people fall into sin, the world loves it, for then it has an opportunity to show its contempt for God. This was what happened in the United States during the 1980s, when certain TV evangelists let God down by their promiscuity and their greed. Then the media had a field day.

Third, Nathan shows us that a true man of God is a person who *applies* God's word. The prophet began by telling this parable, and then he applied it to David:

'There were two men in a certain town, one rich and the other poor. The rich man had a very large number of sheep and cattle, but the poor man had nothing except one little ewe lamb that he had bought. He raised it, and it grew up with him and his children. It shared his food, drank from his cup and even slept in his arms. It was like a daughter to him.

'Now a traveller came to the rich man, but the rich man refrained from taking one of his own sheep or cattle to prepare a meal for the traveller who had come to him. Instead, he took the ewe lamb that belonged to the poor man and prepared it for the one who had come to him.'

David burned with anger against the man and said to Nathan, 'As surely as the Lord lives, the man who did this deserves to die! He must pay for that lamb four times over, because he did such a thing and had no pity.'

Then Nathan said to David, 'You are the man!' (vv. 1-7).

A true man of God will tell you that if you think you will go to heaven because you go to church and have been baptized or because you lead a moral life and do good, you are *not* a Christian and, if you die in your present condition, you will go to hell. He will tell you that a Christian is a person who knows that he has no righteousness of his own and accepts what Jesus has done for him on the cross.

The chief aim of Nathan's parable was to expose David's sin. He knew that this would be easier if he could make David stand back and think objectively. So he told the story of a rich man who abused a poor man to arouse David's sympathy and sense of justice. He succeeded in this, for you will recall that the Bible says: 'David burned with anger against the man and said to Nathan, "As surely as the Lord lives, the man who did this deserves to die!"' Yet it was not until the prophet said 'You are the man!' that David realized the story was a parable and *he* was the rich man.

This amazes me. I would have thought that as David listened the terrible truth would have sunk in. However, he was oblivious to his sin because at the heart of his problem was his self-righteousness.

It is easy to condemn him and say smugly, '*I* would never commit adultery or murder someone like David did.' But that was exactly how *he* reacted to Nathan's parable. He thought, 'How terrible! Fancy that rich man taking away the thing the poor man loved the most! How could anyone do a thing like that!' But the prophet exposed David's self-righteous heart.

I think David's reaction to Nathan's parable teaches us three things about those who are self-righteous.

(1) *Self-righteous people are judgmental.* David condemned the rich man in the parable. We must not point the finger at others, for Jesus said, 'Do not judge, or you too will be judged' (Matt. 7:1).

(2) *Those who are self-righteous are quick to spot sin in others but often fail to detect their own sin.* Self-righteousness blinds us to the truth about ourselves, making it easy for us to judge others. David saw the rich man's sin but did not see his own. However, the Bible says that we are *all* sinners (Rom. 3:23). Not many of us have committed murder and adultery perhaps, but we need the blood of Christ to be applied to our hearts as much as those who have.

(3) *Self-righteous people are unforgiving.* David said the rich man deserved to die. Do you have trouble forgiving others? Perhaps someone has hurt you and you are bitter. But if you do not forgive that person, then, in God's eyes, your sin is as great as his. Since God totally forgives those who repent, should you not show your gratitude to him by forgiving the person who has hurt you?

When Nathan said 'You are the man!' David faced certain indisputable facts:

Fact One: *God had been good to him.* Look at 2 Samuel 12:7-8:

> Then Nathan said to David, 'This is what the Lord, the God of Israel, says: "I anointed you king over Israel, and I delivered you from the hand of Saul. I gave your master's house to you, and your master's wives into your arms. I gave you the house of Israel and Judah. And if all this had been too little, I would have given you even more."'

God had been *very* kind to David, but when Nathan reminded him of it, he felt extremely uncomfortable.

I sense that whenever I say to someone 'God has been good to you', he resents it. However, one thing that will make hell *hell* is that people there will remember God's goodness to them and eternally regret that they refused to acknowledge it in their lifetime.

Fact Two: *He had grieved a holy God.* Read verse 9:

> 'Why did you despise the word of the Lord by doing what is evil in his eyes?'

You need to come to terms with the fact that God is angry with your sin. The Bible tells us that God *hates* sin (Hab. 1:13; Zech. 8:16-17). I do not have the vocabulary to convey to you how much God loathes evil; only the Holy Spirit can do this.

Fact Three: *His sin was exposed.* Read what Nathan said to him in verse 9:

> 'You struck down Uriah the Hittite with the sword . . . '.

As I said earlier, we are all sinners and it is only a matter of time before we are found out (Num. 32:23).

Fact Four: *He had used Bathsheba for his own gratification.* Let us read the remainder of verse 9:

> '. . . and took his wife to be your own.'

If you are having an affair or living with someone to whom you are not married, you may say, 'It is all right; we are in love.' It is *not* love. If you really cared about the other person, you would not use him or her in this way.

Fact Five: *He had brought dishonour upon God's name.* Nathan said:

> 'By doing this you have made the enemies of the Lord show utter contempt . . . ' (v. 14).

You see, what makes sin so bad is what it does to God.

Now if God chastens you for your wrongdoing, it is a good sign, for it *proves* that you are a Christian. Hebrews 12:6 says, 'The Lord disciplines *those he loves, and he punishes everyone he accepts as a son* [my italics].'

I remember when our son T.R. was about four years old, he cut down a tree in our front garden and we had to punish him. 'Why didn't you punish Billy? He helped me.' he said.

'Well, he is not our child, but *you* are,' we replied.

Because David was *his* child, God would not let him get away with his sin, and now Nathan delivered God's judgment, saying:

'Now, therefore, the sword shall never depart from your house . . . ' (v. 10).

Are you a child of God? You can find out, for the proofs you need are here:

- A Christian is a person who has listened to God's minister, who out of concern for God's honour, applied God's word to his situation.

- A Christian is a person who knows that God is holy and sees sin as vile (Hab. 1:13).

- A Christian is a person who sees that pride, lust, greed, envy, hate and unbelief are sin. He knows that the Ten Commandments are right and outline the way in which the people of God are to live their lives (see Exod. 20 1-17).

- A Christian is a person who knows that *he* is a sinner (Rom. 3:23).

- A Christian is a person who is sorry for grieving God. Note, however, if someone confesses his sin but does not change his ways, his repentance was not real. In fact, he is abusing the teaching of 1 John 1:9, which says, 'If we confess our sins, [God] is faithful and just and will forgive us our sins and purify us from all unrighteousness.' When a person is sincere in his repentance, his life will change.

- A Christian is a person who recognizes that he cannot save himself by his good works or by going to church or being baptized. Nathan told David, '*The Lord* has taken away your sin [my italics]', and the Christian accepts that only Jesus Christ, the God-man, can take away *his* sin and it is his blood alone that satisfies God's justice.

- A Christian is a person who has confessed his sin and has received God's pardon.

- A Christian is a person who, if he falls into sin, will come to terms with his or her sin in their lifetime, as David did.

46

Proof That You Are a Christian (Part Two)

2 Samuel 12:1-24

In the previous chapter we saw that one proof that you are a Christian is that you cannot get away with sin. Hebrews 12:6 says, 'The Lord disciplines those whom he loves, and he punishes everyone he accepts as a son.' So if you are a child of God, as surely as night follows day, he will discipline you. In this chapter I want to expand this theme and show you that another proof you are converted is that you accept God's chastening with dignity.

God has three methods of disciplining his children.

First, God speaks through his word and to your heart. We sometimes call this *internal chastening*. This is the least painful way of getting right with him.

However, if you refuse to listen, God tries to reach you through *external chastening*. Then, he uses adverse circumstances, a financial reverse or an illness perhaps, to get your attention. He can be very severe, and while it is happening you may be unable to think clearly or see any end to your troubles. Jonah experienced this kind of chastening when he refused to go to Nineveh and was swallowed by a great fish (Jonah 1).

If external chastening does not work, God uses *terminal chastening*. Terminal chastening is very sad, for it means that he will deal with your sin at the final judgment.

Those who are wise listen to God the *first* time he speaks. Had David done this, he would not have committed adultery and murder and he would not have had to endure God's chastening.

However, two years passed and still the king showed no sign of repentance, so God sent Nathan to confront him. After exposing David's sin, the prophet delivered God's judgment, saying:

'Now, therefore, the sword shall never depart from your house, because you despised me and took the wife of Uriah the Hittite to be your own.

'This is what the Lord says: "Out of your own household I am going to bring calamity upon you. . . . You did it in secret, but I will do this thing in broad daylight before all Israel"' (2 Sam. 12:10-12).

What an awful prospect!

Then Nathan gave David some good news and more bad news. Let us consider the good news first.

David listened with growing horror as the truth came home and he realized how deeply he had offended God. Read verse 13:

Then David said to Nathan. 'I have sinned against the Lord.'

Nathan replied, 'The Lord has taken away your sin. You are not going to die.'

Once David owned his guilt and repented, God forgave him.

Now you cannot solve the problem of your guilt by saying, 'I will try harder and live a better life'; you must stand back and let God deal with your sin in *his* way. He sent his Son into the world to take away your sin and shame. Jesus lived a perfect life and died, still sinless, on the cross. He was your substitute. He paid your debt in full, and all that he did on the cross is yours through faith (2 Cor. 5:21; Rom. 3:22-26).

It is wonderful to know that you are forgiven, and the news that God had forgiven him was music to David's ears.

However, you will recall I said that Nathan gave David more bad news. Read what the prophet had to say in verse 14:

'But because by doing this you have made the enemies of the Lord show utter contempt, the son born to you will die.'

David hoped that Nathan had somehow misunderstood what God had said, but the prophet was not mistaken. The Bible says:

> After Nathan had gone home, the Lord struck the child that Uriah's wife had borne to David, and he became ill. David pleaded with God for the child. He fasted and went into his house and spent the nights lying on the ground. The elders of his household stood beside him to get him up from the ground, but he refused, and he would not eat any food with them.
> On the seventh day the child died (vv. 15-18).

Now proof that you are a Christian is that you accept the consequences of your sin and continue to serve the Lord, even if it causes great hardship. For example, if you have committed a crime, you should confess it to the police. I remember that some years ago a member of the IRA who was converted at Westminster Chapel turned himself in, although he knew he would face a long jail sentence. He accepted his punishment with dignity and went on serving the Lord behind prison walls in Belfast.

Did David accept God's judgment with dignity? Well, the way in which he reacted to the news of his child's death may surprise you. This was what happened:

> David noticed that his servants were whispering among themselves and he realised that the child was dead. 'Is the child dead?' he asked.
> 'Yes,' they replied, 'he is dead.'
> Then David got up from the ground. After he had washed, put on lotions and changed his clothes, he went into the house of the Lord and worshipped. Then he went to his own house, and at his request they served him food, and he ate.
> His servants asked him, 'Why are you acting in this way?

While the child was alive, you fasted and wept, but now that the child is dead, you get up and eat!'

He answered, 'While the child was still alive, I fasted and wept. I thought, "Who knows? The Lord may be gracious to me and let the child live." But now that he is dead, why should I fast? Can I bring him back again? I will go to him, but he will not return to me' (vv. 19-23).

I think that verse 20, which says, 'He went into the house of the Lord and worshipped', is one of the loveliest texts in the Old Testament. Here is further proof that David was truly a child of God, for he worshipped, even though God was disciplining him.

In an earlier chapter I told you how my friend Arthur Blessitt carries a cross around the world as a witness. As you might expect, he has many interesting stories to tell about his experiences. This is one of my favourites. He said:

'I was walking through Northern Israel, and one night I had nowhere to sleep. I came to a bus stop and saw it had a bench. "I'll have to sleep here," I thought. But as it was cold and pouring with rain, I did not relish the prospect. So I looked at the rain and said, "In the name of Jesus, stop!" What do you suppose happened? No. It *didn't* stop. In fact, the rain lashed down three times harder than before! Nevertheless, I said, "Lord, I *love* you."'

When a person worships God no matter what his circumstances are, he has true faith.

What was the essence of David's chastening?

Well, first, we see that there was *exposure*. God said:

'You did it in secret, but I will do this thing in broad daylight before all Israel' (v. 12).

David *thought* that he had covered his tracks well, but he was found out.

Perhaps you have sinned, but you feel pleased because no one knows what you have done. Do not congratulate yourself on this, for it may mean that God will expose your sin at the final judgment. It is far better if he deals with your sin in this life, for it proves that you are his child.

Incidentally, if God had not dealt with David then, it would have sent a signal to all those who live in sin that said, 'Don't worry; it's all right. Anything goes.' Sadly, this is the signal that is broadcast by the media, by parliament and by people in high places today.

Next, we see that there was *equality*. David was a king and a man after God's own heart, but God treated him in the same way he would have treated anyone else. So if you think that, because you have had a special relationship with the Lord over the years, he will not expose your sin, you are mistaken.

Third, we see that there was *expectancy*. Usually, we use this word in the sense that we expect something good will happen. But here I use the word to mean the opposite, for both in the short term and in the long term the outlook for David was unpleasant: his child would soon die and there would be never-ending violence and strife within his family.

I think 'the sword shall never depart from your house' is one of the most disquieting sentences in the Bible. What did David have to look forward to now? Perhaps he exclaimed, 'I would rather *die* than to have to live for the next twenty years with this hanging over me!' This is not recorded in the Bible; nevertheless, I have a feeling that he *did* say something like this because Nathan said, 'You will *not* die [my italics].'

You may wonder why God let David go on living. Well, I believe he did so because he wanted him to be an example to others. Perhaps you have done terrible things and are so ashamed that you wish you were dead. But God wants you to *live*. He has a task for you and says, 'I will put people in your path who have done dreadful things and want to die of shame too. I want you to slip alongside them and say, "I understand because I have been through this myself. Let me help you."'

I promise you on the authority of God's word that, however serious your sin, if you honour what Jesus did for you on the cross you will discover there *is* a life to be lived (see John 10:10). God restored his Holy Spirit to David and continued to use him in his service. In fact, David wrote some of his greatest psalms at this time, and he continued to win victories over God's enemies (see 2 Sam. 12:26-31).

Maybe you say, 'I have let someone down badly, but they know nothing about it. Should I tell them what I have done?' The answer is 'No'. Let me explain. When David pleaded with God for forgiveness he said, 'Against you, you only, have I sinned' (Ps. 51:4). Of course, he had sinned against Bathsheba and Uriah and against other people too, but *God* was the one whom he had hurt the most. Tell *him* that you are sorry; you do not have to confess your sin to anyone else. In fact, speaking from many years of pastoral experience, I have found that those who thought they had to tell all have put themselves (and others) through an unnecessary ordeal and have lived to regret it.

David accepted God's judgment and God gave him courage to face the future with dignity. And if *you* seek his forgiveness and accept the consequences of your sin, God will do the same for you.

47

The Returning Backslider

2 Samuel 12

All of us need something to look forward to; this is the way God made us, but some feel they have nothing to hope for in this life or in the next. What should we do when our situation seems hopeless and we know that we are to blame? Well, I think we can find the answer to this question by studying the story of David in 2 Samuel 12.

One day David would go to heaven, but it seemed that he faced a bleak future on earth. You will recall that he had committed adultery and murder and, as a result, God sent the prophet Nathan to him to confront him with his sin and said:

> 'Now, therefore, the sword shall never depart from your house, because you despised me and took the wife of Uriah the Hittite to be your own' (2 Sam. 12:10).

David felt the anger of God's rod and knew that for the rest of his life he could expect constant trouble in his family and in his kingdom. Maybe he thought, 'I'd rather be dead than face *this!*'

To his credit, David acknowledged his sin immediately and heard Nathan say, 'The Lord has taken away your sin' (v. 13), but God had not finished dealing with David, and Nathan continued:

> 'Because by doing this you have made the enemies of the Lord show utter contempt, the son born to you will die' (v. 14).

Then the prophet left, his mission over.

It was not long before this prophecy was fulfilled, for the Bible says:

> After Nathan had gone home, the Lord struck the child that Uriah's wife had borne to David, and he became ill. . . .
> On the seventh day the child died (vv. 15, 18).

Never think that the death of a baby is owing to someone's sin, but there is no doubt that, in this case, David lost the child as a consequence of his wrongdoing.

Now some would say, 'A true Christian would not sin as seriously as David did.' They are wrong. (However, you should *not* regard this as a licence to sin. In fact, I hope that it will be the *last* thing you will want to do when you see how much David had to suffer as a result of *his* wrongdoing.) David had committed serious sins; nevertheless, God, who sees the end from the beginning, said that he was a man after his own heart (1 Sam. 13:14; Acts 13:22). This proves two things: (1) David was a child of God, and (2) a child of God can make a mess of his life.

I am reminded of a sermon that I heard when I was a student at Trevecca College called 'Don't Miss God's Best for You.' It was the worst sermon that I have ever heard. You see, we have *all* missed 'God's best'. 'God's best' was ruined when Adam and Eve sinned in the Garden of Eden (see Gen. 3). This act resulted in the downfall of the entire human race, and since then all have sinned (Rom. 3:10, 23).

Some sins are undoubtedly worse than others, but you should remember, if you have not sinned as seriously as someone who has really 'gone over the top', it is not because you are any better but because God's restraining grace has prevented you from doing so.

Now the devil loves to come alongside a sinner and say, 'What you have done is so bad that it is pointless for you to think that you can get right with God. He is so angry that he will never have anything to do with you again.' If Satan has said this to you, do not listen; remember, he is a liar (see John 8:44).

In fact, if God has exposed your wrongdoing and made you aware of his displeasure, it is because he loves you and he wants you to know how he feels about sin. Why did he bother to show David what he thought about his sin? It was because he loved him. You see, if you do not care about someone, you do not bother explaining *why* you are angry; you show your contempt by avoiding them. God's anger is a sign of his love.

However, God's chastening can be hard to bear. My heart goes out to David because he had seen days of glory, yet now Nathan seemed to be saying, 'Those days are over.' And on top of that the prophet told him he would lose his child.

David's reaction to the news that his son had become ill almost moves me to tears:

> David pleaded with God for the child. He fasted and went into his house and spent the nights lying on the ground. The elders of his household stood beside him to get him up from the ground, but he refused, and he would not eat any food with them (2 Sam. 12:16–17).

But God did not change his mind and the child died.

However, then David did something wonderful. Read verse 20:

> Then David got up from the ground. After he had washed, put on lotions and changed his clothes, he went into the house of the Lord and worshipped.

This was David's way of saying 'Lord, I love you. You have no reason to love me, but I love you.'

Another thing this story teaches us is how gracious God is to repentant sinners.

Now the purpose of God's chastening is *not* to get even with the one who has offended him. According to the Mosaic Law David deserved the death penalty, for Leviticus 20:10 says: 'If a man commits adultery with another man's wife – with the wife of his neighbour – both the adulterer and the adulteress must be put to death.' But God did not treat David according to the law; he sent Nathan to him to say, 'The Lord has taken away your sin. You are not going to die.' This was why David could write with such feeling in Psalm 103: '[God] does not treat us as our sins deserve or repay us according to our iniquities.'

In fact, God wants to *restore* the backslider. This was what he did when David 'went into the house of the Lord and worshipped'. You may ask, 'How do you *know* what happened then?' Well, David himself tells us in Psalm 51, where he poured out his heart to God in contrition.

Perhaps you have let God down badly and the best news that you could ever hear would be that you belong to him. Well, you can find out whether you are a Christian, for Psalm 51 reveals how a child of God reacts after his sin has been brought home. So let us see what David did.

The first thing David did was to beg God for mercy:

'Have mercy upon me, O God,
    according to your unfailing love;
according to your great compassion . . . (Ps. 51:1).

David knew that what he had done was wrong and he was without excuse. He knew that he could not blame Bathsheba or his parents or the society in which he lived for what he had done. He knew that he could not blame a mid-life crisis and say, 'I simply needed to know that, despite my advancing years, I am still attractive to the opposite sex. God understands that.' He did not try to justify himself: he asked for mercy.

Let me explain why this is important. The only reason you beg someone for mercy is that you realize that you have deeply offended him, but you know that it is up to him to decide whether to be merciful. God is sovereign: he has a will of his own and once said to Moses, 'I will have mercy on whom I will have mercy, and I will have compassion on whom I will have compassion' (Exod. 33:19). The God of the Bible owes you nothing: he could pass you by and still be just. So if you think that you are saved because you have been brought up in a Christian home and you were baptized or because you have such a superior intellect and any church will be lucky to have you, you are *not* a Christian. A proof that you are a child of God is that you ask him for mercy.

The second thing David did was to ask God for cleansing:

'Wash away all my iniquity
    and cleanse me from my sin.
For I know my transgressions,
    and my sin is always before me. . . .

'Cleanse me with hyssop, and I shall be clean;
    wash me, and I shall be whiter than snow' (vv. 2-3, 7).

Hyssop was a branch that the priest would dip in the blood of an animal and sprinkle upon the people at a sacrifice, a ritual that symbolized cleansing. Here, David saw beyond the Mosaic law and realized that his only hope was to plead the blood Jesus would shed on the cross.

The only way *you* can get right with God is by pleading the merit of Jesus' blood. Spurgeon used to say, 'There is no gospel apart from two words: substitution and satisfaction.' Jesus took our punishment on the cross and his blood satisfied God's justice. Accepting this is another proof you are a Christian.

The third thing David did was to acknowledge that the one he hurt most by his sin was God. In verse 4 he said:

'Against you, you only, have I sinned
    and done what is evil in your sight,

> so that you are proved right when you speak
> and justified when you judge.'

Of course, David had wounded others too: he had used Bathsheba to satisfy his lust and murdered her husband; moreover, he had brought shame upon his family and upon his country. However, David knew that it was God, who had entrusted him with his lofty position, whom he had hurt most and he felt deeply ashamed.

If you realize that it is God you have hurt most by your sin, it is another proof that you are a Christian.

The fourth thing David did was to pray for a restoration of joy. Look at verse 12:

> 'Restore to me the joy of your salvation.'

This shows that he had not lost his salvation, but he *had* lost the joy that it had brought him.

Maybe you have become a backslider and have lost the joy of your salvation. Now you may say, 'I'm not a backslider. I haven't done anything nearly as bad as David did.' Then thank God for his restraining grace. However, you should remember that there are times when we all backslide to some extent. You see, there are degrees of backsliding (on a scale of one to ten maybe David was a ten). Maybe you have let God down by becoming self-willed and opinionated, and not only are you making everyone else unhappy but you are miserable too. The good news is that if you ask him God will forgive you and restore the joy that you lost.

The fifth thing David did was to ask God to take him back into his service. He said:

> 'Grant me a willing spirit, to sustain me.
> Then I will teach transgressors your ways,
> and sinners will turn back to you' (vv. 12-13).

In other words he said, 'Let me serve you. I can show sinners the way. I *can* do it, Lord, because I myself have been a great sinner.'

Perhaps you feel that when you ask God to restore you he will say, 'Yes, you can come back to me, but I'm afraid that you must just sit in a corner from now on; I can't use you again.' You are wrong: God says, 'I *want* to use you.' You see, he wants you to *know* he has forgiven you, and this is one of the best ways he has of proving it to you.

David was right when he said in Psalm 103:10: '[God] does not treat us as our sins deserve or repay us according to our iniquities', and when he was renewed to repentance, God affirmed him despite his sin and brought his future under his sovereign will. The Bible says:

> David comforted his wife Bathsheba, and he went to her and lay with her. She gave birth to a son, and they named him Solomon. The Lord loved him; and because the Lord loved him, he sent word through Nathan the prophet to name him Jedidiah (2 Sam. 12:24-25).

Jedidiah means 'beloved of the Lord'. Earlier Nathan had exposed David's sin, but now he returned to say, 'The Lord loves your son. It's all right!'

Think about this for a moment. God was unhappy that David took Bathsheba as his wife and he took the child conceived in adultery, but if God had dealt with David as his sins deserved, he might have said, 'I will not allow you and Bathsheba to have more children.' But he not only gave them another son, he ordained that the Messiah would descend from him. The way in which he treated the couple shows his grace and compassion. Moreover, the fact that he sent his prophet Nathan with the good news proves that he had restored David's reputation within the godly community.

God took David back into his service, and David went on to win further victories over the enemies of God's people (2 Sam. 12:26-31).

It is the devil who wants you to think that you can no longer serve the church. God says, 'Don't listen to Satan's lies; I will restore your reputation within the Christian community.'

The consequences of David's sin were grave, and for the rest of his life he would have to live with God's second best, but that is how we all have to live, for we all have a shadow hanging over us: we all have a skeleton in the cupboard. But God says to the backslider, 'I love you with an everlasting love. I exposed your sin because I want you to return to me. Let me cleanse you and restore you. I have work for you to do.'

48

Fatal Attraction

2 Samuel 13

Do you remember a film called *A Fatal Attraction*? It was about a married man who was attracted by a beautiful woman and had an affair with her that marked the beginning of a long nightmare that ended in bitterness and violent death.

This chapter tells the story of a fatal attraction that also ended in tragedy. David's son Amnon was infatuated with his half-sister Tamar. Having decided that he *had* to have her no matter what, he lied to his father, tricked Tamar into being alone with him and raped her. Then Amnon's passion turned to hatred and he callously threw her out of his house. Two years later her brother Absalom killed him in revenge, and David, the father of all three, mourned for his children.

I believe there are three ways in which we could use this story.

We could use it to show that Nathan's prophecy 'The sword shall never depart from your house' was beginning to be fulfilled (2 Sam. 12:10). Indeed Nathan could have returned and said to David, 'God told you this would happen.' But the Bible tells us that God takes no pleasure in bringing sinners to judgment. 'Do I take any pleasure in the death of the wicked? declares the Sovereign Lord. Rather am I not pleased when they turn from their wicked ways and live?' (Ezek. 18:23).

We could also use this story to show that we are accountable for our own sins. Let me put it like this: at the final judgment it will not do for either Amnon or Absalom to say to God, 'I wouldn't be in this situation if my father hadn't committed adultery and murder.'

However, one would have to admit that David was an imperfect father. It is interesting how somebody can be a great blessing to the world and yet fail as a parent. David was a man after God's own heart (1 Sam. 13:14; Acts 13:22), the writer of many of the psalms, the man through whom Messiah descended, but he was a weak father and he should have seen through Amnon's deception. Nevertheless, God will hold Amnon and Absalom responsible for their sin.

If *you* lose your soul, you will only have yourself to blame. Ezekiel put it like this:

> The word of the Lord came to me: 'What do you people mean by quoting this proverb about the land of Israel:
> '"The fathers eat sour grapes,
> and the children's teeth are set on edge"?
> 'As surely as I live, declares the Sovereign Lord, you will no longer quote this proverb in Israel. For every living soul belongs to me, the father as well as the son – both alike belong to me. *The soul who sins is the one who will die* [my italics]' (Ezek. 18:1-4).

Those who respond to the gospel stop blaming their background, the society in which they live and their psychological make-up for their actions; they acknowledge their guilt and say, 'Lord, I am sorry; wash my sins away with Jesus' blood.' No one who, in their lifetime, has offered up that prayer will stand alone at the judgment, for Jesus Christ, who will be their judge (Acts 17:31), will also be their barrister.

Now sexual lust is not the only fatal attraction. For some, the fatal attraction is a lust for power, although they might not admit it, even to themselves. Sadly, people often delude themselves. The Bible says, 'The heart is deceitful above all things and beyond cure. Who can understand it?' (Jer. 17:9). For others, the fatal attractions are a hedonistic lifestyle, making money or having a prestigious job. For many, the fatal attraction is a new idea. I am reminded of Acts 17:21, which says: 'All the Athenians and the foreigners who lived there spent their time doing nothing but talking about and listening to the latest ideas.' Two thousand years have passed but today people are as fascinated as ever by 'the latest idea'. This is why cults, false religions and the occult have such a popular appeal.

Many people are attracted by liberal theology. I was trained at a seminary where students were taught that it is acceptable to criticize the Bible in the same way as one criticizes the works of writers like Shakespeare or Wordsworth. I have known many young men who were planning to enter the ministry until they were persuaded that the Bible is fallible. Sadly, many of these men gave up their faith. Liberal theology is a fatal attraction, for the Bible *is* the inspired word of God: it is inerrant and infallible. Some of the world's greatest scholars have examined its text thoroughly and have proved that you do not have to commit intellectual suicide to believe in the infallibility of Scripture.

Earlier I said that there are three ways in which we could use this story. I want to use it chiefly to show you how to distinguish the 'Spirit of truth' from the 'spirit of falsehood' (see 1 John 4:6).

Now an unconverted person might say, 'There are so many religions to choose from that I can't see how anyone can say Christianity is the right one.' But Jesus said, '*I* am the way and the truth and the life. *No-one comes to the Father except through me* [my italics]' (John 14:6). Once you deny this claim the way is clear for Satan to get in; should that happen, you would find life a nightmare. Cults and religions other than Christianity are fatal attractions.

I think the story of Amnon and Tamar shows us five ways of recognizing a fatal attraction.

First, a fatal attraction involves *presumption*. By that I mean you presume something is right simply because it appeals to you. Amnon made this mistake. The Bible says:

In the course of time, Amnon son of David fell in love with Tamar, the beautiful sister of Absalom son of David (v. 1).

Noticing that his sister was beautiful, Amnon confused love with physical attraction and thought, 'I trust my feelings, so this *must* be right.'

This was what Eve said to herself in the Garden of Eden when she saw that 'the fruit of the tree was good for food and pleasing to the eye' (Gen 3:6). Eve presumed that because something *looked* good, it must be good. Nowadays such presumption leads people to join cults and explore world religions and leads others to become grasping. Be careful: the consequences of presumption are disastrous.

What Amnon presumed to be love was not love at all. For one thing, the Bible forbids a man to have sexual relations with his sister or even with his half-sister (Lev. 18:9, 11), and, knowing this, Amnon should have put all thoughts of a relationship with Tamar out of his head.

If *you* have a desire that is contrary to the teaching of the Bible, you may be sure that the Holy Spirit did not put it in your heart. For instance, no matter how strong your feelings, you must resist any temptation to have an affair, for the Bible says that adultery is a sin (Exod. 20:14). The same is true of homosexual acts (Lev. 18:22). (Note, the Bible does not condemn people because they feel attracted to the same sex: what it condemns is homosexual *activity*.) Relying on the strength of your feelings rather than relying on God's word is presumption.

Second, a fatal attraction involves *preoccupation.* In other words, like Amnon, you will think of nothing else. Verse 2 says:

Amnon became frustrated to the point of illness on account of his sister Tamar, for she was a virgin, and it seemed impossible for him to do anything to her (2 Sam.13:2).

But the very fact that Amnon's infatuation was making him ill should have been a hint to him that he wanted something that was wrong.

If you have been frustrated because your plans come to nothing, it may be because in his kindness God is trying to prevent you from doing something that is wrong. This being the case, you would be foolish to insist on having your own way.

Third, a fatal attraction involves *peer pressure*. Amnon experienced this. Read verses 3 and 4:

> Now Amnon had a friend named Jonadab son of Shimeah, David's brother. Jonadab was a very shrewd man. He asked Amnon, 'Why do you, the king's son, look so haggard morning after morning? Won't you tell me?'
>
> Amnon said to him, 'I'm in love with Tamar, my brother Absalom's sister.'
>
> 'Go to bed and pretend to be ill,' Jonadab said. 'When your father comes to see you, say to him, "I would like my sister Tamar to come and give me something to eat. Let her prepare the food in my sight so that I may watch her and then eat it from her hand"' (v. 5)

What a friend he turned out to be! He was a 'friend' who said, 'Look, if you feel like having sex with your sister, go ahead.'

The devil has a way of putting 'friends' like that in our path. Foolishly, when we want advice, we often choose to consult those who will tell us what we want to hear. Yet suppose we take their advice and the situation ends in nightmare and tragedy, what will we say to those 'friends' then? Will we say, 'You *made* me do it'? Remember, the Bible says, 'The soul who sins is the one who will die' (Ezek. 18:4).

I have a book entitled *Man the Manipulator*. The author argues that no one can manipulate another unless that person is willing for this to happen. Amnon bowed to peer pressure, but he was willing to do so.

Fourth, a fatal attraction involves *pretence*. Jonadab's advice to Amnon was 'Go to bed and pretend to be ill. . . . When your father comes to see you, say to him, "I would like my sister Tamar to come and give me something to eat"' (v. 5). Amnon's passion was based upon a lie.

Now if you can only get what you want by lying, you may be sure that you are seeking something that is wrong. Are you lying to someone? Shakespeare said, 'To thine own self be true.'

Fifth, a fatal attraction involves *pressure*.

Amnon put pressure on Tamar to sleep with him. Consider the facts.

Fact One: Amnon refused to consider Tamar's feelings. Read verses 12 and 13:

'Don't, my brother!' she said to him. 'Don't force me. Such a thing should not be done in Israel! Don't do this wicked thing. What about me? Where could I get rid of my disgrace?'

He even rejected Tamar's offer of marriage. Tamar said:

'And what about you? You would be like one of the wicked fools in Israel. Please speak to the king; he will not keep me from being married to you.' [As king, David had the power to arrange such a marriage, but had he done so, he would have sinned.] But he refused to listen to her . . .' (v. 13-14).

Are you sleeping with somebody who promises that they will marry you someday? Why do they not do it? Because that person is using you. All extramarital sexual activity is manipulation.

Fact Two: Amnon rejected common sense. He refused to wait. And realizing that he could not *persuade* Tamar to have sex with him, Amnon used force. Read verse 14:

He refused to listen to her, and since he was stronger than she, he raped her.

But when Amnon had finished with Tamar, his 'love' for her suddenly turned to hatred. The Bible says:

> Amnon hated her with intense hatred. In fact, he hated her more than he had loved her. Amnon said to her, 'Get up and get out!'
> 'No!' she said to him. 'Sending me away would be a greater wrong than what you have already done to me.'
> But he refused to listen to her. He called his personal servant and said, 'Get this woman out of here and bolt the door after her. So his servant put her out and bolted the door after her. She was wearing a richly ornamented robe, for this was the kind of garment the virgin daughters of the king wore. Tamar put ashes on her head and tore the ornamented robe she was wearing. She put her hand on her head and went away, weeping aloud as she went (vv. 15-19).

When love is not genuine and one partner sees that he or she has been used, the affair ends in bitterness. The only one way to have peace and a love that endures is to keep sex within the bonds of marriage.

What then is the difference between truth and error? Simply this: truth leads to liberty: the counterfeit leads to drudgery. Jesus said, 'You will know the truth, and the truth will set you free' (John 8:32). The truth leads to life: the counterfeit leads to death. The truth is light: the counterfeit is darkness. The truth is lofty: the counterfeit is degrading.

Just as Amnon callously threw Tamar out when he had no further use for her, when Satan has no further use for you, he will toss you aside and laugh, for he hates you and wants to take you to hell with him.

Jesus will not manipulate you nor will he take you by force: he uses *persuasion*. He simply *invites* you to come to him, saying:

> 'Come to me, all you who are weary and burdened, and I will give you rest' (Matt. 11:28).

'Whoever is thirsty, let him come; and whoever wishes, let him take the free gift of the water of life' (Rev. 22:17).

Jesus will give you peace, dignity, light and eternal life. He is a *blessed* attraction.

49

Skeletons in Your Cupboard

2 Samuel 14

King David was behaving strangely, for he was not on speaking terms with his son Absalom. The *apparent* reason for this was that Absalom had murdered his brother Amnon. Let me remind you of what happened.

Amnon had become so hopelessly infatuated with his half-sister Tamar that he lured her to his house and raped her. Then his passion suddenly died and he callously threw her out onto the street. Deeply distressed, Tamar fled to take refuge with her brother Absalom (2 Sam. 13:20). Realizing that his father was not going to punish Amnon, two years later Absalom took the law into his own hands and killed him. Then he fled to Syria, where he remained for the next three years (2 Sam. 13:23-38).

Note that I said this was the *apparent* cause of David's behaviour, but Joab knew there was another, deeper reason for it. The Bible does not tell us how much the citizens of Jerusalem knew at the time, but Joab knew that his uncle had committed adultery with Bathsheba and murdered her husband to cover it up. In other words, Joab knew that David had a skeleton in his cupboard. And seeing the effect it was having on the king, he decided to put things right and reconcile David with his son. The Bible says:

> Joab son of Zeruiah knew that the king's heart longed for Absalom. So Joab sent someone to Tekoa and had a wise woman brought from there. He said to her, 'Pretend you are in mourning. Dress in mourning clothes, and don't use any cosmetic lotions.

Act like a woman who has spent many days grieving for the dead. Then go to the king and speak these words to him.' And Joab put the words into her mouth.

When the woman from Tekoa went to the king, she fell with her face to the ground to pay him honour, and she said, 'Help me, O king!'

The king asked her, 'What is troubling you?'

'I am indeed a widow; my husband is dead. I your servant had two sons. They got into a fight with each other in the field, and no-one was there to separate them. One struck the other and killed him. Now the whole clan has risen up against your servant; they say, "Hand over the one who struck his brother down, so that we may put him to death for the life of his brother whom he killed; then we will get rid of the heir as well." They would put out the only burning coal I have left, leaving my husband neither name nor descendant on the face of the earth...'

'As surely as the Lord lives,' [David] said, 'not one hair of your son's head will fall to the ground' (2 Sam. 14:1-7, 11).

Seeing that her story had touched the king, the wise woman pressed her point home.

'Why then have you devised a thing like this against the people of God? When the king says this, does he not convict himself, for the king has not brought back his banished son? Like water spilled on the ground, which cannot be recovered, so we must die. But God does not take away life; instead, he devises ways so that a banished person may not remain estranged from him' (vv. 13–14).

David was persuaded to allow Absalom to return to Jerusalem:

The king said to Joab, 'Very well, I will do it. Go, bring back the young man Absalom' (v. 21).

So Absalom returned to Jerusalem. However, although he had not seen his son for two years, David still could not bring himself to speak to him.

Now we may hide the skeleton, but we cannot hide the effect that it has on us, no matter how hard we try. For instance, some people are very prim and proper, as if by their self-righteousness they could atone for their past. Others are moody and irritable or hold a deep grudge. Some people are judgmental, while others are very defensive and quick to take offence. Some have an inordinate hatred for the gospel or for anything that relates to the church. In fact, one's secret past can affect one's whole personality.

Now there are three types of skeleton that we hide in our cupboards.

The first type is what I would call an *imaginary* skeleton. By this, I mean that some people fret about something that exists only in their imagination. For example, here is the person who thinks he has nothing to live for. Here is the one who imagines he has committed the unpardonable sin (see Matt. 12:31), which, as I said in an earlier chapter, is to deny the testimony of the Holy Spirit. (If this is your problem, God wants you to know that if you have affirmed that Jesus is Lord (Rom. 10:9), you have *not* lost your salvation. Satan is lying to you because he wants to drive you to despair.) Here too is the person who cannot believe that God has forgiven him.

I suspect this was David's problem and, despite his prayer of repentance in Psalm 51, he still felt so ashamed that he could not bring himself to discipline his sons or function properly as head of state.

The second type I would call an *involuntary* skeleton. Here we have the person who has done nothing wrong but is suffering because of the wrongdoing of others. For instance, here is the person, who has been sexually abused and feels too ashamed to tell anyone else about it. Victims of sexual abuse often think that they must have done *something* to cause it and suffer needless guilt and shame.

The third type is altogether different. It is what I would call an *incurred* skeleton: you have one because of what you do. For example, here we have the person who is having an affair, here we have the person who is secretly addicted to drink or to drugs. David had committed adultery and murder. Perhaps your skeleton is not so bad as that, but you are equally at pains that nobody knows what you have done.

I want to say three things about this.

First, like the other kinds of skeletons, it is *crippling*.

The skeleton in David's cupboard had certainly crippled him. For one thing, he was not functioning in the way a head of a family should. He was a poor parent, for a loving father should not shrink from disciplining his children. Maybe he could not bring himself to do this because he knew that it was because of his sin that he and Bathsheba had lost their first child (see 2 Sam. 12:13-18) and he was crippled with guilt.

Guilt often affects the way in which we deal with our children. Indeed many parents are so paralyzed with shame that they become ineffective. Some feel guilty that they spend too much time at work and not enough with their families, and, in an effort to compensate, they spoil their children.

Joab could see that David was ineffective in the way he dealt with his children, but his main concern was that David was ineffective in the way he governed the nation. You see, not only was he weak and indecisive but he was setting a poor example to his subjects.

When there is weak leadership in the church, you will often find that the character of the leader is flawed. I know of one man who, although he was a known evangelical, began to dabble in liberal theology and expressed doubts about the infallibility of Scripture and the effectiveness of prayer. Understandably, this upset the members of his church. It turned out that he was having an affair with another man's wife. You see, people will use a theological reason to cover a *moral* deficiency.

We have seen that a skeleton in the cupboard affects the way we function. Perhaps, in your case, you are having difficulties at work or people find it hard to get along with you because you have not dealt with your guilt. Perhaps you are plagued by false guilt – it can happen – but this can be as crippling as true guilt and you need to come to terms with it.

David nursed a grudge against his son so deep that he did not even see his grandchildren, although they lived less than a mile away from his palace. (They are described in 2 Samuel 14:27.) In fact, two more years passed without contact.

Bearing malice is a sin that always grieves the Holy Spirit. Jesus said, 'If you forgive men when they sin against you, your heavenly Father will also forgive you. But if you do not forgive men their sins, your Father will not forgive your sins' (Matt. 6:14-15). Now Jesus was *not* saying that if we do not forgive another we cannot be Christians, he was talking about our fellowship with God. (We should be thankful for this, because if our salvation depended on whether we forgive our enemies, how many of us would go to heaven?)

Grieving the Spirit of God forfeits presence of mind and clear thinking. Writing to the church in Rome, Paul said of the ungodly: 'Their thinking became futile and their foolish hearts were darkened' (Rom. 1:21). If we refuse to forgive others, we are the losers.

Skeletons in the cupboard are not only crippling, they are also *common*. In fact, we all have them, for we have all done things and said things of which we are ashamed. But we tend to wear masks, for we do not want others to know everything about us; we want them to like us.

David was not perfect, but, despite this, he is the only person the Bible describes as a man after God's own heart (1 Sam. 13:14; Acts 13:22). I would not be surprised if the Bible had described Daniel in this way, for we do not know anything about Daniel that was bad; but to think that God, who knew how often David would let him down, would call him a man after his own heart is amazing.

I find it comforting that the Bible does not shrink from revealing the imperfections of the characters in its pages, for if we have a sin that haunts us, Satan will come alongside and whisper, 'You are unique. No one else has ever done anything as bad as that. God can't forgive you. In fact, you aren't a Christian at all!' But as the book of Ecclesiastes says, 'There is nothing new under the sun' (Eccles. 1:9). Satan is a liar (John 8:44).

This brings me to the third thing I want you to know about skeletons in the cupboard: they can be *cleansed*, for in 1 John 1:9 we read: 'If we confess our sins, he is faithful and just and will forgive us our sins and purify us from all unrighteousness.' Now this does not mean we may say glibly, 'Look, Lord, I have done this, but I know you will forgive me', because when we read this verse in context, we see it applies only to those who are sincere in their repentance.

However, when he has forgiven us, God does not want us to continue feeling guilty. In fact, to do so would be to show contempt for what his Son did on the cross, for when Jesus died, he paid our debt in full. God takes no pleasure in our guilty feelings; he rejoices in our acceptance of his pardon.

Joab could see that David was still acting strangely and the only thing that would put the situation right would be a reconciliation with Absalom. So once again he mediated between father and son, and this time he succeeded in persuading David to meet Absalom. The Bible says:

> Then the king summoned Absalom, and he came in and bowed down with his face to the ground before the king. And the king kissed Absalom' (v. 33).

What a moment! David had thought that he could never bring himself to forgive Absalom, but finally he did it, thanks to the intervention of another. David had neither the initiative nor the moral fibre to approach Absalom, but when Joab interceded and reconciled him with his son, David finally came to terms with his feelings.

Do you need someone to reconcile you with God? You must not think for a moment that you can negotiate with him directly and say, 'Look, Lord, I think I am good enough to get into heaven', for he is holy and just one sin is enough to bar your entry. Only one person is worthy to intercede for us: God's own Son Jesus (1 Tim. 2:5). Jesus stepped between sinners and a holy God and bore our sins in his body on the cross (1 Pet. 2:24). His blood satisfied God's justice, and when the Holy Spirit applies it to our hearts, we are reconciled with the Father (Eph. 2:13–18).

Jesus is the perfect intercessor. He alone understands the Father and he also understands us. The Bible says that he sympathizes with our weaknesses (Heb. 4:15). He knows about the guilty secrets that haunt us and says, '"Come to me, all you who are weary and burdened, and I will give you rest" (Matt. 11:28). Let me cleanse you from your sin and lay the skeleton in your cupboard to rest.'

50

How to Accept Yourself After Failure

2 Samuel 15:1–30

I once heard a psychologist say that if he could get his patients to come to terms with their guilt he could cure any psychopathy in ten minutes. Guilt is the most crippling thing in the world.

God does not want us to feel guilty: he wants us to feel at peace. This was why he sent his Son to pay the penalty for our sins on the cross. Perhaps you ask, 'Doesn't God *want* me to be convicted of my sins?' Yes, but only because he wants you to confess them and accept his forgiveness. He shows us that we are sinners simply to point us to Christ.

No one ever felt guiltier than David. He was the greatest king that Israel would *ever* have, but in many ways he was a failure, morally, emotionally, and, for a while, spiritually, for anyone who can live unashamed for two years after committing adultery and murder is in bad shape. David was a failure as a husband and as a parent and, consequently, his family was in shambles. And now, as if all this were not enough, his son Absalom, whom he had kissed and welcomed home at last, gave him more problems.

The Bible makes it clear that Absalom was a man who had uncontrolled ambitions:

> In the course of time, Absalom provided himself with a chariot and horses and with fifty men to run ahead of him. He would get up early and stand by the side of the road leading to the city gate. Whenever anyone came with a complaint to be placed before the king for a decision, Absalom would call out to him, 'What town are you from?' He would answer, 'Your servant is

from one of the tribes of Israel.' Then Absalom would say to him, 'Look, your claims are valid and proper, but there is no representative of the king to hear you.' And Absalom would add, 'If only I were appointed judge in the land! Then everyone who has a complaint or case could come to me and I would see that he receives justice.'

Also, whenever anyone approached him to bow down before him, Absalom would reach out his hand, take hold of him and kiss him. Absalom behaved in this way towards all the Israelites who came to the king asking for justice, and so he stole the hearts of the men of Israel (2 Sam. 15:1–6).

In this way Absalom gained the support he needed for a successful conspiracy against the king.

His disloyalty intensified David's sense of guilt and failure.

How does one cope with failure? Well, the good news is that God gives failures a second chance. Today is the first day of the rest of your life and in it God will give you an opportunity to know his forgiveness afresh. Let the words of the prophet encourage you:

> Because of the Lord's great love
> we are not consumed,
> for his compassions never fail.
> They are new every morning;
> great is your faithfulness (Lam. 3:22–23).

Some years ago I preached a sermon called 'Joseph's Cup and Benjamin's Bag' (now a chapter in my book *God Meant It for Good*). You will recall that Joseph's brothers had sold him into slavery and, as a result, for many years they carried a terrible burden of guilt. But God wanted them to see that he had forgiven them and they could forgive themselves. So he gave them an opportunity to see that they had changed and they could face the future with dignity (see Gen. 44).

Maybe you say, 'I know that God has forgiven me, but I can't forgive myself.' But God does not want you to go on feeling guilty. However, he knows that you have this problem, so he will give you an opportunity to show the graces you failed to show before. If you pass the test, you will see that you have changed and you can face the future unashamed.

This was what he did for David. The Bible says:

> At the end of four years, Absalom said to the king, 'Let me go to Hebron and fulfil a vow I made to the Lord. While your servant was living at Geshur in Aram, I made this vow: "If the Lord takes me back to Jerusalem, I will worship the Lord in Hebron."'
> The king said to him, 'Go in peace.' So he went to Hebron (2 Sam. 15:7–9).

Once he was safely in Hebron, Absalom wasted no time. And in verses 10–13 we read:

> Then Absalom sent secret messengers throughout the tribes of Israel to say, 'As soon as you hear the sound of the trumpets, then say, "Absalom is king in Hebron." Two hundred men from Jerusalem had accompanied Absalom. They had been invited as guests and went quite innocently, knowing nothing about the matter. While Absalom was offering sacrifices, he also sent for Ahithophel the Gilonite, David's counsellor, to come from Giloh, his home town. And so the conspiracy gained strength, and Absalom's following kept on increasing.
> A messenger came and told David, 'The hearts of the men of Israel are with Absalom.'

God had set before David possibly the greatest challenge of his life.

There comes a time when, although a person may have been an adult for some time, he becomes fully mature. In 1 Corinthians 13:11 Paul said, 'When I was a child, I talked liked a child, I thought like a child, I reasoned like a child. When I became a man, I put childish ways behind me.' As we will see, David rose to the challenge and finally became 'a man'.

Now the issue here was greatness versus smallness. Do you know what it is to have to deal with a very small person? Note, I am not referring to a person's physique, I am referring to his character. In this sense, Absalom was a small man. Let us think about this for a moment.

First, we see that Absalom capitalized on his good looks. The Bible says, 'In all Israel there was not a man so highly praised for his handsome appearance as Absalom' (2 Sam. 14:25). Now if anyone has to lean on his appearance, he is a small man.

Second, we see that Absalom capitalized on his personality. He was a politician through and through, and he knew just what to do to steal the hearts of the people. You will recall that as people were on their way to see the king, Absalom would call out to them, 'Where are you going?'

'Oh, I am going to see the king,' they would reply.

'Come here and tell me where you are from and what your problem is.'

Flattered that the prince wanted to talk to them, they would say, 'Well, you see, it is like this.' Then they would pour out their troubles into a seemingly sympathetic ear.

Third, we see that Absalom could only make himself look good by making David look bad, for he would reply, 'Well, the trouble is that the king is a very busy man and he is not interested in that kind of problem. If only I were in charge of things like that!'

To their shame, some Christians try to make themselves look good by criticizing other members of God's family. I recall that once, when Louise and I were in the United States, we switched on the television and began watching some religious programmes. However, eventually, we had to turn off the TV set in disgust because the TV evangelists tried to draw attention to themselves by putting down other ministers.

Do you try to make yourself look good by making somebody else look bad? Politicians seem to do it all the time, especially before an election. If you catch yourself trying to

390

win people's affections by putting others down, then stop. Refuse to be a small person.

Fourth, we see that when he was ready to make his bid for power Absalom feigned a relationship with God. Remember, when he asked his father's permission to go to Hebron, he phrased his request like this:

> 'Let me go to Hebron and fulfil a vow I made to the Lord. While your servant was living at Geshur in Aram, I made this vow: "If the Lord takes me back to Jerusalem, I will worship the Lord in Hebron"' (2 Sam. 15:7-8).

Sadly, like Absalom, those who are about to do something very wicked often appear to be godly.

Fifth, we see that Absalom could not wait for God to exalt him. Had Solomon died, he might have become king one day, but he seized his father's throne. Absalom was a small man; it takes a *big* person to wait patiently.

Are you one of those who cannot wait to get ahead and scramble for power? The Bible says, 'Humble yourselves, therefore, under God's mighty hand, that he may lift you up in due time' (1 Pet. 5:6).

Although he must have been deeply saddened and hurt by his son's rebellion, David saw this as a chance to regain his self-respect and as an opportunity to find out if God was still with him.

Now I want us to see five things about David's reaction to the news of the conspiracy against him.

First, we see that he refused to defend himself. Verse 14 says:

> Then David said to all his officials who were with him in Jerusalem, 'Come! We must flee . . . '.

Running away seems so out of character for David. (Remember, we are talking about one of the greatest and most courageous military leaders that ever lived.) But now he said, 'Whether I abdicate or remain as king is up to God. His will is best. I will let him handle this crisis.'

When someone attacks you and you are tempted to defend yourself, remember that when Abraham Lincoln said, 'He who chooses himself for a lawyer has a fool for a client', he was stating a fact.

Second, we see that David was reluctant to jeopardize others. The Bible says:

> So the king set out, with all the people following him, and they halted at a place some distance away. All his men marched past him, along with all the Kerethites and Pelethites; and all the six hundred Gittites who had accompanied him from Gath marched before the king.
>
> The king said to Ittai the Gittite, 'Why should you come along with us? Go back and stay with King Absalom. You are a foreigner, an exile from your homeland. You came only yesterday. And today shall I make you wander about with us, when I do not know where I am going? Go back, and take your countrymen. May kindness and faithfulness be with you' (vv. 17-20).

By showing concern for these men, David proved that he was the opposite of Absalom, who thought only of himself.

Third, we see that David let go of what was so precious to him, though it hurt him and his followers too, as we see:

> The whole countryside wept aloud as all the people passed by. The king also crossed the Kidron Valley, and all the people moved on towards the desert. . . .
>
> David continued up the Mount of Olives, weeping as he went; his head was covered and he was barefoot (vv. 23, 30).

When we get to heaven and see a video replay of that moment, we will see how hard it was for David to break free from the past.

If you have yet to break free from something that the Holy Spirit has put his finger on, remember that Jesus said, 'Whoever tries to keep his life will lose it, and whoever loses his life will preserve it' (Luke 17:33). God says, 'Leave your old life behind. Let me take care of your future.'

Fourth, we see that David refused to manipulate the glory of God. Look at verses 24 and 25:

> Zadok was there, too, and all the Levites who were with him were carrying the ark of the covenant of God. . . . Then the king said to Zadok, 'Take the ark of God back into the city.'

The ark of the covenant symbolized the glory of God and his presence with his people. Knowing what the ark meant to the Israelites, David could have used it for propaganda purposes, so all the common people would say, 'The ark of the covenant is with David, so we should support him, not Absalom.' But David said, 'Return the ark to Jerusalem.' He knew that it belonged there and he refused to hide behind it.

Fifth, we see that David cast himself upon the mercy and sovereignty of God. Look at the whole of verse 25 and verse 26:

> Then the king said to Zadok, 'Take the ark of God back into the city. If I find favour in the Lord's eyes, he will bring me back and let me see it and his dwelling-place again. But if he says, "I am not pleased with you," then I am ready; let him do to me whatever seems good to him.'

These words move me. Here was a man whose heart had been changed. No longer was David living for his own glory: he wanted to honour God and passed up the chance to save face by keeping the ark with him. He said, 'God has given me an opportunity to prove that I love him. I won't let him down again.' He knew that *God* is the one who exalts people, and realizing that Absalom's rebellion could only have happened with divine permission, he surrendered to God's will.

Paul said that God is sovereign and 'works out everything in conformity with the purpose of his will' (Eph. 1:11). *He* is the one who exalts us. The psalmist put it like this: 'No-one from the east or the west or from the desert can exalt a man. But it is *God* who judges: He brings down one, he exalts another [my italics]' (Ps. 75:6-7).

Are you trying to exalt yourself to a place where God does not want you to be? If so, draw back. David did not seek glory for himself; he wanted to honour God, and this should be your aim too.

Humility is one of the clearest signs of spiritual maturity. After David sinned with Bathsheba, he was self-righteous to the core. Now he recognized that he had no bargaining power with God and he could not say, 'Lord, you can't let this happen to *me*; I am the king!' With great humility, he walked barefoot in sackcloth and ashes across the Kidron Valley.

God wants to bring *you* to a state of brokenness. He wants you to understand that you have no bargaining power, no righteousness of your own and your only hope is to put your trust in what Jesus did for you on the cross.

I am amazed how God allows us to save face – sometimes at the last moment.

God allowed Samson to save face in this way. It is a long story and, here, I can only give you a brief outline. But you can read it for yourself in Judges 16.

Samson was the strongest man who ever lived, but, in response to her constant nagging, he eventually told his treacherous wife Delilah that the secret of his strength was that his head had never been shaved. Delilah promptly sent for the Philistines, who had paid her to betray her husband. Then she persuaded Samson to lie down with his head in her lap, and when he was sound asleep, she called a servant to shave off his hair and bind him with strong rope.

As soon as the Philistines arrived, she woke him, crying, 'Samson the Philistines are upon you!' But Samson had sinned when he told Delilah the secret of his strength, and his superhuman strength had gone. He struggled in vain to free himself, but the Philistines seized him. They gouged out his eyes and imprisoned him. This was what happened when his hair began to grow:

> Now the rulers of the Philistines assembled to offer a great sacrifice to Dagon their god and to celebrate, saying, 'Our god has delivered Samson, our enemy, into our hands'. . . While they were in high spirits, they shouted, 'Bring out Samson to entertain us.' So they called Samson out of prison, and he performed for them.
>
> When they stood him among the pillars, Samson said to the servant who held his hand, 'Put me where I can feel the pillars that support the temple, so that I may lean against them.' . . . Then Samson prayed to the Lord, 'O Sovereign Lord, remember me. O God, please strengthen me just once more.' . . . Then Samson reached towards the two central pillars on which the temple stood. Bracing himself against them, his right hand on the one and his left hand on the other, Samson said, 'Let me die with the Philistines!' Then he pushed with all his might, and down came the temple on the rulers and all the people in it. Thus, he killed many more when he died than while he lived (Jdgs. 16:23, 25-26, 28-30).

At the last minute God graciously allowed Samson to save face and gain a mighty victory over his enemies.

David would live for another twenty years, and in the remaining chapters of this book, we will see that God would be gracious to him.

You may have many years of life ahead of you, but, despite your sin, God wants you to save face too. All you have to do is to repent and put your life into his hands.

51

How to Cope When People Say You Are Finished

2 Samuel 16

God was disciplining David and Nathan's prophecy 'The sword shall never depart from your house' (2 Sam. 12:10) was coming true, for his son Absalom had usurped his throne and David himself was now in exile at Bahurim. His situation seemed desperate and most people thought that he was finished.

If you want to know how to cope when the future seems so bleak and God is disciplining you, you will find the story of David instructive, for, although he would not have known this terminology, David coped by resolving to be Christ-like.

Have you ever been gripped by the desire to be like Jesus? When I made this my goal, I gained an impetus and a strength that has unfailingly seen me through the severest of storms.

My aim is to hear Jesus say to me one day, 'Well done, good and faithful servant!' (see Matt. 25:21). Being successful by worldly standards means nothing compared to this. That was what David wanted to hear God say, and that was what kept him going.

I believe that everything that was happening to David now was God's way of preparing him for eternity and of making the thought of heaven more precious to him.

Perhaps your problem is that you are too attached to worldly things. Maybe you care too much about what others think of you. God wants you to see that the only thing that matters is what *he* thinks of you. The important thing is to take hold of *eternal* life (1 Tim. 6:12).

On earth there are so many injustices, and those who have

all the advantages are those who know the 'right' people and have the 'right' background. But when we stand before the judgment seat of Christ, all that will matter is how closely we resemble him. It is *this* that will determine our eternal reward. And I believe that God increased the reward David would receive in heaven because his aim now was to become more Christ-like.

Let us see how this goal enabled David to face the future.

As if being in exile were not enough for David to bear, God now sent two men to take advantage of his plight. The first was Ziba, to whom David had given the task of caring for Mephibosheth and overseeing his estate (see 2 Sam. 9:9-10). The other was a man called Shimei. These two men had something in common: both were convinced that David was finished and Absalom was the wave of the future.

Absalom was now living in his father's palace, while David, in sackcloth and ashes, walked barefoot across the Kidron Valley weeping openly (see 2 Sam. 15:30). But he did not plead with God to end his humiliation, for he knew it was a fulfilment of Nathan's prophecy. He received his chastening with dignity, though it hurt.

Ziba came to meet David and, oddly enough, flattered him. Why? Because this was the opportune moment to recover the estate that the king had given to Mephibosheth. This was what happened:

> When David had gone a short distance beyond the summit, there was Ziba, the steward of Mephibosheth, waiting to meet him. He had a string of donkeys saddled and loaded with two hundred loaves of bread, a hundred cakes of raisins, a hundred cakes of figs and a skin of wine.
> The king asked Ziba, 'Why have you brought these?'
> Ziba answered, 'The donkeys are for the king's household to ride on, the bread and fruit are for the men to eat, and the wine is to refresh those who become exhausted in the desert.'
> The king then asked, 'Where is your master's grandson?'
> Ziba said to him, 'He is staying in Jerusalem, because he

thinks, "Today the house of Israel will give me back my grandfather's kingdom."'

Then the king said to Ziba, 'All that belonged to Mephibosheth is now yours' (2 Sam. 16:1-4).

Having achieved his purpose, Ziba went on his way. Now if he had the remotest idea that David would return from exile, he would not have lied about Mephibosheth, but he was convinced that David was finished.

Perhaps you believe you are finished. Maybe you have been made redundant or people treat you with contempt and push you aside because you are old. Perhaps you have made a bad mistake and your friends and your family no longer trust you. God is not like that. He loves you so much that if you were the only person in the world he would still have sent his Son to die for you. And if you honour Jesus and say, 'You can have my life; I will do anything you want me to do', he will give you dignity and courage to face the future.

Now we come to Shimei. The Bible tells us that he was 'from the same clan as Saul's family' (v. 5). The Benjamites had accepted David as king, but many were unhappy about it because David was of the tribe of Judah. However, while David was in power, those who resented him had kept quiet. But now they considered him a 'has-been' and felt it was safe to express their feelings.

If you hold a position of responsibility, you can be sure that some people will secretly envy you. However, while you have authority over them, they will keep quiet, but if you make mistakes that result in your downfall, they will not hesitate to tell you exactly what they think of you.

Shimei had that chance now and he made the most of it. David no longer looked like a king: there was no crown on his head; he was in sackcloth and ashes and he was weeping. So he felt it safe to let David know what he thought of him.

The Bible describes Shimei's attack on David in graphic detail:

As King David approached Bahurim, a man from the same clan as Saul's family came out from there. His name was Shimei son of Gera, and he cursed as he came out. He pelted David and all the king's officials with stones, though all the troops and the special guard were on David's right and left. As he cursed, Shimei said, 'Get out, get out, you man of blood, you scoundrel! The Lord has repaid you for all the blood you shed in the household of Saul, in whose place you have reigned. The Lord has handed the kingdom over to your son Absalom. You have come to ruin because you are a man of blood!' (2 Sam. 16:5-8).

Note that Shimei not only claimed to know God better than David did but he also accused David of stealing the kingdom from the house of Saul. Now no one ever seriously thought that David had usurped Saul's throne, but Shimei was of Saul's tribe and he resented a Judaean ruling over him. David had done nothing to injure Shimei personally, although the ferocity of Shimei's attack on him was such that it seemed that way.

It may help you to keep things in perspective if you remember that when people are antagonistic towards you, you may have done nothing to deserve it and the reason they hate you might be that they envy you.

The Bible says that the Jews wanted Jesus out of the way because they envied him (Mark 15:10). This was why, when they arrested him, they sent him to Pontius Pilate, the Roman governor, and demanded that he pass the death sentence on Jesus (see Matt. 27:1-26).

Later, when Jesus hung helpless on the cross, the Jews mocked him, saying, 'He saved others but he can't save himself!' (Mark 15:31. . . . The Roman soldiers also jeered, 'If you are the king of the Jews, save yourself' (Luke 23:37). What had Jesus done to hurt them? Nothing: they were simply getting in on the act. You see, when a person is no longer seen to be successful, cowards come crawling out of the woodwork.

How did David react to Shimei's verbal and physical violence? Well, I want to show you three things.

First, David refused to retaliate, although he had the power to do so. This was what happened:

> Then Abishai son of Zeruiah said to the king, 'Why should this dead dog curse my lord the king? Let me go over and cut off his head.'
>
> But the king said, 'What do you and I have in common, you sons of Zeruiah? If he is cursing because the Lord said to him, "Curse David," who can ask, "Why do you do this?"' (vv. 9-10).

Abishai could so easily have cut Shimei down had David permitted him to do so. But David refused.

When the Roman soldiers crucified Jesus, he could have called ten thousand angels to avenge him. He had the power to do so. In fact, only a few hours earlier, in the Garden of Gethsemane, he used his divine power, *not* to avenge himself, however, but to heal. Read Luke 22:49-51:

> When Jesus' followers saw what was going to happen [i.e. the officers of the temple guard were going to seize Jesus], they said, 'Lord, should we strike with our swords?' And one of them struck the servant of the high priest, cutting off his right ear.
>
> But Jesus answered, 'No more of this!' And he touched the man's ear and healed him.

This shows that Jesus could have easily come down from the cross, but he refused.

Perhaps you have the power to get even with those who have hurt you, but if you want to be like Jesus, you will *not* strike back. The Bible says, 'When they hurled their insults at him, he did not retaliate; when he suffered, he made no threats' (1 Pet. 2:23). In fact, Jesus said, 'Father, forgive them, for they do not know what they are doing' (Luke 23:34).

Second, David regarded the whole episode as God's will. Look again at 2 Samuel 16:10:

> But the king said, 'What do you and I have in common, you
> sons of Zeruiah? If he is cursing because the Lord said to him,
> "Curse David," who can ask, "Why do you do this?"'

This verse reveals that David knew that Shimei was acting in
accordance with God's will and he refused to abort his
chastening. He was looking forward to spending eternity in
heaven and being vindicated *there*.

On the eve of his crucifixion Jesus prayed, 'Father, if you
are willing, take this cup from me; yet not my will, but yours
be done' (Luke 22:42). But God did *not* take the cup from
him, and Jesus fulfilled his Father's purposes and went to the
cross.

If God is testing you, you may be tempted to plead with
him to end your trial as speedily as possible, but David refused
to do that. He said, 'No. This is God's doing. Let my
chastening run its course.'

Third, David thought that if he accepted his chastening
with dignity God might turn it into a blessing, and in verse 12
he said:

> 'It may be that the Lord will see my distress and repay me with
> good for the cursing I am receiving today.'

In other words, he thought, 'Let Shimei carry on cursing me.
The more he curses me the more God may bless me.'

In the Sermon on the Mount Jesus said: 'Blessed are you
when people insult you, persecute you and falsely say all kinds
of evil against you because of me. Rejoice and be glad, because
great is your reward in heaven' (Matt. 5:11-12). So if anyone
is lying about you, take heart: this verse applies to you.

David proved by his reaction to Shimei's abuse that he
was motivated by the desire to be like Jesus and, as a result,
God blessed him. In verse 14 the writer of 2 Samuel put it
like this:

The king and all the people with him arrived at their destination exhausted. And there he refreshed himself.

The Bible does not explain further, but I believe that God blessed David and gave him time to renew his strength.

If you are undergoing a severe test, remember, God knows there is a limit to what you can take. Writing to the church at Corinth, Paul said, 'God is faithful; he will not let you be tempted beyond what you can bear' (1 Cor. 10:13). Moreover, during your trial, he will give you a time of refreshing.

I am reminded of this lovely verse that was inspired by Isaiah 43:2:

When through the deep waters I call thee to go,
The rivers of sorrow shall not overflow,
For I will be with thee, thy trials to bless
And sanctify to thee thy deepest distress.

Did you know that David wrote Psalm 37 and Psalm 23 at this time? In Psalm 23 David expressed his confidence in God's unfailing kindness and compassion, saying:

The Lord is my shepherd, I shall not be in want.
    He makes me lie down in green pastures,
he leads me beside quiet waters,
    he restores my soul.
He guides me in paths of righteousness for his name's sake.
    Even though I walk through the valley of the shadow of death,
I will fear no evil, for you are with me;
    your rod and your staff, they comfort me.
You prepare a table before me in the presence of my enemies.
    You anoint my head with oil; my cup overflows.
Surely goodness and love will follow me all the days of my life,
    and I will dwell in the house of the Lord for ever.

In the midnight of his life he found his greatest inspiration.

At last God had David's undivided attention. The question is, has he got yours?

52

Turning of the Tide

2 Samuel 17

Never, even when he was running from Saul, had David been in a situation as grave as this. His son Absalom had stolen the hearts of the Israelites, seized his throne and driven him into exile. But David knew not to complain about his troubles, for he had committed adultery and murder and God was disciplining him. He had run aground and it seemed that the tide would never turn and lift him from the bottom.

In fact, things went from bad to worse, for David heard some unexpected and very disquieting news:

> Now David had been told, 'Ahithophel is among the conspirators with Absalom' (2 Sam.15:31).

This was indeed bad tidings, for Ahithophel was not only a close friend, he was also a trusted counsellor (1 Chr. 27:33). In fact, 2 Samuel 16:23 says, 'In those days the advice Ahithophel gave was like that of one who enquires of God. That was how both David and Absalom regarded all of Ahithophel's advice.' David was devastated by his defection to Absalom. Perhaps he was thinking of Ahithophel when he wrote Psalm 55 and said:

> If an enemy were insulting me,
>   I could endure it;
> if a foe were raising himself against me,
>   I could hide from him.
> But it is you, a man like myself,
>   my companion, my close friend,

> with whom I once enjoyed sweet fellowship
> as we walked with the throng at the house of God
>
> (vv. 12–14).

Today the tide is out for the church. Few take notice of it or respect its leaders. In fact, according to my latest information, only 4 per cent of the population of the United Kingdom are regular churchgoers and only a small number of these have been converted. I say this with good reason. At Westminster Chapel every Saturday the Pilot Lights go out to witness on London streets and talk to hundreds of passers-by. We ask the few who claim to attend church regularly, 'Do you think you will go to heaven when you die?' Most of them say, 'Yes. You see, I lead a good life and go to church every week.' Sadly, we are living in a day when the gospel is not preached in many of our churches and godlessness and ignorance abound. (Note, I speak of the church *generally*, for in certain churches people are very excited about Jesus.)

What should you do when the tide is out? Well, let us see what David did.

First, we see that David accepted that he could not save himself and his hope of being restored rested on God's sovereign mercy.

You will recall that when he and his followers fled from Jerusalem, they took the ark of God with them, but then David ordered them to take the ark back to the city (2 Sam. 15:25). I find this interesting. You see, the ark of the covenant was precious to the Israelites because it symbolized God's glory and his presence. If David had kept the ark with him, many of the common people would have flocked to his side. But he refused to use the ark for propaganda purposes. Read verses 25 and 26:

> Then the king said to Zadok, 'Take the ark of God back into the city. If I find favour in the Lord's eyes, he will bring me back and let me see it and his dwelling-place again. But if he says, "I

am not pleased with you," then I am ready; let him do to me whatever seems good to him.'

David put his future into God's hands.

Believing that God can turn everything around requires faith. Now if you are not at that point, then it means that, for you, the tide must ebb further. You need to come to the place where you lean on God alone.

Second, we see that when he heard that Ahithophel had defected to Absalom, David fell to his knees. The Bible says:

So David prayed, 'O Lord, turn Ahithophel's counsel into foolishness' (2 Sam. 15:31).

Realizing that he was only reaping what he had sown and he had no bargaining power, David threw himself on God's mercy.

I think we can define prayer as asking God to act. God does things *super*naturally, and when we call on him, he steps into our situation and uses people and events to accomplish his purpose. David asked God to intervene in a situation in which he himself was powerless; for in the capital city Absalom was in control and Ahithophel was with him; he had no link with Jerusalem now.

You too must ask God to do something that is out of your power: you must ask him to save you. Like David, you have no bargaining power and no righteousness of your own; you cannot save yourself; you can only ask God for mercy.

Third, we see that David was open to the surprising way in which God chose to answer his prayer.

Read 2 Samuel 15:32:

When David arrived at the summit, where people used to worship God, Hushai the Arkite was there to meet him, his robe torn and dust on his head.'

David must have been very relieved to see that Hushai had not joined those who had defected to Absalom as Ahithophel had done, for although people around him were kind, they were not in a position to restore him to the throne. He needed the help of someone special, a friend who would remain true and who was in a position to help.

A true friend is someone who, despite the fact he knows all about you, *still* likes you. A true friend is someone who will stand by you when you seem to have no future and can offer nothing in return.

Hushai was one such person. He arrived with 'his robe torn and dust on his head' at a time when it seemed as if David were finished. He was unashamed to show his grief at David's predicament, and he let everyone know where his loyalty lay.

David knew that Hushai was the answer to his prayer and that God had sent him to act as a double agent. Read verses 33 to 37:

> David said to him, 'If you go with me, you will be a burden to me. But if you return to the city and say to Absalom, "I will be your servant, O king; I was your father's servant in the past, but now I will be your servant," then you can help me by frustrating Ahithophel's advice. Won't the priests Zadok and Abiathar be there with you? Tell them anything you hear in the king's palace. Their two sons, Ahimaaz, son of Zadok and Jonathan son of Abiathar, are there with them. Send them to me with anything you hear.'
>
> So David's friend Hushai arrived at Jerusalem as Absalom was entering the city.

Now being a double agent is a dangerous business, and by asking Hushai to risk his life for him, David was stretching his friendship to the limits, for only a very special friend would be prepared to lay his life on the line for you. In fact, Jesus said, 'Greater love has no-one than this, that one lay down his life for his friends' (John 15:13).

Now if you say, 'I have no one who would do that for me',

you are mistaken. The Bible says, 'There is a friend who sticks closer than a brother' (Prov. 18:24) and the good news is that God has sent him to you: he is none other than his own Son. Despite knowing everything about you, Jesus loves you so much that he died for you. Paul said: 'Very rarely will anyone die for a righteous man, though for a good man someone might possibly dare to die. But God demonstrates his own love for us in this: While we were still sinners, Christ died for us' (Rom. 5:7-8).

So Hushai went to Jerusalem and laid his life on the line for David, and the result of his intervention was that the tide began to turn. (We will see how Hushai turned 'Ahithophel's counsel into foolishness' in the next chapter.)

Let me remind you of the signs that indicate the tide is turning.

The first sign is the realization that you are at such a low ebb that you can do nothing but pray. Sometimes God puts us through a terrible ordeal because it is the only way in which he can get our attention. God first tried to get Jonah's attention by *telling* him what to do, but Jonah refused to listen and so God had to take sterner measures. That was why he sent a great fish to swallow him. Even then, it was not until Jonah had spent three days inside the belly of the fish that he cried out to God (see Jonah 2:1). What will it take to get you to pray?

The second sign the tide is turning is the sudden realization that the answer to your prayer is staring you in the face. You see that God has sent his Son to die for you on the cross and he is the only one who can help you. You realize that you must abandon all hope that your own righteousness will save you and say, 'Lord, I need your help. Please forgive my sins. From now on I will put you first and live a life that reflects your holiness and honours your name.' That is the way to talk to God, and that is the way to find peace.

Another sign tells you that the tide *has* turned. For when you put your future in God's hands, you will discover that he will step in to deal with the obstacles in your path. Note that I am *not* saying that you will escape the consequences of your sin or that your problems will disappear overnight. There may be loose ends in your life that need to be tied up, and you may need to discuss your situation with an experienced Christian. What I *am* saying is that whatever your problems are, God will see you through. This was what God did when David threw himself on his mercy.

The plan was that Hushai would send word back to David through Ahimaaz and Jonathan the sons of the priests Zadok and Abiathar. The Bible says:

> Jonathan and Ahimaaz were staying at En Rogel. A servant girl was to go and inform them, and they were to go and tell King David, for they could not risk being seen entering the city. But a young man saw them and told Absalom. So the two of them left quickly and went to the house of a man in Bahurim. He had a well in his courtyard, and they climbed down into it. His wife took a covering and spread it out over the opening of the well and scattered grain over it. No-one knew anything about it.
>
> When Absalom's men came to the woman at the house, they asked, 'Where are Ahimaaz and Jonathan?'
>
> The woman answered them, 'They crossed over the brook.' The men searched but found no-one, so they returned to Jerusalem.
>
> After the men had gone, the two climbed out of the well and went to inform King David (2 Sam. 17:17-21).

Had Absalom's men discovered Ahimaaz and Jonathan things might have turned out very differently for David, but this did not happen because *God* was in control of events.

And when they told David that God had answered his prayer and had frustrated Ahithophel's counsel, he knew that the tide had turned.

At first, the turning of the tide is imperceptible, but no one can stop the incoming waters as they sweep in to cover the shore. One day the tide will turn for the church. Only a few attend its services now, and fewer still have been born again, but God could change this within days and show the world his glory, and then even the most powerful nations on earth would be unable to withstand him.

Indeed the day is coming when everyone will acknowledge his authority. Read Romans 14:11:

> "'As surely as I live,' says the Lord,
>   "Every knee will bow before me;
>   every tongue will confess to God.'"

It is not a question of *whether* you do this but *when*. If the Holy Spirit is calling you to honour Jesus now, do not resist him: acknowledge him as your Saviour and Lord. Then you will see that the tide has turned.

53

Assurance That God Will Use You Again

2 Samuel 17

Have you known better days? Can you recall a time when you had a sense of personal dignity, a time when you knew God was with you and your future looked promising? Perhaps things are different now and those days have gone.

Of course, there may be more than one explanation for this. For instance, maybe you are getting old and have been pushed aside; maybe you have let God down and fallen into sin, and you wonder, 'What is the use? Why does God keep me here? I know that he has forgiven me, but surely he will never *use* me again.'

That was how David felt. Here was a man who, perhaps, had known greater glory than anyone who had ever lived, but he had fallen into sin and now he was paying dearly for it, for his own son had rebelled against him and seized his throne. God had forgiven David, but Nathan's prophecy that the sword would never leave his house was being fulfilled (see 2 Sam. 12:10).

Perhaps you think it was unfair that God dealt with David so severely, but God had been good to him. Jesus said that God exercises discernment in judgment. He put it like this: 'From everyone who has been given much, much will be demanded; and from the one who has been entrusted with much, much more will be asked' (Luke 12:48).

Now, accompanied by a few loyal friends, the exiled king was walking barefoot across the Kidron Valley weeping. Most people thought that he was finished, but David knew that God was disciplining him and he accepted his chastening with dignity.

However, the news that his close friend and counsellor Ahithophel had defected to Absalom was hard to bear. Then, David fell to his knees and begged God to intervene. The Bible says:

So David prayed, 'O Lord, turn Ahithophel's counsel into foolishness' (2 Sam. 15:31).

This was a key moment in David's life, and he knew that if God answered his prayer, it would change everything.

I do not know how much prayer means to you, but I was brought up to believe that it is vitally important. Although my father was a layperson, he would not think of spending less than half an hour alone with God before setting off for work. To me that was normal. And when I was a teenager, I spent one or two hours in prayer daily and thought that all youngsters who loved the Lord did the same.

Are you in a crisis? Have you prayed about your situation? David's prayer: 'O Lord, turn Ahithophel's counsel into foolishness' shows the importance of praying in detail and making a specific request of God.

David was a man of prayer and he instinctively turned to God. It is true that there were people around him who were doing their best to encourage him, but the only thing that mattered was that *God* answered him, for it would show that he still had a future in God's service.

However, he had no assurance that God *would* hear him. Now some Christians *can* tell when they pray that God will grant their request. I wish I could, but I would say that when I pray, 99 per cent of the time I feel nothing. Like David, sometimes we just have to wait and see what God will do.

You cannot always judge what is happening by the way you feel. When you invite Jesus Christ into your life, you may expect a highly emotional experience but, in fact, at the time you may feel *nothing* and wonder if God has really saved you. It is true that some weep when the Holy Spirit convicts them of sin or cry with joy when they realize they have been forgiven, but others feel nothing and still have a valid conversion. You may recall that Dr Springer, our dentist in Fort Lauderdale, and his wife felt no emotion when they accepted Christ, yet they went on to win many souls for him (see Chapter Two of this book). What matters is not the number of tears you shed but the sincerity of your repentance. What matters is not what you *feel* but what has actually happened.

We cannot always judge by appearances. Two thousand years ago no one watching the crucifixion realized that God's own Son was paying the penalty for our sin; nevertheless, God *was* at work that day.

You will recall that God *did* answer David's prayer, for suddenly his friend Hushai appeared and agreed to go to Jerusalem and nullify Ahithophel's advice to Absalom (2 Sam. 15:32-37). I want us to see now that, although David did not know what God was doing for him in the background, in fact, he was at work.

In Jerusalem Ahithophel gave Absalom this evil counsel:

> Ahithophel said to Absalom, 'I would choose twelve thousand men and set out tonight in pursuit of David. I would attack him while he is weary and weak. I would strike him with terror, and then all the people with him will flee. I would strike down only the king and bring all the people back to you. The death of the man you seek will mean the return of all; all the people will be unharmed.' This plan seemed good to Absalom and to all the elders of Israel (2 Sam. 17:1-4).

Had Absalom followed this advice, David would, almost certainly, have been killed. But God prompted Absalom to get a second opinion:

> Absalom said, 'Summon also Hushai the Arkite, so that we can hear what he has to say' (v. 5).

415

That was the moment that altered the course of history. Note, it was Absalom himself who asked for Hushai's advice. This shows that God can do *anything*: he can intervene in a way that causes even our enemies to act on an impulse that will change everything.

When Hushai answered Absalom's summons, God gave him the tact and eloquence he needed to refute Ahithophel's advice.

Hushai replied to Absalom, 'The advice Ahithophel has given is, not good this time. . . .' (v. 7).

This was a diplomatic way of saying that *usually* Ahithophel gave good advice, but *this* time Absalom ought to consider one or two other things.

What Hushai said was untrue, for Ahithophel's advice was sound. Now I do not justify telling a lie, but another phenomenon was at work here. The Bible tells us there were times when God put a 'lying spirit' into the mouths of his prophets (1 Kgs. 22:23; 2 Chr. 18:22).

One of the most awesome verses I know is 2 Thessalonians 2:11, which says that when people listen to Satan and deliberately reject the truth, God sends them 'a powerful delusion so that they will believe the lie'. As we will see, Absalom was led to believe a lie because he did not believe the truth.

Hushai then set out to shake Absalom's confidence in Ahithophel's scheme. He began by playing upon Absalom's fears, reminding him of his father's formidable courage and experience as a warrior.

'You know your father and his men; they are fighters, and as fierce as a wild bear robbed of her cubs. Besides, your father is an experienced fighter; he will not spend the night with the troops. Even now, he is hidden in a cave or some other place. If he should attack your troops first, whoever hears about it will say, "There has been a slaughter among the troops who follow Absalom." Then even the bravest soldier, whose heart is like the heart of a lion, will melt with fear, for all Israel knows that your father is a fighter and that those with him are brave' (vv. 8–10).

Next Hushai appealed to Absalom's pride by telling him that his people ought to see him at the head of his troops leading them into battle.

'So I advise you: Let all Israel, from Dan to Beersheba – as numerous as the sand on the seashore – be gathered to you, with you yourself leading them into battle. Then we will attack him wherever he may be found, and we will fall on him as dew settles on the ground. Neither he nor any of his men will be left alive' (vv. 11–12).

The Bible tells us that Absalom was a very handsome man and was very proud of his long hair (see 2 Sam. 14:25–26). Picturing himself at the head of his army, acknowledging the cheers of an admiring crowd, Absalom was won over. Little did he know that God had used Hushai to persuade him to adopt a plan that would mean his defeat.

If the devil is attacking you and you are at the end of your tether, remember, he always overreaches himself. This was what happened here.

I have often wondered *why* Satan goes too far; one would think that he would learn from his past mistakes. However, I have concluded that he is prepared to take the risk because he delights that for those he uses the consequences are disastrous. Sadly, some do not even believe that the devil exists and he finds them easy prey, but when he has finished with them, he laughs at their misery.

Ahithophel turned out to be the Judas Iscariot of the Old Testament and met with the same end. You will recall that after he betrayed Jesus Judas 'went away and hanged himself' (Matt. 27:5), and when Ahithophel realized that Absalom had not followed his advice and he was no longer needed, he did the same (2 Sam. 17:23). Satan did nothing to stop him: he laughed.

We would do well to remember, however, that Satan can only work through people who do not love one another. So the surest way to avoid being his instrument is to be filled with love. You see, when someone you love hurts you, you are prepared to forgive them. Then, finding that he cannot make you bitter, Satan will leave you alone, but if you bear malice, he will use you. The devil found it easy to work through Absalom and Ahithophel for both were consumed with hatred.

The new regime in Israel did not honour God: Absalom's only concern was his own glory. He and his followers did not seek God in prayer, nor did Ahithophel advise them that they should. But what Ahithophel and Absalom had forgotten was that *David* was a man of prayer. As I said, Satan always goes too far.

Are you receiving advice from anyone now? Has this person told you to seek the Lord? Now if you say, 'I *am* trying to find God, but he does not seem to be there!' remember, the Bible says, 'If . . . you seek the Lord your God, you will find him if you look for him *with all your heart and with all your soul* [my italics]' (Deut. 4:29).

I want to remind you of three more things about David.

First, David was a forgiven man.

God says to you, 'No matter how great your sin, if you repent, I will forgive you.' If you say, 'I've asked him to forgive me, but I don't *feel* any different', remember that if your repentance is sincere, he *has* forgiven you. Do not trust your feelings: trust God's word. The Bible says, 'If we confess our sins, he is faithful and just and *will* forgive us our sins and purify us from all unrighteousness [my italics]' (1 John 1:9).

Second, David accepted his chastening with dignity. He did not complain, 'Lord, I don't deserve this! You are going too far! I can't take any more!'

When God disciplines you, it proves that you are his child.

The Bible says, 'The Lord disciplines those he loves, and he punishes everyone he accepts as a son' (Heb. 12:6). So accept God's chastening with dignity and say, 'No matter *what* happens, I will trust him.' Job said, 'Though he slay me, yet will I hope in him' (Job. 13:15). It takes a lot of faith to say that.

Third, David prayed that God would use him again. Read Psalm 51:10–13:

> Create in me a pure heart, O God,
>   and renew a steadfast spirit within me.
> Do not cast me from your presence
>   or take your Holy Spirit from me.
> Restore to me the joy of your salvation
>   and grant me a willing spirit to sustain me.
>
> Then I will teach transgressors your ways,
>   and sinners will turn back to you.'

You see, when God forgives us our sins, he takes our future on board and he will use us in his service.

Hushai sent Ahimaaz the son of Zadok the priest and Jonathan the son of Abiathar to David with news of Absalom's intentions (2 Sam. 17:17–21). The two men arrived at David's camp suddenly, probably in the middle of the night, with this message:

> 'Set out and cross the river at once; Ahithophel has advised such and such against you' (v. 21).

Absalom had rejected Ahithophel's counsel, but Hushai was taking no chances. So he told David what Ahithophel had advised in case Absalom changed his mind and took twelve thousand men to hunt him down and kill him after all. Hushai reasoned that if David were prepared, he could defend himself, whichever plan Absalom decided to adopt.

It was the best news David had heard for years, for he could see that God *had* answered his prayer and he was still with him. That was all he needed to know. From that moment on he could cope.

I am reminded of when Elijah prayed on Mount Carmel that God would end a three-year drought in Israel. The Bible says:

> Elijah said to Ahab [the king], 'Go, eat and drink, for there is the sound of heavy rain.' So Ahab went off to eat and drink, but Elijah climbed to the top of Carmel, bent down to the ground and put his face between his knees.
>
> 'Go and look towards the sea,' he told his servant. And he went up and looked.
>
> 'There is nothing there,' he said.
>
> Seven times Elijah said, 'Go back.'
>
> The seventh time the servant reported, 'A cloud as small as a man's hand is rising from the sea' (1 Kgs. 18:41-44).

Elijah knew then he could sit back and just watch God at work.

> So Elijah said, 'Go and tell Ahab, "Hitch up your chariot and go down before the rain stops you."'
>
> Meanwhile, the sky grew black with clouds, the wind rose, a heavy rain came on . . . (vv. 44-45).

When David heard his two spies say, 'Set out and cross the river at once; Ahithophel has advised such and such against you', he knew that from then on he could leave everything to God.

God now brought new friends into David's life. The Bible says:

> When David came to Mahanaim, Shobi son of Nahash from Rabbah of the Ammonites, and Makir son of Ammiel from Lo Debar, and Barzillai the Gileadite from Rogelim brought bedding and bowls and articles of pottery. They also brought wheat and barley, flour and roasted grain, beans and lentils, honey and

curds, sheep, and cheese from cows' milk for David and his people to eat. For they said, 'The people have become hungry and tired and thirsty in the desert' (vv. 27-29).

These people came out of the blue to help him and he enjoyed every minute of their company because he knew that God had sent them.

When God gives you a fresh start, you will find he will bring new friends into your life too. You should welcome them, for they will encourage you and you will enjoy Christian fellowship.

The fact that all this happened at Mahanaim would not have been lost on David. Every Israelite knew that when Jacob was going through a time of trial God sent angels to encourage him and he named the place where they met him 'Mahanaim', saying, 'This is the camp of God' (Gen 32:1-2). Mahanaim was a reminder to David of God's graciousness, for Jacob had often let God down too, but, despite this, God used him to accomplish his divine purpose. And David knew that God would do the same for him.

None of us is perfect, as John Calvin said, 'In every saint there is something reprehensible.' But God wants to cleanse and restore those who fall. He has a plan for *your* life, and if you ask him, he will wash your sins away and take care of your future.

54

Why You Can Afford to Be Gracious

2 Samuel 18:1-7

Has someone treated you unjustly? Are you waiting for a chance to get even? If so, I want to tell you that, like David, you can afford to be gracious.

David had been the victim of a grave injustice when his son Absalom seized his throne and drove him into a humiliating exile. To make matters worse, his close friend and counsellor Ahithophel defected to Absalom. However, when David prayed, God stepped in and sent Hushai to nullify Ahithophel's advice to Absalom. Because of Hushai's intervention the tide began to turn and David knew that God would restore him.

It became apparent that not all the Israelites had defected to Absalom, and God prompted thousands of loyal troops to join the king at Mahanaim. David had left the palace with a handful of bodyguards, but now he had the welcome task of organizing an army. The Bible says:

> David mustered the men who were with him and appointed over them commanders of thousands and commanders of hundreds. David sent the troops out – a third under the command of Joab, a third under Joab's brother Abishai son of Zeruiah, and a third under Ittai the Gittite. The king told the troops, 'I myself will surely march out with you' (2 Sam. 18:1-2).

Here we see a new David: God had disciplined him and he had changed.

The Bible says, 'The Lord disciplines those he loves, and

he punishes everyone he accepts as a son' (Heb. 12:6). Why does he chasten us? Do you think that God enjoys putting us through hard times? Do you think that he looks down from heaven, saying, 'I am going to make that person suffer for what he did'? No. The writer to the Hebrews explains that he chastens us for one reason: 'God disciplines us for our good, that we may share in his holiness. No discipline seems pleasant at the time, but painful. Later on, however, it produces a harvest of righteousness and peace for those who have been trained by it' (Heb. 12:10-11). God wants to mould us and transform us into his own likeness (2 Cor. 3:18). However, this does not happen simply because we *say*, 'I have decided to pray to be more like Jesus'; sometimes we need to go through a time of trial, and that alone will change us.

One effect of God's chastening is that we become more gracious in the way we deal with others. This was the effect it had on David, who showed his graciousness in three ways.

First, David became vulnerable. He told his men, 'I myself will surely march out with you.' This was a courageous gesture, because he was an experienced warrior and knew that those in the front line face the greatest risk of being killed. But he wanted to show his gratitude to his troops by leading them into battle personally, and so he dismissed all thought of his own importance and was prepared to lay his life on the line.

One aspect of graciousness is that you refuse to take yourself so seriously. You can tell in a minute when someone has a high opinion of himself but is so sensitive that you have to handle him with kid gloves. But are *you* like that? Do you think that the world will collapse if no one exalts you? God wants you to stop setting such store on your life; he wants you to see that you can afford to be gracious. Jesus said, 'Whoever finds his life will lose it, and whoever loses his life for my sake will find it' (Matt. 10:39).

Second, David was teachable. Read verses 3 and 4:

The men said, 'You must not go out; if we are forced to flee, they won't care about us. Even if half of us die, they won't care; but you are worth ten thousand of us. It would be better now for you to give us support from the city.'

The king answered, 'I will do whatever seems best to you.'

Once David might have said, 'Who are these people to tell *me* what to do? I am the king!' But now he admitted his need of sound advice and changed his mind. In other words, David became teachable.

Do you have Christian friends? What are they saying to you? Are they all telling you the same thing? Proverbs 11:14 says, 'Many advisers make victory sure.' If you are receiving the same signal from those who understand your situation and know you best, are you sufficiently gracious to accept that you need good counsel? Are you teachable?

When you admit that you need advice, you take the first step towards conversion. You take the second step when you see that what your friends have been telling you is right. You realize that you are a sinner and that you cannot save yourself, no matter how good a life you lead; your only hope is to plead the merit of the blood that God's Son shed for you on the cross, humbling though that may be. To put it another way, you change your mind and become teachable. The Bible calls this repentance.

Something that new Christians often find frustrating is that they are excited about Jesus and want their friends and their families to get to know him too, yet, try as they might, they cannot get them to see what they see. But repentance is the work of the Holy Spirit in the heart of an individual; it is not something that we can bring about.

Third, David became gentle. After agreeing to stay behind, he gave a very strict order to the three men whom he had put in charge.

The king commanded Joab, Abishai and Ittai, 'Be gentle with the young man Absalom for my sake' (v. 5).

Because God was with him, David *knew* what the outcome of the battle would be, but he was worried about what would happen to Absalom. He knew that his arrogant son had behaved appallingly and would have to pay for his sin; however, he wanted *God* to be the one to deal with him, and so he instructed his three commanders to treat him gently.

Maybe your attitude towards your enemy has led you to say, 'As soon as I get the chance, I'll get even with him.' But Jesus said that we should be gracious to our enemies. He put it like this:

'You have heard that it was said, "Love your neighbour and hate your enemy." But I tell you: Love your enemies and pray for those who persecute you, that you may be sons of your Father in heaven' (Matt. 5:43-45).

Have you prayed, 'Lord, bless my enemy; deal gently with him'? If you are not ready to offer up this prayer, your chastening will continue. Remember, Jesus also said:

'If you forgive men when they sin against you, your heavenly Father will also forgive you. But if you do not forgive men their sins, your Father will not forgive your sins' (Matt. 6:14-15).

The proof that you have forgiven your enemy totally is that you say, 'Lord, bless him', and *mean* it. This *proves* that you are a new person.

I believe there were four reasons why David behaved so graciously.

First, David remembered that he was chosen from the pasture (Ps. 78:70). He could never forget that he had not reached his lofty position through merit. He had been a simple shepherd. He knew that he had done nothing to deserve his lofty position; it was *God* who had exalted him.

Heaven is populated by people who know that they do not deserve to be there. A Christian is a person who wonders, 'Why has God been so gracious to me? What did I do to deserve salvation?' God has been good to *me*, for I am going to heaven: most people are not. 'That is an awful thing to say!' you may exclaim. But it was Jesus himself who said that few find 'the road that leads to life' (Matt. 7:14). I do not know why God saves some but not others; I wish that he would save everyone. But he knows what he is doing. He has given me eternal life. What have I done to deserve it? Nothing.

Second, David could afford to be gracious because he knew that he had abused the privilege that God had given him. He had sinned: he had committed adultery with Bathsheba and he had murdered her husband to cover it up. Then for two years he had lived unashamed until God sent Nathan to confront him with his sin and say, 'The sword shall never depart from your house' (2 Sam. 12:10). David knew that prophecy was being fulfilled and it was his own sin that was responsible for his son's rebellion. How could he judge Absalom? He could afford to be gracious.

Jesus said, 'Do not judge, or you too will be judged' (Matt. 7:1). If you are judgmental, I guarantee that it will be only a matter of time before God shows you that you are no better than your enemy. Until you learn not to point the finger, your chastening will continue.

Third, David could afford to be gracious to Absalom because he himself was a forgiven man. According to the Law, the punishment for adultery and murder was death (Lev. 20:10; Num. 35:16). But David knew that God had not dealt with him according to the Law, so how could he ask him to deal harshly with another when he himself had received such mercy!

Perhaps you are angry and bitter because someone has treated you badly. Maybe someone has lied about you or cheated you out of money, and you lie awake at night fantasizing about the day you will get even. If so, stop; think what God has done for you. Knowing that your sins nailed his Son to the cross and yet he freely forgave you, do you really want him to punish your enemy? You can afford to be gracious.

Do you remember the Parable of the Unmerciful Servant (Matt. 18:23-35)? Jesus said:

'The kingdom of heaven is like a king who wanted to settle accounts with his servants. As he began the settlement, a man who owed him ten thousand talents was brought to him. Since he was not able to pay, the master ordered that he and his wife and his children and all that he had be sold to repay the debt.

'The servant fell on his knees before him. "Be patient with me," he begged, "and I will pay back everything." The servant's master took pity on him, cancelled the debt and let him go.

'But when that servant went out, he found one of his fellow-servants who owed him a hundred denarii. He grabbed him and began to choke him. "Pay back what you owe me!" he demanded.

'His fellow servant fell to his knees and begged him, "Be patient with me and I will pay you back."

'But he refused. Instead he went off and had the man thrown into prison until he could pay the debt. When the other servants saw what had happened, they were greatly distressed and went and told their master everything that had happened.

'Then the master called the servant in. "You wicked servant," he said, "I cancelled all that debt of yours because you begged me to. Shouldn't you have had mercy on your fellow-servant just as I had on you?" In anger his master turned him over to the jailers to be tortured, until he should pay back all he owed.'

God hates it if you refuse to forgive another when he has forgiven you so much.

Indeed if you bear malice, *you* are the loser; *you* are the one who will feel tormented, and the bitterness inside you will affect your health and your appearance. It is so foolish to harbour a grudge.

Now when you forgive someone, you should not go up to that person and say, 'I forgive you.' In fact, sometimes that is the *worst* thing you can do. I have known those who have gone up to another and said, 'I have decided to forgive you for what you have done to me', but the very fact that they say that shows that they have *not* forgiven that person; they simply want him to know how angry they feel. It is a way of returning to the attack. When you forgive someone, he or she can tell by your expression and by the tone of your voice that you have done so; you do not have to say anything.

Fourth, David could afford to be gracious because he knew that God was turning the tide and victory was certain; only the details of how God would bring this about were lacking.

If you are a Christian, you have God's promise that you will go to heaven (see John 3:16). You do not know all the details concerning the last days and the Second Coming of Jesus, but you do know that he *is* coming and you will spend eternity with him. With the promise of such a glorious future, do you *really* want vengeance? You can afford to be gracious.

We have seen that David became gentle, vulnerable and teachable. He knew that God had forgiven him so much and he would be a fool to be otherwise. And so would you.

55

If Only . . . !

2 Samuel 18:4–33

David waited in Mahanaim as his army marched out to fight Absalom and his forces. He was certain of the *outcome* of the battle, but he was concerned about Absalom's safety. The Bible says:

> The king stood beside the gate while all the men marched out in units of hundreds and of thousands. The king commanded Joab, Abishai and Ittai [the commanders of his army], 'Be gentle with the young man Absalom for my sake.' And all the troops heard the king giving orders concerning Absalom to each of the commanders' (2 Sam. 18:4–5).

But, in the end, David's orders were ignored:

> The army marched into the field to fight Israel, and the battle took place in the forest of Ephraim. There the army of Israel was defeated by David's men, and the casualties that day were great – twenty thousand men. The battle spread out over the whole countryside, and the forest claimed more lives that day than the sword.
>
> Now Absalom happened to meet David's men. He was riding his mule, and as the mule went under the thick branches of a large oak, Absalom's head got caught in the tree. He was left hanging in mid-air, while the mule he was riding kept on going.
>
> When one of the men saw this, he told Joab, 'I have just seen Absalom hanging in an oak tree.'
>
> Joab said to the man who had told him this, 'What! You saw him? Why didn't you strike him to the ground right there? Then I would have had to give you ten shekels of silver and a warrior's belt.'

But the man replied, 'Even if a thousand shekels were weighed out into my hands, I would not lift my hand against the king's son. In our hearing the king commanded you and Abishai and Ittai, "Protect the young man Absalom for my sake." And if I had put my life in jeopardy—and nothing is hidden from the king—you would have kept your distance from me.'

Joab said, 'I am not going to wait like this for you.' So he took three javelins in his hand and plunged them into Absalom's heart while Absalom was still alive in the oak tree. And ten of Joab's armour-bearers surrounded Absalom, struck him and killed him (2 Sam. 18:6–15).

Absalom's downfall had only been a matter of time. When Jesus said, 'Whoever exalts himself will be humbled, and whoever humbles himself will be exalted' (Matt. 23:12), he stated an eternal truth. In Psalm 103 David said, 'The Lord is compassionate and gracious, slow to anger, abounding in love' (v. 8). God is patient: it takes a lot to make him angry, and he warns an arrogant person repeatedly before he brings him down. However, unless that person heeds God's warnings, eventually God will humble him. Proverbs 16:18 says, 'Pride goes before destruction, a haughty spirit before a fall.'

Such verses are appropriate when we think of Absalom, who was so full of his own importance. The Bible gives us an illustration of his vanity:

During his life-time Absalom had taken a pillar and erected it in the King's Valley as a monument to himself, for he thought, 'I have no son to carry on the memory of my name.' He named the pillar after himself, and it is called Absalom's Monument to this day' (2 Sam. 18:18).

Can you imagine anyone building his own monument! Someone once said that the man who deserves a monument does not need one, and the man who needs one does not deserve it. Absalom's attempt to perpetuate his name was so sad. However, the source of Absalom's pride was the cause of his downfall. If you read 2 Samuel 14:25–26, you will see that the source of his pride was his long hair:

> In all Israel there was not a man so highly praised for his handsome appearance as Absalom. From the top of his head to the sole of his foot there was no blemish in him. Whenever he cut the hair of his head—he used to cut his hair from time to time when it became too heavy for him—he would weigh it, and its weight was two hundred shekels by the royal standard [about 2.5 kg].

Absalom was so proud of his hair that he refused to roll it up or wear a helmet. He wanted everyone to see it streaming behind him as he rode into battle at the head of his army. How ironic that it became entangled in a tree and he was dragged from his mule and left dangling, a helpless target!

Beware of championing the gifts God gives you. If he has made you beautiful, kill your pride. Being good-looking has its pitfalls.

You may remember that in an earlier chapter I said Ahithophel was the Judas Iscariot of the Old Testament, but I believe Absalom is also an Old Testament picture of Judas. The Bible says that when Judas betrayed Jesus, Satan entered into him (Luke 22:3). I think that the devil took up residence in *Absalom's* heart too. You see, some kinds of sin are so unspeakable that you have to conclude that demonic forces are involved.

I think that the story of Absalom shows us four ways in which the devil can gain entry into our hearts and minds.

First, Satan gets in when our ambitions are not sanctified. Now being ambitious is not wrong. An ambitious person can be highly motivated and get things done. Martin Luther used to say, 'God uses ambition to drive a man to service.' However, unless we pray that the blood of Christ cleanses our ambition, Satan will try to ensure that it controls us. Then we can become so obsessed with getting what we want that the consequences will be disastrous. For example, the person who thinks of nothing else but making money may become so greedy and impatient that eventually he becomes involved in all kinds of shady dealings. As Paul said, 'The love of money is a root of all kinds of evil' (1 Tim. 6:10).

Second, Satan gets in when we do not allow God to heal our wounds. Maybe you know what it is to have somebody walk all over you or lie about you, and you cry, 'Lord, why did this happen? How *could* they treat me like that!' But if you keep picking at your wounds and you refuse to forgive your enemy, at some imperceptible point the devil will get in. Then you will become so obsessed with getting even that you begin to do things that once would have been inconceivable.

Third, Satan gets in when our gift is not sanctified. Now if you say, 'I don't have a gift', you are wrong. God has endowed all of us with certain gifts. Moreover, he has given each of us a gift that is unique. We sometimes say, 'When God made so-and-so, he threw the mould away.' Well, when he made *you*, he threw the mould away. God has equipped you for a task that you alone can do.

God equipped Daniel for a task that only he could do. One gift that Daniel received from God was the ability to interpret visions. We find one example of how Daniel used this gift in Daniel 5.

Do you remember what happened at Belshazzar's banquet? The Bible says:

> Suddenly the fingers of a human hand appeared and wrote on the plaster of the wall, near the lampstand in the royal palace. The king watched the hand as it wrote. His face turned pale and he was so frightened that his knees knocked together and his legs gave way.
>
> The king called out for the enchanters, astrologers and diviners to be brought . . . .
>
> Then all the king's wise men came in, but they could not read the writing or tell the king what it meant. So King Belshazzar became even more terrified and his face grew more pale. His nobles were baffled.

The queen, hearing the voices of the king and his nobles, came into the banquet hall. 'O king, live for ever!' she said. 'Don't be alarmed! Don't look so pale! There is a man in your kingdom who has the spirit of the holy gods in him. In the time of your father he was found to have insight and intelligence and wisdom like that of the gods. . . . Call for Daniel, and he will tell you what the writing means' (Dan. 5:5–12).

They found Daniel, for he alone could interpret the writing, which warned Belshazzar that God had weighed him on his scales and found him wanting.

God had a task for Daniel and he has a task for each of us. However, he cannot use us unless we ask him to sanctify our gift; in fact, it would cause our downfall.

Fourth, Satan gets in if our bodies are not the Lord's. Paul said, 'Do you not know that your body is a temple of the Holy Spirit, who is in you, whom you have received from God? You are not your own; you were bought at a price' (1 Cor. 6:19–20). This means that our bodies belong to God. Now this verse *chiefly* relates to sexual conduct, and Paul went on to say, 'The body is not meant for sexual immorality, but for the Lord, and the Lord for the body' (1 Cor. 6:13). The Bible condemns sex outside marriage. You may say, 'Well, I have certain needs that must be satisfied.' I understand that, but with God's help you can resist temptation. In 1 Corinthians 10:13 we read: 'No temptation has seized you except what is common to man. And God is faithful; he will not let you be tempted beyond what you can bear. But when you are tempted, he will also provide a way out so that you can stand up under it.' The danger is, if we do not resist sexual temptation, our lusts will become unsatiable and demonic forces will take control.

As I said, I believe that Absalom was controlled by Satan. How could a man do what he did without the devil's help? No wonder that David feared for his son and anxiously waited for news. The Bible says:

While David was sitting between the inner and outer gates, the watchman went up to the roof of the gateway by the wall. As he looked out, he saw a man running alone. The watchman called out to the king and reported it.

The king said, 'If he is alone, he must have good news.' And the man came closer and closer.

Then the watchman saw another man running, and he called down to the gatekeeper, 'Look, another man running alone!'

The king said, 'He must be bringing good news, too' (2 Sam. 18:24–26).

In a way it *was* good news, for the messenger, who happened to be Ahimaaz, shouted:

'All is well!' He bowed down before the king with his face to the ground and said, 'Praise be to the Lord your God! He has delivered up the men who lifted their hands against my lord the king' (v. 28).

But David wanted news of his *son*:

The king asked, 'Is the young man Absalom safe?'

Ahimaaz was reluctant to tell him that Absalom was dead and his reply was vague. He said:

'I saw great confusion just as Joab was about to send the king's servant and me, your servant, but I don't know what it was' (v. 29).

It was not until a second messenger, a Cushite sent by Joab, arrived that David learnt the truth.

The king asked the Cushite, 'Is the young man Absalom safe?'

The Cushite replied, 'May the enemies of my lord the king and all who rise up to harm you be like that young man.'

The king was shaken. He went up to the room over the

gateway and wept. As he went, he said: 'O my son Absalom! My son, my son Absalom! If only I had died instead of you—O Absalom, my son, my son!' (vv. 32–33).

What are we to make of David's cry?

Well, first, I see it as a cry of a parent who realizes that his child is eternally lost. Above all else, Christian parents want the assurance that their children are converted. You see, the Bible teaches that only those who have accepted Jesus as their Saviour can enter heaven when they die. Perhaps your parents are praying that you will become a Christian. If you want to know how they will feel if you die unconverted, you have only to think of how David wept over Absalom: 'O my son Absalom! My son, my son Absalom! If only I had died instead of you – O Absalom, my son, my son!' Christian parents cannot bear the thought of their children spending eternity in hell.

When I was a teenager, I had a newspaper round. One evening I looked on the front page of *The Ashland Daily Independent* and saw that somebody I knew had been killed in the Korean war. I stood rooted to the spot in shock, for he was only a year or two older than I was; moreover, he had been my idol, for he had been the star basketball and baseball player of the Ashland Tomcats.

I went home and showed the report to my parents because his mother was a member of our church. My father said, 'We must go round and see if there's anything we can do.' So we set off. But when we arrived we found that other people had had the same idea and there were so many cars parked in the street that we had to park in the next block. When we got out of the car, although we were some distance away, we heard a terrible, despairing wail coming from the direction of her house. I will never forget that awful sound if I live to be a hundred! We hurried to the house and someone let us in, but the bereaved woman did not know that we were there. She just sat rocking and moaning aloud.

Second, David's cry was the cry of one who knew that all which happened was traceable to *his* sin. 'If only I hadn't committed adultery! If only I hadn't tried to cover it up by committing murder! If only I repented sooner!' he thought. 'Absalom received the punishment that *I* deserved.' And when David cried, 'My son, my son Absalom! If only I had died instead of you!' he meant it.

Yet what David *wished* that he could have done Jesus *did*. He was not responsible for our disobedience, but he paid the penalty for it. Isaiah put it like this:

> He was pierced for *our* transgressions,
>   he was crushed for *our* iniquities;
> the punishment that brought us peace was upon *him*,
>   and by his wounds we are healed.
> We all, like sheep, have gone astray,
>   each of us has turned to his own way;
>   and the Lord has laid on him the iniquity of us all [my italics]
> (Isa. 53:5–6).

Jesus said, 'Greater love has no-one than this, that he lay down his life for his friends' (John 15:13).

A few days before his crucifixion, on the first Palm Sunday, in fact, Jesus wept over Jerusalem. Read Luke 19:41–44:

> As [Jesus] approached Jerusalem and saw the city, he wept over it and said, 'If you, even you, had only known on this day what would bring you peace – but now it is hidden from your eyes. The days will come upon you when your enemies will build an embankment against you and encircle you and hem you in on every side. They will dash you to the ground, you and the children within your walls. They will not leave one stone on another, because you did not recognise the time of God's coming to you.'

Israel was the apple of God's eye (Deut. 32:10; Zech. 2:8). God had chosen Israel from all the other nations and promised to send it a Messiah. The Jews longed for the Messiah to come, and every Sabbath they would hear this scripture read in the synagogue: 'Oh, that you would rend the heavens and come down' (Isa. 64:1). But when Jesus, the God-man, came, he did not fit Jewish preconceptions of the Messiah and they rejected him. The time of their visitation came and they missed it. No wonder Jesus wept.

I recall witnessing to a young man from Scotland who said, 'Everybody seems to be talking to me about God today.'

'Well,' I said, 'this is not something that will happen to you every day because most people don't care about Jesus. Will you pray to receive him?'

'Another time, perhaps,' he replied.

'Look,' I said, 'God is obviously trying to get your attention, but if you don't accept Christ today, you may *never* do it.'

I was concerned for him because if a person obstinately refuses to respond to the gospel, eventually, God will *stop* trying to get through to him. God said, 'My Spirit will not contend with man for ever' (Gen. 6:3). Then, although that person may hear preaching that once would have driven him to tears or made him tremble with fear, he will just shrug his shoulders and say, 'I wonder why *that* ever bothered me?'

If you are still unconverted, I want you to know that Jesus has come to you *today*. This is the time of your visitation. Do not miss it. 'Seek the Lord while he may be found; call on him while he is near' (Isa. 55:6). You see, at the final judgment those who rejected Christ will cry in despair, 'If only . . .!' but it will be too late.

56

How to Cope with Guilty Feelings

2 Samuel 19:1–8

When Absalom seized his throne, David longed for God to vindicate him. However, when God intervened and gave him the victory, David was devastated, for he learnt that Absalom had been killed (see 2 Sam. 18:31–33). The Bible says:

> The king was shaken. He went up to the room over the gateway and wept. As he went, he said: 'O my son Absalom! My son, my son Absalom! If only I had died instead of you – O Absalom, my son, my son!' (2 Sam. 18:33).

The news that at last God had turned the tide did not bring David the happiness that he had expected.

When the revival that we long for comes, it will not bring the unmitigated joy that many Christians expect. In fact, I think that we will find some things about it unpleasant. For instance, I believe that many of those who profess to be God's friends, people who we expected would become actively involved in his work, will actually oppose it.

I say this with good reason. When Arthur Blessitt first came to Westminster Chapel, we experienced a touch of revival – not the great revival we were praying for, but a work of the Holy Spirit, nevertheless. I was deeply moved and I could not understand why everyone else did not feel the same way. It was obvious what we *ought* to be doing, but, sadly, Arthur's visit marked the beginning of a period of bitter opposition.

Another deep disappointment about the revival may be that so many remain unconverted. (We do not understand why the Holy Spirit passes some by, but we must remember that God is sovereign.)

One would have expected David's vindication to bring him great joy, but the news that his son had died brought him great sorrow. In fact, he was inconsolable, and he was so wrapped up in his grief that he spared no thought for the troops returning from the battle, but shut himself away, moaning constantly, 'O my son Absalom! My son, my son Absalom!' The Bible says:

> For the whole army the victory that day was turned into mourning, because on that day the troops heard it said, 'The king is grieving for his son.' The men stole into the city that day as men steal in who are ashamed when they flee from battle (Sam. 19: 2–3).

David should have put his grief aside and thanked the men who had fought so hard to save him. Sorrow, however poignant, should not hinder us from doing our duty.

However, I believe that David was paralyzed by a sense of pseudo-guilt (false guilt), and it is this that I want to talk about in this chapter. I want you to see four things: (1) the *presence* of pseudo-guilt, (2) the *peril* of pseudo- guilt, (3) the *proof* of pseudo-guilt, and (4) the *provision* God made for dealing with our sin.

First, I want to talk about the *presence* of pseudo-guilt.

You may ask, 'What is the difference between false guilt and true guilt?' Well, the sense of true guilt stems from God. He makes you feel guilty so you will see your need of the Saviour and find peace. Pseudo-guilt is quite different. It does *not* come from God: it is self-inflicted. It is an attempt to punish ourselves, and it does not lead to peace but to torment.

David was punishing himself: God was not doing it. You see, God had forgiven him for committing adultery with Bathsheba and murdering her husband, so David had no reason to feel guilty (see 2 Sam. 12:13), but he had never forgiven himself. As a result he had failed to discipline his children effectively and to bring them up to respect God's laws. Now he thought, 'If only I had been a better father Absalom would still be alive today! This is all my fault.'

Now you will probably say, 'But David was grief-stricken. Surely that is not wrong!' Of course not. But David went too far and called attention to his feelings. You see, David would not have kept on crying, 'O Absalom, my son, my son!' if he thought that no one could hear him.

I have taken many funeral services and I believe that those whose grief is deepest seldom make a great fuss. I have known widows who showed little sign of their sorrow yet took months to recover from their loss, while other friends and relatives, feeling guilty about the way they treated the deceased in his lifetime perhaps, would make a great fuss but would recover almost immediately.

Next, I want to talk about the *peril* of pseudo-guilt. I believe that it is dangerous for two reasons.

First, it is a subtle form of self-atonement, for if you feel guilty despite knowing that Jesus Christ paid your debt on the cross, you show contempt for his grace. You see, you are really saying, 'What Jesus did is not good enough for me.' Now if you still say, 'But I *can't* forgive myself', I ask, are you more righteous than God? He forgives you. The Bible says, 'If we confess our sins, he is faithful and just and will forgive us our sins and purify us from all unrighteousness' (1 John 1:9). 'Well,' you may say, 'Surely it is *right* that I should feel bad.' But your guilty feelings can *never* atone for your sin. In his famous hymn 'Rock of Ages' Augustus Toplady put it like this:

Not the labour of my hands
Can fulfil Thy law's demands;
Could my zeal no respite know,
Could my tears for ever flow,
All for sin could not atone:
Thou must save, and Thou alone.

Pseudo-guilt is an unconscious attempt to atone by grief. Tears sometimes make people feel better, but they can be phony. Those who think that a few tears will impress God are mistaken. After the gospel service at Westminster Chapel sometimes people come to me and say, 'Your sermon made me cry tonight.'

'Did you accept Christ?' I reply.

'Well, no. But I was deeply moved.'

Their tears had simply given them a religious feeling, a feeling that they had done something good.

Second, pseudo-guilt is dangerous because it is counterproductive. You see, Satan will get in and then you will become paralyzed with grief and self-pity. You will be unable to get on with your life and you will shut out the friends who try to help you.

This was what happened to David. As we have seen, he shut himself in the room over the gateway, moaning, 'O Absalom, my son, my son!' No one dared to approach him. Everyone tiptoed around whispering, 'Oh, isn't it awful! Just listen to the poor king grieving for his son.'

However, Joab saw that David had to be shaken out of his self-pity, so he marched into the room over the gateway and spoke bluntly. The Bible says:

> Then Joab went into the house to the king and said, 'Today you have humiliated all your men, who have just saved your life and the lives of your sons and daughters and the lives of your wives and concubines. You love those who hate you and hate those who love you. You have made it clear today that the commanders and their men mean nothing to you. I see that you would be pleased if Absalom were alive today and all of us were dead. Now go out and encourage your men. I swear by the Lord that if you don't go out, not a man will be left with you by nightfall. This will be worse for you than all the calamities that have come upon you from your youth till now' (2 Sam. 19:5–7).

Third, I want to show you the *proof* of pseudo-guilt. In verse 8 we have proof that David was afflicted by false guilt. It says:

> So the king got up and took his seat in the gateway. When the men were told, 'The king is sitting in the gateway,' they all came before him.

When Joab said, 'You must snap out of it', David did so immediately. You see, pseudo-guilt is a display. As I said earlier, David knew that he had an audience and that was why he displayed his grief in the way he did. He had not forgiven himself for his sin, and he wanted everyone to know that he felt terrible.

Those who are afflicted by pseudo-guilt are controlled by what others might think. Because they cannot forgive themselves, they want others to know that they feel guilty. However, as I said, the danger is that Satan will then get in and keep them in that state. Joab did David a favour, for pseudo-guilt needs to be smashed.

Finally, I want you to see the *provision* that God made for dealing with our sin. God does not want us to live with a burden of guilt, so he sent his Son to die on a cross to take our guilt away. Isaiah said:

> We all, like sheep, have gone astray,
>   each of us has turned to his own way;
>   and the Lord has laid on him the iniquity of us all (Isa. 53:6–7).

If you realized how much God hates sin, you would see how sickening it is for him to hear you moan about the past. In fact, if you think that by punishing yourself you do something that parallels what Jesus did at Calvary, you make God angry, and he will say, 'I punished my Son for your sin. If only you knew what it cost him!'

On the cross Jesus suffered unimaginable physical torture,

but the spiritual agony he endured was far worse. The Bible says that for a time he was separated from his Father, a punishment so terrible that he cried aloud, 'My God, my God, why have you forsaken me?' (Matt. 27:46).

Perhaps over the years you have beaten yourself black and blue to atone for your unworthiness, but the only atonement for sin that God recognizes is what his Son did on the cross. Pseudo-guilt is the devil's way of paralyzing you, but if you could accept that God has forgiven you, your life would be transformed.

You may say, 'But no one else will forgive me for what I have done.' That is their problem. God says, 'I want my word to be the only thing that matters to you. I have forgiven you. I accept you. Will I do? I don't want you to feel guilty. Leave your past to me and step into the future with your head high.'

57

Eating Humble Pie

2 Samuel 19

If you have authority over others, you will have enemies, and should something happen that results in your downfall, these people will not hesitate to tell you exactly what they think of you.

You may remember that this was what happened when David fled into exile. Let me remind you of what happened. A man called Shimei, who was from the same tribe as Saul, had long resented the fact that David, who was of the tribe of Judah, ruled Israel. However, while David was in power, he had kept quiet. But *now* David seemed to be finished and Shimei made an appalling verbal and physical assault on him. The Bible says:

> Shimei son of Gera . . . cursed as he came out. He pelted David and all the king's officials with stones, though all the troops and the special guard were on David's right and left. As he cursed, Shimei said, 'Get out, get out, you man of blood, you scoundrel! The Lord has repaid you for all the blood you shed in the household of Saul, in whose place you have reigned. The Lord has handed the kingdom over to your son Absalom. You have come to ruin because you are a man of blood!' (2 Sam. 16:5-8).

'It's all right,' Shimei thought. 'David won't be back.' But, as we will see, he was wrong.

Hundreds of years later the Roman soldiers who crucified Jesus jeered, 'If you are the king of the Jews, save yourself' (Luke 23:37). They did not imagine for a second that one day they would see the man dying on the cross again, so they thought it safe to show their contempt. Nevertheless, one day those men will find themselves face to face with their victim, for Jesus is coming back.

On the Isle of Patmos John had a vision in which he saw Jesus' Second Coming. He described the scene like this:

Look, he is coming with the clouds,
 and every eye will see him,
even those who pierced him [my italics] (Rev. 1:7).

Can you imagine their terror?

But the Roman soldiers will not be the only ones to be filled with horror on that final day, for John went on to say:

All the peoples of the earth will mourn because of him.

The unconverted will be in a state of shock and wail aloud, for no one will care what others think of them then. They will have but one thought: 'There he is! It's all over.' Too late they will cry, 'Lord, I'm sorry; I didn't know! *Please* don't send me to hell!'

Their reaction to the sight of Jesus will contrast sharply with that of Christians. One famous hymn writer summed up their response like this:

Look, ye saints, the sight is glorious!
See the Man of Sorrows now.
                              Rev. T. Kelly

Overjoyed, God's people will exclaim, 'Can this *really* be happening? It's wonderful!'

We will all see Jesus one day. In Matthew 24:44 Jesus said, 'You ... must be ready, because the Son of Man will come at an hour when you do not expect him.' This verse applies to the time of our deaths or to the Second Coming, whichever happens first. None of us know *when* Jesus will return and none of us know exactly *when* we will die. It is true that some become terminally ill and have an opportunity to get right with God, but many die suddenly. We should take no chances. You see, it is only during our lifetimes that repentance is possible (see 2 Cor. 6:2). The important thing is to be prepared.

Now eating humble pie is something that we all have to do at some time. It is not a question of *whether* we do it but *when*. Those of us who are wise, humble ourselves now and say, 'Lord, I repent. Please forgive me.' Tragically, those who do not eat humble pie now, will do so at the final judgment, but, as I said, it will be too late.

Sadly, some would rather die than say, 'I am sorry; I was wrong.' Ahithophel, who had defected to Absalom, saw what would happen when Absalom rejected his advice, but rather than eat humble pie, he hanged himself (see 2 Sam. 17:23). And in New Testament times Judas Iscariot, filled with remorse because he had betrayed an innocent man, did the same (see Matt. 27:3-10).

Humble pie was the dish of the day for many as David made his way back to Jerusalem. The first to sample it was the tribe of Judah.

Strangely, it was the tribes of Israel who called for David to return to rule over them and David's own tribe dragged their heels (2 Sam. 19:9-10). So David tried to rally their support.

First he reminded them that they were his own kin:

King David sent this message to Zadok and Abiathar the priests: 'Ask the elders of Judah, "Why should you be the last to bring the king back to his palace, since what is being said throughout Israel has reached the king at his quarters? You are my brothers, my own flesh and blood. So why should you be the last to bring back the king?"' (2 Sam. 19:11-12).

Then he made an ingenious diplomatic move, saying:

> 'And say to Amasa [formerly, the commander-in-chief of Absalom's forces], "Are you not my own flesh and blood? May God deal with me, be it ever so severely, if from now on you are not the commander of my army in place of Joab"' (v. 13).

By making Amasa commander-in-chief in place of Joab, David placated those who had supported Absalom. The Bible says:

> He won over the hearts of all the men of Judah as though they were one man. They sent word to the king, 'Return, you and all your men' (v. 14).

His diplomacy succeeded, but David must have felt sad that it should have been necessary to persuade his *own* people to support him.

When Jesus came to this earth, he came to his own people. The apostle Paul said, 'I am not ashamed of the gospel, because it is the power of God for the salvation of everyone who believes: first for the Jew, then for the Gentile' (Rom. 1:16). The Jews were the ones who should have had the advantage of everything that Jesus did on the cross, but they rejected him and the gospel was preached to the Gentiles. Through the prophet Isaiah God said, 'I revealed myself to those who did not ask for me; I was found by those who did not seek me' (Isa. 65:1).

I think that when the revival comes, we will find that many Christians who ought to enjoy it most will oppose it and be put to one side.

I am reminded of the Parable of the Prodigal Son. Jesus told the story of the young man who could not wait until his father died to receive his share of the inheritance, so he persuaded his father to give him his share immediately, and then he went away and wasted it in extravagant living. Jesus said:

'After he had spent everything, there was a severe famine in that whole country, and he began to be in need. So he went and hired himself out to a citizen of that country, who sent him to his fields to feed pigs. He longed to fill his stomach with the pods that the pigs were eating, but no-one gave him anything.

'When he came to his senses, he said, "How many of my father's hired men have food to spare, and here I am starving to death! I will set out and go back to my father and say to him: 'Father, I have sinned against heaven and against you. I am no longer worthy to be called your son; make me like one of your hired men.' " So he got up and went to his father.

'But while he was still a long way off, his father saw him and was filled with compassion for him; he ran to his son, threw his arms around him and kissed him.

'The son said to him, "Father, I have sinned against heaven and against you. I am no longer worthy to be called your son."

'But the father said to his servants, "Quick! Bring the best robe and put it on him. Put a ring on his finger and sandals on his feet. Bring the fattened calf and kill it. Let's have a feast and celebrate. For this son of mine was dead and is alive again; he was lost and is found." So they began to celebrate.

'Meanwhile, the older son was in the field. When he came near the house, he heard music and dancing. So he called one of the servants and asked him what was going on. "Your brother has come," he replied, "and your father has killed the fattened calf because he has him back safe and sound."

'The older brother became angry and refused to go in. So his father went out and pleaded with him. But he answered his father, "Look! All these years I've been slaving for you and never disobeyed your orders. Yet you never gave me even a young goat so that I could celebrate with my friends. But when this son of yours who has squandered your property with prostitutes comes home, you kill the fattened calf for him!"

'"My son," the father said, "you are always with me, and everything I have is yours. But we had to celebrate and be glad, because this brother of yours was dead and is alive again; he was lost and is found"' (Luke 15:14-32).

This is the way it will be when the church experiences revival, and like the envious elder brother who refused to join in the party to welcome the prodigal home, certain Christians will refuse to join in because they were not the first.

The second party to eat humble pie was Shimei.

Now if you are one of those who say, 'I couldn't face the humiliation of admitting that I was wrong', think of him. As we have seen, he was the man who had most to fear from David's return. But interestingly, when he heard that David was returning, Shimei did not go into hiding, he 'hurried down' to meet him. The Bible says:

> Now the men of Judah had come to Gilgal to go out and meet the king and bring him across the Jordan. Shimei son of Gera, the Benjamite from Bahurim, hurried down with the men of Judah to meet King David. . . .
>
> When Shimei son of Gera crossed the Jordan, he fell prostrate before the king and said to him, 'May my lord not hold me guilty. Do not remember how your servant did wrong on the day my lord the king left Jerusalem. May the king put it out of his mind. For I your servant know that I have sinned, but today I have come here as the first of the whole house of Joseph to come down and meet my lord the king' (vv. 15–20).

Jesus *is* coming back. What will you do? Well, you have two options.

One option is to do nothing. However, this would be an act of the utmost folly, for when Jesus returned you would be numbered among those whom John described in his vision of the Second Coming. He said:

> Then the kings of the earth, the princes, the generals, the rich, the mighty, and every slave and every free man hid in the caves and among the rocks of the mountains. They called to the mountains and the rocks, 'Fall on us and hide us from the face of him who sits on the throne and from the wrath of the Lamb! For the great day of their wrath has come, and who can stand?' (Rev. 6:15-17).

The second option is to do what Shimei did. He did not wait until David returned to Jerusalem; he 'hurried down' to meet the king and prostrated himself before him, saying, 'I am without excuse. I am guilty. I am so sorry.'

In the Sermon on the Mount Jesus said:

> 'Settle matters quickly with your adversary who is taking you to court. Do it while you are still with him on the way, or he may hand you over to the judge, and the judge may hand you over to the officer, and you may be thrown into prison. I tell you the truth, you will not get out until you have paid the last penny' (Matt. 5: 25-26).

This verse also applies not only to our relationships with others but also to our relationship with God. If you are unconverted, *he* is your enemy. 'But I thought God loved me?' you may reply. He *does* love you. In fact, God loves you so much that he sent his Son to die for you. But unless you repent of your sins and plead the merit of the blood that Jesus shed on the cross, God's wrath will remain on you (see John 3:36).

However, there were three parties who had to eat humble pie that day. The third to do so was Abishai, who harboured a grudge against Shimei. Indeed, as we see in 2 Samuel 19:21, Abishai wanted to execute him on the spot:

> Then Abishai son of Zeruiah said, 'Shouldn't Shimei be put to death for this? He cursed the Lord's anointed.'

Abishai hated the thought that David might forgive Shimei and welcome him among them.

In the Parable of the Workers in the Vineyard (Matt. 20:1-16) Jesus told the story of labourers brought in to harvest the grapes who resented the fact that others who were brought in at the last minute received the same wages as those who had worked all day long.

Are you like that? Do you resent it when a great sinner is converted and is warmly welcomed into the church? Do you think, 'He doesn't *deserve* to be saved.' The scandal of the Christian faith is that the greatest sinners are given a free pardon, not on the basis of anything that they have done but on the basis of Jesus' sacrifice on the cross.

David had no time for Abishai's churlishness and delivered a strong rebuke:

> 'What do you and I have in common, you sons of Zeruiah?' This day you have become my adversaries! Should anyone be put to death in Israel today? Do I not know that today I am king over Israel?' (v. 22).

Then, turning to Shimei, he showed him compassion:

> The king said to Shimei, 'You shall not die.' And the king promised him on oath (v. 23).

If you say, 'Lord, I am so ashamed. I beg you for mercy', Jesus will give you a free pardon (see 1 John 1:9), not because of any good you have done but because he died to save you. Not only will you receive his forgiveness, you will spend eternity with him in heaven, for he said:

> 'In my Father's house are many rooms; if it were not so, I would have told you. I am going there to prepare a place for you. And if I go and prepare a place for you, I will come back and take you to be with me that you also may be where I am' (John 14:2-3).

As we have seen, when Jesus returns, *everyone* will see him. For those who did not eat humble pie and repent of their sins in their lifetime the humiliation of that moment will be unbearable; in fact, no greater horror can be conceived. So I urge you to run to the Saviour while you are 'on the way' and throw yourself on his mercy. The Bible says, '*Now* is the time of God's favour, *now* is the day of salvation [my italics]' (2 Cor. 6:2). Remember God said, 'My Spirit will not contend with man for ever' (Gen. 6:3).

58

How to Cope When Someone Lies About You

2 Samuel 19:24-30

A good name is a precious thing. The book of Proverbs says, 'A good name is more desirable than great riches' (Prov. 22:1). Perhaps Shakespeare was thinking of this verse when he wrote:

'Who steals my purse steals trash; 'tis something, nothing;
'Twas mine, 'tis his, and has been slave to thousands;
But he that filches from me my good name
Robs me of that which not enriches him,
And makes me poor indeed' (*Othello* Act 3, Sc. 3).

Mephibosheth's good name was taken from him.

Do you remember Mephibosheth, the invalid son of Jonathan, who, until his death at the hands of the Philistines, had been David's closest friend? When David was firmly established as king of Israel he had asked, 'Is there anyone still left of the house of Saul to whom I can show kindness for Jonathan's sake?' (2 Sam. 9:1). And learning that Mephibosheth was in need, he sent for him and said, 'Don't be afraid . . . for I will surely show you kindness for the sake of your father Jonathan. I will restore to you all the land that belonged to your grandfather Saul, and you will always eat at my table' (v. 7). Mephibosheth was overwhelmed. He had expected nothing, but suddenly he was given dignity, respect and recognition; moreover, he was adopted into David's family as a royal son.

The loser in all this was Ziba, who had managed to acquire quite an estate for himself out of the royal holdings left by his former master King Saul. Now, to Ziba's chagrin, David handed the entire estate over to Saul's grandson Mephibosheth. Furthermore, because Mephibosheth was disabled, David ordered Ziba and his sons to take care of him and oversee his estate (vv. 9-10).

However, after Absalom's coup and David's flight into exile, Ziba, ever the opportunist, saw his chance to recover the property that David had made him turn over to Mephibosheth. This was what happened:

> When David had gone a short distance beyond the summit, there was Ziba, the steward of Mephibosheth, waiting to meet him. He had a string of donkeys saddled and loaded with two hundred loaves of bread, a hundred cakes of raisins, a hundred cakes of figs and a skin of wine.
>
> The king asked Ziba, 'Why have you brought these?'
>
> Ziba answered, 'The donkeys are for the king's household to ride on, the bread and fruit are for the men to eat, and the wine is to refresh those who become exhausted in the desert' (2 Sam. 16:1-2).

At this time David was very vulnerable, and he was fooled by this seemingly magnanimous gesture. Then, realizing that Mephibosheth was absent, the king asked:

> 'Where is your master's grandson?'
>
> Ziba said to him, 'He is staying in Jerusalem, because he thinks, "Today the house of Israel will give me back my grandfather's kingdom"' (v. 3).

Nothing could be further from the truth: Mephibosheth had been overcome with grief when David was forced into exile. In fact, the Bible says: 'He had not taken care of his feet or trimmed his moustache or washed his clothes from the day the king left until the day he returned safely' (2 Sam. 19:24).

Perhaps you know what it is like to be lied about. Perhaps you did not realize what was happening; all you knew was that your friends suddenly and inexplicably distanced themselves from you, and it was months before you discovered the reason.

Mephibosheth was the victim of a lie, for, sadly, David did not wait to check Ziba's story:

> Then the king said to Ziba, 'All that belonged to Mephibosheth is now yours.'
> 'I humbly bow,' Ziba said. 'May I find favour in your eyes, my lord the king' (2 Sam. 16:4).

Then Ziba went away, delighted with the success of his mission.

However, as David approached Jerusalem, Mephibosheth went to meet him:

> The king asked him, 'Why didn't you go with me, Mephibosheth?'
> He said, 'My lord the king, since I your servant am lame, I said, "I will have my donkey saddled and will ride on it, so that I can go with the king." But Ziba my servant betrayed me. And he has slandered your servant to my lord the king. My lord the king is like an angel of God; so do whatever pleases you. All my grandfather's descendants deserved nothing but death from my lord the king, but you gave your servant a place among those who sat at your table. So what right do I have to make any more appeals to the king?'
> The king said to him. 'Why say more? I order you and Ziba to divide the fields.'
> Mephibosheth said to the king, 'Let him take everything, now that my lord the king has arrived home safely' (2 Sam. 19:25-30).

Had David been more discerning then, he would have realized that Ziba had lied, for Mephibosheth was clearly touched to see him return and was so grateful for his past kindness to him. But others, including David's own son Absalom and his friend and counsellor Ahithophel, had betrayed his trust, so it is little wonder that he was unsure where Mephibosheth's loyalties lay.

Let us think about what David's response meant to Mephibosheth. After his father and grandfather died, disabled and unable to earn a living, Mephibosheth had lived in poverty. Now, again, he had nothing. However, what made this so painful was that he sincerely loved and respected his benefactor. God, who had prompted David to act with such generosity, seemed to be hiding his face.

Eventually, every Christian discovers that, occasionally, God withdraws the *sense* of his presence. (Note, I speak of the *sense* of God's presence, for he never actually leaves us.) Isaiah experienced this and said, 'Truly you are a God who hides himself' (Isa. 45:15). Perhaps you ask, 'Why does God do this?' Well, I believe one reason that God hides himself is to test our faith.

Soon after we began the Pilot Light work, I witnessed to one man and was thrilled when he prayed to receive Christ. He gave me his address and promised, 'I will be at church tomorrow.' When he did not turn up, I thought, 'Well, perhaps he will come *next* Sunday.' But he did not come. Thinking that he might be discouraged, Tony Gaylor and I drove to Battersea to find him. It was a wasted journey: he had given me a fictitious address. Yet that man had prayed to receive Jesus, and his conversion had seemed so authentic. We often experience disappointments like this.

Some people say, 'If God were *really* behind the Pilot Light work, all those people who prayed to receive Christ would have come to church. In fact, Westminster Chapel would be bursting at the seams!' My answer is, if we know that we are acting in accordance with God's will, we must press on in faith, despite having no *evidence* that he is at work.

If you are a Christian, you will experience disappointments. There may come a time when you lose your job or fail to get the promotion you feel you deserve. Perhaps your best friend will turn against you or your spouse will be unfaithful to you.

Maybe you even develop a terminal illness. All kinds of things can happen, and you may wonder why God does not seem to be with you any longer. But it is in times like these that you discover whether your faith is strong enough to stand up to the test.

In this life there is so much injustice: bad things happen to good people and good things happen to bad people. Solomon put it like this: 'Righteous men . . . get what the wicked deserve, and wicked men . . . get what the righteous deserve' (Eccles. 8:14). And we wonder why God allows these things to happen.

I remember preaching a sermon called 'There Must Be a Heaven Somewhere'. I took the title from an old Negro spiritual that the slaves sang as they toiled in the cotton fields of Georgia and Alabama. The Negro spirituals were mostly about heaven. You see, those slaves who had Christian owners were allowed to go to church and sit in the gallery. There, they heard that everyone who puts their trust in Jesus goes to heaven when they die. They liked that. You see, they had nothing here on earth to look forward to.

However, tragically, many people suffer in this world and have nothing to look forward to in the next. Many of the slaves in the Deep South suffered terribly at the hands of their owners, but only those who trusted in what Jesus did for them on the cross have eternal life. The Bible says, 'For God so loved the world that he gave his one and only Son, that *whoever believes in him* shall not perish but have eternal life [my italics]' (John 3:16).

You may ask, 'Why does God promise salvation only to those who *believe*?' Because the highest compliment you can pay another is to say, 'I believe you.' When someone says that to me I know that they trust me completely. God wants us to affirm him like that.

Mephibosheth must have felt hurt that David did not affirm him, but the way in which he reacted shows us how we can cope when someone lies about us. I want to use this story to show you four things.

First, I want you to see that Mephibosheth detached himself from earthly things. Remember, he said, 'Let [Ziba] take everything, now that my lord the king has arrived home safely.'

Now if your ambition is happiness on earth, then being lied about will seem like the end of the world, because, for you, *this* world is all there is. But the Bible makes it clear that we should set our sights on things *eternal*. Read 1 John 2:15-17. John said:

> Do not love the world or anything in the world. If anyone loves the world, the love of the Father is not in him. For everything in the world – the cravings of sinful man, the lust of his eyes and the boasting of what he has and does – comes not from the Father but from the world. The world and its desires pass away, but the man who does the will of God lives for ever.

You see, all Christians will go to heaven; in view of a glorious future, what does it matter if our names are not cleared on earth? Paul said, 'If only for this life we have hope in Christ, we are to be pitied more than all men' (1 Cor. 15:19).

I think that one of the worst things that has happened to Christianity is the so-called health and wealth gospel. God does *not* promise us heaven on earth. Now if you say in your testimony 'Wonderful things have happened to me since God saved me', then praise him, but remember that prosperity is a bonus. I preach a gospel that says heaven awaits the Christian when he *dies*.

Second, Mephibosheth did not *strive* to defend himself. When David said, 'Why didn't you go with me?' Mephibosheth simply said, 'My lord the king, since I your servant am lame, I said, "I will have my donkey saddled and will ride on it, so that I can go with the king." But Ziba my servant betrayed me. And he has slandered your servant to my lord the king.' He did not protest his innocence again.

I have often said that the greatest freedom is having nothing to prove. Abraham Lincoln once said, 'If the end brings me out all right, what is said against me won't amount to anything. If the end brings me out wrong, ten angels swearing I was right would make no difference.'

Now you may think that Ziba got away with his sin, but Proverbs 11:21 says, 'Be sure of this: The wicked will not go unpunished'; one day Ziba will answer to God and Mephibosheth will be vindicated.

If someone has lied about you, you must not try to vindicate yourself. God says, 'It is mine to avenge; I will repay' (Rom. 12:19). In fact, this is a strain that runs right through the Bible (see Deut. 32:35; Ps. 94:1; Heb. 10:30). God will vindicate you brilliantly, so you would be very foolish to take matters into your own hands.

Now sometimes God avenges his children in their lifetime, but he does not *promise* to do this. Paul said:

> Among God's churches we boast about your perseverance and faith in all the persecutions and trials you are enduring.
> All this is evidence that God's judgment is right, and as a result you will be counted worthy of the kingdom of God, for which you are suffering. God is just: He will pay back trouble to those who trouble you and give relief to you who are troubled, and to us as well. This will happen when the Lord Jesus is revealed from heaven in blazing fire with his powerful angels. He will punish those who do not know God and do not obey the gospel of our Lord Jesus (2 Thess. 1:4-8).

God *will* vindicate you: you have his word, but you must leave the timing to him.

Third, although Mephibosheth might have said, 'I don't want to have anything to do with the king since he won't give me what I want', he rejoiced that he was returning to rule over his people.

Suppose God does not give you everything you want. Suppose, for instance, you are sick and he does not heal you or he does not give you the promotion that you have longed for or someone has lied about you and he does not clear your name, will you *still* love and honour him? Mephibosheth was simply glad that, once again, the king would be honoured by his people. Is God's honour *your* deepest concern?

Fourth, Mephibosheth cherished the peace that he had by rejoicing in the truth. He never forgot that, although he did not deserve the king's favour, he had been adopted into his family and that was enough.

59

So Near and Yet So Far

2 Samuel 20:1-22

So near and yet so far. Could this be said of you? Are you so close to the heart of the things that can change the world, yet so far from what *really* matters that should you die now no one will be *sure* that you were truly converted? In other words, in this respect are you like Joab?

Joab was the commander-in-chief of David's forces, a brilliant military strategist. He was a colourful, complex and enigmatic character. At times he was sympathetic, courageous, caring and conscientious, yet at other times he was disobedient, arrogant, disrespectful, deceitful, despicable, cold and heartless.

Perhaps you wonder why David kept Joab so close to him. I think it was simply because he depended on Joab's fanatical loyalty. No one served the king more loyally than Joab or understood him so well. In fact, sometimes Joab would act without asking permission first, knowing that David could not openly approve of his actions but would be secretly pleased with the outcome. Yet no one caused David more grief and agony than Joab did because in many ways he was so unlike him.

Now you could say that one of the tragic things about Joab was that he was *too* familiar with the king. You see, as David lay dying, assuming that David wanted his *eldest* son to succeed him, Joab supported Adonijah when he made a bid for his father's throne. But this time he miscalculated: David intended *Solomon* to become the next king of Israel. And when David heard what Adonijah had done, he abdicated and made

Solomon king in his place (see 1 Kings 1).

Joab's error of judgment eventually resulted in his execution. After his father's death, because Adonijah continued to be a threat, Solomon put him to death (see 1 Kgs. 2:25). Joab knew then that he himself did not have long to live. The Bible says:

> When the news reached Joab, who had conspired with Adonijah though not with Absalom, he fled to the tent of the Lord and took hold of the horns of the altar. King Solomon was told that Joab had fled to the tent of the Lord and was beside the altar. Then Solomon ordered Benaiah son of Jehoiada, 'Go, strike him down!' . . .
>
> So Benaiah son of Jehoiada went up and struck down Joab and killed him, and he was buried on his own land in the desert (1 Kgs. 2:28-29, 34).

Similarly, a person can be familiar with holy things, yet never receive Christ. It is possible to hold an office in the church, to be a church member or a teacher of the Bible and make the fatal error of believing that this will guarantee that he will go to heaven. So near and yet so far.

Will we see Joab in heaven? Well, let us consider some of the things that he did.

He was a fearless soldier. As you may recall, he was the man who so courageously captured Jerusalem (see 1 Chr. 11:4-9). Moreover, he was so loyal to the king that he was prepared to carry out his orders without question. For instance, when David sent Joab a sealed letter, ordering him to send Bathsheba's husband to certain death in the front line in the war against the Ammonites, he obeyed immediately (see 2 Sam. 11:14-16).

Later, when David and his son Absalom were not on speaking terms, Joab interceded for Absalom. No one else *dared* to interfere, but Joab managed to reconcile the king with his son (see 2 Sam. 14). Then, when Absalom seized the throne and David fled into the wilderness, Joab stayed with him, and under his command David's forces defeated those of Absalom (see 2 Sam. 18).

David had ordered that no harm should come to his wayward son (v. 5), but it was not in Joab's nature to show compassion to anyone who rose up against the king. And learning that, as Absalom fled, his long hair had become entangled in the branches of an oak tree and he was dangling helplessly in mid-air, Joab killed him (see vv. 9-15).

Joab was so devoted to the king that he was prepared to be tough with him. And when David shut himself away, crying, 'O Absalom, my son, my son!' (v. 33), oblivious to the needs of others, it was he who, again, did what no one else would dare do. Joab told David bluntly, 'Stop wallowing in self-pity and go out and encourage your troops or your whole kingdom will turn against you' (see 2 Sam. 19:5-7). These were shock tactics, but they worked, for David pulled himself together.

In 2 Samuel 20 there is another story that illustrates how ruthless Joab was, yet how useful he was to David.

Unable to forget that Joab had killed Absalom, David demoted him and appointed Amasa, whom he had pardoned for commanding Absalom's forces, as his commander-in-chief instead (2 Sam. 19:13). Then David set out for Jerusalem. But his troubles were still not over. The Bible says:

Now a troublemaker named Sheba son of Bicri, a Benjamite, happened to be there. He sounded the trumpet and shouted,

'We have no share in David,
no part in Jesse's son!
Every man to his tent, O Israel!'

So all the men of Israel deserted David to follow Sheba son of Bicri. But the men of Judah stayed by their king all the way from the Jordan to Jerusalem. . . .

Then the king said to Amasa, 'Summon the men of Judah to come to me within three days, and be here yourself.' But when

465

Amasa went to summon Judah, he took longer than the time the king had set for him (2 Sam. 20:1-2, 4-5).

David realized that something would have to be done quickly and he could not wait for Amasa, so he turned to Abishai and said:

'Now Sheba son of Bicri will do us more harm than Absalom did. Take your master's men and pursue him, or he will find fortified cities and escape from us.' So Joab's men and the Kerethites and the Pelethites and all the mighty warriors went out under the command of Abishai. They marched out from Jerusalem to pursue Sheba son of Bicri.

While they were at the great rock in Gibeon, Amasa came to meet them (vv. 6-8).

Seeing a chance to get rid of his rival, Joab stepped forward:

Joab was wearing his military tunic, and strapped over it at his waist was a belt with a dagger in its sheath. As he stepped forward, it dropped out of its sheath.

Joab said to Amasa, 'How are you, my brother?' Then Joab took Amasa by the beard with his right hand to kiss him. Amasa was not on his guard against the dagger in Joab's hand, and Joab plunged it into his belly, and his intestines spilled out on the ground. Without being stabbed again, Amasa died. Then Joab and his brother Abishai pursued Sheba son of Bicri (vv. 8-10).

Eventually, Joab and Abishai tracked Sheba down to Abel Beth Maacah and promptly laid siege to the city. As they began to batter down its walls, a wise woman poked her head over the rampart and appealed to Joab to spare them. The wily Joab struck a bargain with her, saying:

'Hand over this one man [Sheba], and I'll withdraw from the city.'

The woman said to Joab, 'His head will be thrown to you from the wall.'

Then the woman went to all the people with her wise advice, and they cut off the head of Sheba son of Bicri and threw it to Joab (vv. 21–22).

Then Joab returned triumphantly to Jerusalem, knowing that, because he had gained a much needed victory, David would ignore the fact that he had murdered Amasa and had acted without authority. He was right. In fact, David rewarded Joab by giving him his old job back as commander-in- chief of his forces (see v. 23).

The question is, do you expect to see a man like that in heaven? Here was the man who had killed Abner, Absalom and Amasa in cold blood. Here was the man who supported Adonijah.

Now if you say, 'I don't see how Joab could possibly go to heaven after all he did', I would remind you that no one *deserves* eternal life: we are not saved by works but by grace. Paul put it like this: 'For it is by grace you have been saved, through faith – and this not from your selves, it is the gift of God – not by works, so that no-one can boast' (Eph. 2: 8–9).

Have you committed a serious sin? Perhaps someone reading this is living in adultery or has stolen money or has even committed murder and thinks, 'There is no hope for me.' You are wrong. You *do* have hope, for we are not saved by our works but by grace, God's unmerited favour.

However, once you repent and invite Christ into your heart, your life will change. You see, the Bible teaches that when someone becomes a Christian the work of sanctification (the process of being made holy) begins (see 2 Tim. 1:9). When someone receives Jesus as Saviour and Lord, the Holy Spirit comes to indwell him, and he gives that person a desire to please God. This means that a Christian will try to keep God's commands (see John 14:15).

So far we have little evidence that Joab's heart was right with God. Is there anything further we can say about him?

Someone once seemed to have had high hopes for Joab,

because they gave him a name that means 'Yahweh [Jehovah] is Father'. What a start in life, to have a name like that! So Joab probably had a background that was the equivalent of a Christian home today. Moreover, he was a nephew of the king, who was a man after God's own heart (1 Sam. 13:14; Acts 13:22). However, the probability that Joab came from a godly home and the fact that he had a prestigious background would not save him.

Have you had a good start in life? Have you come from a Christian home? If so, do not make the mistake of thinking that *this* makes you a Christian. You may be grateful for a Christian upbringing, but it will not save you. You yourself must accept Jesus as your Lord and Saviour.

However, some may argue that there is *some* evidence that Joab was a child of God and point us to 2 Samuel 12:26–28:

> Joab fought against Rabbah of the Ammonites and captured the royal citadel. Joab then sent messengers to David, saying, 'I have fought against Rabbah and taken its water supply. Now muster the rest of the troops and besiege the city and capture it. Otherwise I shall take the city, and it will be named after me.'

Joab wanted David to have all the credit for the victory, which shows that he had some semblance of humility. But if you say, 'Only a Christian could be like that', you are mistaken: many unconverted heroes have been equally self-effacing.

Some may argue that Joab's horrified response when David ordered him to take a census is evidence that he was a child of God. (We shall deal with this in more detail in a later chapter.) The Bible says:

> The king said to Joab and the army commanders with him, 'Go throughout the tribes of Israel from Dan to Beersheba and enrol the fighting men, so that I may know how many there are.'
> But Joab replied to the king, 'May the Lord your God multiply the troops a hundred times over, and may the eyes of

my lord the king see it. But why does my lord the king want to do such a thing?' (2 Sam. 24:2–3).

Here, Joab, concerned at David's lack of trust that God would fight Israel's battles for them, undoubtedly displayed a flash of spiritual insight and piety. 'Surely, *this* tells us something about Joab!' You may say. Yes, but having a flash of spiritual insight does not make one a Christian.

We cannot be certain that we will see Joab in heaven; nevertheless, in the final moments of his life, he did something that makes me hope that we *will* see him there, for when he realized that Solomon would put him to death for supporting Adonijah, he 'fled to the tent of the Lord and took hold of the horns of the altar'. Now the horns of the altar were sprinkled with blood offered for the sins of the people. Perhaps Joab knew that his only hope was to plead the blood of the sacrifice. If he did that, despite all the evil in his past, we will see him in heaven.

If you were to die tomorrow, would people reflect on the things that you have done and wonder if you were in heaven? Christians *should* lead holy lives, but what *really* matters is not what people say about you; what really matters is that you put your faith in the sacrifice Jesus made for you on the cross. If you repent of your sins and plead the merit of Jesus' blood, you will go to heaven.

60

Does God Judge Nations Today?

2 Samuel 21:1-14

The British nation has experienced one disaster after another. On 18 November 1987 thirty people died in the inferno in the King's Cross underground station. Then, the country was horrified by two disasters in nine days. On 12 December 1988 thirty-six people were killed near Clapham Junction, when a packed commuter train ran into the back of another and an empty train ploughed into the wreckage. A few days later a terrorist bomb ripped apart Pan Am Flight 103 over the little village of Lockerbie in Scotland, killing all 259 passengers on board and 11 people on the ground. Then on 15 April 1989 we watched our televisions in disbelief as dozens of people were crushed to death in the Hillsborough football stadium.

There are two ways of regarding these catastrophes. One way is to say, 'If God exists, he's not all-powerful, all-knowing and all-loving or he would have intervened.' The other way to look at these events is to say, 'God must have had a reason for allowing these things to happen.'

That was how David viewed the situation when disaster came to Israel. Read 2 Samuel 21:1:

> During the reign of David, there was a famine for three successive years; so David sought the face of the Lord.

Now you may say, 'I don't know why David turned to *God*. Natural disasters – droughts, famines, floods, earthquakes and the like – are always happening somewhere or another. Israel was simply unfortunate.' Well, I would point out two things.

First, David knew that the famine did *not* happen by chance. You see, each year Israel has two rainy seasons – one in the spring and one in the autumn. The famine lasted for three years, which meant that the rains failed *six* times in succession. Second, David knew that sometimes God does bring judgment upon a sinful nation. He knew that God had destroyed Sodom and Gomorrah because of their wickedness (see Gen. 19:23-25) and had punished Egypt for its sin against the Israelites (see Exod. 7 – 14). And realizing that it was likely that God was using the drought to send a signal to the generation living in his day, David asked him what it meant.

The relationship between God and nations is an aspect of theology that has long been neglected. This saddens me, for God not only notices what individuals do, but he notices what the *nations* do. Isaiah put it like this:

> Surely the nations are like a drop in a bucket;
> they are regarded as dust on the scales;
> he weighs the islands as though they were fine dust (Isa. 40:15).

In fact, a strain runs right through the Bible showing that God is concerned about the righteousness of a people. You may remember that God said to Jonah, 'Go to the great city of Nineveh and preach against it, because its wickedness has come up before me' (Jonah 1:1).

The Bible says, 'Man is destined to die once, and after that to face judgment' (Heb. 9:27). So we will all stand before the judgment seat of Christ. But God will not only judge individuals, he will judge the nations. Jesus said:

> 'When the Son of Man comes in his glory, and all the angels with him, he will sit on his throne in heavenly glory. All the nations will be gathered before him, and he will separate the people one from another as a shepherd separates the sheep from the goats' (Matt. 25:31-32).

It seems that when we get to heaven God's concern for the nations will continue. Describing his vision of heaven in the book of Revelation, John said:

> Then the angel showed me the river of the water of life, as clear as crystal, flowing from the throne of God and of the Lamb down the middle of the great street of the city. On each side of the river stood the tree of life, bearing twelve crops of fruit, yielding its fruit every month. *And the leaves of the tree are for the healing of the nations* [my italics] (Rev. 22:1–2).

Now although I do not understand everything in 2 Samuel 21, I want you to notice four things.

First, I want you to see that here is a picture of a responsible leader.

The Bible says, 'During the reign of David, there was a famine for three successive years; so *David sought the face of the Lord* [my italics].' Now the proof that the leader of a nation is responsible is not that he or she can hold inflation at a certain level or reduce unemployment; it is this: when major calamities happen that might be a signal from God, the leader of the nation concerned asks God what he is saying.

The Bible says, 'Righteousness exalts a nation, but sin is a disgrace to any people' (Prov. 14:34). 'Blessed is the nation whose God is the Lord' (Ps. 33:12). But do you know of any national or public figure who has asked God why so many disasters are happening in Britain now? As far as I know, the leaders of the government and the leaders of the church have done nothing.

Second, I want you to see the possibility of a revealed leading.

When David asked God why he had sent the famine, God answered him. The Bible does not tell us *how* David discovered God's reason for sending the famine. Perhaps God sent a trusted prophet or a priest to him – Zadok or Abiathar, for instance – to reveal his purpose. However, what we *do* know is that God answered David.

Would it surprise you if we asked God why these disasters are happening and he answered us? God invited Jeremiah to question him, and said, 'Call to me and I will answer you and tell you great and unsearchable things you do not know' (Jer. 33:3). It is wonderful to know that God might reveal his purpose to his people.

There *is* an explanation for these tragedies; there *is* a God in heaven, a God who cares. The question is, do people *want* to know what it is? As you know, on Saturdays at Westminster Chapel we go out as Pilot Lights to witness on the streets. Almost every week someone will ask us, 'Why is God allowing these disasters to happen?' But they do not want a reply; they want to put God on the spot.

Third, I want you to see the penalty for a rescinded loyalty. We have a God who remembers.

When God answered David's question, he said:

'It is on account of Saul and his blood-stained house; it is because he put the Gibeonites to death' (2 Sam. 21:1).

Let me explain what had happened. About two hundred years earlier Joshua had formed an alliance with the Gibeonites, who, although they were not a part of the Israeli nation, lived among them. Joshua swore an oath to those people, binding for all time, that the Israelites would not harm them (see Josh. 9). The Israelites had respected this oath until Saul became king. Then, eager to impress his subjects, he foolishly ignored the sacred bond between the two races and tried to exterminate the foreigners. Now God regards the failure to honour a vow as a serious matter. In fact, he said, 'It is better not to vow than to make a vow and not fulfil it' (Eccles. 5:5). But Saul thought he could put himself above God's word.

There have always been those who thought that they could set themselves above God's word and say, 'Yes, the word of God applies *generally*, but he did not mean it to apply to *me*.' This is the most foolish remark a person can make.

'Well,' you may say, 'if I make God angry, no doubt he will soon let me know.' Not necessarily. I am convinced that the angrier God is, the longer he waits to show it. Forty years passed after Saul broke that oath before God brought judgment on Israel. 'That's unfair!' you may say. 'It was *Saul* who broke the oath, not the Israelites living in David's reign. Many of them were not even born when Saul sinned.' That is true, but the fact is, we are responsible for our origins.

Historically, Britain is a Christian nation. Now I say this guardedly, for I do *not* mean that everyone living there is a Christian; nevertheless, there is a certain recognition here for the God of the Bible, and God notices things like that. However, although national leaders and church leaders in Britain today know that former generations were characterized by their fear of God and their respect for his word, they do not feel obliged to honour that. But the Bible warns, 'Do not move an ancient boundary stone set up by your forefathers' (Prov. 22:28). We are responsible for our origins.

Maybe you were brought up in a Christian family, but you grew up to resent it, feeling that you were not getting as much fun out of life as others were. But you should honour the Christian background that God has given you. Remember, Jesus said, 'From everyone who has been given much, much will be demanded; and from the one who has been entrusted with much, much more will be asked' (Luke 12:48).

God remembers things that a new generation may disregard, and in Exodus 34:6–7 he said:

'The Lord, the Lord, the compassionate and gracious God, slow to anger, abounding in love and faithfulness, maintaining love to thousands, and forgiving wickedness, rebellion and sin. Yet he does not leave the guilty unpunished; he punishes the children and their children for the sin of the fathers to the third and fourth generation' (see also Num. 14:18).

This passage clearly shows that God holds us accountable for the sins of a former generation. We have a retrospective liability. The fact that God held Israel responsible for the sin its people committed forty years earlier is sobering. If you still think that this is unfair, remember that through the prophet Isaiah God said:

> 'My thoughts are not your thoughts,
>   neither are your ways my ways . . . .
> As the heavens are higher than the earth,
>   so are my ways higher than your ways
> and my thoughts than your thoughts (Isa. 55:8–9).

God does not make mistakes: he knows what he is doing. And the day will come when God will clear his name and you will realize that he is 'righteous in all his ways' (see Ps. 145:17).

Fourth, we see the provision of a righteous law. In 2 Samuel 21 we read:

> The king summoned the Gibeonites and spoke to them. . . . David asked the Gibeonites, 'What shall I do for you? How shall I make amends so that you will bless the Lord's inheritance?'
>
> The Gibeonites answered him, 'We have no right to demand silver or gold from Saul or his family, nor do we have the right to put anyone in Israel to death.'
>
> 'What do you want me to do for you?' David asked (vv. 2–4).

Interestingly, the Gibeonites who had survived the slaughter did not want *financial* compensation for Saul's sin against their people: they wanted satisfaction by *substitution*.

> They answered the king, 'As for the man who destroyed us and plotted against us so that we have been decimated and have no place anywhere in Israel, let seven of his male descendants be

given to us to be killed and exposed before the Lord at Gibeah of Saul – the Lord's chosen one' (vv. 5–6).

In other words, although Saul's family were innocent, they had to pay the price for his sin. Sparing Jonathan's son Mephibosheth because of the oath he had sworn to Jonathan (v. 7; see also 1 Sam. 20:16–17), David chose seven of Saul's descendants:

> He handed them over to the Gibeonites, who killed and exposed them on a hill before the Lord (v. 9).

This is a picture of the way God brought about our salvation. Peter said:

> For you know that it was not with perishable things such as silver or gold that you were redeemed from the empty way of life handed down to you from your forefathers, but with the precious blood of Christ . . . (1 Pet. 1:18).

We cannot *buy* our salvation; God demands satisfaction by substitution. As I said in a previous chapter, we can never match the standard of righteousness God requires, for he requires perfection in thought, in word and in deed 60 seconds a minute, 60 minutes an hour, 24 hours a day, 365 days of the year, all the days of our life. This was why he sent his sinless Son to take our place on the cross. Paul said, 'God made him who had no sin to be sin for us, so that in him we might become the righteousness of God' (2 Cor. 5:21).

The Bible tells us that when the seven men had paid the price for Saul's sin, God lifted the curse from Israel. Read verse 14:

> After that, God answered prayer on behalf of the land.

In 2 Chronicles 7:14 we read: 'If my people, who are called by my name, will humble themselves and pray and seek my face and turn from their wicked ways, then will *I hear from heaven and will forgive their sin and will heal their land* [my italics].' Three thousand years have passed since God made this promise, but it is valid today.

God created the world: it is his. Psalm 24:1 says, 'The earth is the Lord's, and everything in it.' He is sovereign and has always judged the nations, and Britain is under his judgment now.

Yet the worst kind of judgment a nation can experience is not an earthquake or a plane falling from the sky; it is not soaring inflation, rising unemployment or an Aids epidemic: it is what the prophet Amos called 'a famine of hearing the words of the Lord' (Amos 8:11). Generally speaking, Christian ministers are not preaching the gospel today. Indeed some church leaders who have the ear of the media make fun of the Bible and scoff at such things as the virgin birth, the resurrection and the ascension.

Perhaps you say, 'Well, I don't believe the Bible either, so I am in good company!' But that does not excuse you. The leaders of the church are failing in their duty to urge the nation to call upon the name of God in times like these, but at the final judgment you will not be able to blame them; you will answer to God *personally*.

God owes you nothing, and yet he has been so good to you, and he stoops to ask, 'Will you listen? Will you turn in repentance to me?'

61

Famous Last Words

2 Samuel 23

In 2 Samuel 23 is the psalm (not included in the psalter) known as 'David's last words'. No one knows whether they are *literally* his last words, but this seems unlikely, particularly when we read the first two chapters of 1 Kings and find him making pertinent decisions. Many theologians think that this passage of Scripture is comparable to a last will and testament and was David's final legacy to God's people. It offers wonderful encouragement to us all, for it proves that one can die victoriously, *despite* a life that went badly wrong.

Now you may think that I have passed over 2 Samuel 22, a chapter that, with only minor differences, is Psalm 18. I am not going to do an exposition of this psalm, but I will refer to it.

I think we can best examine David's last words by dividing the passage of Scripture into three sections. (Please note that I use the Authorised Version here.)

In the first section David spoke of how God used him.

Now these be the last words of David.
David the son of Jesse said,
And the man who was raised up on high,
The anointed of the God of Jacob,
And the sweet psalmist of Israel, said,
The Spirit of the Lord spake by me,
And his word was in my tongue (vv. 1–2).

Apart from the assurance that God has given us eternal life, can anything be more satisfying than the knowledge that God has used us?

Let us return to Psalm 18 for a moment. Theologians believe that David wrote this psalm forty years earlier perhaps, after God delivered him from the hand of Saul, eight years after he had killed Goliath. If this were the case, then David would have been only about twenty-five years old when he wrote it, and his whole life stretched before him.

Now it was no accident that the writer of 2 Samuel inserted Psalm 18 immediately before David's last words. I think he intended to show us that, at the end of David's life, his testimony had changed. Let me explain.

In Psalm 18 David recorded his *early* experiences of God. For example, he says:

> [God] brought me out into a spacious place [Jerusalem or Israel perhaps];
>> he rescued me because he delighted in me.
> The Lord has dealt with me according to my righteousness;
>> according to the cleanness of my hands he has rewarded me.
> For I have kept the ways of the Lord;
>> I have not done evil by turning from my God (vv. 19–21).

Here is the testimony of a young man who, although not perfect, until then had lived cleanly and not committed the serious sins of adultery and murder and other acts of violence. He could truly say, 'I have not done evil by turning from my God.'

However, in 2 Samuel 23 are the words of a man who knew he would die very soon, a man who was reflecting on his life and knew that he had grieved God.

The first thing that David said was this:

> 'The Spirit of the Lord spake by me,
> And his word was in my tongue' (v. 2).

Jesus affirmed David as a prophet. For instance, in Matthew 21:42, when he said, 'Have you never read in the Scriptures:

"The stone the builders rejected has become the capstone"?' he was quoting the prophecy that David made about him in Psalm 118:22. Jesus affirmed David again when he asked the Pharisees:

'What do you think about the Christ? Whose son is he?'

'The son of David,' they replied.

He said to them, 'How is it then that David, *speaking by the Spirit*, calls him Lord? [my italics]' (Matt. 22:41–44).

Later, Peter, preaching on the day of Pentecost, also referred to David as a prophet (see Acts 2:30). And when the disciples prayed in Acts 4, they said, '[Lord] you spoke by the Holy Spirit through the mouth of your servant, our father David' (v. 25). So at times, David spoke for God.

The second section of David's last words relate to his reign and to the covenant (a promise made binding by an oath) that God made with him.

'The God of Israel said,
The Rock of Israel spake to me,
He that ruleth over men must be just,
Ruling in the fear of God.
And he shall be as the light of the morning, when the sun riseth,
Even a morning without clouds;
As the tender grass springing out of the earth
By clear shining after rain.
Although my house be not so with God;
Yet he hath made with me an everlasting covenant,
Ordered in all things, and sure;
For this is all my salvation, and all my desire,
Although he make it not to grow' (vv. 3–5).

Note, David said that God requires those in positions of authority to rule justly and lead godly lives. Now this applies not only to the leaders of a nation but to those who hold positions of authority in the church. Paul said, 'If anyone sets his heart on being an overseer, he desires a noble task. Now the overseer must be above reproach . . .' (1 Tim. 3:1-2). As Jesus said, 'From everyone who has been given much, much will be demanded' (Luke 12:48).

Yet then came words of regret. David said, 'Although my house be not so with God'. Here is his admission of where he went wrong. I have often said that the marvel of the Bible is that it does not gloss over the imperfections of God's people, and here the Bible records David's admission that he had failed as head of his family. No longer was he saying, as he had forty years earlier, 'The Lord has dealt with me according to my righteousness'; he was saying, 'Would to God that I had *always* lived righteously!' David knew that had he not committed adultery and murder things would have turned out very differently. Nathan the Prophet had said, 'The sword shall never depart from your house' (2 Sam. 12:10). How true those words were!

Are you still young? Then I want you to know that if you avoid falling into serious sin one day you will be so thankful. You may say, 'Well, I think I ought to have a chance to sow my wild oats just like everyone else.' But I urge you to resist the temptation to go the way of the world, for if you succumb and fall into sin, eventually, you will rue the day.

Maybe you are older and you have not fallen into serious sin, but who among us does not regret *something* that he or she has done in the past? When we were young, perhaps, like David did, we could have said, 'The Lord has dealt with me according to my righteousness', but none of us want to talk like that when our lives are drawing to a close.

When David realized that his life was almost over he did not speak of his righteousness; he spoke of the covenant that God had made with him, saying:

'He hath made with me an everlasting covenant,
Ordered in all things, and sure' (2 Sam. 23:5).

You see, in Acts 2:30 Peter said that God swore an oath to David. The apostle put it like this:

'[David] was a prophet and knew that God had promised him on oath that he would place one of his descendants on his throne.'

David foresaw the day when God would send the Messiah, whose human ancestry would be of his line. He knew that he was going to heaven, but he also knew that he was a sinner and his hope of eternal life rested solely on the covenant.

You may say, 'A man like that does not deserve eternal life.' But none of us deserves to go to heaven. The marvel is, we are saved by *grace* (Eph. 2:8-9). Grace is God's unmerited favour and it is based upon the *new* covenant. You see, having fulfilled the covenant that he made with David by sending Jesus Christ to this earth, God made a covenant with us. This covenant is conditional. Its terms are these: if we trust what Jesus did for us on the cross and repent of our sins, God will pardon us and give us eternal life.

The third section of David's last words is a solemn warning to God's enemies:

But the sons of Belial [a nickname for the devil] shall be all of them as thorns thrust away,
Because they cannot be taken with hands:
But the man that shall touch them
Must be fenced with iron and the staff of a spear;
And they shall be utterly burned with fire in the same place (vv. 6–7).

David foresaw that God will punish those who reject Jesus Christ and that those who refuse to accept the gospel will be eternally doomed.

I have a small book called *The Last Words of Five Hundred Remarkable Persons*, which contains the last words of some well-known Christians. Their comments show that eternity held no terrors for them. Let me give you some examples:

- The Puritan John Preston's last words were, 'Though I change my place, I shall not change my company, for I walked with God all these years.'

- John Bradford, who was burned at the stake in Smithfield, told his friends, 'I am going to have a merry supper with the Lord tonight.'

- John Wesley's last words were these: 'Best of all, God is with us.'

- The Puritan Dr Goodwin said, 'Ah! Is this dying? Have I dreaded as an enemy this smiling friend?'

- After bidding his family farewell, Jonathan Edwards said, 'Now where is Jesus of Nazareth, my never-failing friend?'

These men knew that they were going to heaven, not as a reward for their righteousness but because they trusted in the new covenant. On what do you base *your* hope of eternal life?

62

Oh No, Not Again!

2 Samuel 24:1–14

If you have struggled long and hard to overcome a particular sin and thought, 'Victory at last! I will never do that again!' only to succumb to temptation shortly after, I think you will find this chapter encouraging. You see, as I said in the previous chapter, the wonderful thing about the Bible is that it does not hide the frailty of its heroes. It reveals that the best of God's people were weak and sometimes sinned grievously, even when they had sworn, 'Never again!'

Another wonderful thing about the Bible is that it tells us of God's *grace* to repentant sinners. Paul put it like this: 'For it is by grace you have been saved, through faith – and this not from yourselves, it is the gift of God – not by works, so that no-one can boast' (Eph. 2:8-9). If God judged people by their works, King David would have had no chance of entering heaven, and neither would we: we are saved by grace.

However, God does not save us that we might continue to sin. In Psalm 130:4 David said:

There is forgiveness with thee,
That thou mayest be *feared* [my italics]' (AV).

The word 'repentance' means 'a change of mind'. It means that we resolve to turn our backs on sin. It is on this basis alone that God forgives us.

A wonderful feeling of peace steals over the Christian when he experiences God's forgiveness. Yet it is equally true that when he realizes that he has sinned, he feels ashamed. You

485

see, God makes a sinner feel guilty, but only because he wants that person to repent and return to him.

When David committed adultery and murder (see 2 Sam. 11), you will remember that he lived unashamed for two years, but then God sent the prophet Nathan to him to expose his sin and David was devastated (see 2 Sam. 12).

David repented and God forgave him (2 Sam. 12:13); nevertheless, as we have seen, his sin cost him dearly, for he had to endure God's chastening. As we saw in earlier chapters, the consequences of his sin were severe. First, God took the baby who was conceived in adultery (vv. 14-19). Then Nathan's prophecy 'The sword shall never depart from your house' (2 Sam. 12:10) began to be fulfilled. David's son Amnon raped his half-sister Tamar and was murdered by Absalom (2 Sam. 13) and then Absalom, who had seized his father's throne, was defeated in battle and killed by Joab (2 Sam. 15; 18:1-18).

However, God gave David a second chance and not only restored him to the throne but renewed him spiritually (2 Sam. 15–19). It seemed then as though it would be plain sailing all the way. Surely, one would think, David had learned his lesson.

However, in this chapter we see that again he committed a sin that he would regret. You see, he counted the warriors in Israel. 'What is so bad about that?' you may ask. Well, Israel was a theocracy. The Israelites were *God's* people and *he* fought their battles for them. When David decided to take this census, it was as if he were telling God, 'I no longer trust you; I prefer to rely on the numerical strength of my army.'

I want to show you five things about David's sin:

First, I want you to see the mystery of temptation. I put it this way because the Bible is infallible and 2 Samuel 24:1 presents us with a difficulty. It says:

> Again the anger of the Lord burned against Israel, and he incited David against them, saying, 'Go and take a census of Israel and Judah.'

However, in 1 Chronicles 21 is another account of the same
event, which begins like this:

> Satan rose up against Israel and incited David to take a census
> of Israel (v. 1).

Now those who do not believe that the Bible is inerrant and
infallible say, 'These verses are proof that the Bible contradicts
itself.' But I prefer to refer to the mystery of temptation.
Let us consider these verses in the light of other scriptures.
First, we go to the New Testament, where James said:

> When tempted, no-one should say, 'God is tempting me.' For
> God cannot be tempted by evil, nor does he tempt anyone; but
> each one is tempted when, by his own evil desire, he is dragged
> away and enticed. Then, after desire has conceived, it gives birth
> to sin; and sin, when it is full-grown, gives birth to death (Jas.
> 1:13–15).

James clearly says that *God* does not tempt anyone.
Now consider this passage from the book of Job:

> One day the angels came to present themselves before the Lord,
> and Satan also came with them. The Lord said to Satan, 'Where
> have you come from?'
>
> Satan answered the Lord, 'From roaming through the earth
> and going to and fro in it.'
>
> Then the Lord said to Satan, 'Have you considered my servant
> Job? There is no one on earth like him; he is blameless and
> upright, a man who fears God and shuns evil.'
>
> 'Does Job fear God for nothing?' Satan replied, 'Have you
> not put a hedge around him and his household and everything
> he has? You have blessed the work of his hands, so that his
> flocks and herds are spread throughout the land. But stretch out
> your hand and strike everything he has, and he will surely curse
> you to your face.'
>
> The Lord said to Satan, 'Very well, then, everything he has
> is in your hands, but on the man himself, do not lay a finger'
> (Job 1:6–12).

Satan had to get God's permission before laying a finger on Job. In other words, *Satan* is the tempter, but he can do nothing without God's consent.

You see, the Bible does *not* contradict itself, and what we have in 2 Samuel 24 is a situation where God *allowed* Satan to tempt David. Satan was – and is still – God's *tool*.

Let me give you another example of how God used Satan to accomplish his divine purpose. First, I ask you this. Who was responsible for crucifying Jesus? Was it Satan, who entered into the heart of Judas Iscariot and prompted him to betray the Son of God? Was it the wicked men who hammered in the nails? You may say, 'They all were.' But on the day of Pentecost, addressing the Jews, Peter said this:

> '[Jesus] was handed over to you *by God's set purpose and foreknowledge*; and you, with the help of wicked men, put him to death by nailing him to the cross [my italics]' (Acts 2:23).

There was a threefold rule in operation here: (1) Satan always overreaches himself; (2) when Satan is up to something, so too is God, and (3) when Satan is up to something big, God is up to something bigger. God allowed the devil to bring about the death of Jesus on the cross, and, unwittingly, Satan advanced God's plan of salvation.

This threefold rule was also in operation when God permitted Satan to tempt David to number the fighting men.

The second thing that I want you to see is the providence of God's warning. Consider 2 Samuel 24:2–3:

> So the king said to Joab and the army commanders with him, 'Go throughout the tribes of Israel from Dan to Beersheba and enrol the fighting men, so that I may know how many there are.'
>
> But Joab replied to the king, 'May the Lord your God multiply the troops a hundred times over, and may the eyes of my lord the king see it. But why does my lord the king want to do such a thing?'

Amazingly, Joab, who so often grieved God, was the one to warn David not to sin.

Before anyone sins, he receives a warning. Did you know that David received a warning before he committed adultery with Bathsheba? Read 2 Samuel 11:2–3:

> One evening David got up from his bed and walked around on the roof of the palace. From the roof he saw a woman bathing. The woman was very beautiful, and David sent someone to find out about her. The man said, 'Isn't this Bathsheba, the daughter of Eliam and the wife of Uriah the Hittite?'

In other words, the servant said, 'It's bad news, your majesty: the lady is married.' I call that a warning, and it should have stopped David in his tracks.

Now if we ignore God's warning, we are without excuse. This was why Jesus said to the disciples in the Garden of Gethsemane, 'Watch and pray so that you will not fall into temptation' (Matt. 26:41). Did you notice the order? Jesus said, 'Watch and pray'. He did not say, 'Pray and watch'. Do you know why? Because he knew that some of us would say, 'Well, I prayed about this situation and look what happened!' We all like to blame God for the things we do. But remember, James said:

> No-one should say, 'God is tempting me.' For God cannot be tempted by evil nor does he tempt anyone; but each one is tempted when, by his own evil desire, he is dragged away and enticed. Then, after desire has conceived, it gives birth to sin; and sin, when it is full-grown gives birth to death (Jas. 1:13–15).

The onus to resist temptation rests with us.

The third thing I want you to see is that sorrow always follows sin. That is to say, if you sin, eventually you will regret it. Read 2 Samuel 24:10:

David was conscience-stricken after he had counted the fighting men, and he said to the Lord, 'I have sinned greatly in what I have done. Now, O Lord, I beg you, take away the guilt of your servant. I have done a very foolish thing.'

Filled with remorse, David asked for forgiveness.

Now if you realize that you have sinned and repent quickly, it is a *good* sign, for it means that the Holy Spirit is dealing with you now. Sadly, some people feel no remorse in this life, but, as I said, sorrow always follows sin, and when they stand before God at the final judgment they will beg him for mercy, but it will be too late.

The fourth thing I want you to see is the certainty of chastening. The word 'chastening' means 'correction by punishment' – the Greek word means *enforced learning.* Hebrews 12:6 says, 'The Lord disciplines those he loves, and he punishes everyone he accepts as a son.' So if you are a child of God, he will discipline you. He might slap you on the wrist; he may shake you by the shoulders, or he might put you flat on your back. But the purpose of God's chastening is not to get even. The writer to the Hebrews says, 'God disciplines us for our good, that we may share in his holiness' (Heb. 12:10). It is God's way of getting our attention and of letting us know that he hates sin.

Again, we see that, although David was a man after God's own heart (1 Sam. 13:14; Acts 13:22), God did not bend the rules for him. The Bible says:

Before David got up the next morning, the word of the Lord had come to Gad the prophet, David's seer: 'Go and tell David, "This is what the Lord says: I am giving you three options. Choose one of them for me to carry out against you."'

So Gad went to David and said to him, 'Shall there come upon you three years of famine in your land? Or three months of fleeing from your enemies while they pursue you? Or three days of plague in your land? Now then, think it over and decide how I should answer the one who sent me' (2 Sam. 24:11-13).

Now if God would not bend the rules for David, he will not bend the rules for us.

The fifth thing I want you to see is God's graciousness. Filled with remorse, David said:

> 'I am in deep distress. Let us fall into the hands of the Lord, for his mercy is great; but do not let me fall into the hands of men' (v.14).

David preferred to put himself into God's hands rather than into the hands of men, for he knew that God was compassionate and kind. In Psalm 103 he put it like this:

> The Lord is compassionate and gracious,
> slow to anger, abounding in love.
> He will not always accuse,
> nor will he harbour his anger for ever;
> he does not treat us as our sins deserve
> or repay us according to our iniquities.
> For as high as the heavens are above the earth,
> so great is his love for those who fear him;
> as far as the east is from the west,
> so far has he removed our transgressions from us.
> As a father has compassion on his children,
> so the Lord has compassion on those who fear him;
> for he knows how we are formed,
> he remembers that we are dust (vv. 8-13).

'He knows how we are formed, he remembers that we are dust.' These words almost move me to tears, for I have let God down so often and so often have had to say, 'Lord, I have done it again. I am so sorry.' And then I turn to this verse and hear God say, 'I know how weak you are. I forgive you.'

You may say, ' I know that if I repent, God will forgive me, but I still don't understand *why* he allows us to be tempted and to fall into sin.' Well, I believe that he does so that we may see what we are capable of doing without his restraining hand upon us. God does not want us to become self-righteous and overconfident and to think that we can do without him: he wants to keep us humble.

63

What Is a Christian?

2 Samuel 24

Would it surprise you to learn that David was a Christian? You may say, 'That is impossible: David lived a thousand years before Christ came.' Well, let me explain what we mean by the term 'Christian'.

The word 'Christian' was a nickname coined in the first century by unbelievers, who used it as a term of derision to show their hatred of Jesus Christ and his followers. It is used only three times in the Bible. The first time the word 'Christian' occurs is in Acts 11:26, which says, 'The disciples were called Christians first at Antioch.' The second occasion it is used is in Acts 26:28, where King Agrippa said to Paul, 'Do you think that in such a short time you can persuade me to be a Christian?' The last time it occurs is in 1 Peter 4:16, where Peter said, 'If you suffer as a Christian, do not be ashamed, but praise God that you bear that name.'

Later the recipients used the term themselves to denote those who come to God and are given the assurance that they have eternal life. Such people existed before Jesus came, so one could call them Christians, although this term did not exist in their day. David was a child of God and so he was a Christian.

Are you a Christian? You can find out, for in this chapter I shall use the events described in 2 Samuel 24 to give you seven proofs.

First, a Christian is one who experiences God's discipline (or chastening). (I have dealt with God's chastening in previous chapters, but I want to say more about it here.) If God disciplines you, rejoice, for it is a sign that you are his child. You see, the Bible says, 'The Lord disciplines those he loves, and he punishes everyone he accepts as a son (Heb. 12:6).

Now as Christians we must be *self*-disciplined. Let me explain what I mean by self-discipline.

Someone once came to me and said, 'I find it so *difficult* to read the Bible and pray. I wish I could enjoy it more.' I responded by reminding him of 2 Timothy 4:2, the verse in which Paul said, 'Be prepared in season and out of season'. I explained that 'in season' denotes those times when we feel such an outpouring of the Holy Spirit that we can hardly wait to read our Bibles and pray and 'out of season' denotes those times when we have no sense of the presence of God and we find it hard to pray and read the Scriptures. I said it is in times like these, when we discipline ourselves and pray despite our feelings, that we show how much we love the Lord, rather than in those times when the word of God almost leaps from the page and prayer flows easily.

If you are a Christian, you should read the Bible and pray regularly. In fact, I would urge you to read at least one chapter of the Bible and to spend at least half an hour in prayer daily. Now if you say, 'But after just *two* minutes, I find myself at a loss for words', it is because you do not have sufficient concern for God's glory and you have not discovered the joy of interceding for others.

God wants you to lead a holy life, and if you are a Christian and do not discipline yourself to spend time with him, *he* will discipline you. For instance, he may withhold success from you or cause you to have a financial setback to get your attention and to make you see that you are grieving him.

Unfortunately, David did not see that by numbering the fighting men he would grieve God. It was not until Joab and the other army commanders had carried out his wishes that he was 'conscience-stricken' (2 Sam. 24:10).

As we saw in the previous chapter, because of David's sin God disciplined him. The Bible says:

The Lord sent a plague on Israel from that morning until the end of the time designated, and seventy thousand of the people from Dan to Beersheba died (v. 15).

David accepted his chastening with dignity because he knew that God was disciplining him for his good.

Second, a Christian is one who takes responsibility for his own sin.

God sent a plague on the Israelites, but verse 17 reveals that David pleaded with him to spare the people:

When David saw the angel who was striking down the people, he said to the Lord, 'I am the one who has sinned and done wrong. These are but sheep. What have they done? Let your hand fall upon me and my family.'

Now the truth is, 'the anger of the Lord burned against *Israel* [my italics]' (v. 1), but David said, '*I* am the one who has sinned, Lord. Punish me.'

Similarly, a Christian refuses to blame his parents, his teachers or the society in which he lives for his wrongdoing; he says, 'It's all my fault, Lord. I am sorry.' The old Negro spiritual puts it like this:

Not my brother, nor my sister, but it's me, O Lord,
Standin' in the need of prayer.

Not the preacher, nor the deacon, but it's me, O Lord,
Standin' in the need of prayer.

Not my father, nor my mother, but it's me, O Lord,
Standin' in the need of prayer.

Not the stranger, nor my neighbour, but it's me, O Lord
Standin' in the need of prayer.

Third, the Christian is a person who meets God at the place he has appointed.

God made it clear to David where he was to meet him. Verse 18 says:

> On that day Gad went to David and said to him, 'Go up and build an altar to the Lord on the threshing-floor of Araunah the Jebusite.' So David went up as the Lord had commanded through Gad.

God sometimes likes to show his glory in the place where he has done so before. Araunah's threshing floor was on Mount Moriah (known today as the Temple Mount in Jerusalem). It was here that hundreds of years earlier God told Abraham to sacrifice Isaac (see Gen 22:2).

God *still* wants his people to meet him at the place he has appointed. It is not enough to choose a place of worship simply because it has a wonderful history and is an architectural masterpiece, for these things are artificial and superficial. God wants Christians to worship him in the place of *his* choosing, a place where he meets with his people.

Fourth, a Christian is one who has an immediate affinity with those whose hearts God has touched.

As far as we know Araunah was a total stranger to David; nevertheless, their conversation reveals that they had an immediate rapport:

> Araunah said, 'Why has my lord the king come to his servant?'
> 'To buy your threshing floor,' David answered, 'so that I can build an altar to the Lord, that the plague on the people may be stopped.'
> Araunah said to David, 'Let my lord the king take whatever pleases him and offer it up. Here are oxen for the burnt offering, and here are threshing sledges and ox yokes for the wood. O king, Araunah gives all this to the king.' Araunah also said to him, 'May the Lord your God accept you' (vv. 21-23).

When one Christian meets another, the colour of the other's skin, his social background, his politics and financial status are irrelevant, for, as God's children, they have a common bond.

A Christian does not need to know another for years before he enjoys fellowship. When Louise and I went to the Soviet Union, the Christians we met were complete strangers to us. We did not even speak the same language, but we understood each other, nevertheless. And when the time came to say goodbye, our new friends simply pointed to the sky. You see, they knew that, although we were unlikely ever to meet again on earth, one day we would renew our friendship in heaven.

Fifth, a Christian is one who knows that only a blood sacrifice can atone for his sin. Running right through the Bible is a scarlet thread. On every page you will find either a direct or an indirect reference to the blood of the sacrifice. Why? Because no matter how good a life we lead, we cannot atone for our own sin; a sacrifice is necessary. The Bible says, 'Without the shedding of blood there is no forgiveness' (Heb. 9:22).

David recognized that only a sacrifice would satisfy God's justice. The Bible says:

> But the king replied to Araunah, 'No, I insist on paying you for it. I will not sacrifice to the Lord my God burnt offerings that cost me nothing.'
> So David bought the threshing floor and the oxen and paid fifty shekels of silver for them. David built an altar to the Lord there and sacrificed burnt offerings and fellowship offerings (2 Sam. 24:24).

The Old Testament sacrifice of an animal was a shadow of what was to come a thousand years later, when Jesus, the Lamb of God, shed his blood on the cross and satisfied God's justice (1 Cor. 5:7). The Christian is one who does not trust his good works to get him into heaven; he trusts in the blood of Jesus' sacrifice.

Sixth, a Christian is one who knows that he owes his

497

salvation to Jesus and does what he can to show his gratitude to God.

Did you notice that David insisted on paying for the threshing floor and the oxen (see 2 Sam. 24:24)? You may say, 'How can I thank God for saving me?' The answer is, by living a godly life that brings honour to his name. Take care not to sin deliberately and try to please him in all you do. I am speaking of the doctrine of sanctification or the doctrine of gratitude.

Finally, a Christian is a person who enjoys fresh beginnings.

When David counted the fighting men he grieved God, but he repented and pleaded the blood of the sacrifice. The Bible says:

> Then the Lord answered prayer on behalf of the land, and the plague on Israel was stopped (v. 25).

The Bible says, '[God's] compassions never fail. They are new every morning' (Lam. 3:22-23). And in his kindness God gave David a new beginning.

God promises a new beginning to *all* who turn in repentance to him, for the Bible says, 'If we confess our sins, he is faithful and just and will forgive us our sins and purify us from all unrighteousness' (1 John 1:9).

64

How God Answers Prayer

1 Kings 1:22-53

On 31 October 1955, as I was driving to the Nazarene College in Trevecca, I had what I can only describe as a Damascus Road experience, for it was almost as extraordinary as the conversion of Saul of Tarsus. Jesus became more real to me then than my *own* existence. The afterglow of this experience lasted for months, and I have never been quite the same since. In the weeks that followed God promised me that some day he would use me. I did not know *where* he wanted me to serve him, but I could see this would not be in my old denomination, for the Holy Spirit had given me a new theology.

Some months later I went home and told my family and my friends what had happened and what God had said, but they were convinced that I was wrong and their reaction stunned me.

The summer of 1956 was awful. My father, who loved me and had dedicated me to the Lord before I was born, felt that God's hand was no longer upon me. My grandmother had given me a car, but now she asked me to give it back. My friends did not understand what had happened either and distanced themselves from me. At one time one person was particularly critical of me, and seeing God's blessing on him and no evidence of it on me, everyone said, 'You should be like him.' In fact, life became so difficult that one hot August afternoon I lay on my grandmother's bed and wept. I could not understand why this was happening to me; I was simply obeying God. I had never experienced anything so painful.

All this came to mind as I prepared to preach on 1 Kings 1, for I think that, in sense, my experience is similar to that of Solomon when his half-brother Adonijah tried to usurp the throne that their father David had promised him.

As we study this story, I want to show you the way in which God often answers prayer. Now you may say, 'But the Bible story does not mention prayer.' That is true; nevertheless, this story is a *picture* of the way in which God usually works. In fact, one could say that it reveals the pattern underlying the way in which he generally works.

I want you to notice four things about this pattern.

First, I want you to notice the promise and the excitement that begin the pattern.

Read 1 Chronicles 22:7-10, the passage describing how David summoned his seventeen-year-old son Solomon and spoke to him about building a temple for the Lord:

> David said to Solomon: 'My son, I had it in my heart to build a house for the Name of the Lord my God. But this word of the Lord came to me: "You have shed much blood and have fought many wars. You are not to build a house for my Name, because you have shed much blood on the earth in my sight. But you will have a son who will be a man of peace and rest, and I will give him rest from all his enemies on every side. His name will be Solomon, and I will grant Israel peace and quiet during his reign. He is the one who will build a house for my Name. He will be my son, and I will be his father. And I will establish the throne of his kingdom over Israel for ever."'

What great news! Solomon had God's promise that he would use him in a truly wonderful way.

It is exciting when God witnesses to us so powerfully, for one of the great truths in the Bible is that when God makes a vow he *will* fulfil it. You see, it is impossible for him to lie (Heb. 6:18).

Now this brings me to the second thing I want to say about the pattern that underlies the way in which God answers prayer: before he steps in, there is often a delay.

You see, God may not act immediately. Through the prophet Isaiah God once said: 'Sing, O barren woman, you who never bore a child; burst into song, shout for joy, you who were never in labour; because more are the children of a desolate woman than of her who has a husband' (Isa. 54:1). The verses that follow contain one of the most marvellous promises in the Bible. But it was a long time before that promise was fulfilled and referred to in the New Testament (see Gal. 4:27).

Of course, sometimes God *does* respond immediately. There have been times when I have prayed for something in the morning and received a glorious answer before sundown. However, generally speaking, my experience has been that God makes us wait. The problem is, we are often so impatient and when all our hopes and dreams seem to be shattered, we feel confused and betrayed.

I was overjoyed when God promised that he would use me, but dark days lay ahead. You may remember that my father asked me, 'When do you think this will happen, son?' and I replied, 'Within a year, Dad.' But twelve months later I was not working for God: I was selling baby equipment. My father was heartbroken. He would go to bed weeping wondering what had gone wrong, for only a few months earlier I had been seen by some as the wave of the future as far as my denomination was concerned. But I was even more hurt because I could not understand why God had not fulfilled his promise to me.

Solomon must have felt like this when it seemed that the promises that David had made to him had come to nothing. This was what had happened:

> Now Adonijah, whose mother was Haggith, put himself forward and said, 'I will be king.' So he got chariots and horses ready, with fifty men to run ahead of him (1 Kgs. 1:5).

People probably thought, 'David will step in soon and put an end to this nonsense', but he did nothing. Read verse 6:

> His father had never interfered with him by asking, 'Why do you behave as you do?'

As we have seen, David was not a perfect father: he distanced himself from his children and failed to discipline them when they were young, and he did not check Adonijah's behaviour now, making it easy for him to carry out his plan to set himself up as king. The Bible says:

> Adonijah conferred with Joab son of Zeruiah and with Abiathar the priest, and they gave him their support. But Zadok the priest, Benaiah the son of Jehoiada, Nathan the prophet, Shimei and Rei and David's special guard did not join Adonijah.
> Adonijah then sacrificed sheep, cattle and fattened calves at the Stone of Zoheleth near En Rogel. He invited all his brothers, the king's sons, and all the men of Judah who were royal officials, but he did not invite Nathan the prophet or Benaiah or the special guard or his brother Solomon (1 Kgs. 1:7-10).

Did you notice that Adonijah excluded Solomon from the celebrations? Have you ever been deliberately excluded from something? Do you know what it feels like to be left on the sidelines? After my Damascus Road experience, I seemed to have no future in the ministry. People who once thought that I had a bright future in the Nazarene church would ask, 'What are doing now, R.T.?'

'I am a salesman,' I would reply.

'Good! Praise the Lord!' they would say. But I knew they were thinking that I was finished, and I felt confused and betrayed by God.

Many of the greatest saints have experienced this 'dark night of the soul', as someone has called it. For example, God promised Moses that he would use him to deliver the people of Israel from slavery in Egypt (see Exod. 3). When Moses told the Israelites that they would soon be free, they were thrilled. The Bible says:

> When [the people] heard that the Lord was concerned about them and had seen their misery, they bowed down and worshipped (Exod. 4:31).

However, when Moses went to Pharaoh and asked him to set the slaves free, Pharaoh refused and made them work harder than ever. Can you imagine their sense of betrayal? Exodus 5:22-33 reveals how disillusioned Moses himself felt by God's failure to intervene:

> Moses returned to the Lord and said, 'O Lord, why have you brought trouble upon this people? Is this why you sent me? Ever since I went to Pharaoh to speak in your name, he has brought trouble upon this people, and you have not rescued your people at all.'

The lesson for us here is that even after God makes a great promise, sometimes things get worse before they get better.

The third thing we see in this story is what happens when the godly community is stirred up.

Now Abiathar the priest and Joab supported Adonijah's bid for power, but Nathan the prophet was indignant and went to see Bathsheba:

> Nathan asked Bathsheba, Solomon's mother, 'Have you not heard that Adonijah, the son of Haggith, has become king without our lord David's knowing it? Now then, let me advise you how you can save your own life and the life of your son Solomon. Go in to King David and say to him, "My lord the king, did you not swear to me your servant: 'Surely Solomon your son shall be king after me, and he will sit on my throne'? Why then has Adonijah become king?" While you are still there talking to the king, I will come in and confirm what you have said' (1 Kgs. 1:11-14).

You may say, 'Why did Nathan ask Bathsheba to speak to David?' Well, I believe that here Nathan was applying an important biblical principle. Jesus expressed it like this: 'If two of you on earth agree about anything you ask for, it will be done for you by my Father in heaven' (Matt. 18:19).

When Louise and I have a particular need we pray together and claim this promise. Then I record it in my spiritual journal and put the date. God's faithfulness has never failed to amaze us.

When T.R. and Missy were children sometimes I would promise them a treat, but they would get up to mischief and I would say, 'Well, you certainly don't deserve it now.' But they knew they could always get to my heart by saying, 'But Daddy, you *promised.*' And I would say, 'You are right. I will keep my word.'

The great sixteenth-century reformer John Calvin said, 'The best way to pray is to quote God's word back to him, because God will honour his word.' Calvin was right: we *may* say, 'Lord, I am leaning on your promise.' God *will* keep his word because his integrity is at stake. It is said that in the Hebridean revival in the late 1940s one man knelt in his pew and sobbed his heart out, crying, 'Lord, your *honour* is at stake!' Perhaps the reason that God delays and allows baffling things to happen is that he wants the godly community to pray in faith and lean on his word.

We come now to my fourth point about the way in which God often answers prayer: finally he himself is stirred up.

When Bathsheba and then Nathan reminded David of his promise to Solomon, at last David took action. The Bible says:

> Then King David said, 'Call in Bathsheba.' So she came into the king's presence and stood before him.
> The king then took an oath: 'As surely as the Lord lives, who has delivered me out of every trouble, I will surely carry out today what I swore to you by the Lord, the God of Israel: Solomon your son shall be king after me, and he will sit on my throne in my place' (1 Kgs. 1:28–30).

True to his word, David immediately made arrangements for Solomon to be proclaimed king.

King David said, 'Call in Zadok the priest, Nathan the prophet and Benaiah son of Jehoiada.' When they came before the king, he said to them: 'Take your lord's servants with you and set Solomon my son on my own mule and take him down to Gihon. There shall Zadok the priest and Nathan the prophet anoint him king over Israel. Blow the trumpet and shout, "Long live King Solomon!" Then you are to go up with him, and he is to come and sit on my throne and reign in my place. I have appointed him ruler over Israel and Judah' (vv. 32–35).

So Zadok the priest, Nathan the prophet, Benaiah son of Jehoiada, the Kerethites and the Pelethites went down and put Solomon on King David's mule and escorted him to Gihon. Zadok the priest took the horn of oil from the sacred tent and anointed Solomon. Then they sounded the trumpet and all the people shouted, 'Long live King Solomon!' and all the people went up after him, playing flutes and rejoicing greatly, so that the ground shook with the sound (vv. 38–40).

The noise reached the ears of Adonijah and his guests as they were finishing their feast. When they discovered the reason for it, all the guests dispersed in alarm and Adonijah himself fled in terror too and took hold of the horns of the altar, pleading for his life (vv. 49–53). In a matter of hours the situation was turned around. Do you know what made the difference? Nathan got the king's attention.

Sometimes it seems difficult to get God's attention. David found this to be the case, and in Psalm 78:65 he said: 'Then the Lord awoke as from sleep.' David knew that God never sleeps (Ps. 121:4): what he was saying was that there are times when it *seems* as if he has been asleep.

I do not fully understand why God delays answering our prayers and sometimes takes us to the edge of our endurance before he intervenes, but I know that when he does, he can transform a situation that, humanly speaking, is hopeless.

When God rescued the Israelites from slavery in Egypt, he *literally* took them to the brink, for he led them to the shore of the Red Sea. Behind them, in hot pursuit, was Pharaoh's army and before them was the water. It seemed as if God's promise of freeing his people from slavery had come to nothing. The Bible says:

> As Pharaoh approached, the Israelites looked up, and there were the Egyptians, marching after them. They were terrified and cried out to the Lord. . . .
> Then the Lord said to Moses, 'Why are you crying out to me?' Tell the Israelites to move on. Raise your staff and stretch out your hand over the sea to divide the water so that the Israelites can go through the sea on the dry ground.' . . .
> Then Moses stretched out his hand over the sea, and all that night the Lord drove the sea back with a strong east wind and turned it into dry land. The waters were divided, and the Israelites went through the sea on dry ground, with a wall of water on their right and on their left (Exod. 14:10, 15–16, 21–22).

I remember that after Louise and I were first married, we were heavily in debt. (It was my fault, not hers.) We needed help and every day when I came home from work I would ask her, 'Has the answer come?'

'Not yet,' she would reply.

But God knew there was a limit to what we could bear, and at last the day came when he intervened and turned our situation around. I do not know why he waited so long before answering our prayers, but I *do* know that his timing is perfect.

What God did for me he can for you. You may think that your situation is hopeless, but Jesus said, 'With God all things are possible' (Matt. 19:26). When God steps in, he will transform your life.

One night in that summer of 1956 when I was at my lowest ebb, as I was drifting into sleep, I heard a voice inside me saying, 'Turn to Acts 4:11.' I woke up immediately and thought, 'I will read this verse now.' So I switched on the bedside light, picked up my Bible to find that it said: 'This is the stone which was set at nought of you builders, which is become the head of the corner' (AV).

At that time I was being 'set at nought', particularly by the man I mentioned earlier who was exalted by others in the church. However, although he was a good man at heart, a few years later he got into some kind of trouble and became so depressed that he committed suicide.

In fact, over the years I have watched the Adonijahs of this world go forward to public acclaim and it seemed as if I was left on the sidelines. But I learnt that if I waited God would do things that I never dreamed possible.

In 1963 I was the pastor of a church in Ohio. But because I preached that Jesus Christ is God in the flesh – God as though he were not man, and man as though he were not God – they charged me with heresy. The church treasurer started a petition for my dismissal and encouraged other members to sign it. They got all but one name on the petition that they needed to fire me, but I did not stay. I learnt later that the treasurer's wife died within the year and he married a Jehovah's Witness, a member of a sect that denies the deity of Christ, and shortly after, he himself died a shameful death. I also heard that another member of the church who would stand up and defy me openly while I was preaching lost his reason.

You see, God has a way of letting us think for a while that we are outnumbered and Adonijah will defeat us, but when he intervenes, suddenly, everything changes and the breakthrough that we have longed for comes.

SUBJECT INDEX